TESTIMONIES FOR THE CHURCH

VOLUME SIX

TESTIMONIES

FOR

THE CHURCH

VOLUME SIX

Comprising Testimony Number 34

by

ELLEN G. WHITE

PACIFIC PRESS PUBLISHING ASSOCIATION

Mountain View, California

Omaha, Nebraska   Oshawa, Ontario

PACIFIC
PRESS
PUB.
ASSN.

PRINTED
IN U·S·A·

CONTENTS

PAGE

The Times of Volume Six 3

SECTION ONE
The Outlook

God's Purpose in the Church 9
The Work for This Time 14
Extension of the Work in Foreign Fields 23

SECTION TWO
Evangelistic Work

The Camp Meeting 31
    Reaching the Masses 33
    An Object Lesson 34
    Securing Attendance 35
    Attendance of Church Members 38
    Preparation of Heart 41
    Business Matters 44
    Ministerial Help 46
    All to Be Workers 48
    Prayer and Counsel 50
    Needs of the Church 52
    How to Present the Message 53
    The Last Warning 60
    Praise Meetings 62
    Revival Efforts 64
    Personal Labor 68
    Bible Studies 68
    A Word in Season 69
    Raising Funds 70
    Results of Camp Meeting Work 70
After the Camp Meeting 72
    The Work of the Evangelist 76
    In the Highways and Hedges 76
    Caring for Our Own Poor 85
    Church Officers and Workers 85
Less Preaching, More Teaching 87

Ministerial Institutes 89
Baptism 91
  Meaning of the Ordinance 91
  Preparation for Baptism 91
  Examination of Candidates 95
  Administration of the Ordinance 97
  After Baptism 98
The Building of Meetinghouses 100
Children's Meetings and Church Schools 105
The Temperance Work 110
Object Lessons in Health Reform 112
Women to Be Gospel Workers 114
Teaching Home Religion 119
Meeting Opposition 120
Parable of the Straying Sheep 124

SECTION THREE

Education

The Need of Educational Reform 126
  The Third Angel's Message in Our Schools 127
  Bible Study 131
  The Training of Workers 133
  Missionary Teachers 136
  Elements of Success 139
Hindrances to Reform 141
  To Teachers and Managers 145
Character and Work of Teachers 152
  Deficiencies of Teachers 155
  The Teacher's Work 156
  A Personal Appeal 157
Words From a Heavenly Instructor 162
School Homes 168
  Domestic Duties 169
  Christian Sociability and Courtesy 172
  Religious Exercises 174
Industrial Reform 176
The Avondale School Farm 181
  The Work Before Us 182

The Land to Be Reserved 183
A Panorama 185
God and Nature 185
An Object Lesson 188
Missionary Labor the Highest Training 189
Church Schools 193
The Work of Church Schools 193
Separation From the World 194
The Children Neglected 196
Church Schools Needed 198
The Character of Church Schools and of Their Teachers . 200
Results of Church School Work 202
School Management and Finance 206
Freedom From Debt 207
Economy 208
Good Management 210
Low Tuitions 210
Assisting Worthy Students 213
Teaching Self-Reliance 214
Duty of Our Conferences 215
Inspection by General Conference Auditor 216
The Church Schools 216

SECTION FOUR
Medical Missionary Work

God's Design in Our Sanitariums 219
The Physician's Work for Souls 229
Unity in Our Work 235
Responsibilities of Medical Workers 243
Conformity to the World 248
Prayer 252
The World's Need 254
The Church's Need 261
The Message of Isaiah Fifty-Eight 265
Our Duty to the Household of Faith 269
New Sabbathkeepers 269
The Poor, the Sick, and the Aged 270
Our Duty to the World 273

The Care of Orphans 281
  A Christlike Work 283
  Ministers' Wives Adopting Orphans 285
  Orphans' Homes 286
The Medical Missionary Work and the Third Angel's
  Message 288
  Medical Missionary Workers 291
  "Press Together" 292
Neglect by the Church and the Ministry 294
  Opportunities Slighted 294
  Results of Neglect 296
  Need of Repentance 297
  Neglect by the Ministry 298
The Reward of Service 305

SECTION FIVE

Canvassing

Importance of the Work 313
Qualifications of the Canvasser 317
The Canvasser a Gospel Worker 321
United Effort in Canvassing 326
Revival of the Canvassing Work 329

SECTION SIX

Cautions and Counsels

Showing Hospitality 341
The Observance of the Sabbath 349
  Reform in Sabbath Observance 351
  Preparation for the Sabbath 353
  The Sabbath in the Home 356
  Traveling on the Sabbath 359
  Sabbath Meetings 360
A Revival in Health Reform 369
  Obedience to Physical Law 369
  The Church and Health Reform 370
  Diet 372
  Extremes in Diet 373

True Temperance 374
Ministers to Teach Health Reform 376
The Importance of Voice Culture 380
Giving to God His Own 384
The First Fruits 384
Remember the Poor 385
All Things Belong to God 385
Another Opportunity 387
Without Excuse 387
The Blessing 388
The Complainers 389
"They That Feared the Lord" 390
Christ in All the Bible 392
Our Attitude Toward the Civil Authorities 394
Love Among Brethren 398
Present Truth With Gentleness 400
God's Word to Be Supreme 402
Preparation for the Final Crisis 404

Section Seven
Calls to Service

Young Men in the Ministry 411
The Church and the Ministry 417
The Home Missionary Work 421
A Warning From the Church of Ephesus 421
The Result of Inaction 424
Winning Souls the Chief Aim 427
Begin With Those Nearest 427
The Example of Philip With Nathanael 428
The Family a Missionary Field 429
Instruct the Church in Missionary Work 431
Set the Church Members to Work 432
The Uneducated to Be Workers 433
Arouse the Idlers 434
The Youth to Be Missionaries 435
Let the Churches Awake 436
The Increase of Facilities 440
Help for Mission Fields 445

The Publishing House in Norway 454
Our Danish Sanitarium 463
The Relief of Our Schools 468
  An Example of Liberality 468
  The Lord's Plan 469
  All to Co-operate 469
  Preparation for the Work 471
  The Work in All Lands 473
  Results of the Work 475
  Be Not Weary in Well-Doing 477
The Claim of Redemption 479
Scriptural Index 483
General Index 486

THE TIMES OF VOLUME SIX

THIS volume presents testimonies penned by Ellen G. White during her sojourn in Australia. Except for an occasional reference to the local field, the reader would not detect that the writer was in another continent, for the instruction is world wide in its scope. It is a fact, nevertheless, that the revelations given to Mrs. White had a direct bearing on current issues and the development of the work at the time of writing. It is understandable, therefore, that there are represented in this volume topics which were related to the lines of work being developed in the Australasian field during this period. Publication of the book took place late in the year 1900, shortly after Mrs. White had returned to the United States.

In its topical arrangement, volume 6 is quite different from the preceding five volumes. Up to this time the testimonies had first appeared in pamphlets and small books as counsel was progressively given for the church. The articles were printed largely in chronological order, and dealt with almost every phase of Christian experience and every line of denominational work. As the content of these thirty-three publications was reprinted in volumes 1 to 5, the original order was left unchanged. A number of the articles were communications addressed first to individuals and later published for the church because the cases presented illustrated the experience of many others. Some of the articles dealt with local situations and special issues. There was some repetition of thought, as important lines of truth were stressed again and again as the church was in danger of neglecting some line of work or of letting slip some church standard. These testimonies bore rich fruit in the lives of Seventh-day Adventists and in the work of the denomination.

With the publication of volume 6, eleven years after volume 5 was issued, the *Testimonies for the Church* took on a new form. The work of the denomination, now becoming world wide in its scope, presented needs and problems which called forth considerable counsel and instruction in certain particular lines. This represented largely an amplification of lines of instruction presented in earlier years and a re-emphasis of counsel. Consequently it was not difficult, when the articles for volume 6 were gathered for publication, to arrange them in topical order.

That Mrs. White might assist in the starting of a training school in Australia, she was asked to go to that field in 1891. She led out in the appeals for the school and assisted in laying plans for the work. Being in a new field, there was little by way of past experience or precedent to influence the plans. Under these favorable circumstances, and with the spirit of prophecy counsels to guide and guard, the Australasian Missionary College was established in a backward country region. From this training center, Australian youth, with the practical education gained at Avondale, were to serve in the home fields and to penetrate the far-flung islands of the South Pacific. In its rural environment, in its broad industrial program, and in some other features the Avondale school was to become a pattern school. As the instruction concerning the conduct of our educational work was presented anew to guide and mold this institution, entering into the many details of location, finance, curriculum, discipline, and administration, it was included in this volume for the benefit of the church around the world.

When Mrs. White reached Australian shores, she found a work well begun, but still in its infancy. In the aggressive evangelistic program which was developed and fostered, not only the evangelists themselves were engaged in service, but in not a few cases they were joined by their wives in giving Bible studies and sometimes in preaching. Several well-planned evangelistic camp meetings were held, which were carefully followed up so as to conserve the harvest. There were many conversions, followed by baptisms and the organizing of new churches and the building of meetinghouses.

Not only in the planning for the work was the influence of the spirit of prophecy felt, but Mrs. White herself took an active part in preaching, in personal work, and in assisting in the raising of money for the new church buildings. Counsel regarding these phases of our work is found in this volume.

It was in the times of volume 6 that Seventh-day Adventists became more fully mission conscious and accepted the whole world as a field of labor. The building and launching of the mission boat, "Pitcairn," in California in 1890 fired the imagination of young and old alike and focused attention on an around-the-world mission program. The reports of the voyages of the "Pitcairn," as it pioneered mission work in the South Sea Islands, were eagerly watched by all.

It was not long until colporteur evangelists entered India with our literature, and in 1894 our missionaries in Africa pushed up into distinctively native territories and established the Solusi Mission, our first foreign mission among heathen peoples. Ministers were also soon sent into South America. Then, too, Mrs. White's presence in Australia for nine years as a pioneer worker helped to keep the eyes of Seventh-day Adventists on the ends of the earth and to place emphasis on the admonition given on page 31 of this volume: "It is our work to give to the whole world,—to every nation, kindred, tongue, and people,—the saving truths of the third angel's message." Throughout the volume various mission fields are mentioned by name, and appeals for men and means are presented, together with counsel and encouragement concerning the work in different lands.

A number of colleges and worker training schools were started during the times of volume 6. Early in the period Union College at Lincoln, Nebraska, was opened in 1891 and Walla Walla College in the State of Washington in 1892. The others were in Australia, South Africa, and Denmark. Sanitariums were also opened at Boulder, Colorado, in 1896, in Denmark and South Africa in 1897, and at South Lancaster,

Massachusetts, in 1899. Two new publishing houses were added to the list of institutions, one in Hamburg, Germany, in 1895, and the other in Buenos Aires, South America, in 1897. Church schools presenting elementary work were also begun in several places.

Though many warnings were given against large denominational centers and centralizing tendencies, the steadily growing work seemed to require more people and larger facilities at our denominational headquarters at Battle Creek, Michigan, and plans were even initiated to bring certain lines of denominational work under central control at Battle Creek. Thus instead of the plans for the work of various sections of the field being laid by those on the ground, they were directed largely from the home offices in Battle Creek. This had the appearance of business efficiency, yet it actually was a serious menace to efficiency and vital leadership in the work of God. Through the nineties these tendencies developed rapidly, but in God's own time and in His own way they were checked.

It was in these times and under the influence of the spirit of prophecy counsels that the ground structure was laid for organizational changes in the administration of the denomination's world work. As the cause was pioneered and developed rapidly under the favorable conditions of Australia, steps were taken to bind the local conference organizations into a "union conference," thus establishing an organizational unit between the local conference and the General Conference. This made possible, on-the-ground planning by the group of workers close to the problems, and thus relieved the General Conference of many minor details. The result was encouraging and formed the pattern which was soon to be followed throughout the denomination.

In the lines of medical evangelism a beginning was made in Australia during this period, but in the United States it was a time of great expansion. A medical college was set in operation which attracted an increasing number of Seventh-day

Adventist youth desiring preparation as medical missionaries. New branch institutions were opened, receiving their guidance, finance, and personnel from the great parent institution at Battle Creek. A large work was also launched for the fallen and unfortunate. But good enterprises are often threatened with the danger of overemphasis, thereby bringing an unbalance into the work of God as a whole. So now it seemed that the medical missionary work, which had been designated as the right arm of the message, threatened to become the body.

Too, while there was great advance in the development of medical missionaries and medical missionary work in connection with the Battle Creek Sanitarium, there was growing indifference on the part of some Seventh-day Adventists to the basic principles of healthful living. These conditions help us to understand the significance of the repeated appeals in volume 6 calling the people to higher standards of living, urging a united medical and evangelistic ministry, delineating our duty to orphans and the aged of the household of faith, and cautioning against an unbalanced work.

As the denominational work developed in many fields, literature found an ever increasingly important place. Colporteur evangelists constituted an army, with the individual colporteur a part of the recognized staff of gospel heralds in each section of the world field. In not a few instances these literature evangelists had formed the spearhead of attack in carrying the message to new and distant lands. Volume 6 sets forth the dignity and importance of the colporteur ministry.

This eleven-year period between the publication of volumes 5 and 6 of the *Testimonies* marked the issuance of several important E. G. White books. In 1890 *Patriarchs and Prophets* came from the press. *Steps to Christ* was published in 1892, and what is today known as "the old edition" of *Gospel Workers* was also printed that year. *Christian Education,* the forerunner of *Education,* was issued in 1894, and two years later *Thoughts From the Mount of Blessing* and *Christ Our Sav-*

iour were printed. Work on the manuscript for *The Desire of Ages* was completed and the book printed in 1898, and in 1900 *Christ's Object Lessons* was published.

In an effort to relieve our institutions of the heavy indebtedness which they were carrying, Mrs. White donated the manuscript for *Christ's Object Lessons* and urged our church members and workers to join in its wide sale to their neighbors and friends. Hundreds of thousands of dollars were thus brought into the cause through this relief book campaign, and thousands of copies of this truth-filled book were distributed.

A type of work was in this way initiated which led large numbers of lay members to call from house to house in behalf of the work of the church. Thus the way was paved for the "ingathering" campaigns which were to develop a few years later into a source of revenue to the work of God, yielding millions of dollars.

Of course, all through this twelve-year period, scores and hundreds of communications bearing warnings, counsels, and encouragement were penned by the messenger of the Lord and were sent into the field in letters and in articles in the journals of the denomination. While many of these dealt with subjects already presented less comprehensively in the earlier *Testimonies,* some new phases of counsel were set forth and former counsels emphasized. These are found in such general sections as "Cautions and Counsels" and "Calls to Service." Among the important articles comprising these sections are such as deal with "The Observance of the Sabbath," "A Revival in Health Reform," "Our Attitude Toward the Civil Authorities," "Preparation for the Final Crisis," and "The Relief of Our Schools." The adding of this new volume to the growing series of *Testimonies for the Church* deeply impressed Seventh-day Adventists with the direct way in which God was continuing to guide and lead His people.

THE TRUSTEES OF THE
ELLEN G. WHITE PUBLICATIONS.

THE OUTLOOK

"Lift up your eyes, and look
on the fields; for they are
white already to harvest."

GOD'S PURPOSE IN THE CHURCH

It is God's purpose to manifest through His people the principles of His kingdom. That in life and character they may reveal these principles, He desires to separate them from the customs, habits, and practices of the world. He seeks to bring them near to Himself, that He may make known to them His will.

This was His purpose in the deliverance of Israel from Egypt. At the burning bush Moses received from God the message for the king of Egypt: "Let My people go, that they may serve Me." Exodus 7:16. With a mighty hand and an outstretched arm God brought out the Hebrew host from the land of bondage. Wonderful was the deliverance He wrought for them, punishing their enemies, who refused to listen to His word, with total destruction.

God desired to take His people apart from the world and prepare them to receive His word. From Egypt He led them to Mount Sinai, where He revealed to them His glory. Here was nothing to attract their senses or divert their minds from God; and as the vast multitude looked at the lofty mountains towering above them, they could realize their own nothingness in the sight of God. Beside these rocks, immovable except by the power of the divine

(9)

will, God communicated with men. And that His word might ever be clear and distinct in their minds, He proclaimed amid thunder and lightning and with terrible majesty the law which He had given in Eden and which was the transcript of His character. And the words were written on tables of stone by the finger of God. Thus the will of the infinite God was revealed to a people who were called to make known to every nation, kindred, and tongue the principles of His government in heaven and in earth.

To the same work He has called His people in this generation. To them He has revealed His will, and of them He requires obedience. In the last days of this earth's history the voice that spoke from Sinai is still saying to men: "Thou shalt have no other gods before Me." Exodus 20:3. Man has set his will against the will of God, but he cannot silence this word of command. The human mind can never fully comprehend its obligation to the higher power, but it cannot evade the obligation. Profound theories and speculations may abound, men may try to set science in opposition to revelation, and thus do away with the law of God; but stronger and still stronger will the Holy Spirit bring before them the command: "Thou shalt worship the Lord thy God, and Him only shalt thou serve." Matthew 4:10.

How is the world treating the law of God? Everywhere men are working against the divine precepts. In their desire to evade the cross bearing attendant on obedience, even the churches are taking sides with the great apostate in claiming that the law of God has been changed or abrogated. Men in their blindness boast of wonderful progress and enlightenment; but the heavenly watchers see the earth filled with corruption and violence. Because of sin the atmosphere of our world has become as the atmosphere of a pesthouse.

A great work is to be accomplished in setting before men the saving truths of the gospel. This is the means ordained by God to stem the tide of moral corruption. This is His means of restoring His moral image in man. It is His remedy for universal disorganization. It is the power that draws men together in unity. To present these truths is the work of the third angel's message. The Lord designs that the presentation of this message shall be the highest, greatest work carried on in the world at this time.

Satan is constantly urging men to accept his principles. Thus he seeks to counterwork the work of God. He is constantly representing the chosen people of God as a deluded people. He is an accuser of the brethren, and his accusing power he is constantly using against those who work righteousness. The Lord desires through His people to answer Satan's charges by showing the result of obedience to right principles.

All the light of the past, all the light which shines in the present and reaches forth into the future, as revealed in the word of God, is for every soul who will receive it. The glory of this light, which is the very glory of the character of Christ, is to be manifested in the individual Christian, in the family, in the church, in the ministry of the word, and in every institution established by God's people. All these the Lord designs shall be symbols of what can be done for the world. They are to be types of the saving power of the truths of the gospel. They are agencies in the fulfillment of God's great purpose for the human race.

God's people are to be channels for the outworking of the highest influence in the universe. In Zechariah's vision the two olive trees which stand before God are represented as emptying the golden oil out of themselves through golden tubes into the bowl of the sanctuary. From this the lamps of the sanctuary are fed, that they may give a continuous bright and shining light. So from the anointed ones that stand in God's presence the fullness of divine light and love and power is imparted to His people, that they may impart to others light and joy and refreshing. They are to become channels through which divine instrumentalities communicate to the world the tide of God's love.

The purpose which God seeks to accomplish through His people today is the same that He desired to accomplish through Israel when He brought them forth out of Egypt. By beholding the goodness, the mercy, the justice, and the love of God revealed in the church, the world is to have a representation of His character. And when the law of God is thus exemplified in the life, even the world will recognize the superiority of those who love and fear and serve God above every other people on the earth. The Lord has His eye upon every one of His people; He has His plans concerning each. It is His purpose that those who practice His holy precepts shall be a distinguished people. To the people of God today as well as to ancient Israel belong the words written by Moses through the Spirit of Inspiration: "Thou art an holy people unto the Lord thy God: the Lord thy God hath chosen thee to be a special people unto Himself, above all people that are upon the face of the earth." Deuteronomy 7:6. "Behold, I have taught you statutes and judgments, even as the Lord my God commanded me, that ye should do so in the land whither ye go to possess it. Keep therefore and do them; for this is your wisdom and your understanding in the sight of the nations, which shall hear all these statutes, and say, Surely this great nation is a wise and understanding people. For what nation is there so great, who hath God so nigh unto them, as the Lord our

God is in all things that we call upon Him for? And what nation is there so great, that hath statutes and judgments so righteous as all this law, which I set before you this day?" Deuteronomy 4:5-8.

Even these words fail of expressing the greatness and the glory of God's purpose to be accomplished through His people. Not to this world only but to the universe are we to make manifest the principles of His kingdom. The apostle Paul, writing by the Holy Spirit, says: "Unto me, who am less than the least of all saints, is this grace given, that I should preach among the Gentiles the unsearchable riches of Christ; and to make all men see what is the fellowship of the mystery, which from the beginning of the world hath been hid in God, who created all things by Jesus Christ: to the intent that now unto the principalities and powers in heavenly places might be [made] known by the church the manifold wisdom of God." Ephesians 3:8-10.

Brethren, "we are made a spectacle unto the world, and to angels, and to men." "What manner of persons ought ye to be in all holy conversation and godliness, looking for and hasting the coming of the day of God?" 1 Corinthians 4:9; 2 Peter 3:11, 12, margin.

———

In order to manifest the character of God, in order that we may not deceive ourselves, the church, and the world by a counterfeit Christianity, we must become personally acquainted with God. If we have fellowship with God, we are His ministers, though we may never preach to a congregation. We are workers together with God in presenting the perfection of His character in humanity.

THE WORK FOR THIS TIME

WE are standing upon the threshold of great and solemn events. Prophecies are fulfilling. Strange, eventful history is being recorded in the books of heaven. Everything in our world is in agitation. There are wars and rumors of wars. The nations are angry, and the time of the dead has come, that they should be judged. Events are changing to bring about the day of God, which hasteth greatly. Only a moment of time, as it were, yet remains. But while already nation is rising against nation, and kingdom against kingdom, there is not now a general engagement. As yet the four winds are held until the servants of God shall be sealed in their foreheads. Then the powers of earth will marshal their forces for the last great battle.

Satan is busily laying his plans for the last mighty conflict, when all will take sides. After the gospel has been proclaimed in the world for nearly two thousand years, Satan still presents to men and women the same scene that he presented to Christ. In a wonderful manner he causes the kingdoms of the world in their glory to pass before them. These he promises to all who will fall down and worship him. Thus he seeks to bring men under his dominion.

Satan is working to the utmost to make himself as God and to destroy all who oppose his power. And today the world is bowing before him. His power is received as the power of God. The prophecy of the Revelation is being fulfilled, that "all the world wondered after the beast." Revelation 13:3.

Men in their blindness boast of wonderful progress and enlightenment; but to the eye of Omniscience are revealed the inward guilt and depravity. The heavenly watchers see the earth filled with violence and crime. Wealth is obtained by every species of robbery, not robbery of men only, but of God. Men are using His means to gratify their selfishness. Everything they can grasp is made to minister to their greed. Avarice and sensuality prevail. Men cherish the attributes of the first great deceiver. They have accepted him as God, and have become imbued with his spirit.

But the cloud of judicial wrath hangs over them, containing the elements that destroyed Sodom. In his visions of things to come the prophet John beheld this scene. This demon worship was revealed to him, and it seemed to him as if the whole world were standing on the brink of perdition. But as he looked with intense interest he beheld the company of God's commandment-keeping people. They had upon their foreheads the seal of the living God, and he said: "Here is the patience of the saints: here are they that keep the commandments of God, and the faith of Jesus. And I heard a voice from heaven saying unto me, Write, Blessed are the dead which die in the Lord from henceforth: Yea, saith the Spirit, that they may rest from their labors; and their works do follow them. And I looked, and behold a white cloud, and upon the cloud One sat like unto the Son of man, having on His head a golden crown, and in His hand a sharp sickle. And another angel came out of the temple, crying with a loud voice to Him that sat on the cloud, Thrust in Thy sickle, and reap: for the time is come for Thee to reap; for the harvest of the earth is ripe. And He that sat on the cloud thrust in His sickle on the earth; and the earth was reaped. And another angel came out of the temple which is in heaven, he also having a sharp sickle. And another angel came out from the altar, which had power over fire; and cried with a loud cry to him that had the sharp sickle, saying, Thrust in thy sharp sickle, and gather the clusters of the vine of the earth; for her grapes are fully ripe. And the angel thrust in his sickle into the earth, and gathered the vine of the earth, and cast it into the great winepress of the wrath of God." Revelation 14:12-19.

When the storm of God's wrath breaks upon the world, it will be a terrible revelation for souls to find that their house is being swept away because it is built upon the sand. Let the warning be given them before it is too late. We should now feel the responsibility of laboring with intense earnestness to impart to others the truths that God has given for this time. We cannot be too much in earnest.

The heart of God is moved. Souls are very precious in His sight. It was for this world that Christ wept in agony; for this world He was crucified. God gave His only-begotten Son to save sinners, and He desires us to love others as He has loved us. He desires to see those who have a knowledge of the truth imparting this knowledge to their fellow men.

Now is the time for the last warning to be given. There is a special power in the presentation of the truth at the present time; but how long will it continue? Only a little while. If there was ever a crisis, it is now.

All are now deciding their eternal destiny. Men need to be aroused to realize the solemnity of the time, the nearness of the day when human probation shall be ended. Decided efforts should be made to bring the message for this time prominently before the people. The third angel is to go forth with great power. Let none ignore this work or treat it as of little importance.

The light we have received upon the third angel's message is the true light. The mark of the beast is exactly what it has been proclaimed to be. Not all in regard to this matter is yet understood, nor will it be understood until the unrolling of the scroll; but a most solemn work is to be accomplished in our world. The Lord's command to His servants is: "Cry aloud, spare not, lift up thy voice like a trumpet, and show My people their transgression, and the house of Jacob their sins." Isaiah 58:1.

There is to be no change in the general features of our work. It is to stand as clear and distinct as prophecy has made it. We are to enter into no confederacy with the world, supposing that by so doing we could accomplish more. If any stand in the way, to hinder the advancement of the work in the lines that God has appointed, they will displease God. No line of truth that has made the Seventh-day Adventist people what they are is to be weakened. We have the old landmarks of truth, experience, and duty, and we are to stand firmly in defense of our principles, in full view of the world.

It is essential that men be raised up to open the living oracles of God to all peoples. Men of all ranks and capacities, with their various gifts, are to co-operate harmoniously for a common result. They are to unite in the work of bringing the truth to the people, each worker fulfilling his own special appointment.

The three angels of Revelation 14 are represented as flying in the midst of heaven, symbolizing the work of those who proclaim the first, second, and third angels' messages. All are linked together. The evidences of the abiding, everliving truth of these grand messages, that mean so much to the church, that have awakened such intense opposition from the religious world, are not extinct. Satan is constantly seeking to cast a shadow about these messages, so that the people of God shall not clearly discern their import, their time and place; but they live and are to exert their power upon our religious experience while time shall last.

The influence of these messages has been deepening and widening, setting in motion the springs of action in thousands of hearts, bringing into existence institutions of learning, publishing houses, and health institutions. All these are instrumentalities of God to co-operate in the grand work represented by the first, second, and third angels, the work of warning the inhabitants of the world that Christ is coming the second time with power and great glory.

————

Brethren and sisters, would that I might say something to awaken you to the importance of this time, the significance of the events that are now taking place. I point you to the aggressive movements now being made for the restriction of religious liberty. God's sanctified memorial has been torn down, and in its place a false sabbath, bearing no sanctity, stands before the world. And while the powers of darkness are stirring up the elements from beneath, the Lord God of heaven is sending power from above to meet the emergency by arousing His living agencies to exalt the law of heaven. Now, just now, is our time to work in foreign countries. As America, the land of religious liberty, shall unite with the papacy in forcing the conscience and compelling men to honor the false sabbath, the people of every country on the globe will be led to follow her example. Our people are not half awake to do all in their power, with the facilities within their reach, to extend the message of warning.

The Lord God of heaven will not send upon the world His judgments for disobedience and transgression until He has sent His watchmen to give the warning. He will not close up the period of probation until the message shall be more distinctly proclaimed. The law of God is to be magnified; its claims must be presented in their true, sacred character, that the people may be brought to decide for or against the truth. Yet the work will be cut short in righteousness. The message of Christ's righteousness is to sound from one end of the earth to the other to prepare the way of the Lord. This is the glory of God, which closes the work of the third angel.

———

There is no work in our world so great, so sacred, and so glorious, no work that God honors so much, as this gospel work. The message presented at this time is the last message of mercy for a fallen world. Those who have the privilege of hearing this message, and who persist in refusing to heed the warning, cast away their last hope of salvation. There will be no second probation.

The word of truth, "It is written," is the gospel we are to preach. No flaming sword is placed before this tree of life. All who will may partake of it. There is no power that can prohibit any soul from taking of its fruit. All may eat, and live forever.

———

Mysteries into which angels desire to look, which prophets and kings and righteous men desired to understand, the remnant church will carry in messages from God to the world. The prophets prophesied of these things, and they longed to understand that which they foretold; but to them this privilege was not given. They longed to see what we see, and to hear what we hear; but they could not. They will know all when Christ shall come the second time; when, surrounded by a multitude which no man can number, He explains the deliverance wrought out by the great sacrifice He made.

The truths of the third angel's message have been presented by some as a dry theory; but in this message is to be presented Christ the Living One. He is to be revealed as the first and the last, as the I AM, the Root and the Offspring of David, and the bright and morning Star. Through this message the character of God in Christ is to be manifested to the world. The call is to be sounded: "O Jerusalem, that bringest good tidings, lift up thy voice with strength; lift it up, be not afraid; say unto the cities of Judah, Behold your God! Behold, the Lord God will come with strong hand, and His arm shall rule for Him: behold, His reward is with Him, and His work before Him. He shall feed His flock like a shepherd: He shall gather the lambs with His arm, and carry them in His bosom." Isaiah 40:9-11.

Now, with John the Baptist, we are to point men to Jesus, saying: "Behold the Lamb of God, which taketh away the sin of the world." John 1:29. Now as never before is to be sounded the invitation: "If any man thirst, let him come unto Me, and drink." "The Spirit and the bride say, Come. And let him that heareth say, Come. And let him that is athirst come. And whosoever will, let him take the water of life freely." John 7:37; Revelation 22:17.

There is a great work to be done, and every effort possible must be made to reveal Christ as the sin-pardoning Saviour, Christ as the Sin Bearer, Christ as the bright and morning Star; and the Lord will give us favor before the world until our work is done.

————

While the angels hold the four winds, we are to work with all our capabilities. We must bear our message without any delay. We must give evidence to the heavenly universe, and to men in this degenerate age, that our religion is a faith and a power of which Christ is the Author and His word the divine oracle. Human souls are hanging in the balance. They will either be subjects for the kingdom of God or slaves to the despotism of Satan. All are to have the privilege of laying hold of the hope set before them in the gospel, and how can they hear without a preacher? The human family is in need of a moral renovation, a preparation of character, that they may stand in God's presence. There are souls ready to perish because of the theoretical errors which are prevailing, and which are calculated to counterwork the gospel message. Who will now fully consecrate themselves to become laborers together with God?

As you see the peril and misery of the world under the working of Satan, do not exhaust your God-given energies in idle lamentations, but go to work for yourselves and for others. Awake, and feel a burden for those who are perishing. If they are not won to Christ they will lose an eternity of bliss. Think of what it is possible for them to gain. The soul that God has created and Christ has redeemed is of great value because of the possibilities before it, the spiritual advantages that have been granted it, the capabilities it may possess if vitalized by the word of God, and the immortality which through the Life-giver it may obtain if obedient. One soul is of more value to heaven than a whole world of property, houses, lands, money. For the conversion of one soul we should tax our resources to the utmost. One soul won to Christ will flash heaven's light all around him, penetrating the moral darkness and saving other souls.

If Christ left the ninety and nine, that He might seek and save the one lost sheep, can we be justified in doing less? Is not a neglect to work even as Christ worked, to sacrifice as He sacrificed, a betrayal of sacred trusts, an insult to God?

Sound an alarm throughout the length and breadth of the earth. Tell the people that the day of the Lord is near and hasteth greatly. Let none be left unwarned. We might have been in the place of the poor souls that are in error. We might have been placed among barbarians. According to the truth we have received above others, we are debtors to impart the same to them.

We have no time to lose. The end is near. The passage from place to place to spread the truth will soon be hedged with dangers on the right hand and on the left. Everything will be placed to obstruct the way of the Lord's messengers, so that they will not be able to do that which it is possible for them to do now. We must look our work fairly in the face and advance as fast as possible in aggressive warfare. From the light given me of God I know that the powers of darkness are working with intense energy from beneath, and with stealthy tread Satan is advancing to take those who are now asleep, as a wolf taking his prey. We have warnings now which we may give, a work now which we may do; but soon it will be more difficult than we can imagine. God help us to keep in the channel of light, to work with our eyes fastened on Jesus our Leader, and patiently, perseveringly press on to gain the victory.

EXTENSION OF THE WORK IN
FOREIGN FIELDS

THE word comes to me in the night season to speak to the churches that know the truth: "Arise, shine; for thy light is come, and the glory of the Lord is risen upon thee." Isaiah 60:1.

The words of the Lord in the fifty-fourth chapter of Isaiah are for us: "Enlarge the place of thy tent, and let them stretch forth the curtains of thine habitations: spare not, lengthen thy cords, and strengthen thy stakes; for thou shalt break forth on the right hand and on the left; and thy seed shall inherit the Gentiles, and make the desolate cities to be inhabited. Fear not; for thou shalt not be ashamed: neither be thou confounded; for thou shalt not be put to shame. . . . For thy Maker is thine husband; the Lord of hosts is His name; and thy Redeemer the Holy One of Israel; The God of the whole earth shall He be called." Isaiah 54:2-5.

And the words of Christ to His disciples are also for His people today: "Say not ye, There are yet four months, and then cometh harvest? behold, I say unto you, Lift up your eyes, and look on the fields; for they are white already to harvest. And he that reapeth receiveth wages, and gathereth fruit unto life eternal: that both he that soweth and he that reapeth may rejoice together." John 4:35, 36.

God's people have a mighty work before them, a work that must continually rise to greater prominence. Our efforts in missionary lines must become far more extensive. A more decided work than has been done must be done prior to the second appearing of our Lord Jesus

(23)

Christ. God's people are not to cease their labors until they shall encircle the world.

The vineyard includes the whole world, and every part of it is to be worked. There are places which are now a moral wilderness, and these are to become as the garden of the Lord. The waste places of the earth are to be cultivated, that they may bud and blossom as the rose. New territories are to be worked by men inspired by the Holy Spirit. New churches must be established, new congregations organized. At this time there should be representatives of present truth in every city and in the remote parts of the earth. The whole earth is to be illuminated with the glory of God's truth. The light is to shine to all lands and all peoples. And it is from those who have received the light that it is to shine forth. The daystar has risen upon us, and we are to flash its light upon the pathway of those in darkness.

A crisis is right upon us. We must now by the Holy Spirit's power proclaim the great truths for these last days. It will not be long before everyone will have heard the warning and made his decision. Then shall the end come.

It is the very essence of all right faith to do the right thing at the right time. God is the great Master Worker, and by His providence He prepares the way for His work to be accomplished. He provides opportunities, opens up lines of influence and channels of working. If His people are watching the indications of His providence, and stand ready to co-operate with Him, they will see a great work accomplished. Their efforts, rightly directed, will produce a hundredfold greater results than can be accomplished with the same means and facilities in another channel where God is not so manifestly working. Our work is reformative, and it is God's purpose that the excellence of the work in all lines shall be an object lesson to the people. In new fields especially it is important that the work be so established as to give a correct representation of the truth. In all our plans for missionary operations these principles should be kept in mind.

Certain countries have advantages that mark them as centers of education and influence. In the English-speaking nations and the Protestant nations of Europe it is comparatively easy to find access to the people, and there are many advantages for establishing institutions and carrying forward our work. In some other lands, such as India and China, the workers must go through a long course of education before the people can understand them, or they the people. And at every step there are great difficulties to be encountered in the work. In America, Australia, England, and some other European countries, many of these impediments do not exist. America has many institutions to give character to the work. Similar facilities should be furnished for England, Australia, Germany, and Scandinavia, and other Continental countries as the work advances. In these countries the Lord has able workmen, laborers of experience. These can lead out in the establishment of institutions, the training of workers, and the carrying forward of the work in its different lines. God designs that they shall be furnished with means and facilities. The institutions established would give character to the work in these countries, and would give opportunity for the training of workers for the darker heathen nations. In this way the efficiency of our experienced workers would be multiplied a hundredfold.

There is a great work to be done in England. The light radiating from London should beam forth in clear, distinct rays to regions beyond. God has wrought in England, but this English-speaking world has been terribly neglected. England has needed many more laborers and much more means. London has been scarcely touched. My heart is deeply moved as the situation in that great city is presented before me. It pains me to think that greater facilities are not provided for the work throughout Europe. I have sore heartache as I think of the work in Switzerland, Germany, Norway, and Sweden. Where there are one or two men struggling to carry forward the different branches of the cause, there should be hundreds at work. In the city of London alone no fewer than one hundred men should be engaged. The Lord marks the neglect of His work, and there will be a heavy account to settle by and by.

If the workers in America will impart to others of their great mercies, they will see prosperity in England. They will sympathize with the workers who are struggling with difficulties there, and will have the heart to say, not only in word but in action: "All ye are brethren." Matthew 23:8. They will see a great work done in London, all through the cities of England, and throughout the different European countries.

God calls upon us to push the triumphs of the cross in Australia. New fields are opening. For want of workers and money the work has been hindered, but it must be hindered no longer. Of all countries, Australia most resembles America. All classes of people are there. And the warning message has not been presented and rejected. There are thousands of honest souls praying for light. God's watchmen are to stand on the walls of Zion and to give the warning: "The morning cometh, and also the night"—the night wherein no man can work. While the angels are holding the four winds, the message is to enter every field in Australia as fast as possible.

The strengthening of the work in these English-speaking countries will give our laborers a hundredfold more influence than they have had to plant the standard of truth in many lands.

While we are trying to work these destitute fields, the cry comes from far-off countries: "Come over and help us." These are not so easily reached, and not so ready for the harvest, as are the fields more nearly within our sight; but they must not be neglected.

The poverty of the missions in Africa has recently been opened before me. The missionaries sent from America to the natives of Africa have suffered and are still suffering for the necessaries of life. God's missionaries, who carry the message of mercy to heathen lands, are not properly sustained in their work.

Our brethren have not discerned that in helping to advance the work in foreign fields they would be helping the work at home. That which is given to start the work in one field will result in strengthening the work in other places. As the laborers are freed from embarrassment, their efforts can be extended; as souls are brought to the truth and churches are established, there will be increasing financial strength. Soon these churches will be able not only to carry on the work in their own borders, but to impart to other fields. Thus the burden resting on the home churches will be shared.

The home missionary work will be farther advanced in every way when a more liberal, self-denying, self-sacrificing spirit is manifested for the prosperity of foreign missions; for the prosperity of the home work depends largely, under God, upon the reflex influence of the evangelical work done in countries afar off. It is in working actively to supply the necessities of the cause of God that we bring our souls in touch with the Source of all power.

Although the work in foreign fields has not advanced as it should have advanced, yet that which has been accomplished affords reason for gratitude and ground for encouragement. Much less means has been spent in these fields than in the home fields, and the work has been done under the hardest pressure and without proper facilities. Yet, considering the help that has been sent to these fields, the result is indeed surprising. Our missionary success has been fully proportionate to our self-denying, self-sacrificing effort. God alone can estimate the work accomplished as the gospel message has been proclaimed in clear, straight lines. New fields have been entered, and aggressive work has been done. The seeds of truth have been sown, the light has flashed upon many minds, bringing enlarged views of God and a more correct estimate as to the character to be formed. Thousands have been brought to a knowledge of the truth as it is in Jesus. They have been imbued with the faith that works by love and purifies the soul.

The value of these spiritual advantages is beyond our comprehension. What line can sound the depths of the word preached? What balances can correctly weigh the influence of those who are converted to the truth? In their turn they become missionaries to work for others. In many places houses of worship have been erected. The Bible, the precious Bible, is studied. The tabernacle of God is with men, and He dwells with them.

Let us rejoice that a work which God can approve has been done in these fields. In the name of the Lord let us lift up our voices in praise and thanksgiving for the results of work abroad.

And still our General, who never makes a mistake, says to us: "Advance. Enter new territory. Lift up the standard in every land. 'Arise, shine; for thy light is come, and the glory of the Lord is risen upon thee.' "

Our watchword is to be: Onward, ever onward. The angels of God will go before us to prepare the way. Our burden for the "regions beyond" can never be laid down until the whole earth shall be lightened with the glory of the Lord.

———

The missionary spirit needs to be revived in our churches. Every member of the church should study how to help forward the work of God, both in home missions and in foreign countries. Scarcely a thousandth part of the work is being done that ought to be done in missionary fields. God calls upon His workers to annex new territory for Him. There are rich fields of toil waiting for the faithful worker. And ministering angels will co-operate with every member of the church who will labor unselfishly for the Master.

———

The church of Christ on earth was organized for missionary purposes, and the Lord desires to see the entire church devising ways and means whereby high and low, rich and poor, may hear the message of truth. Not all are called to personal labor in foreign fields, but all can do something by their prayers and their gifts to aid the missionary work.

An American businessman who was an earnest Christian, in conversation with a fellow worker remarked that he himself worked for Christ twenty-four hours of the day. "In all my business relations," he said, "I try to represent my Master. As I have opportunity, I try to win others to Him. All day I am working for Christ. And at night, while I sleep, I have a man working for Him in China."

In explanation he added: "In my youth I determined to go as a missionary to the heathen. But on the death of my father I had to take up his business in order to provide for the family. Now, instead of going myself, I support a missionary. In such a town of such a province of China, my worker is stationed. And so, even while I sleep, I am, through my representative, still working for Christ."

Are there not Seventh-day Adventists who will do likewise? Instead of keeping the ministers at work for the churches that already know the truth, let the members of the churches say to these laborers: "Go work for souls that are perishing in darkness. We ourselves will carry forward the services of the church. We will keep up the meetings, and, by abiding in Christ, will maintain spiritual life. We will work for souls that are about us, and we will send our prayers and our gifts to sustain the laborers in more needy and destitute fields."

Why should not the members of a church or of several small churches unite to sustain a missionary in foreign fields? If they will deny themselves of selfish indulgences, dispense with needless and hurtful things, they can do this. Brethren and sisters, will you not help in this work? I beseech you to do something for Christ, and to do it now. Through the teacher whom your money shall sustain in the field, souls may be saved from ruin to shine as stars in the Redeemer's crown.

EVANGELISTIC WORK

> "How beautiful upon the mountains are the feet of him that bringeth good tidings, that publisheth peace; . . . that saith unto Zion, Thy God reigneth."

THE CAMP MEETING

THE camp meeting is one of the most important agencies in our work. It is one of the most effective methods of arresting the attention of the people and reaching all classes with the gospel invitation. The time in which we live is a time of intense excitement. Ambition and war, pleasure and money-making, absorb the minds of men. Satan sees that his time is short, and he has set all his agencies at work, that men may be deceived, deluded, occupied, and entranced, until probation shall be ended and the door of mercy be forever shut. It is our work to give to the whole world—to every nation, kindred, tongue, and people—the saving truths of the third angel's message. But it has been a difficult problem to know how to reach the people in the great centers of population. We are not allowed entrance to the churches. In the cities the large halls are expensive, and in most cases but few will come out to the best halls. We have been spoken against by those who were not acquainted with us. The reasons of our faith are not understood by the people, and we have been regarded as fanatics who were ignorantly keeping Saturday for Sunday. In our work we have been perplexed to know how to break through the barriers of worldliness and prejudice, and bring before the people

(31)

the precious truth which means so much to them. The Lord has instructed us that the camp meeting is one of the most important instrumentalities for the accomplishment of this work.

We must plan wisely, that the people may have an opportunity of hearing for themselves the last message of mercy to the world. The people should be warned to make ready for the great day of God, which is right upon them. We have no time to lose. We must do our utmost to reach men where they are. The world is now reaching the boundary line in impenitence and disregard for the laws of the government of God. In every city of our world the warning must be proclaimed. All that can be done should be done without delay.

And our camp meetings have another object, preparatory to this. They are to promote spiritual life among our own people. The world in its wisdom knows not God. The world cannot see the beauty, the loveliness, the goodness, the holiness of divine truth. And in order that men may understand this, there must be a channel through which it shall come to the world. The church has been constituted that channel. Christ reveals Himself to us that we may reveal Him to others. Through His people are to be manifested the riches and glory of His unspeakable gift.

God has committed to our hands a most sacred work, and we need to meet together to receive instruction, that we may be fitted to perform this work. We need to understand what part we shall individually be called upon to act in building up the cause of God in the earth, in vindicating God's holy law, and in lifting up the Saviour as "the Lamb of God, which taketh away the sin of the world." John 1:29. We need to meet together and receive the divine touch, that we may understand our work in the home. Parents need to understand how they may send forth from the sanctuary of the home their sons and daughters so trained and educated that they will be fitted to shine as lights in the world. We need to understand in regard to the division of labor and how each part of the work is to be carried forward. Each one should understand the part he is to act, that there may be harmony of plan and of labor in the combined work of all.

REACHING THE MASSES

In the Sermon on the Mount Christ said to His disciples: "Ye are the light of the world. A city that is set on an hill cannot be hid. Neither do men light a candle, and put it under a bushel, but on a candlestick; and it giveth light unto all that are in the house. Let your light so shine before men, that they may see your good works, and glorify your Father which is in heaven." Matthew 5:14-16. If our camp meetings are conducted as they should be, they will indeed be a light in the world. They should be held in the large cities and towns where the message of truth has not been proclaimed. And they should continue for two or three weeks. It may sometimes be advisable to hold a camp meeting for several successive seasons in the same place; but as a rule the place of meeting should be changed from year to year. Instead of having mammoth camp meetings in a few localities, more good would be done by having smaller meetings in many places. Thus the work will be constantly extending into new fields. Just as soon as the standard of truth is lifted in one locality, and it is safe to leave the new converts, we must plan to enter other new fields. Our camp meetings are a power, and when held in a place where the community can be stirred, they will have far greater power than when for the convenience of our own people they are located where, because of previous meetings and the rejection of truth, the public interest is deadened.

A mistake has been made in holding camp meetings in out-of-the-way places and in continuing in the same place year after year. This has been done to save expense and labor, but the saving should be made in other lines. In new fields especially, a dearth of means often makes it difficult to meet the expense of a camp meeting. Careful economy should be exercised and inexpensive plans devised, for much can be saved in this way. But let not the work be crippled. This method of presenting the truth to the people is by the devising of our God. When souls are to be labored for, and the truth is to be brought before those who know it not, the work must not be hindered in order to save expense.

Our camp meetings should be so conducted as to accomplish the greatest possible amount of good. Let the truth be properly presented and represented by those who believe it. It is light, the light of heaven, that the world needs, and whatever manifests the Lord Jesus Christ is light.

AN OBJECT LESSON

Every camp meeting should be an object lesson of neatness, order, and good taste. We must give careful regard to economy, and must avoid display; but everything connected with the grounds should be neat and tidy. Taste and tact do much to attract. And in all our work we should present the discipline of organization and order.

Everything should be so arranged as to impress both our own people and the world with the sacredness and importance of the work of God. The regulations observed in the encampment of the Israelites are an example to us. It was Christ who gave those special instructions to Israel, and He intended them for us also, upon whom the ends of the world are come. We should study carefully the specifications of God's word and practice these directions as the will of God. Let everything connected with the encampment be pure, wholesome, and cleanly. Special attention should be given to all sanitary arrangements, and men of sound judgment and discernment should see that nothing is permitted to sow the seeds of sickness and death throughout the encampment.

The tents should be securely staked, and whenever there is liability of rain, every tent should be trenched. On no account let this be neglected. Serious and even fatal illness has been contracted through neglect of this precaution.

We should feel that we are representatives of truth of heavenly origin. We are to show forth the praises of Him who has called us out of darkness into His marvelous light. We should ever bear in mind that angels of God are walking through the encampment, beholding the order and arrangement in every tent. To the large numbers of people who come to the ground, all the arrangements are an illustration of the belief and principles of the people conducting the meeting. It should be the very best illustration possible. All the surroundings should be a lesson. Especially should the family tents, in their neatness and order, giving a glimpse of home life, be a constant sermon as to the habits, customs, and practices of Seventh-day Adventists.

SECURING ATTENDANCE

As we were preparing to hold a camp meeting near a large city where our people were but little known, I seemed one night to be in an assembly met for consultation as to the work to be done before the meeting. It was proposed to make large efforts, and incur heavy expense for distributing notices and papers. Arrangements were being made to do this, when One who is wise in counsel said: "Set your tents, begin your meetings, then advertise; and more will be accomplished.

"The truth as spoken by the living preacher will have greater influence than the same matter will have when published in the papers. But both methods combined will have still greater force. It is not the best plan to follow one line of effort year after year. Change the order of things. When you give time and opportunity, Satan is prepared to rally his forces, and he will work to destroy every soul possible. Do not arouse opposition before the people have had opportunity to hear the truth and know what they are opposing. Reserve your means to do a strong work after the meeting rather than before. If a press can be secured to be worked during the meeting, printing leaflets, notices, and papers for distribution, it will have a telling influence."

At some of our camp meetings strong companies of workers have been organized to go out into the city and its suburbs to distribute literature and invite people to the meetings. By this means hundreds of persons were secured as regular attendants during the last half of the meeting who otherwise might have thought little about it.

We must take every justifiable means of bringing the light before the people. Let the press be utilized, and let every advertising agency be employed that will call attention to the work. This should not be regarded as nonessential. On every street corner you may see placards and notices calling attention to various things that are going on, some of them of the most objectionable character; and shall those who have the light of life be satisfied with feeble efforts to call the attention of the masses to the truth?

Those who become interested have to meet sophistry and misrepresentation from popular ministers, and they know not how to answer these things. The truth presented by the living preacher should be published in as compact a form as possible, and circulated widely. As far as practicable, let the important discourses given at our camp meetings be published in the newspapers. Thus the truth which was placed before a limited number may find access to many minds. And where the truth has been misrepresented, the people will have an opportunity of knowing just what the minister said.

Put your light on a candlestick, that it may give light to all who are in the house. If the truth has been given to us, we are to make it so plain to others that the honest in heart may recognize it and rejoice in its bright rays.

Nathanael prayed that he might know whether or not the One announced by John the Baptist as the Messiah was indeed the Lamb of God that taketh away the sin of the world. While he was laying his perplexities before God and asking for light, Philip called him, and in earnest, joyful tones exclaimed: "We have found Him, of whom Moses in the law, and the prophets, did write, Jesus of Nazareth, the son of Joseph." John 1:45.

But Nathanael was prejudiced against the Nazarene. Through the influence of false teaching, unbelief arose in his heart, and he asked: "Can there any good thing come out of Nazareth?" Philip did not try to combat his prejudice and unbelief. He said: "Come and see." This was wise; for as soon as Nathanael saw Jesus, he was convinced that Philip was right. His unbelief was swept

away, and faith, firm, strong, and abiding, took possession of his soul. Jesus commended the trusting faith of
Nathanael.

There are many in the same condition as was Nathanael. They are prejudiced and unbelieving because they
have never come in contact with the special truths for
these last days or with the people who hold them, and it
will require but attendance upon a meeting full of the
Spirit of Christ to sweep away their unbelief. No matter
what we have to meet, what opposition, what effort to
turn souls away from the truth of heavenly origin, we
must give publicity to our faith, that honest souls may see
and hear and be convinced for themselves. Our work is
to say, as did Philip: "Come and see."

We hold no doctrine that we wish to hide. To those
who have been educated to keep the first day of the
week as a sacred day, the most objectionable feature of
our faith is the Sabbath of the fourth commandment.
But does not God's word declare that the seventh day
is the Sabbath of the Lord our God? True, it is not an
easy matter to make the required change from the first
to the seventh day. It involves a cross. It clashes with
the precepts and practices of men. Learned men have
taught the people tradition till they are full of unbelief
and prejudice. Yet we must say to these people: "Come
and see." God requires us to proclaim the truth and
let it discover error.

ATTENDANCE OF CHURCH MEMBERS

It is important that the members of our churches
should attend our camp meetings. The enemies of truth
are many; and because our numbers are few, we should
present as strong a front as possible. Individually you
need the benefits of the meeting, and God calls upon you
to number one in the ranks of truth.

Some will say: "It is expensive to travel, and it would be better for us to save the money and give it for the advancement of the work where it is so much needed." Do not reason in this way; God calls upon you to take your place among the rank and file of His people. Strengthen the meeting all you possibly can by being present with your families. Put forth extra exertion to attend the gathering of God's people.

Brethren and sisters, it would be far better for you to let your business suffer than to neglect the opportunity of hearing the message God has for you. Make no excuse that will keep you from gaining every spiritual advantage possible. You need every ray of light. You need to become qualified to give a reason of the hope that is in you with meekness and fear. You cannot afford to lose one such privilege.

Anciently the Lord instructed His people to assemble three times a year for His worship. To these holy convocations the children of Israel came, bringing to the house of God their tithes, their sin offerings, and their offerings of gratitude. They met to recount God's mercies, to make known His wonderful works, and to offer praise and thanksgiving to His name. And they were to unite in the sacrificial service which pointed to Christ as the Lamb of God that taketh away the sin of the world. Thus they were to be preserved from the corrupting power of worldliness and idolatry. Faith and love and gratitude were to be kept alive in their hearts, and through their association together in this sacred service they were to be bound closer to God and to one another.

In the days of Christ these feasts were attended by vast multitudes of people from all lands; and had they been kept as God intended, in the spirit of true worship, the light of truth might through them have been given to all the nations of the world.

With those who lived at a distance from the tabernacle, more than a month of every year must have been occupied in attendance upon these holy convocations. The Lord saw that these gatherings were necessary for the spiritual life of His people. They needed to turn away from their worldly cares, to commune with God, and to contemplate unseen realities.

If the children of Israel needed the benefit of these holy convocations in their time, how much more do we need them in these last days of peril and conflict! And if the people of the world then needed the light which God had committed to His church, how much more do they need it now!

This is a time for everyone to come up to the help of the Lord, to the help of the Lord against the mighty. The forces of the enemy are strengthening, and as a people we are misrepresented. We desire the people to become acquainted with our doctrines and work. We want them to know what we are, and what we believe. We must find our way to their hearts. Let the army of the Lord be on the ground to represent the work and cause of God. Do not plead an excuse. The Lord has need of you. He does not do His work without the co-operation of the human agent. Go to the camp meeting, even though you have to make a sacrifice to do so. Go with a will to work. And make every effort to induce your friends to go, not in your place, but to go with you, to stand on the Lord's side and obey His commandments. Help those who are interested to attend, if necessary providing them with food and lodging. Angels who are commissioned to minister to those who are heirs of salvation will accompany you. God will do great things for His people. He will bless every effort to honor His cause and advance His work.

PREPARATION OF HEART

At these gatherings we must ever remember that two forces are at work. A battle unseen by human eyes is being waged. The army of the Lord is on the ground, seeking to save souls. Satan and his host are also at work, trying in every possible way to deceive and destroy. The Lord bids us: "Put on the whole armor of God, that ye may be able to stand against the wiles of the devil. For we wrestle not against flesh and blood, but against principalities, against powers, against the rulers of the darkness of this world, against spiritual wickedness in high places." Ephesians 6:11, 12. Day by day the battle goes on. If our eyes could be opened to see the good and evil agencies at work, there would be no trifling, no vanity, no jesting or joking. If all would put on the whole armor of God and fight manfully the battles of the Lord, victories would be gained that would cause the kingdom of darkness to tremble.

None of us should go to the camp meeting depending on the ministers or the Bible workers to make the meeting a blessing to us. God does not want His people to hang their weight on the minister. He does not want them to be weakened by depending on human beings for help. They are not to lean, like helpless children, upon someone else as a prop. As a steward of the grace of God, every church member should feel personal responsibility to have life and root in himself. Each one should feel that in a measure the success of the meeting depends upon him. Do not say: "I am not responsible. I shall have nothing to do in this meeting." If you feel thus, you are giving Satan opportunity to work through you. He will crowd your mind with his thoughts, giving you something to do in his lines. Instead of gathering with Christ, you will scatter abroad.

The success of the meeting depends on the presence and power of the Holy Spirit. For the outpouring of the Spirit every lover of the cause of truth should pray. And as far as lies in our power, we are to remove every hindrance to His working. The Spirit can never be poured out while variance and bitterness toward one another are cherished by the members of the church. Envy, jealousy, evil surmising, and evilspeaking are of Satan, and they effectually bar the way against the Holy Spirit's working. Nothing else in this world is so dear to God as His church. Nothing is guarded by Him with such jealous care. Nothing so offends God as an act that injures the influence of those who are doing His service. He will call to account all who aid Satan in his work of criticizing and discouraging.

Those who are destitute of sympathy, tenderness, and love cannot do Christ's work. Before the prophecy can be fulfilled, The weak shall be "as David," and the house of David "as the angel of the Lord" (Zechariah 12:8), the children of God must put away every thought of suspicion in regard to their brethren. Heart must beat in unison with heart. Christian benevolence and brotherly love must be far more abundantly shown. The words are ringing in my ears: "Draw together, draw together." The solemn, sacred truth for this time is to unify the people of God. The desire for pre-eminence must die. One subject of emulation must swallow up all others—who will most nearly resemble Christ in character? who will most entirely hide self in Jesus?

"Herein is My Father glorified," Christ says, "that ye bear much fruit." John 15:8. If there was ever a place where the believers should bear much fruit, it is at our camp meetings. At these meetings our acts, our words, our spirit, are marked, and our influence is as far-reaching as eternity.

Transformation of character is to be the testimony to the world of the indwelling love of Christ. The Lord expects His people to show that the redeeming power of grace can work upon the faulty character and cause it to develop in symmetry and abundant fruitfulness.

But in order for us to fulfill God's purpose, there is a preparatory work to be done. The Lord bids us empty our hearts of the selfishness which is the root of alienation. He longs to pour upon us His Holy Spirit in rich measure, and He bids us clear the way by self-renunciation. When self is surrendered to God, our eyes will be opened to see the stumbling stones which our un-Christlikeness has placed in the way of others. All these God bids us remove. He says: "Confess your faults one to another, and pray one for another, that ye may be healed." James 5:16. Then we may have the assurance that David had when, after confession of his sin, he prayed: "Restore unto me the joy of Thy salvation; and uphold me with Thy free Spirit. Then will I teach transgressors Thy ways; and sinners shall be converted unto Thee." Psalm 51:12, 13.

When the grace of God reigns within, the soul will be surrounded with an atmosphere of faith and courage and Christlike love, an atmosphere invigorating to the spiritual life of all who inhale it. Then we can go to the camp meeting not merely to receive, but to impart. Everyone who is a partaker of Christ's pardoning love, everyone who has been enlightened by the Spirit of God and converted to the truth, will feel that for these precious blessings he owes a debt to every soul with whom he comes in contact. Those who are humble in heart the Lord will use to reach souls whom the ordained ministers cannot approach. They will be moved to speak words which reveal the saving grace of Christ.

And in blessing others they will themselves be blessed.

God gives us opportunity to impart grace, that He may refill us with increased grace. Hope and faith will strengthen as the agent for God works with the talents and facilities that God has provided. He will have a divine agency to work with him.

BUSINESS MATTERS

As far as possible our camp meetings should be wholly devoted to spiritual interests. They should not be made occasions for the transaction of business.

At the camp meetings, workers are gathered from all parts of the field, and it seems a favorable opportunity for considering business matters connected with the various branches of the work and for the training of workers in different lines. All these different interests are important, but when they have been attended to at a camp meeting, but little opportunity remains for dealing with the practical relation of truth to the soul. Ministers are diverted from their work of building up the children of God in the most holy faith, and the camp meeting does not meet the end for which it was appointed. Many meetings are conducted in which the larger number of the people have no interest, and if they could attend them all they would go away wearied instead of being refreshed and benefited. Many are disappointed at the failure of their expectation to receive help from the camp meeting. Those who came for enlightenment and strength return to their homes little better fitted to work in their families and churches than before attending the meeting.

Business matters should be attended to by those especially appointed for this work. And as far as possible they should be brought before the people at some other time than the camp meeting. Instruction in canvassing, in Sabbath school work, and in the details of tract and missionary work should be given in the home churches or in meetings specially appointed. The same principle applies to cooking schools. While these are all right in their place, they should not occupy the time of our camp meetings.

The presidents of conferences and the ministers should give themselves to the spiritual interests of the people and should therefore be excused from the mechanical labor attendant upon the meeting. The ministers should be ready to act as teachers and leaders in the work of the camp when occasion requires, but they should not be wearied out. They should feel refreshed and be in a cheerful frame of mind, for this is essential for the best good of the meeting. They should be able to speak words of cheer and courage, and to drop seeds of spiritual truth into the soil of honest hearts, to spring up and bear precious fruit.

The ministers should teach the people how to come to the Lord and how to lead others to Him. Methods must be adopted, plans must be carried out, whereby the standard shall be uplifted, and the people shall be taught how they may be purified from iniquity and elevated by adherence to pure and holy principles.

There must be time for heart searching, for soul culture. When the mind is occupied with matters of business, there must necessarily be a dearth of spiritual power. Personal piety, true faith, and heart holiness must be kept before the mind until the people realize their importance.

We must have the power of God in our camp meetings, or we shall not be able to prevail against the enemy of souls. Christ says: "Without Me ye can do nothing."

Those who gather at camp meetings must be impressed with the fact that the object of the meetings is to attain to a higher Christian experience, to advance in the knowledge of God, to become strengthened with spiritual vigor;

and unless we realize this, the meetings will to us be fruitless.

MINISTERIAL HELP

In camp meetings or tent efforts in or near the large cities there should be an abundance of ministerial help. In all our camp meetings the ministerial force should be as strong as possible. It is not wise to allow a constant strain upon one or two men. Under such a strain they become physically and mentally exhausted, and are unable to do the work appointed them. In order that they may have the strength required for the meetings, ministers should arrange beforehand to leave their fields of labor in safe hands, with those who, though they may not be able to preach, can carry forward the work from house to house. In God many can do valiantly, and for their labor will see returns the richness of which will surprise them.

In our large meetings a variety of gifts is needed. Fresh capabilities should be brought into the work. Opportunity must be given for the Holy Spirit to work on the mind. Then the truth will be presented with freshness and power.

In conducting the important interests of meetings near a large city, the co-operation of all the workers is essential. They should keep in the very atmosphere of the meetings, becoming acquainted with the people as they come in and go out, showing the utmost courtesy and kindness, and tender regard for their souls. They should be ready to speak to them in season and out of season, watching to win souls. Oh, that Christ's workers would show one half as much vigilance as does Satan, who is always on the track of human beings, always wide awake, watching to lay some gin or snare for their destruction.

Let every succeeding day be made the most important day of labor. That day, that evening, may be the only opportunity which some soul may have to hear the warning message. Keep this ever in mind.

When ministers allow themselves to be called away from their work to visit the churches, not only do they exhaust their physical strength, but they rob themselves of the time needed for study and prayer and for silence before God in self-examination. Thus they are unfitted to do the work when and where it should be done.

There is nothing more needed in the work than the practical results of communion with God. We should show by our daily lives that we have peace and rest in God. His peace in the heart will shine forth in the countenance. It will give to the voice a persuasive power. Communion with God will impart a moral elevation to the character and to the entire course of action. Men will take knowledge of us, as of the first disciples, that we have been with Jesus. This will impart to the minister's labors a power even greater than that which comes from the influence of his preaching. Of this power he must not allow himself to be deprived. Communion with God through prayer and the study of His word must not be neglected, for here is the source of his strength. No work for the church should take precedence of this.

We have too slight a hold upon God and upon eternal realities. If men will walk with God, He will hide them in the cleft of the Rock. Thus hidden, they can see God, even as Moses saw Him. With the power and light that God imparts, they can comprehend more and accomplish more than they had before deemed possible.

More ability, tact, and wisdom are needed in presenting the word and feeding the flock of God than many suppose.

A dry, lifeless presentation of the truth belittles the most sacred message that God has given to men.

Those who teach the word must themselves live in hourly contact, in conscious, living communion with God. The principles of truth and righteousness and mercy must be within them. They must draw from the Fountain of all wisdom moral and intellectual power. Their hearts must be alive with the deep movings of the Spirit of God.

The source of all power is limitless; and if in your great need you seek for the Holy Spirit to work upon your own soul, if you shut yourself in with God, be assured that you will not come before the people dry and spiritless. Praying much and beholding Jesus, you will cease to exalt self. If you patiently exercise faith, trusting God implicitly, you will recognize the voice of Jesus saying: "Come up higher."

ALL TO BE WORKERS

"And He gave some, apostles; and some, prophets; and some, evangelists; and some, pastors and teachers; for the perfecting of the saints, for the work of the ministry, for the edifying of the body of Christ: till we all come in the unity of the faith, and of the knowledge of the Son of God, unto a perfect man, unto the measure of the stature of the fullness of Christ." Ephesians 4:11-13.

This scripture presents a large program of work that may be brought into our camp meetings. All these gifts are to be in exercise. Every faithful worker will minister for the perfecting of the saints.

Those who are in training for work in the cause in any line should improve every opportunity to work at the camp meetings. Wherever camp meetings are held, young men who have received an education in medical lines should feel it their duty to act a part. They should be encouraged not only to work in medical lines, but also to speak upon the points of present truth, giving the reason why we are Seventh-day Adventists. These young men, if given an opportunity to work with older ministers, will receive much help and blessing.

There is something for everyone to do. Every soul that believes the truth is to stand in his lot and place, saying: "Here am I; send me." Isaiah 6:8. By engaging in work at the camp meeting, all may be learning how to work successfully in their home churches.

Properly conducted, the camp meeting is a school where pastors, elders, and deacons can learn to do more perfect work for the Master. It should be a school where the members of the church, old and young, are given opportunity to learn the way of the Lord more perfectly, a place where believers can receive an education that will help them to help others.

Parents who come to camp meeting should take special heed to the lessons given for their instruction. Then, in the home life, by precept and example, let them impart these lessons to their children. As they thus strive to save their children from the corrupting influences of the world, they will see an improvement in their families.

The best help that ministers can give the members of our churches is not sermonizing, but planning work for them. Give each one something to do for others. Help all to see that as receivers of the grace of Christ they are under obligation to work for Him. And let all be taught how to work. Especially should those who are newly come to the faith be educated to become laborers together with God. If set to work, the despondent will soon forget their despondency; the weak will become strong, the ignorant intelligent, and all will be prepared to present the truth as it is in Jesus. They will find an unfailing helper in Him who has promised to save all that come unto Him.

PRAYER AND COUNSEL

Those who labor at camp meetings should frequently engage together in prayer and counsel, that they may labor intelligently. At these meetings there are many things that demand attention. But the ministers should take time to meet together for prayer and counsel every day. You should know that all things are drawing in even lines, "that you are standing," as the words were spoken to me, "shoulder to shoulder, marching right ahead, and not drawing off." When the work is carried on in this way, there is unity of heart, and there will be harmony of action. This will be a wonderful means of bringing the blessing of God upon the people.

Before giving a discourse, ministers should take time to seek God for wisdom and power. In earlier times the ministers would often go away and pray together, and they would not cease until the Spirit of God responded to their prayers. Then they would return from the place of prayer with their faces lighted up; and when they spoke to the congregation, their words were with power. They reached the hearts of the people because the Spirit that gave them the blessing prepared hearts to receive their message. There is far more being done by the heavenly universe than we realize in preparing the way that souls may be converted. We are to work in harmony with the messengers of heaven. We want more of God; we are not to feel that our talking and sermonizing can do the work. Unless the people are reached through God, they will never be reached. We are to rely wholly upon God, pleading His promise: "Not by might, nor by power, but by My Spirit, saith the Lord of hosts." Zechariah 4:6.

When those to whom God has entrusted responsibilities as leaders fear and tremble before Him because of the responsibility of the work, when they feel their own unworthiness and seek the Lord in humility, when they purify themselves from all that is displeasing to Him, when they plead with Him until they know that they have forgiveness and peace, then God will manifest Himself through them. Then the work will go forward with power.

Fellow laborers, we must have Jesus, the precious Jesus, abiding in our own hearts much more fully if we are to meet with success in presenting Him to the people. We are in great need of the heavenly influence, God's Holy Spirit, to give power and efficiency to our work. We need to open the heart to Christ. We need much firmer faith and more fervent devotion. We need to die to self, and in mind and heart to cherish an adoring love for our Saviour. When we will seek the Lord with all the heart we shall find Him, and our hearts will be all aglow with His love. Self will sink into insignificance, and Jesus will be all and in all to the soul.

Christ presents to us who are athirst the water of life, that we may drink freely; when we do this we have Christ within us as a well of water springing up into everlasting life. Then our words are full of moisture. We are prepared to water others.

We must draw nigh to God. We must be laborers together with Him, else weakness and mistakes will be seen in all we undertake. If it were left to us to manage the interests of the cause of God in our own way, we would not have reason to expect much; but if self is hid in Christ, all our work will be wrought in God. Let us have faith in God at every step. While we realize our own weakness, let us not be faithless, but believing.

If we will take God at His word, we shall see of His salvation. The gospel that we present to save perishing souls must be the very gospel that saves our own souls. We must receive the word of God. We must eat the word, live the word; it is the flesh and blood of the Son of God. We must eat His flesh and drink His blood—receive by faith His spiritual attributes.

We must receive light and blessing, that we may have something to impart. It is the privilege of every worker first to talk with God in the secret place of prayer and then to talk with the people as God's mouthpiece. Men and women who commune with God, who have an abiding Christ, make the very atmosphere holy, because they are co-operating with holy angels. Such witness is needed for this time. We need the melting power of God, the power to draw with Christ.

NEEDS OF THE CHURCH

Many come to camp meeting with hearts full of murmuring and complaining. Through the work of the Holy Spirit these must be led to see that their murmuring is an offense to God. They must be led to feel self-reproach because they have allowed the enemy to control their mind and judgment. Complaining must be turned to repentance, uncertainty and despondency to the earnest inquiry: "How shall I become true in faith?"

When man is a partaker of the divine nature, the love of Christ will be an abiding principle in the soul, and self and its peculiarities will not be exhibited. But it is sad to see those who should be vessels unto honor indulging in the gratification of the lower nature and walking in paths that conscience condemns. Men professing to be followers of Christ fall to a low level, always mourning over their shortcomings, but never overcoming and bruising Satan under their feet. Guilt and condemnation constantly burden the soul, and the cry of such might well be: "O wretched man that I am! who shall deliver me from the body of this death?" Romans 7:24. Through indulgence in sin, self-respect is destroyed; and when that is gone, respect for others is lessened; we think that others are as unrighteous as we are ourselves.

At our yearly convocations these things should be set before the people, and they should be encouraged to find in Christ deliverance from the power of sin. He says: "When ye shall search for Me with all your heart, . . . I will be found of you." Jeremiah 29:13, 14. The standard should be elevated, and the preaching should be of the most spiritual character, that the people may be led to see the reason of their weakness and unhappiness. Many are unhappy because they are unholy. Purity of heart, innocence of mind, only can be blessed of God. When sin is cherished, it can in the end produce nothing but unhappiness; and the sin which leads to the most unhappy results is pride of heart, the lack of Christlike sympathy and love.

HOW TO PRESENT THE MESSAGE

Everywhere there are hearts crying out for the living God. Discourses unsatisfying to the hungry soul have been given in the churches. In these discourses there is not that divine manifestation which touches the mind and creates a glow in the soul. The hearers cannot say: "Did not our heart burn within us, while He talked with us by the way, and while He opened to us the Scriptures?" Luke 24:32. Much of the teaching given is powerless to awaken the transgressor or convict souls of sin. The people who come to hear the word need a plain, straightforward presentation of truth. Some who have once tasted of the word of God have dwelt long in an atmosphere where there is no God, and they long for the divine presence.

The very first and most important thing is to melt and

subdue the soul by presenting our Lord Jesus Christ as the sin-pardoning Saviour. Never should a sermon be preached, or Bible instruction in any line be given, without pointing the hearers to "the Lamb of God, which taketh away the sin of the world." John 1:29. Every true doctrine makes Christ the center, every precept receives force from His words.

Keep before the people the cross of Calvary. Show what caused the death of Christ—the transgression of the law. Let not sin be cloaked or treated as a matter of little consequence. It is to be presented as guilt against the Son of God. Then point the people to Christ, telling them that immortality comes only through receiving Him as their personal Saviour.

Arouse the people to see how far they have departed from the Lord's ordinances by adopting worldly policy and conforming to worldly principles. These have brought them into transgression of God's law.

———

Many in the world set their affections on things that in themselves are not evil; but they become satisfied with these things, and do not seek the greater and higher good that Christ desires to give them. Now we must not rudely seek to deprive them of what they hold dear. Reveal to them the beauty and preciousness of truth. Lead them to behold Christ in His loveliness; then they will turn from everything that would draw their affections away from Him. This is the principle of the Saviour's dealing with men; it is the principle that must be brought into the church.

Christ came into the world to "bind up the broken-hearted, to proclaim liberty to the captives, and the opening of the prison to them that are bound." Isaiah 61:1. The Sun of Righteousness shall "arise with healing in

His wings." Malachi 4:2. The world is full of men and women who are carrying a heavy burden of sorrow and suffering and sin. God sends His children to reveal to them Him who will take away the burden and give them rest. It is the mission of Christ's servants to help, to bless, and to heal.

Christ's favorite theme was the paternal character and abundant love of God. This knowledge of God was Christ's own gift to men, and this gift He has committed to His people to be communicated by them to the world.

In presenting to the people the various lessons and warnings of the special message for this time, we must bear in mind that not all are equally appropriate for the congregations that assemble at our camp meetings. Even Jesus said to His disciples, who had been with Him for three years: "I have yet many things to say unto you, but ye cannot bear them now." John 16:12. We must endeavor to present the truth as the people are prepared to hear it and to appreciate its value. The Spirit of God is working upon the minds and hearts of men, and we are to work in harmony with it.

Of some truths the people already have a knowledge. There are some in which they are interested, of which they are ready to learn more. Show them the significance of these truths and their relation to others which they do not understand. Thus you will arouse a desire for greater light. This is "rightly dividing the word of truth." 2 Timothy 2:15.

Let the message for this time be presented, not in long,

labored discourses, but in short talks, right to the point. Do not think when you have gone over a subject once that you can pass right on to other points, and the hearers will retain all that has been presented. There is danger of passing too rapidly from point to point. Give short lessons, in plain, simple language, and let them be often repeated.

Do not immediately follow one discourse with another, but let a period of rest intervene, that the truth may be fastened in the mind, and that opportunity for meditation and prayer may be given for both ministers and people. Thus there will be growth in religious knowledge and experience.

Keep the mind concentrated on a few vital points. Do not bring unimportant ideas into your discourses. God would not have you think that you are impressed by His Spirit when you fly from your subject, bringing in foreign matters that have no connection with your text. By wandering from straight lines, and bringing in that which calls the mind off the subject, you lose your bearing, and weaken all that you have previously said. Give your hearers pure wheat, thoroughly winnowed.

Be careful never to lose a sense of the presence of the divine Watcher. Remember that you are speaking, not only before an assembly of men, but before One whom you should ever recognize. Speak as if the whole heavenly universe were before you.

One night, previous to an important meeting, I seemed

in my sleeping hours to be in meeting with my brethren, listening to One who spoke as having authority. He said: "Many souls will attend this meeting who are honestly ignorant of the truths that will be presented. They will listen and become interested, because Christ is drawing them; conscience tells them that what they hear is true, for it has the Bible for its foundation. The greatest care is needed in dealing with these souls.

"Let such portions of the message be dealt out to them as they may be able to grasp and appropriate. Though it should appear strange and startling, many will recognize with joy that new light is shed on the word of God; whereas if new truths were presented in so large a measure that they could not comprehend them, some would go away and never come again. Some, in their efforts to tell it to others, would misrepresent what they had heard. Some would so wrest the Scriptures as to confuse other minds.

"Those who will study the manner of Christ's teaching, and educate themselves to follow His way, will attract and hold large numbers now, as Christ held the people in His day. At every meeting, Satan will be on the ground, that with his hellish shadow he may obtrude himself between man and God to intercept every ray of light that might shine on the soul. But when the truth in its practical character is urged upon the people because you love them, souls will be convicted, because the Holy Spirit of God will impress their hearts.

"Arm yourselves with humility; pray that angels of God may come close to your side to impress the mind; for it is not you that work the Holy Spirit, but the Holy Spirit must work you. It is the Holy Spirit that makes the truth impressive. Keep practical truth ever before the people."

Do not make prominent those features of the message which are a condemnation of the customs and practices of the people, until they have an opportunity to know that we are believers in Christ, that we believe in His divinity and in His pre-existence. Let the testimony of the world's Redeemer be dwelt upon. He says: "I Jesus have sent Mine angel to testify unto you these things in the churches." Revelation 22:16.

————

At the Queensland camp meeting in 1898, instruction was given me for our Bible workers. In the visions of the night, ministers and workers seemed to be in a meeting where Bible lessons were being given. We said, "We have the Great Teacher with us today," and we listened with interest to His words. He said: "There is a great work before you in this place. You will need to present truth in its simplicity. Bring the people to the waters of life. Speak to them the things which most concern their present and eternal good. Let not your study of the Scriptures be of a cheap or casual order. In all that you say, know that you have something which is worthy of the time you take to say it, and of the time of the hearers to hear. Speak of those things which are essential, those things which will instruct, bringing light with every word.

"Learn to meet the people where they are. Do not present subjects that will arouse controversy. Let not your instruction be of a character to perplex the mind. Do not cause the people to worry over things which you may understand but which they do not see, unless these are of vital consequence to the saving of the soul. Do not present the Scriptures in a way to exalt self and encourage vainglory in the one who opens the word. The work for this time is to train students and workers to deal with subjects in a plain, serious, and solemn manner. There must be no time uselessly employed in this great work. We must not miss the mark. Time is too short for us to undertake to reveal all that might be opened to view. Eternity will be required for us to know all the length and breadth, the depth and height, of the Scriptures. There are some souls to whom certain truths are of more importance than other truths. Skill is needed in your education in Scriptural lines. Read and study Psalm 40:7, 8; John 1:14; 1 Timothy 3:16; Philippians 2:5-11; Colossians 1:14-17; Revelation 5:11-14.

"To the apostle John on the Isle of Patmos were revealed the things which God desired him to give to the people. Study these revelations. Here are themes worthy of our contemplation, large and comprehensive lessons which all the angelic host are now seeking to communicate. Behold the life and character of Christ, and study His mediatorial work. Here is infinite wisdom, infinite love, infinite justice, infinite mercy. Here are depths and heights, lengths and breadths, for our consideration. Numberless pens have been employed in presenting to the world the life, the character, and the mediatorial work of Christ, and yet every mind through which the Holy Spirit has worked has presented these themes in a light that is fresh and new."

We desire to lead the people to understand what Christ is to them and what are the responsibilities they are called upon to accept in Him. As His representatives and witnesses, we ourselves need to come to a full understanding of the saving truths gained by an experimental knowledge.

Teach the great practical truths that must be stamped upon the soul. Teach the saving power of Jesus, "in whom we have redemption through His blood, even the forgiveness of sins." Colossians 1:14. It was at the cross that mercy and truth met together, that righteousness and truth kissed each other. Let every student and every worker study this again and again, that they, setting forth the Lord crucified among us, may make it a fresh subject to the people. Show that the life of Christ reveals an infinitely perfect character. Teach that "as many as received Him, to them gave He power to become the sons of God, even to them that believe on His name." John 1:12. Tell it over and over again. We may become the sons of God, members of the royal family, children of the heavenly King. Let it be known that all who accept Jesus Christ and hold the beginning of their confidence firm to the end will be heirs of God and joint heirs with Christ "to an inheritance incorruptible, and undefiled, and that fadeth not away, reserved in heaven for you, who are kept by the power of God through faith unto salvation ready to be revealed in the last time." 1 Peter 1:4, 5.

THE LAST WARNING

The third angel's message is to be given with power. The power of the proclamation of the first and second messages is to be intensified in the third. In the Revelation John says of the heavenly messenger who unites with the third angel: "I saw another angel come down from heaven, having great power; and the earth was lightened with his glory. And he cried mightily with a strong voice." Revelation 18:1, 2. We are in danger of giving the third angel's message in so indefinite a manner that it does not impress the people. So many other interests are brought in that the very message which should be proclaimed with power becomes tame and voiceless. At our camp meetings a mistake has been made. The Sabbath question has been touched upon, but has not been presented as the great test for this time. While the churches profess to believe in

Christ, they are violating the law which Christ Himself proclaimed from Sinai. The Lord bids us: "Show My people their transgression, and the house of Jacob their sins." Isaiah 58:1. The trumpet is to give a certain sound.

When you have a congregation before you for only two weeks, do not defer the presentation of the Sabbath question until everything else is presented, supposing that you thus pave the way for it. Lift up the standard—the commandments of God and the faith of Jesus. Make this the important theme. Then, by your strong arguments, make it of still greater force. Dwell more on the Revelation. Read, explain, and enforce its teaching.

Our warfare is aggressive. Tremendous issues are before us, yea, and right upon us. Let our prayers ascend to God that the four angels may still hold the four winds, that they may not blow to injure or destroy until the last warning has been given to the world. Then let us work in harmony with our prayers. Let nothing lessen the force of the truth for this time. The present truth is to be our burden. The third angel's message must do its work of separating from the churches a people who will take their stand on the platform of eternal truth.

Our message is a life-and-death message, and we must let it appear as it is, the great power of God. We are to present it in all its telling force. Then the Lord will make it effectual. It is our privilege to expect large things, even the demonstration of the Spirit of God. This is the power that will convict and convert the soul.

The perils of the last days are upon us, and in our work we are to warn the people of the danger they are in. Let not the solemn scenes which prophecy has revealed be left untouched. If our people were half awake, if they realized the nearness of the events portrayed in the Revelation, a reformation would be wrought in our churches, and many more would believe the message. We have no time to lose; God calls upon us to watch for souls as they that must give an account. Advance new principles, and crowd in the clear-cut truth. It will be as a sword cutting both ways. But be not too ready to take a controversial attitude. There will be times when we must stand still and see the salvation of God. Let Daniel speak, let the Revelation speak, and tell what is truth. But whatever phase of the subject is presented, uplift Jesus as the center of all hope, "the Root and the Offspring of David, and the bright and morning Star." Revelation 22:16.

PRAISE MEETINGS

In our camp meeting services there should be singing and instrumental music. Musical instruments were used in religious services in ancient times. The worshipers praise God upon the harp and cymbal, and music should have its place in our services. It will add to the interest. And every day a praise meeting should be held, a simple service of thanksgiving to God. There would be much more power in our camp meetings if we had a true sense of the goodness, mercy, and long-suffering of God, and if more praise flowed forth from our lips to the honor and glory of His name. We need to cultivate more fervor of soul. The Lord says: "Whoso offereth praise glorifieth Me." Psalm 50:23.

It is Satan's work to talk of that which concerns himself, and he is delighted to have human beings talk of his power, of his working through the children of men. Through indulgence in such conversation the mind becomes gloomy and sour and disagreeable. We may become channels of communication for Satan, through which flow words that bring no sunshine to any heart. But let us decide that this shall not be. Let us decide not to be channels through which Satan shall communicate gloomy, disagreeable thoughts. Let our words be not a savor of death unto death, but of life unto life.

In the words we speak to the people and in the prayers we offer, God desires us to give unmistakable evidence that we have spiritual life. We do not enjoy the fullness of blessing which the Lord has prepared for us, because we do not ask in faith. If we would exercise faith in the word of the living God we should have the richest blessings. We dishonor God by our lack of faith; therefore we cannot impart life to others by bearing a living, uplifting testimony. We cannot give that which we do not possess.

If we will walk humbly with God, if we will work in the spirit of Christ, none of us will carry heavy burdens. We shall lay them upon the great Burden Bearer. Then we may expect triumphs in the presence of God, in the communion of His love. From the beginning to the end every camp meeting may be a love feast, because God's presence is with His people.

All heaven is interested in our salvation. The angels of God, thousands upon thousands, and ten thousand times ten thousand, are commissioned to minister to those who shall be heirs of salvation. They guard us against evil and press back the powers of darkness that are seeking our destruction. Have we not reason to be thankful every moment, thankful even when there are apparent difficulties in our pathway?

The Lord Himself is our helper. "Sing, O daughter of Zion; shout, O Israel; be glad and rejoice with all the heart, O daughter of Jerusalem." "The Lord thy God in the midst of thee is mighty; He will save, He will rejoice over thee with joy; He will rest in His love, He will joy over thee with singing." Zephaniah 3:14, 17. This is the testimony the Lord desires us to bear to the world. His praise should continually be in our hearts and upon our lips.

Such a testimony will have an influence upon others. As we seek to turn men from their self-indulgent efforts to secure happiness, we must show them that we have something better than that which they are seeking. When Jesus talked with the Samaritan woman, He did not reprove her for coming to draw from Jacob's well, but He presented something of far greater value. In comparison with Jacob's well He presented the fountain of living waters. "If thou knewest the gift of God," He said, "and who it is that saith to thee, Give Me to drink; thou wouldest have asked of Him, and He would have given thee living water. . . . Whosoever drinketh of the water that I shall give him shall never thirst; but the water that I shall give him shall be in him a well of water springing up into everlasting life." John 4:10-14.

The church needs the fresh, living experience of members who have habitual communion with God. Dry, stale testimonies and prayers, without the manifestation of Christ in them, are no help to the people. If everyone who claims to be a child of God were filled with faith and light and life, what a wonderful witness would be given to those who come to hear the truth! And how many souls might be won to Christ!

REVIVAL EFFORTS

At our camp meetings there are far too few revival efforts made. There is too little seeking of the Lord. Revival services should be carried from the beginning to the close of the meeting. The most determined efforts should be made to arouse the people. Let all see that you are in earnest because you have a wonderful message from heaven. Tell them that the Lord is coming in judgment, and that neither kings nor rulers, wealth nor influence, will avail to ward off the judgments soon to fall. At the close of every meeting, decisions should be called for. Hold fast to those interested, until they are confirmed in the faith.

We must be more decidedly in earnest. We must talk the truth in private and in public, presenting every argument, urging every motive of infinite weight, to draw men to the Saviour uplifted on the cruel cross. God desires every man to attain unto eternal life. Mark how all through the word of God there is manifest the spirit of urgency, of imploring men and women to come to Christ, to deny appetites and passions that corrupt the soul. With all our powers we must urge them to look unto Jesus and to accept His life of self-denial and sacrifice. We must show that we expect them to give joy to the heart of Christ by using every one of His gifts in honoring His name.

Many who come to the meeting are weary and heavy-laden with sin. They do not feel safe in their religious faith. Opportunity should be given for those who are troubled and want rest in spirit to find help. After a discourse those who wish to follow Christ should be invited to signify their desire. Invite all who are not satisfied that they are prepared for Christ's coming, and all who feel burdened and heavy-laden, to come apart by themselves. Let those who are spiritual converse with these souls. Pray with and for them. Let much time be spent in prayer and close searching of the word. Let all obtain the real facts of faith in their own souls through belief that the Holy Spirit will be imparted to them because they have a real hungering and thirsting after righteousness. Teach them how to surrender themselves to God, how to believe, how to claim the promises. Let the deep love of God be expressed in words of encouragement, in words of intercession.

Let there be far more wrestling with God for the salvation of souls. Work disinterestedly, determinedly, with a spirit never to let go. Compel souls to come in to the marriage supper of the Lamb. Let there be more praying, believing, and receiving, and more working together with God.

There is the most distressing indifference and neglect in regard to the great salvation. The careless must be awakened, else they are lost. Since God has given His own Son to save the guilty sinner, He means through His agents to counterwork the human and satanic agencies that are united to destroy the soul. The Lord has made every provision that the uplifted Saviour may be revealed to sinners. Although they are dead in trespasses and sins, their attention must be aroused by the preaching of Christ and Him crucified. Men must be convicted of the evil of sin. The eyes of the transgressor must be enlightened. Let all who have been drawn to Christ tell the story of His love. Let everyone who has felt the converting power of Christ upon his own soul do what he can in the name of the Lord.

The infinite value of the sacrifice required for our redemption reveals the fact that sin is a tremendous evil. God might have wiped out this foul blot from His creation by sweeping the sinner from the face of the earth. But He "so loved the world, that He gave His only-begotten Son, that whosoever believeth in Him should not perish, but have everlasting life." John 3:16. Why are not all who claim to love God seeking to enlighten their neighbors and their associates, that they may not longer neglect this great salvation?

Christ gave Himself to a shameful, agonizing death,

showing His great travail of soul to save the perishing. Oh, Christ is able, Christ is willing, Christ is longing, to save all who will come unto Him! Talk to souls in peril and get them to behold Jesus upon the cross, dying to make it possible for Him to pardon. Talk to the sinner with your own heart overflowing with the tender, pitying love of Christ. Let there be deep earnestness; but not a harsh, loud note should be heard from the one who is trying to win the soul to look and live. First have your own soul consecrated to God. As you look upon our Intercessor in heaven, let your heart be broken. Then, softened and subdued, you can address repenting sinners as one who realizes the power of redeeming love. Pray with these souls, by faith bringing them to the foot of the cross; carry their minds up with your mind, and fix the eye of faith where you look, upon Jesus the Sin Bearer. Get them to look away from their poor, sinful selves to the Saviour, and the victory is won. They behold for themselves the Lamb of God that taketh away the sin of the world. They see the Way, the Truth, the Life. The Sun of Righteousness sheds its bright beams into the heart. The strong tide of redeeming love pours into the parched and thirsty soul, and the sinner is saved to Jesus Christ.

Christ crucified—talk it, pray it, sing it, and it will break and win hearts. This is the power and wisdom of God to gather souls for Christ. Formal, set phrases, the presentation of merely argumentative subjects, is productive of little good. The melting love of God in the hearts of the workers will be recognized by those for whom they labor. Souls are thirsting for the waters of life. Do not be empty cisterns. If you reveal the love of Christ to them, you may lead the hungering, thirsting ones to Jesus, and He will give them the bread of life and the water of salvation.

PERSONAL LABOR

The Lord's servants must not only preach the word from the pulpit, but must come in personal contact with the people. When a discourse is given, precious seed is sown. But if personal effort is not made to cultivate the soil, the seed does not take root. Unless the heart is softened and subdued by the Spirit of God, much of the discourse is lost. Observe those in the congregation who seem to be interested, and speak to them after the service. A few words spoken in private will often do more good than the whole discourse has done. Inquire how the subjects presented appear to the hearers, whether the matter is clear to their minds. By kindness and courtesy show that you have a real interest in them and a care for their souls. Many have been led to think that as a people we do not believe in conversion. When we appeal to them to come to Christ, hearts will be softened, and prejudice will be swept away.

BIBLE STUDIES

Whenever practicable, every important discourse should be followed by a Bible study. Here the points that have been presented can be applied, questions can be asked, and right ideas inculcated. More time should be devoted to patiently educating the people, giving them opportunity to express themselves. It is instruction that men need, line upon line, and precept upon precept.

Special meetings also should be held for those who are becoming interested in the truths presented and who need instruction. To these meetings the people should be invited, and all, both believers and unbelievers, should have an opportunity to ask questions on points not fully understood. Give all an opportunity to speak of their perplexities, for they will have them. In all the sermons and in all the Bible studies, let the people see that on every point a plain "Thus saith the Lord" is given for the faith and doctrines which we advocate.

This was the method of Christ's teaching. As He spoke to the people, they would question as to His meaning. To those who were humbly seeking for light, He was always ready to explain His words. But Christ did not encourage criticism or caviling, nor should we. When men try to provoke a discussion of controverted points of doctrine, tell them that the meeting was not appointed for that purpose.

When you do answer a question, be sure to have the hearers see and acknowledge that it is answered. Do not let a question drop, telling them to ask it again. Feel your way step by step, and know how much you have gained.

In such meetings those who understand the message can ask questions which will bring out light on points of truth. But some may not have wisdom to do this. When any put questions that serve only to confuse the mind and sow the seeds of doubt, they should be advised to refrain from such questioning. We must learn when to speak and when to keep silent, learn to sow the seeds of faith, to impart light, not darkness.

A WORD IN SEASON

Those who keep in a prayerful frame of mind will be able to speak a word in season to those who are brought within the sphere of their influence; for God will give wisdom whereby they may serve the Lord Jesus. "When wisdom entereth into thine heart, and knowledge is pleasant unto thy soul; discretion shall preserve thee, understanding shall keep thee." Proverbs 2:10, 11. You will open your mouth with wisdom, and in your tongue will be the law of kindness.

If those who claim to be Christians will heed the word of Christ, all who come in contact with them will acknowledge that they have been with Jesus and have learned of Him. They will represent Christ, and eternal things will be their theme. The realities of eternity will be brought near. They will watch for souls as they that must give an account. This means much more than many seem to think. It means to go out and search for the lost sheep.

RAISING FUNDS

None are to take advantage of the camp meetings, when the greatest number of people may be reached, in order to introduce special interests or to raise means for the various benevolent objects that are becoming so numerous. The work of God in the ministry of the word, the promulgation of the truth in the regions beyond, the great interests of educational work in new fields, and the establishment of sanitariums in connection with the work of the gospel ministry—these are objects that should be presented to the people at our camp meetings.

RESULTS OF CAMP MEETING WORK

A great work is to be accomplished by our camp meetings. The Lord has specially honored these gatherings, which He has called "holy convocations." To these meetings come thousands of people, many merely from curiosity to see and hear some new thing. But as they hear the message of truth and come in contact with those who believe it, many are impressed. They see that this people are not what they have been represented. Prejudice, opposition, and indifference are swept away, and with candid interest they listen to the word spoken.

The Lord has His representatives in all the churches. These persons have not had the special testing truths for these last days presented to them under circumstances that brought conviction to heart and mind; therefore they have not, by rejecting light, severed their connection with God. Many there are who have faithfully walked in the light that has shone upon their pathway. They hunger to know more of the ways and works of God. All over the world men and women are looking wistfully to heaven. Prayers and tears and inquiries go up from souls longing for light, for grace, for the Holy Spirit. Many are on the very verge of the kingdom, waiting only to be gathered in.

As the lessons of Christ, the truths of the Bible in their simplicity, are placed before these souls, they recognize the light and rejoice in it. Their perplexities vanish before the light of truth as dew before the morning sun. Their conceptions of Bible truth are expanded, and the revelation of God in Christ comes to them, showing them the depth, breadth, and height of divine, spiritual mystery that they did not before discern, that cannot be explained, but only exemplified in Christlike character.

Many who are not connected with any church, and who appear wholly unmindful of the claims of God, are not at heart as indifferent as they seem. Even the most irreligious have their hours of conviction, when there comes to them a longing for something they have not. In every town and city there are large numbers who do not attend any place of worship. Many of these are attracted to the camp meeting. Many come who are slaves of sin, the helpless victims of evil habits. Many are convicted and converted. As they by faith grasp the promise of God for the forgiveness of their sins, the bondage of habit is broken. Forsaking their sinful indulgences, they become freemen in Christ Jesus, and rejoice in the liberty of the sons of God. This is the work to be done in all our camp meetings. Through this means thousands will be won to Christ.

AFTER THE CAMP MEETING

By camp meetings held in the cities thousands will be called out to hear the invitation to the feast: "Come; for all things are now ready." Luke 14:17. After arousing the interest of the people, we should not cut these meetings short, pulling down all the tents and giving the impression that the meeting is over. Just at the time when hundreds have become interested, the greatest good may be accomplished by faithful and earnest work. Therefore the meetings should be so managed that the public interest may be maintained.

After one of the camp meetings the question as to the continuance of tent meetings was under consideration. I told the brethren a dream I had had. I dreamed that I saw a partially completed building. The workmen were gathering up their tools, preparing to leave it unfinished; but I entreated them to consider the matter. "The building is not finished," I said; "come back, and keep at work until it is roofed." Then they came back and continued the work. So the brethren heeded my counsel to remain and continue the work of the camp meeting. As the result a number accepted the truth.

There need not be so many failures in the expensive efforts put forth in camp meetings and tent meetings; there need not be so few sheaves to bring to the Master. In places where the standard of present truth has never been lifted, more souls will now be converted as the result of a certain amount of work than ever before. For everyone whose hands seem to be weakening and losing their hold I have the word: "Grasp the standard more firmly." Faith says: "Go forward." You must not fail nor be discouraged. There is no weakness of faith in him who is constantly advancing.

After a camp meeting it may sometimes be difficult to hold the principal speakers for several weeks to develop the interest awakened. It may be expensive to retain the ground and to keep a sufficient number of the family tents standing to maintain the appearance of a camp meeting. It may be at a sacrifice that several families remain on the ground to assist the ministers and Bible workers in visiting and Bible study with those who come to the meetings, and in visiting the people at their homes, telling of the blessings received at the meetings and inviting them to come. No doubt it will be difficult to secure a sufficient number of workers to carry forward the work successfully. But the results will justify the effort. It is by such earnest and energetic efforts as these that some of our camp meetings have been instrumental in raising up strong working churches. And it is by just such earnest work that the third angel's message must be carried to the people of our cities.

Sometimes a large number of speakers attend a camp meeting for a few days, and just when the interest of the people is fully aroused, nearly all hurry away to another meeting, leaving two or three speakers behind to struggle against the depressing influence of the tearing down and removal of the family tents. How much better it would be if the meetings were continued for a longer time; if persons would come from each church prepared to remain a month or longer, helping in the meetings and learning how to labor acceptably. Then they could carry a valuable experience to their churches when they return home. How much better if some of the same speakers who aroused the interest of the people during the largest attendance at the meeting would remain to follow up the work by a thoroughly organized protracted effort. To conduct meetings in this way would require that several be in progress at the same time, and this would not permit a few men to attend all the meetings. But we must remember that the work is to be accomplished "not by might, nor by power, but by My Spirit, saith the Lord of hosts." Zechariah 4:6.

The work should not stop when the meetings on the camp ground close. Doctrines have been presented that are new and strange to the people. Those who are convicted and who desire to accept the truth, will have to meet the most determined and subtle opposition. Ministers, friends, and acquaintances will put forth every effort to catch away the seeds of truth sown in the heart. We must not leave the seed to be thus caught away. We must not allow it to wither for want of moisture.

Changes tend to weaken the influence of the meetings. Continue the meetings on the camp ground whenever practicable. But when it seems advisable to move, let the large tent be removed to some favorable location, and let the services in it be continued. A mission should be established. Secure a suitable place, and let a number of workers unite to form a mission family. This should be in charge of a man and his wife who are persons of ability and consecration and whose influence will give character to the work.

In following up the interest after a camp meeting, helpers are needed in various lines, and these occasions should be as a training school for workers. Let young men work in connection with experienced laborers who will pray with them and patiently instruct them. Consecrated women should engage in Bible work from house to house. Some of the workers should act as colporteurs, selling our literature and giving judiciously to those who cannot buy.

Let some of the workers attend religious gatherings in

other churches and, as there is opportunity, take part in them. Jesus when only twelve years old went into the school of the priests and rabbis at the temple and asked questions. In this temple school, studies were conducted daily, somewhat as we conduct Bible studies. Jesus asked questions as a learner, but His questions furnished new matter for those learned priests to think upon. Similar work might be done today. Judicious young men should be encouraged to attend the meetings of the Young Men's Christian Association, not for the sake of contention, but to search the Scriptures with them and suggest helpful questions.

Had work in these various lines been done earnestly and vigorously after all our camp meetings, many more souls would have been gathered in as the fruit of the seed sown at the meetings.

Let the workers become acquainted with the people and read to them the precious words of Christ. Lift up Jesus crucified among them, and soon those who have listened to the messages of warning from the ministers at the tent, and have been convicted, will be drawn out to ask for further information. This is the time to present the reasons of our faith with meekness and fear; not a slavish fear, but a cautious fear lest we speak unadvisedly. Present the truth in all its loveliness, in simplicity and sincerity, giving meat in due season, and to everyone his portion of meat.

This work requires you to watch for souls as they that must give an account. The tenderness of Christ must pervade the heart of the worker. If you have a love for souls you will reveal a tender solicitude for them. You will offer humble, earnest, heartfelt prayers for those whom you visit. The fragrance of Christ's love will be revealed in your work. He who gave His own life for the life of the world will co-operate with the unselfish worker to make an impression upon human hearts.

THE WORK OF THE EVANGELIST

Teaching the Scriptures, praying in families—this is the work of the evangelist, and this work is to be mingled with preaching. If it is omitted, preaching will, to a great extent, be a failure. Come close to the people by personal efforts. Teach them that the love of God must come into the sanctuary of the home life.

Take no glory whatever to yourself. Do not work with a divided mind, trying to serve self and God at the same time. Keep self out of sight. Let your words lead the weary and heavy-laden to carry their burdens to Jesus. Work as seeing Him who is at your right hand, ready to give you His efficiency and omnipotent power in every emergency. The Lord is your Counselor, your Guide, the Captain of your salvation. He goes before your face, conquering and to conquer.

IN THE HIGHWAYS AND HEDGES

The command of Christ to His people is: "Go out into the highways and hedges, and compel them to come in, that My house may be filled." Luke 14:23.

The call to the gospel feast is first to be given in the highways. It must be given to those who claim to be in the highways of Christian experience—to the members of the different churches. "He that hath an ear, let him hear what the Spirit saith unto the churches." Revelation 2:7. In these churches there are true worshipers and there are false worshipers. A work must be done for those who have fallen from their first love, who have lost their first zeal and interest in spiritual things. We must bring the warning before professed Christians who are transgressors of the law of God. To them the message must be given.

The Lord says: "Unto the angel of the church in Sardis write; These things saith He that hath the seven Spirits of God, and the seven stars; I know thy works, that thou hast a name that thou livest, and art dead. Be watchful, and strengthen the things which remain, that are ready to die: for I have not found thy works perfect before God. Remember therefore how thou hast received and heard, and hold fast, and repent. If therefore thou shalt not watch, I will come on thee as a thief, and thou shalt not know what hour I will come upon thee." Revelation 3:1-3.

The warning for the last church also must be proclaimed to all who claim to be Christians. The Laodicean message, like a sharp, two-edged sword, must go to all the churches: "I know thy works, that thou art neither cold nor hot: I would thou wert cold or hot. So then because thou art lukewarm, and neither cold nor hot, I will spew thee out of My mouth. Because thou sayest, I am rich, and increased with goods, and have need of nothing; and knowest not that thou art wretched, and miserable, and poor, and blind, and naked: I counsel thee to buy of Me gold tried in the fire, that thou mayest be rich; and white raiment, that thou mayest be clothed, and that the shame of thy nakedness do not appear; and anoint thine eyes with eyesalve, that thou mayest see. As many as I love, I rebuke and chasten: be zealous therefore, and repent." Verses 15-19. It is our work to proclaim this message. Are we putting forth every effort that the churches may be warned?

We have a work to do for the ministers of other churches. God wants them to be saved. They, like ourselves, can have immortality only through faith and obedience. We must labor for them earnestly that they may obtain it. God wants them to have a part in His special work for this time. He wants them to be among the number who are giving to His household meat in due season. Why should they not be engaged in this work?

Our ministers should seek to come near to the ministers of other denominations. Pray for and with these men, for whom Christ is interceding. A solemn responsibility is theirs. As Christ's messengers we should manifest a deep, earnest interest in these shepherds of the flock.

The call to be given in "the highways" is to be proclaimed to all who have an active part in the world's work, to the teachers and leaders of the people. Those who bear heavy responsibilities in public life—physicians and teachers, lawyers and judges, public officers and businessmen—should be given a clear, distinct message. "What shall it profit a man, if he shall gain the whole world, and lose his own soul? Or what shall a man give in exchange for his soul?" Mark 8:36, 37.

We talk and write much of the neglected poor; should not some attention be given also to the neglected rich? Many look upon this class as hopeless, and they do little to open the eyes of those who, blinded and dazed by the power of Satan, have lost eternity out of their reckoning. Thousands of wealthy men have gone to their graves unwarned because they have been judged by appearance and passed by as hopeless subjects. But, indifferent as they may appear, I have been shown that most of this class are soul-burdened. There are thousands of rich men who are starving for spiritual food. Many in official life feel their need of something which they have not. Few among them go to church, for they feel that they receive no benefit. The teaching they hear does not touch the soul. Shall we make no personal effort in their behalf?

Some will ask: Can we not reach them with publications? There are many who cannot be reached in this way.

It is personal effort that they need. Are they to perish without a special warning? It was not so in ancient times. God's servants were sent to tell those in high places that they could find peace and rest only in the Lord Jesus Christ.

The Majesty of heaven came to our world to save lost, fallen humanity. His efforts included not merely the outcasts but those in places of high honor. Ingeniously He worked to obtain access to souls in the higher classes who knew not God and did not keep His commandments.

The same work was continued after Christ's ascension. My heart is made very tender as I read of the interest manifested by the Lord in Cornelius. Cornelius was a man in high position, an officer in the Roman army, but he was walking in strict accordance with all the light he had received. The Lord sent a special message from heaven to him, and by another message directed Peter to visit him and give him light. It ought to be a great encouragement to us in our work to think of the compassion and tender love of God for those who are seeking and praying for light.

There are many who are represented to me as being like Cornelius, men whom God desires to connect with His church. Their sympathies are with the Lord's commandment-keeping people. But the threads that bind them to the world hold them firmly. They have not the moral courage to take their position with the lowly ones. We are to make special efforts for these souls, who are in need of special labor because of their responsibilities and temptations.

From the light given me I know that a plain "Thus saith the Lord" should now be spoken to men who have influence and authority in the world. They are stewards to whom God has committed important trusts. If they will accept His call, God will use them in His cause.

There are men of the world who have God-given powers of organization that are needed in the carrying forward of the work for these last days. Men are needed who can take the management of institutions, men who can act as leaders and educators in our conferences. God calls for men who can look ahead and discern the work that needs to be done, who can act as faithful financiers, men who will stand firm as a rock to principle in every peril and crisis that may arise.

The cause of God needs now, as it has needed in past years, talent which it was God's purpose that it should have. But so much selfishness has been woven into our institutions that the Lord has not wrought to connect with the work those who should be connected with it. He has seen that they would not be properly recognized and appreciated.

God calls for earnest, humble workers who will carry the truth to the higher classes. It is by no casual, accidental touch that wealthy, world-loving, world-worshiping souls can be drawn to Christ. Decided personal effort must be put forth by men and women imbued with the missionary spirit, those who will not fail nor be discouraged.

We should hold convocations for prayer, asking the Lord to open the way for the truth to enter the strongholds where Satan has set up his throne, and dispel the shadow he has cast athwart the pathway of those whom he is seeking to deceive and destroy. We have the assurance: "The effectual fervent prayer of a righteous man availeth much." James 5:16.

Solicit prayer for the souls for whom you labor; present them before the church as subjects for their supplication. It will be just what the members of the church need, to have their minds called from their petty difficulties, to feel a great burden, a personal interest, for a soul that is ready to perish. Select another and still another soul, daily seeking guidance from God, laying everything before Him in earnest prayer, and working in divine wisdom. As you do this, God will give you the Holy Spirit to convict and convert the soul.

There are some who are especially fitted to work for the higher classes. These should seek the Lord daily, making it a study how to reach these persons, not to have merely a casual acquaintance with them, but to lay hold of them by personal effort and living faith, manifesting a deep love for their souls, a real concern that they shall have a knowledge of the truth as it is in the word of God.

In order to reach these classes, believers themselves must be living epistles, "known and read of all men." 2 Corinthians 3:2. We do not represent as fully as we might the elevating, ennobling character of the truth. We are in danger of becoming narrow and selfish. With fear and trembling lest we fail, we should ever remember this.

Let those who work for the higher classes bear themselves with true dignity, remembering that angels are their companions. Let them keep the treasure house of mind and heart well filled with "It is written." Hang in memory's hall the precious words of Christ. They are to be valued far above silver or gold.

We are not to conceal the fact that we are Seventh-day Adventists. The truth may be ashamed of us because our course of action is not in harmony with its pure principles, but we need never be ashamed of the truth. As you have opportunity, confess your faith. When anyone asks you, give him a reason of the hope that is in you, with meekness and fear.

It is the constant realization of the preciousness of Christ's atoning sacrifice in our behalf that qualifies us to point others to the Lamb of God that taketh away the sin of the world. We must become exponents of the efficacy of the blood of Christ, by which our own sins have been forgiven. Only thus can we reach the higher classes.

In this work many discouragements will be presented, many heartsickening revelations will be made. Christ has said that it is easier for a camel to go through the eye of a needle than for a rich man to enter the kingdom of God. But all things are possible with God. He can and will work through human agencies upon the minds of rich men whose lives have been devoted to money getting.

The heavenly universe has long been waiting to co-operate with human agents in this work which they have shunned and neglected. Many who have attempted the work have given up in discouragement, when, had they persevered, they would have been largely successful. Those who faithfully do this work will be blessed of God. The righteousness of Christ will go before them, and the glory of the Lord will be their rearward.

There are miracles to be wrought in genuine conversion, miracles that are not now discerned. The greatest men of the earth are not beyond the power of a wonder-working God. If those who are workers together with Him will be men of opportunity, doing their duty bravely and faithfully, God will convert men who occupy responsible places, men of intellect and influence. Through the power of the Holy Spirit, many will accept the divine principles. Beholding Jesus in His loveliness, in His self-denial and self-sacrifice, the self-sufficient rich man will see himself in contrast as wretched, and miserable, and poor, and blind, and naked, and will become so small in his own estimation that he will prefer Christ to himself, and will lay hold on eternal life.

Converted to the truth, he will become an agent in the hand of God to communicate the light. He will have a special burden for other souls of this neglected class. He will feel that a dispensation of the gospel is committed to him for those who have made this world their all. Time and money will be consecrated to God, means will be brought into His treasury, talent and influence will be converted to the truth, and new efficiency and power will be added to the church.

Christ instructs His messengers to go also to those in the byways and hedges, to the poor and lowly of the earth. Many of these do not understand what they must do to be saved. Many are sunken in sin. Many are in distress. Disease of every type afflicts them, both in body and in soul. They long to find a solace for their troubles, and Satan tempts them to seek it in lusts and pleasures that lead to ruin and death. They are spending their money for that which is not bread, and their labor for that which satisfieth not. These souls must not be passed by.

With the work of advocating the commandments of God and repairing the breach that has been made in His law, we are to mingle compassion for suffering humanity. We are to show supreme love to God; we are to exalt His memorial, which has been trodden down by unholy feet; and with this work we are to manifest mercy, benevolence, and the tenderest pity for the suffering and the sinful.

In every place where the truth is presented, earnest efforts should be made from the first to preach the gospel to the poor and to heal the sick. This work, faithfully done, will add to the church many souls of such as shall be saved.

Those who engage in house-to-house labor will find opportunities for ministry in many lines. They should pray for the sick and should do all in their power to relieve them from suffering. They should work among the lowly, the poor, and the oppressed. We should pray for and with the helpless ones who have not strength of will to control the appetites that passion has degraded. Earnest, persevering effort must be made for the salvation of those in whose hearts an interest is awakened. Many can be reached only through acts of disinterested kindness. Their physical wants must first be relieved. As they see evidence of our unselfish love, it will be easier for them to believe in the love of Christ.

Missionary nurses are best qualified for this work; but others should be connected with them. These, although not specially educated and trained in nursing, can learn from their fellow workers the best manner of labor.

Talk, pharisaism, and self-praise are abundant; but these will never win souls to Christ. Pure, sanctified love, such love as was expressed in Christ's lifework, is as a sacred perfume. Like Mary's broken box of ointment, it fills the whole house with fragrance. Eloquence, knowledge of truth, rare talents, mingled with love, are all precious endowments. But ability alone, the choicest talents alone, cannot take the place of love.

This love must be manifested by God's workers. Love for God and for those for whom Christ has died will do a work that we can scarcely comprehend. Those who do not cherish and cultivate this love cannot be successful missionaries.

Let all who decide for Christ be set to work for others who are dead in trespasses and sins. Wherever the truth has been proclaimed and people have been awakened and converted, the believers are at once to unite in exercises of charity. Wherever Bible truth has been presented, a work of practical godliness is to be begun. Wherever a church is established, missionary work is to be done for the helpless and the suffering.

CARING FOR OUR OWN POOR

We are commanded to "do good unto all men, especially unto them who are of the household of faith." Galatians 6:10. In our benevolent work special help should be given to those who, through the presentation of the truth, are convicted and converted. We must have a care for those who have the moral courage to accept the truth, who lose their situations in consequence, and are refused work by which to support their families. Provision should be made to aid the worthy poor and to furnish employment for those who love God and keep His commandments. They should not be left without help, to feel that they are forced to work on the Sabbath or starve. Those who take their position on the Lord's side are to see in Seventh-day Adventists a warmhearted, self-denying, self-sacrificing people, who cheerfully and gladly minister to their brethren in need. It is of this class especially that the Lord speaks when He says: "Bring the poor that are cast out to thy house." Isaiah 58:7.

CHURCH OFFICERS AND WORKERS

Great care should be exercised in selecting officers for the new churches. Let them be men and women who are thoroughly converted. Let those be chosen who are best qualified to give instruction, those who can minister both in word and in deed. There is a deep-seated necessity for work in every line.

Never allow the interest to flag. Devise methods that will bring a deep and living interest into the new churches. All connected with the church should feel an individual responsibility. All should work to the utmost of their ability to strengthen the church and make the meetings so full of life that outsiders will be attracted and interested. All should feel it a sin to let the interest wane when we have such sacred, solemn truths from the living oracles to repeat over and over again. Impress upon all the necessity of the baptism of the Holy Spirit, the sanctification of the members of the church, so that they will be living, growing, fruit-bearing trees of the Lord's planting.

God calls for self-denying, self-sacrificing workers. Those who devote their God-given time to hunting for souls, travailing for souls, watching for souls as they that must give an account, will obtain a rich experience. As they communicate the precious truths of God's word to others, their own hearts will be opened for the entrance of the word. They will be instructed by the Great Teacher.

Christ has opened a fountain for the sinful, suffering world, and the voice of divine mercy is heard: "Come, all ye thirsting souls; come and drink." You may take of the water of life freely. Let him that heareth say, Come; and whosoever will, let him come. Let every soul, women as well as men, sound this message. Then the work will be carried to the waste places of the earth. The scripture will be fulfilled: In that day the Lord shall open fountains in the valleys, and "rivers in the desert," and "with joy shall ye draw water out of the wells of salvation." Isaiah 41:18; 43:19, 20; 12:3.

LESS PREACHING, MORE TEACHING

At our camp meetings one or two laborers should not be required to do all the preaching and all the teaching in Bible lines. At times greater good can be accomplished by breaking up the large congregation into sections. Thus the educator in Bible truth can come closer to the people than in a large assembly.

At our camp meetings there is much more preaching than there should be. This brings a heavy burden upon the ministers, and as a consequence much that requires attention is neglected. Many little things that open the door to serious evils are passed by unnoticed. The minister is robbed of physical strength and deprived of the time he needs for meditation and prayer in order to keep his own soul in the love of God. And when so many discourses are crowded in, one after another, the people have no time to appropriate what they hear. Their minds become confused, and the services seem to them tedious and wearisome.

There should be less preaching and more teaching. There are those who want more definite light than they receive from hearing the sermons. Some need a longer time than do others to understand the points presented. If the truth presented could be made a little plainer, they would see it and take hold of it, and it would be like a nail fastened in a sure place.

It has been shown me that our camp meetings are to increase in interest and success. As we approach nearer the end, I have seen that in these meetings there will be less preaching and more Bible study. There will be little groups all over the ground with their Bibles in their hands, and different ones leading out in a free, conversational study of the Scriptures.

(87)

This was the method that Christ taught His disciples. When the great throngs gathered about the Saviour, He would give instruction to the disciples and to the multitude. Then after the discourse the disciples would mingle with the people and repeat to them what Christ had said. Often the hearers had misapplied Christ's words, and the disciples would tell them what the Scriptures said and what Christ had taught that they said.

If the man who feels that he is called of God to be a minister will humble himself and learn of Christ, he will become a true teacher. What we need in our camp meetings is a ministry vivified by the Holy Spirit. There must be less sermonizing and more tact to educate the people in practical religion. They must be impressed with the fact that Christ is salvation to all who believe. "God so loved the world, that He gave His only-begotten Son, that whosoever believeth in Him should not perish, but have everlasting life." John 3:16. There are grand themes on which the gospel minister may dwell. Christ has said: "He that believeth on Me hath everlasting life." John 6:47.

If the minister's lips are touched with a coal from off the altar, he will lift up Jesus as the sinner's only hope. When the heart of the speaker is sanctified through the truth, his words will be living realities to himself and to others. Those who hear him will know that he has been with God and has drawn near to Him in fervent, effectual prayer. The Holy Spirit has fallen upon him, his soul has felt the vital, heavenly fire, and he will be able to compare spiritual things with spiritual. Power will be given him to tear down the strongholds of Satan. Hearts will be broken by his presentation of the love of God, and many will inquire: "What must I do to be saved?"

MINISTERIAL INSTITUTES

"Go ye into all the world, and preach the gospel to every creature," is the Saviour's command to His workers. But this plain direction has been disregarded. Though the light has been given again and again, men have been called from their fields of labor to spend weeks in attending a ministerial institute. There was a time when this was necessary, because our own people opposed the work of God by refusing the light on the righteousness of Christ by faith. This they should have received and should have imparted with heart and voice and pen, for it is their only efficiency. They should have labored under the Holy Spirit's direction to give the light to others.

The holding of so many Biblical institutes among our own people is not wise. The object is good, but there is a more urgent work to be done in carrying the light of truth into regions where it has not penetrated. The laborers held to work for those who already have a knowledge of the truth are kept away from the people who know it not. By devoting much time year after year to ministerial institutes, our brethren have neglected fields that are white already to harvest. Souls in spiritual blindness, prejudiced by those who misrepresent the truth, have been left unwarned. Oh, the neglect that will be charged against individuals, organizations, and churches in that day when every man shall be judged according to the deeds done in the body! Then it will be seen how great was the measure of responsibility for failing to extend the work into the regions beyond.

An attendance upon so many institutes has not brought

the greatest benefit to the workers themselves. Talent is best developed where it is most needed. Ministers called from their fields to attend ministerial institutes are not so well prepared for the work as if they gave themselves to consecrated labor in the destitute fields where the standard of truth is to be uplifted. If they studied the word of God with a teachable spirit, praying, and watching unto prayer, and working as well as praying, angels of God would open their understanding to perceive truth in its beauty.

As the knowledge of the truth is received, let it be imparted to those who are in darkness, without God and without hope in the world. In such labor there is a variety of minds to deal with, and God will greatly bless His servants as they look to Him for wisdom. The Holy Spirit will come to all who are begging for the bread of life to give to their neighbors.

Instead of holding institutes to fit ministers for their work, let these ministers be given work to do in places where camp meetings have been held. After being fed with the bread of life by a miracle of God's mercy, let them work to feed others.

The large amount of means required for ministerial institutes would have brought far greater returns had it been expended in maintaining the ministers in actual labor in missionary fields.

There are in the ministry men of faith and prayer, men who can say: "That which was from the beginning, which we have heard, which we have seen with our eyes, which we have looked upon, and our hands have handled, of the Word of life; . . . that which we have seen and heard declare we unto you." 1 John 1:1-3. These men are to instruct others. Let workers be trained by actual labor in connection with experienced men.

BAPTISM

MEANING OF THE ORDINANCE

THE ordinances of baptism and the Lord's Supper are two monumental pillars, one without and one within the church. Upon these ordinances Christ has inscribed the name of the true God.

Christ has made baptism the sign of entrance to His spiritual kingdom. He has made this a positive condition with which all must comply who wish to be acknowledged as under the authority of the Father, the Son, and the Holy Spirit. Before man can find a home in the church, before passing the threshold of God's spiritual kingdom, he is to receive the impress of the divine name, *"The Lord our Righteousness."* Jeremiah 23:6.

Baptism is a most solemn renunciation of the world. Those who are baptized in the threefold name of the Father, the Son, and the Holy Spirit, at the very entrance of their Christian life declare publicly that they have forsaken the service of Satan and have become members of the royal family, children of the heavenly King. They have obeyed the command: "Come out from among them, and be ye separate, . . . and touch not the unclean thing." And to them is fulfilled the promise: "I will receive you, and will be a Father unto you, and ye shall be My sons and daughters, saith the Lord Almighty." 2 Corinthians 6:17, 18.

PREPARATION FOR BAPTISM

There is need of a more thorough preparation on the part of candidates for baptism. They are in need of more faithful instruction than has usually been given them. The principles of the Christian life should be made plain to those who have newly come to the truth. None can depend upon their profession of faith as proof that they have a saving connection with Christ. We are not only to say, "I believe," but to practice the truth. It is by conformity to the will of God in our words, our deportment, our character, that we prove our connection with Him. Whenever one renounces sin, which is the transgression of the law, his life will be brought into conformity to the law, into perfect obedience. This is the work of the Holy Spirit. The light of the word carefully studied, the voice of conscience, the strivings of the Spirit, produce in the heart genuine love for Christ, who gave Himself a whole sacrifice to redeem the whole person, body, soul, and spirit. And love is manifested in obedience. The line of demarcation will be plain and distinct between those who love God and keep His commandments, and those who love Him not and disregard His precepts.

Faithful Christian men and women should have an intense interest to bring the convicted soul to a correct knowledge of righteousness in Christ Jesus. If any have allowed the desire for selfish indulgence to become supreme in their life, the faithful believers should watch for these souls as they that must give an account. They must not neglect the faithful, tender, loving instruction so essential to the young converts that there may be no halfhearted work. The very first experience should be right.

Satan does not want anyone to see the necessity of an entire surrender to God. When the soul fails to make this surrender, sin is not forsaken; the appetites and passions are striving for the mastery; temptations confuse the conscience, so that true conversion does not take place. If all had a sense of the conflict which each soul must wage with satanic agencies that are seeking to ensnare,

entice, and deceive, there would be much more diligent
labor for those who are young in the faith.

These souls, left to themselves, are often tempted and
do not discern the evil of the temptation. Let them feel
that it is their privilege to solicit counsel. Let them seek
the society of those who can help them. Through association with those who love and fear God they will receive
strength.

Our conversation with these souls should be of a spiritual, encouraging character. The Lord marks the conflicts
of every weak, doubting, struggling one, and He will help
all who call upon Him. They will see heaven open before
them, and angels of God descending and ascending the
ladder of shining brightness which they are trying to
climb.

The Parents' Work. Parents whose children desire to
be baptized have a work to do, both in self-examination
and in giving faithful instruction to their children. Baptism is a most sacred and important ordinance, and there
should be a thorough understanding as to its meaning.
It means repentance for sin, and the entrance upon a new
life in Christ Jesus. There should be no undue haste to
receive the ordinance. Let both parents and children
count the cost. In consenting to the baptism of their children, parents sacredly pledge themselves to be faithful
stewards over these children, to guide them in their character building. They pledge themselves to guard with
special interest these lambs of the flock, that they may not
dishonor the faith they profess.

Religious instruction should be given to children from
their earliest years. It should be given, not in a condemnatory spirit, but in a cheerful, happy spirit. Mothers
need to be on the watch constantly, lest temptation shall
come to the children in such a form as not to be recog-

nized by them. The parents are to guard their children with wise, pleasant instruction. As the very best friends of these inexperienced ones, they should help them in the work of overcoming, for it means everything to them to be victorious. They should consider that their own dear children who are seeking to do right are younger members of the Lord's family, and they should feel an intense interest in helping them to make straight paths in the King's highway of obedience. With loving interest they should teach them day by day what it means to be children of God and to yield the will in obedience to Him. Teach them that obedience to God involves obedience to their parents. This must be a daily, hourly work. Parents, watch, watch and pray, and make your children your companions.

When the happiest period of their life has come, and they in their hearts love Jesus and wish to be baptized, then deal faithfully with them. Before they receive the ordinance, ask them if it is to be their first purpose in life to work for God. Then tell them how to begin. It is the first lessons that mean so much. In simplicity teach them how to do their first service for God. Make the work as easy to be understood as possible. Explain what it means to give up self to the Lord, to do just as His word directs, under the counsel of Christian parents.

After faithful labor, if you are satisfied that your children understand the meaning of conversion and baptism, and are truly converted, let them be baptized. But, I repeat, first of all prepare yourselves to act as faithful shepherds in guiding their inexperienced feet in the narrow way of obedience. God must work in the parents that they may give to their children a right example, in love, courtesy, and Christian humility, and in an entire giving up of self to Christ. If you consent to the baptism of your children and then leave them to do as they choose, feeling no special duty to keep their feet in the straight path, you yourselves are responsible if they lose faith and courage and interest in the truth.

The Pastor's Work. Candidates who have grown to manhood and womanhood should understand their duty better than do the younger ones; but the pastor of the church has a duty to do for these souls. Have they wrong habits and practices? It is the duty of the pastor to have special meetings with them. Give them Bible readings, converse and pray with them, and plainly show the claims of the Lord upon them. Read to them the teaching of the Bible in regard to conversion. Show what is the fruit of conversion, the evidence that they love God. Show that true conversion is a change of heart, of thoughts and purposes. Evil habits are to be given up. The sins of evil-speaking, of jealousy, of disobedience, are to be put away. A warfare must be waged against every evil trait of character. Then the believing one can understandingly take to himself the promise: "Ask, and it shall be given you." Matthew 7:7.

EXAMINATION OF CANDIDATES

The test of discipleship is not brought to bear as closely as it should be upon those who present themselves for baptism. It should be understood whether they are simply taking the name of Seventh-day Adventists, or whether they are taking their stand on the Lord's side, to come out from the world and be separate, and touch not the unclean thing. Before baptism there should be a thorough inquiry as to the experience of the candidates. Let this inquiry be made, not in a cold and distant way, but kindly, tenderly, pointing the new converts to the Lamb of God that taketh away the sin of the world. Bring the requirements of the gospel to bear upon the candidates for baptism.

One of the points upon which those newly come to the faith will need instruction is the subject of dress. Let the new converts be faithfully dealt with. Are they vain in dress? Do they cherish pride of heart? The idolatry of dress is a moral disease. It must not be taken over into the new life. In most cases, submission to the gospel requirements will demand a decided change in the dress.

There should be no carelessness in dress. For Christ's sake, whose witnesses we are, we should seek to make the best of our appearance. In the tabernacle service, God specified every detail concerning the garments of those who ministered before Him. Thus we are taught that He has a preference in regard to the dress of those who serve Him. Very specific were the directions given in regard to Aaron's robes, for his dress was symbolic. So the dress of Christ's followers should be symbolic. In all things we are to be representatives of Him. Our appearance in every respect should be characterized by neatness, modesty, and purity. But the word of God gives no sanction to the making of changes in apparel merely for the sake of fashion, that we may appear like the world. Christians are not to decorate the person with costly array or expensive ornaments.

The words of Scripture in regard to dress should be carefully considered. We need to understand that which the Lord of heaven appreciates in even the dressing of the body. All who are in earnest in seeking for the grace of Christ will heed the precious words of instruction inspired by God. Even the style of the apparel will express the truth of the gospel.

All who study the life of Christ and practice His teachings will become like Christ. Their influence will be like

His. They will reveal soundness of character. As they walk in the humble path of obedience, doing the will of God, they exert an influence that tells for the advancement of the cause of God and the healthful purity of His work. In these thoroughly converted souls the world is to have a witness to the sanctifying power of truth upon the human character.

The knowledge of God and of Jesus Christ, expressed in character, is an exaltation above everything that is esteemed in earth or in heaven. It is the very highest education. It is the key that opens the portals of the heavenly city. This knowledge it is God's purpose that all who put on Christ by baptism shall possess. And it is the duty of God's servants to set before these souls the privilege of their high calling in Christ Jesus.

ADMINISTRATION OF THE ORDINANCE

Whenever possible, let baptism be administered in a clear lake or running stream. And give to the occasion all the importance and solemnity that can be brought into it. At such a service angels of God are always present.

The one who administers the ordinance of baptism should seek to make it an occasion of solemn, sacred influence upon all spectators. Every ordinance of the church should be so conducted as to be uplifting in its influence. Nothing is to be made common or cheap, or placed on a level with common things. Our churches need to be educated to greater respect and reverence for the sacred service of God. As ministers conduct the services connected with God's worship, so they are educating and training the people. Little acts that educate and train and discipline the soul for eternity are of vast consequence in the uplifting and sanctifying of the church.

In every church, baptismal robes should be provided for the candidates. This should not be regarded as a needless outlay of means. It is one of the things required in obedience to the injunction: "Let all things be done decently and in order." 1 Corinthians 14:40.

It is not well for one church to depend upon borrowing robes from another. Often when the robes are needed, they are not to be found; some borrower has neglected to return them. Every church should provide for its own necessities in this line. Let a fund be raised for this purpose. If the whole church unite in this, it will not be a heavy burden.

The robes should be made of substantial material, of some dark color that water will not injure, and they should be weighted at the bottom. Let them be neat, well-shaped garments, made after an approved pattern. There should be no attempt at ornamentation, no ruffling or trimming. All display, whether of trimming or ornaments, is wholly out of place. When the candidates have a sense of the meaning of the ordinance, they will have no desire for personal adornment. Yet there should be nothing shabby or unseemly, for this is an offense to God. Everything connected with this holy ordinance should reveal as perfect a preparation as possible.

AFTER BAPTISM

The vows which we take upon ourselves in baptism embrace much. In the name of the Father, the Son, and the Holy Spirit we are buried in the likeness of Christ's death and raised in the likeness of His resurrection, and we are to live a new life. Our life is to be bound up with the life of Christ. Henceforth the believer is to bear in mind that he is dedicated to God, to Christ, and to the Holy Spirit. He is to make all worldly considerations secondary to this new relation. Publicly he has declared that he will no longer live in pride and self-indulgence.

He is no longer to live a careless, indifferent life. He has made a covenant with God. He has died to the world. He is to live to the Lord, to use for Him all his entrusted capabilities, never losing the realization that he bears God's signature, that he is a subject of Christ's kingdom, a partaker of the divine nature. He is to surrender to God all that he is and all that he has, employing all his gifts to His name's glory.

The obligations in the spiritual agreement entered into at baptism are mutual. As human beings act their part with wholehearted obedience, they have a right to pray: "Let it be known, Lord, that Thou art God in Israel." The fact that you have been baptized in the name of the Father, the Son, and the Holy Spirit is an assurance that, if you will claim Their help, these powers will help you in every emergency. The Lord will hear and answer the prayers of His sincere followers who wear Christ's yoke and learn in His school His meekness and lowliness.

"If ye then be risen with Christ, seek those things which are above, where Christ sitteth on the right hand of God. Set your affection on things above, not on things on the earth. For ye are dead, and your life is hid with Christ in God." Colossians 3:1-3.

"Put on therefore, as the elect of God, holy and beloved, bowels of mercies, kindness, humbleness of mind, meekness, long-suffering; forbearing one another, and forgiving one another, if any man have a quarrel against any: even as Christ forgave you, so also do ye. And above all these things put on charity, which is the bond of perfectness. And let the peace of God rule in your hearts, to the which also ye are called in one body; and be ye thankful. . . . And whatsoever ye do in word or deed, do all in the name of the Lord Jesus, giving thanks to God and the Father by Him." Verses 12-17.

THE BUILDING OF MEETINGHOUSES

WHEN an interest is aroused in any town or city, that interest should be followed up. The place should be thoroughly worked until a humble house of worship stands as a sign, a memorial of God's Sabbath, a light amid the moral darkness. These memorials are to stand in many places as witnesses to the truth. God in His mercy has provided that the messengers of the gospel shall go to all countries, tongues, and peoples until the standard of truth shall be established in all parts of the inhabited world.

———

Wherever a company of believers is raised up, a house of worship should be built. Let not the workers leave the place without accomplishing this.

In many places where the message has been preached and souls have accepted it, they are in limited circumstances and can do but little toward securing advantages that would give character to the work. Often this renders it difficult to extend the work. As persons become interested in the truth, they are told by the ministers of other churches—and these words are echoed by the church members: "These people have no church, and you have no place of worship. You are a small company, poor and unlearned. In a short time the ministers will go away, and then the interest will die down. Then you will give up all these new ideas which you have received."

Can we suppose that this will not bring strong temptation to those who see the reasons of our faith and are convicted by the Spirit of God in regard to present truth? It has to be often repeated that from a small beginning large interests may grow. If wisdom and sanctified judgment and skillful generalship are manifested by us in building up the interests of our Redeemer's kingdom, we shall do all in our power to assure the people of the stability of our work. Humble sanctuaries will be erected where those who accept the truth may find a place to worship God according to the dictates of their own conscience.

———

Whenever it is possible, let our church buildings be dedicated to God free of debt. When a church is raised up, let the members arise and build. Under the direction of a minister who is guided by the advice of his fellow ministers, let the newly converted ones work with their own hands, saying: "We need a meetinghouse, and we must have it." God calls upon His people to make cheerful, united efforts in His cause. Let this be done, and soon will be heard the voice of thanksgiving: "See what the Lord hath wrought."

There are some cases, however, in which a young church may not be able at once to bear the whole burden of erecting a house of worship. In these cases let the brethren in other churches help them. In some cases it may be better to hire some money than not to build. If a man has money, and, after giving what he can, will make a loan, either without interest or at a low rate, it would be right to use the money until the indebtedness can be lifted. But I repeat: If possible, church buildings should be dedicated free of debt.

In our churches the pews should not be rented. The wealthy are not to be honored above the poor. Let no distinction be made. "All ye are brethren."

In none of our buildings should we seek to make a display; for this would not advance the work. Our economy should testify to our principles. We should employ methods of work that are not transient. Everything should be done solidly for time and for eternity.

———

The lax way which some churches have of incurring debts and keeping in debt was presented before me. In some cases a continual debt is upon the house of God. There is continual interest to be paid. These things should not, and need not, be. If there is that wisdom and tact and zeal manifested for the Master which God requires, there will be a change in these things. The debts will be lifted. God calls for offerings from those who can give, and even the poorer members can do their little. Self-denial will enable all to do something. Both old and young, parents and children, are to show their faith by their works. Let the necessity of each acting a part be most strenuously impressed upon the members of the church. Let everyone do his best. When there is a will to do, God will open the way. He does not design that His cause shall be trammeled with debt.

God calls for self-sacrifice. This will bring not only financial but spiritual prosperity. Self-denial and self-sacrifice will work wonders in advancing the spirituality of the church.

———

It is displeasing to God for our churches to be burdened with debt. "The silver is Mine, and the gold is Mine, saith the Lord of hosts." Haggai 2:8. When that gold and silver is used for selfish purposes, to gratify ambition or pride or desire for any selfish indulgence, God is dishonored. When the people chosen by God embellish their own houses and invest His money in selfish gratification, leaving His cause to languish, they cannot be blessed.

When you place the Lord first, and determine that His house shall no longer be dishonored by debt, God will bless you. Every week endeavor to lay aside something for this object, something in addition to your tithe money. Have a box for this purpose. Explain to your children that it is the self-denial box, in which you place every dollar and every penny that is not required for actual necessities. It is for the Lord's house, to lift the heaven-dishonoring debt from the place of worship. In making this offering, every member of the family will receive a blessing.

God reads every thought. He notes every action. Everything done with sincere purpose for the advancement of His work will be blessed by Him. The two mites, the cup of cold water, presented in sympathy and love, will be made effective in doing good here and will bring a reward hereafter.

The test question for every Christian to ask himself is: "Have I, in my inmost soul, supreme love for Christ? Do I love His tabernacle? Will not the Lord be honored by my making His sacred institution my first consideration? Is my love for God and my Redeemer strong enough to lead me to deny self? When tempted to indulge in pleasure and selfish enjoyment, shall I not say: No, I will spend nothing for my own gratification while the house of God is burdened with debt?"

Our Redeemer claims far more than we give Him. Self interposes its desire to be first; but the Lord claims the whole heart, the entire affections. He will not come in as second. And should not Christ have our first and highest consideration? Should He not demand this token of our respect and loyalty? These things underlie our very heart life, in the home circle and in the church. If the heart, the soul, the strength, the life, are surrendered wholly to God, if the affections are given wholly to Him, we shall make Him supreme in all our service. When we are in harmony with God, the thought of His honor and glory comes before everything else. No person is preferred before Him in our gifts and offerings. We have a sense of what it means to be partners with Christ in the sacred firm.

The house where God meets with His people will be dear and sacred to every one of His loyal children. It will not be left crippled with debt. To allow such a thing would appear almost like a denial of your faith. You will be ready to make a great personal sacrifice if only you may have a house free from debt, where God can meet with and bless His people.

Every debt upon every house of worship among us may be paid if the members of the church will plan wisely and put forth earnest, zealous effort to cancel the debt. And in every case where a debt is lifted, let there be a service of thanksgiving, which shall be as a rededication to God of His house.

God tries the faith of His people to test their character. Those who in times of emergency are willing to make sacrifices for Him are the ones whom He will honor with a partnership in His work. Those who are unwilling to practice self-denial in order to carry out God's purposes will be tested, that their course may appear to human eyes as it appears to the eyes of Him who reads the heart.

When the Lord sees His people restricting their imaginary wants, practicing self-denial, not in a mournful, regretful spirit, as Lot's wife left Sodom, but joyfully for Christ's sake, then the work will go forward with power.

CHILDREN'S MEETINGS AND CHURCH SCHOOLS

At all our camp meetings, work should be done for the children and youth. A children's meeting or Bible kindergarten should be held daily under the direction of teachers qualified for the work. In simple language, lessons should be given both from the Bible and from nature. Kindergarten methods and object lessons from nature will be of great advantage in interesting the little ones. At some of our camp meetings children's meetings have been held twice a day. After the morning lesson, on pleasant days, teachers and children would take a long walk, and during the walk, by the banks of a river or in the grassy fields, a halt would be called and a short lesson from nature given. In such lessons as these the children can be taught the parables of Christ. The truth will be fastened in their minds as a nail in a sure place.

In our work for the children the object should be not merely to educate and entertain them, but to work for their conversion. We should ask the blessing of God on the seed sown, and the conviction of the Holy Spirit will take hold of even the little ones. If we exercise faith in God, we shall be enabled to lead them to the Lamb of God that taketh away the sin of the world.

This is a work of the greatest consequence to the younger members of the Lord's family. In these meetings even children who are favored with Christian instruction at home can learn much that will be a great help to them. If the children are taught in the simplicity of Christ, they will receive the knowledge; and as they return to their homes, they will bring forth from the treasure house of the heart precious lessons.

The youth should be given opportunity to become more fully instructed in the word of God. Bible truth should be made plain to them. Those who have an experience in the truth should search the Scriptures with them. This will be as seed sown in good ground.

Such meetings for children and youth, if rightly conducted, will be attended by many who are not of our faith, and the lessons learned at the meetings will be repeated at home. Through the children the parents may be reached. At our camp meetings in Australia these meetings have been the means of great good.

Following is a brief account of work done in this line at an Australian camp meeting, as written out by one who had a part in the work:

"On the first Sabbath the children were organized into departments and classes, and the teachers began their work. At the beginning there were six children in the primary department and about fifteen in the kindergarten. As soon as the children living in the neighborhood learned of the meetings being held for them, they began to attend, and each day found many new ones added to the classes. The average daily attendance from the outside was between eighty and one hundred, and on Sundays there was a larger number present. Most of the children were very regular in their attendance. The same spirit of earnestness, attention, and order that characterized the services among the older ones marked the children's meetings. Both in the classwork and in the general review exercises the work was so arranged that the children had a part in doing as well as listening, and in this way they soon felt at home, and their eagerness to bear some part in the work testified to their interest.

"Each lesson opened with a general exercise, which was followed by the class studies; and at the close all assembled for a brief review and song. In the opening exercises, after the song and prayer, the motto and all the memory verses previously learned were recited, either in concert or individually, or both. A short, appropriate reading or recitation was given by one of the children who had previously volunteered to prepare it. The 'Scripture alphabet' was learned and recited by the children, each choosing his own letter and verse. The selection and learning of the verses were done at home, and these responsibilities placed upon the children proved an additional incentive for them to be present the following day and to be regular in attendance.

"The ready responses in the review exercises testified that the interest in classwork had been marked, and that many valuable truths had found their way into the minds and hearts of the children. As the children returned to their homes, the parents were surprised and pleased to hear them repeat the whole lesson. Many parents expressed, in various ways, their appreciation of the work that had been done for the children and regretted that the meetings must close so soon.

"Several teachers from Sunday schools attended the meetings and expressed themselves as greatly pleased and benefited by the work done. Parents sometimes came with their children and seemed as much interested as the little ones. Others, though not in harmony with our views, took the trouble to dress their children neatly and allowed them to come. Some parents remarked that they did not know what we did with their children, but one thing was certain, the children would come, and they could not keep them at home. Some of the children came long distances, and we have every reason to believe that much of the seed sown fell into good ground."

───────

The good seed sown in these meetings should not be left to perish for want of care. Many parents would rejoice if the instruction given to their children at the camp meeting could be continued. They would gladly place their children in a school where the same principles were taught and practiced. While the interest of both parents and children is awakened, it is a golden opportunity for the establishment of a school at which the work begun at the camp meeting can be carried forward.

And as believers are raised up and churches organized, such a school will be found of great value in promoting the permanence and stability of the work. Workers in new territory should not feel free to leave their field of labor till the needed facilities have been provided for the churches under their care. Not only should a humble house of worship be erected, but all necessary arrangements should be made for the permanent establishment of the church school.

This matter has been plainly presented before me. I saw in different places new companies of believers being raised up and meetinghouses being erected. Those newly come to the faith were helping with willing hands, and those who had means were assisting with their means. In the basement of the church, above ground, I was shown a room provided for a school where the children could be educated in the truths of God's word. Consecrated teachers were selected to go to these places. The numbers in the school were not large, but it was a happy beginning.

As the work was being pressed forward, I heard the voices of children and parents singing:

> "Except the Lord build the house,
> They labor in vain that build it:
> Except the Lord keep the city,
> The watchman waketh but in vain."

> "Praise ye the Lord.
> Praise the Lord, O my soul.

While I live will I praise the Lord:
I will sing praises unto my God while I have any being.
Put not your trust in princes,
Nor in the son of man, in whom there is no help."

"Praise ye the Lord from the heavens:
Praise Him in the heights.
Praise ye Him, all His angels:
Praise ye Him, all His hosts.
Praise ye Him, sun and moon:
Praise Him, all ye stars of light."

Psalms 127:1; 146:1-3; 148:1-3.

The establishing of churches and the erection of meetinghouses and school buildings was extended from city to city. In each place the believers were making a united, persevering effort, and the Lord was working to increase His forces. Something was being established that would publish the truth.

This is the work to be done in America, in Australia, in Europe, and wherever companies are brought into the truth. The companies that are raised up need a place of worship. Schools are needed where Bible instruction may be given to the children. The schoolroom is needed just as much as is the church building. The Lord has persons to engage in the work of establishing church schools as soon as something is done to prepare the way for them.

———

In localities where believers are few, let two or three churches unite in erecting a humble building for a church school. Let all share the expense. It is high time for Sabbathkeepers to separate their children from worldly associations and place them under the very best teachers, who will make the Bible the foundation of all study.

THE TEMPERANCE WORK

In our work more attention should be given to the temperance reform. Every duty that calls for reform involves repentance, faith, and obedience. It means the uplifting of the soul to a new and nobler life. Thus every true reform has its place in the work of the third angel's message. Especially does the temperance reform demand our attention and support. At our camp meetings we should call attention to this work and make it a living issue. We should present to the people the principles of true temperance and call for signers to the temperance pledge. Careful attention should be given to those who are enslaved by evil habits. We must lead them to the cross of Christ.

Our camp meetings should have the labors of medical men. These should be men of wisdom and sound judgment, men who respect the ministry of the word and who are not victims of unbelief. These men are the guardians of the health of the people, and they are to be recognized and respected. They should give instruction to the people in regard to the dangers of intemperance. This evil must be more boldly met in the future than it has been in the past. Ministers and doctors should set forth the evils of intemperance. Both should work in the gospel with power to condemn sin and exalt righteousness. Those ministers or doctors who do not make personal appeals to the people are remiss in their duty. They fail of doing the work which God has appointed them.

In other churches there are Christians who are standing in defense of the principles of temperance. We should seek to come near to these workers and make a way for them to stand shoulder to shoulder with us. We should call upon great and good men to second our efforts to save that which is lost.

If the work of temperance were carried forward by us as it was begun thirty years ago; if at our camp meetings we presented before the people the evils of intemperance in eating and drinking, and especially the evil of liquor drinking; if these things were presented in connection with the evidences of Christ's soon coming, there would be a shaking among the people. If we showed a zeal in proportion to the importance of the truths we are handling, we might be instrumental in rescuing hundreds, yea thousands, from ruin.

Only eternity will reveal what has been accomplished by this kind of ministry — how many souls, sick with doubt, and tired of worldliness and unrest, have been brought to the Great Physician, who longs to save to the uttermost all who come unto Him. Christ is a risen Saviour, and there is healing in His wings.

————

As we see men going where the liquid poison is dealt out to destroy their reason, as we see their souls imperiled, what are we doing to rescue them? Our work for the tempted and fallen will achieve real success only as the grace of Christ reshapes the character and the man is brought into living connection with the infinite God. This is the purpose of all true temperance effort. We are called upon to work with more than human energy, to labor with the power that is in Jesus Christ. The One who stooped to take human nature is the One who will show us how to conduct the battle. Christ has left His work in our hands, and we are to wrestle with God, supplicating day and night for the power that is unseen. It is laying right hold of God through Jesus Christ that will gain the victory.

OBJECT LESSONS IN HEALTH REFORM

THE large gatherings of our people afford an excellent opportunity of illustrating the principles of health reform. Some years ago at these gatherings much was said in regard to health reform and the benefits of a vegetarian diet; but at the same time flesh meats were furnished at the tables in the dining tent, and various unhealthful articles of food were sold at the provision stand. Faith without work is dead; and the instruction upon health reform, denied by practice, did not make the deepest impression. At later camp meetings those in charge have educated by practice as well as by precept. No meat has been furnished at the dining tent, but fruits, grains, and vegetables have been supplied in abundance. As visitors ask questions in regard to the absence of meat, the reason is plainly stated, that flesh is not the most healthful food.

As we near the close of time we must rise higher and still higher upon the question of health reform and Christian temperance, presenting it in a more positive and decided manner. We must strive continually to educate the people, not only by our words, but by our practice. Precept and practice combined have a telling influence.

At the camp meeting, instruction on health topics should be given to the people. At our meetings in Australia, lectures on health subjects were given daily, and a deep interest was aroused. A tent for the use of physicians and nurses was on the ground; medical advice was given freely, and was sought by many. Thousands of people attended the lectures, and at the close of the camp meeting the people were not satisfied to let the matter drop with what they had already learned. In several cities where camp meetings were held, some of the leading citizens urged that a branch sanitarium be established, promising their co-operation. In several cities the work has been started, with good success. A health institution, rightly conducted, gives character to our work in new fields. And not only is it a benefit to the people, but the workers connected with it can be a help to the laborers in evangelistic lines.

In every city where we have a church there is need of a place where treatment can be given. Among the homes of our church members there are few that afford room and facilities for the proper care of the sick. A place should be provided where treatment may be given for common ailments. The building might be inelegant and even rude, but it should be furnished with facilities for giving simple treatments. These, skillfully employed, would prove a blessing not only to our people, but to their neighbors, and might be the means of calling the attention of many to health principles.

It is the Lord's purpose that in every part of our world health institutions shall be established as a branch of the gospel work. These institutions are to be His agencies for reaching a class whom nothing else will reach. They need not be large buildings, but should be so arranged that effective work may be done.

Beginnings might be made in every prominent place where camp meetings are held. Make small beginnings, and enlarge as circumstances may demand. Count the cost of every undertaking, that you may be sure of being able to finish. Draw as little as possible from the treasury. Men of faith and financial ability are needed to plan economically. Our sanitariums must be erected with a limited outlay of means. Buildings in which to begin the work can often be secured at low cost.

WOMEN TO BE GOSPEL WORKERS

THE work that has been begun in helping our sisters feel their individual accountability to God is a good and necessary work. Long has it been neglected. The Lord would have us ever urge the worth of the human soul upon those who do not understand its value. And when this work is laid out in clear, simple, definite lines, we may expect that the home duties, instead of being neglected, will be done much more intelligently.

If we can arrange to have regular, organized companies instructed intelligently in regard to the part they should act as servants of the Master, our churches will have a vitality that they have long needed. The excellence of the soul that Christ died to save will be appreciated. Our sisters generally have a hard time with their increasing families and their unappreciated trials. I have so longed for women who could be educated to help our sisters rise from their discouragement and feel that they could do a work for the Lord. This will bring rays of sunshine into their own lives, which will be reflected into the lives of others. God will bless all who unite in this grand work.

Many youth as well as older sisters appear shy of religious conversation. They do not appreciate their opportunities. They close the windows of the soul that should be opened heavenward, and open their windows wide earthward. But when they see the excellence of the human soul they will close the windows earthward, which depend on worldly amusements and associations in folly and sin, and will open the windows heavenward to behold spiritual things. The word of God must be their assurance, their hope, their peace. Then they can say: "I will receive the light of the Sun of Righteousness, that it may shine forth to others."

The most successful toilers are those who cheerfully take up the work of serving God in little things. Every human being is to work with his life thread, weaving it into the fabric to help complete the pattern.

The work of Christ was largely made up of personal interviews. He had a faithful regard for the one-soul audience. From that one soul the intelligence received was carried to thousands.

We should educate the youth to help the youth; and as they seek to do this work they will gain an experience that will qualify them to become consecrated workers in a larger sphere. Thousands of hearts can be reached in the most simple, humble way. The most intellectual, those who are looked upon and praised as the world's most gifted men and women, are often refreshed by the simple words that flow from the heart of one who loves God and who can speak of that love as naturally as the worldling speaks of the things which his mind contemplates and feeds upon. Often the words well prepared and studied have little influence. But the true, honest words of a son or daughter of God, spoken in natural simplicity, will open the door to hearts that have long been locked.

The wails of a world's sorrow are heard all around us. Sin is pressing its shadow upon us, and our minds must be ready for every good word and work. We know that we have the presence of Jesus. The sweet influence of His Holy Spirit is teaching and guiding our thoughts, leading us to speak words that will cheer and brighten the pathway of others. If we can speak to our sisters often, and instead of saying, "Go," lead them ourselves to do as we would do, to feel as we would feel, there will be a growing appreciation of the value of the human soul. We are learners, that we may be teachers. This thought must be impressed on the mind of every church member.

We fully believe in church organization; but this is not to prescribe the exact way in which we should work, for not all minds are to be reached by the same methods. Nothing is to be allowed to keep the servant of God from his fellow men. The individual believer is to labor for the individual sinner. Each person has his own light to keep burning; and if the heavenly oil is emptied into these lamps through the golden pipes; if the vessels are emptied of self, and prepared to receive the holy oil, light will be shed on the sinner's path to some purpose. More light will be shed on the pathway of the wanderer by one such lamp than by a whole procession of torchlights gotten up for show. Personal consecration and sanctification to God will bring better results than the most imposing display.

Teach our sisters that their question should be each day: "Lord, what wilt Thou have me to do this day?" Each consecrated vessel will daily have the holy oil emptied into it to be emptied out into other vessels.

———

If the life we live in this world is wholly for Christ, it is a life of daily surrender. He has the freewill service, and each soul is His own jewel. If we can impress upon our sisters the good which it is in their power to do through Christ, we shall see a large work accomplished. If we can arouse the mind and heart to co-operate with the divine Worker, we shall, through the work they may accomplish, gain great victories. But self must be hidden; Christ must appear as the worker.

There must be an interchange of taking in and giving out, receiving and imparting. This links us up as laborers together with God. This is the lifework of the Christian. He that will lose his life shall find it.

The capacity for receiving the holy oil from the two olive trees is increased as the receiver empties that holy oil out of himself in word and action to supply the necessities of other souls. Work, precious, satisfying work—to be constantly receiving and constantly imparting.

We need and must have fresh supplies every day. And how many souls we may help by communicating to them! All heaven is waiting for channels through which can be poured the holy oil, to be a joy and a blessing to others. I have no fear that any will make blundering work if they will only become one with Christ. If He is abiding with us, we shall work continuously and solidly, so that our work will abide. The divine fullness will flow through the consecrated human agent to be given forth to others.

The Lord has a work for women as well as men to do. They may accomplish a good work for God if they will first learn in the school of Christ the precious, all-important lesson of meekness. They must not only bear the name of Christ, but possess His Spirit. They must walk even as He walked, purifying their souls from everything that defiles. Then they will be able to benefit others by presenting the all-sufficiency of Jesus.

Women may take their places in the work at this crisis, and the Lord will work through them. If they are imbued with a sense of their duty, and labor under the influence of the Spirit of God, they will have just the self-possession required for this time. The Saviour will reflect upon these self-sacrificing women the light of His countenance, and this will give them a power which will exceed that of men. They can do in families a work that men cannot do, a work that reaches the inner life. They can come close to the hearts of those whom men cannot reach. Their labor is needed.

———————

A direct necessity is being met by the work of women who have given themselves to the Lord and are reaching out to help a needy, sin-stricken people. Personal evangelistic work is to be done. The women who take up this work carry the gospel to the homes of the people in the highways and the byways. They read and explain the word to families, praying with them, caring for the sick, relieving their temporal necessities. They present before families and individuals the purifying, transforming influence of the truth. They show that the way to find peace and joy is to follow Jesus.

———————

All who work for God should have the Martha and the Mary attributes blended—a willingness to minister and a sincere love of the truth. Self and selfishness must be put out of sight. God calls for earnest women workers, workers who are prudent, warmhearted, tender, and true to principle. He calls for persevering women who will take their minds from self and their personal convenience, and will center them on Christ, speaking words of truth, praying with the persons to whom they can obtain access, laboring for the conversion of souls.

Oh, what is our excuse, my sisters, that we do not devote all the time possible to searching the Scriptures, making the mind a storehouse of precious things, that we may present them to those who are not interested in the truth? Will our sisters arise to the emergency? Will they work for the Master?

TEACHING HOME RELIGION

THOSE who bear the last message of mercy to the world should feel it their duty to instruct parents in regard to home religion. The great reformatory movement must begin in presenting to fathers and mothers and children the principles of the law of God. As the claims of the law are presented, and men and women are convicted of their duty to render obedience, show them the responsibility of their decision, not only for themselves but for their children. Show that obedience to God's word is our only safeguard against the evils that are sweeping the world to destruction. Parents are giving to their children an example either of obedience or of transgression. By their example and teaching, the eternal destiny of their households will in most cases be decided. In the future life the children will be what their parents have made them.

If parents could be led to trace the results of their action, and could see how by their example and teaching they perpetuate and increase the power of sin or the power of righteousness, a change would certainly be made. Many would break the spell of tradition and custom.

Let ministers urge this matter upon their congregations. Press home upon the consciences of parents the conviction of their solemn duties, so long neglected. This will break up the spirit of pharisaism and resistance to the truth as nothing else can. Religion in the home is our great hope and makes the prospect bright for the conversion of the whole family to the truth of God.

MEETING OPPOSITION

Our ministers and teachers are to represent the love of God to a fallen world. With hearts melted in tenderness let the word of truth be spoken. Let all who are in error be treated with the gentleness of Christ. If those for whom you labor do not immediately grasp the truth, do not censure, do not criticize or condemn. Remember that you are to represent Christ in His meekness and gentleness and love. We must expect to meet unbelief and opposition. The truth has always had to meet these elements. But though you should meet the bitterest opposition, do not denounce your opponents. They may think, as did Paul, that they are doing God's service, and to such we must manifest patience, meekness, and long-suffering.

Let us not feel that we have heavy trials to bear, severe conflicts to endure, in representing unpopular truth. Think of Jesus and what He has suffered for you, and be silent. Even when abused and falsely accused, make no complaint; speak no word of murmuring; let no thought of reproach or discontent enter your mind. Take a straightforward course, "having your conversation honest among the Gentiles: that, whereas they speak against you as evildoers, they may by your good works, which they shall behold, glorify God in the day of visitation." 1 Peter 2:12.

"Love as brethren, be pitiful, be courteous: not rendering evil for evil, or railing for railing: but contrariwise blessing; knowing that ye are thereunto called, that ye should inherit a blessing. For he that will love life, and see good days, let him refrain his tongue from evil, and his lips that they speak no guile: let him eschew evil, and do good; let him seek peace, and ensue it. For the eyes of the Lord are over the righteous, and His ears are open unto their prayers: but the face of the Lord is against them that do evil. And who is he that will harm you, if ye be followers of that which is good? But and if ye suffer for righteousness' sake, happy are ye: and be not afraid of their terror, neither be troubled; but sanctify the Lord God in your hearts: and be ready always to give an answer to every man that asketh you a reason of the hope that is in you with meekness and fear." 1 Peter 3:8-15.

You should conduct yourself with meekness toward those who are in error, for were not you yourself recently in blindness in your sins? And because of the patience of Christ toward you, should you not be tender and patient toward others? God has given us many admonitions to manifest great kindness toward those who oppose us, lest we influence a soul in the wrong direction.

Our life must be hid with Christ in God. We must know Christ personally. Then only can we rightly represent Him to the world. Let the prayer constantly ascend: "Lord, teach me how to do as Jesus would do were He in my place." Wherever we are we must let our light shine forth to the glory of God in good works. This is the great, important interest of our life.

––––––––

The Lord wants His people to follow other methods than that of condemning wrong, even though the condemnation be just. He wants us to do something more than to hurl at our adversaries charges that only drive them further from the truth. The work which Christ came to do in our world was not to erect barriers and constantly thrust upon the people the fact that they were wrong.

He who expects to enlighten a deceived people must come near to them and labor for them in love. He must become a center of holy influence.

In the advocacy of the truth the bitterest opponents should be treated with respect and deference. Some will not respond to our efforts, but will make light of the gospel invitation. Others—even those whom we suppose to have passed the boundary of God's mercy—will be won to Christ. The very last work in the controversy may be the enlightenment of those who have not rejected light and evidence, but who have been in midnight darkness and have in ignorance worked against the truth. Therefore treat every man as honest. Speak no word, do no deed, that will confirm any in unbelief.

If anyone shall seek to draw the workers into debate or controversy on political or other questions, take no heed to either persuasion or challenge. Carry forward the work of God firmly and strongly, but in the meekness of Christ and as quietly as possible. Let no human boasting be heard. Let no sign of self-sufficiency be made. Let it be seen that God has called us to handle sacred trusts; preach the word, be diligent, earnest, and fervent.

The influence of your teaching would be tenfold greater if you were careful of your words. Words that should be a savor of life unto life may by the spirit which accompanies them be made a savor of death unto death. And remember that if by your spirit or your words you close the door to even one soul, that soul will confront you in the judgment.

Do not, when referring to the *Testimonies,* feel it your duty to drive them home. In reading the *Testimonies* be sure not to mix in your filling of words, for this makes it impossible for the hearers to distinguish between the word of the Lord to them and your words. Be sure that you do not make the word of the Lord offensive. We long to see reforms, and because we do not see that which we desire, an evil spirit is too often allowed to cast drops of gall into our cup, and thus others are embittered. By our ill-advised words their spirit is chafed, and they are stirred to rebellion.

Every sermon you preach, every article you write, may be all true; but one drop of gall in it will be poison to the hearer or the reader. Because of that drop of poison, one will discard all your good and acceptable words. Another will feed on the poison; for he loves such harsh words; he follows your example, and talks just as you talk. Thus the evil is multiplied.

Those who present the eternal principles of truth need the holy oil emptied from the two olive branches into the heart. This will flow forth in words that will reform, but not exasperate. The truth is to be spoken in love. Then the Lord Jesus by His Spirit will supply the force and the power. That is His work.

———

Place yourselves in the divine current, where you can receive the heavenly inspiration, for you may have it; then point the weary, the heavy-laden, the poor, the brokenhearted, the perplexed soul, to Jesus, the Source of all spiritual strength. Be faithful minutemen to show forth the praises of Him who has called you out of darkness into His marvelous light. Tell it with pen and voice that Jesus lives to make intercession for us.

PARABLE OF THE STRAYING SHEEP

THE parable of the straying sheep should be treasured as a motto in every household. The divine Shepherd leaves the ninety and nine, and goes out into the wilderness to seek the one that is lost. There are thickets, quagmires, and dangerous crevices in the rocks, and the Shepherd knows that if the sheep is in any of these places, a friendly hand must help it out. As He hears its bleating afar off, He encounters any and every difficulty that He may save His sheep that is lost. When He discovers the lost one, He does not greet it with reproaches. He is only glad that He has found it alive. With firm yet gentle hand He parts the briers or takes it from the mire; tenderly He lifts it to His shoulders and bears it back to the fold. The pure, sinless Redeemer bears the sinful, the unclean.

The Sin Bearer carries the befouled sheep; yet so precious is His burden that He rejoices, singing: "I have found My sheep which was lost." Luke 15:6. Let every one of you consider that your individual self has thus been borne upon Christ's shoulders. Let none entertain a masterly spirit, a self-righteous, criticizing spirit; for not one sheep would ever have entered the fold if the Shepherd had not undertaken the painful search in the desert. The fact that one sheep was lost was enough to awaken the sympathy of the Shepherd and start Him on His quest.

This speck of a world was the scene of the incarnation and suffering of the Son of God. Christ did not go to worlds unfallen, but He came to this world, all seared and marred with the curse. The outlook was not favorable, but most discouraging. Yet "He shall not fail nor be dis-

couraged, till He have set judgment in the earth." Isaiah
42:4. We must bear in mind the great joy manifested by
the Shepherd at the recovery of the lost. He calls upon
His neighbors: "Rejoice with Me; for I have found My
sheep which was lost." And all heaven echoes the note
of joy. The Father Himself joys over the rescued one with
singing. What a holy ecstasy of joy is expressed in this
parable! That joy it is your privilege to share.

Are you, who have this example before you, co-operating with Him who is seeking to save the lost? Are you
colaborers with Christ? Can you not for His sake endure
suffering, sacrifice, and trial? There is opportunity for
doing good to the souls of the youth and the erring. If
you see one whose words or attitude shows that he is separated from God, do not blame him. It is not your work
to condemn him, but come close to his side to give him
help. Consider the humility of Christ, and His meekness
and lowliness, and work as He worked, with a heart full
of sanctified tenderness. "At the same time, saith the
Lord, will I be the God of all the families of Israel, and
they shall be My people. Thus saith the Lord, The people which were left of the sword found grace in the
wilderness; even Israel, when I went to cause him to rest.
The Lord hath appeared of old unto me, saying, Yea, I
have loved thee with an everlasting love: therefore with
loving-kindness have I drawn thee." Jeremiah 31:1-3.

In order for us to work as Christ worked, self must
be crucified. It is a painful death; but it is life, life to
the soul. "For thus saith the high and lofty One that
inhabiteth eternity, whose name is Holy; I dwell in the
high and holy place, with him also that is of a contrite
and humble spirit, to revive the spirit of the humble, and
to revive the heart of the contrite ones." Isaiah 57:15.

EDUCATION

> "The Lord giveth wisdom: out of His mouth cometh knowledge and understanding."

THE NEED OF EDUCATIONAL REFORM

"AND they shall build the old wastes, they shall raise up the former desolations, and they shall repair the waste cities, the desolations of many generations." "And thou shalt be called, The repairer of the breach, The restorer of paths to dwell in." Isaiah 61:4; 58:12. These words of Inspiration present before believers in present truth the work that should now be done in the education of our children and youth. When the truth for these last days came to the world in the proclamation of the first, second, and third angels' messages, we were shown that in the education of our children a different order of things must be brought in; but it has taken much time to understand what changes should be made.

Our work is reformatory; and it is the purpose of God that through the excellence of the work done in our educational institutions the attention of the people shall be called to the last great effort to save the perishing. In our schools the standard of education must not be lowered. It must be lifted higher and still higher, far above where it now stands; but the education given must not be confined to a knowledge of textbooks merely. The study of textbooks alone cannot afford students the discipline they need, nor can it impart true wisdom. The object of our schools is to provide places where the younger members of the Lord's family may be trained according to His plan of growth and development.

Satan has used the most ingenious methods to weave his plans and principles into the systems of education, and thus gain a strong hold on the minds of the children and youth. It is the work of the true educator to thwart his devices. We are under solemn, sacred covenant to God to bring up our children for Him and not for the world; to teach them not to put their hands into the hand of the world, but to love and fear God, and to keep His commandments. They should be impressed with the thought that they are formed in the image of their Creator and that Christ is the pattern after which they are to be fashioned. Most earnest attention must be given to the education which will impart a knowledge of salvation, and will conform the life and character to the divine similitude. It is the love of God, the purity of soul woven into the life like threads of gold, that is of true worth. The height man may thus reach has not been fully realized.

For the accomplishment of this work a broad foundation must be laid. A new purpose must be brought in and find place, and students must be aided in applying Bible principles in all they do. Whatever is crooked, whatever is twisted out of the right line, is to be plainly pointed out and avoided; for it is iniquity not to be perpetuated. It is important that every teacher should love and cherish sound principles and doctrines, for this is the light to be reflected upon the pathway of all students.

THE THIRD ANGEL'S MESSAGE IN OUR SCHOOLS

In the book of Revelation we read of a special work that God desires to have His people do in these last days. He has revealed His law and shown us the truth for this time. This truth is constantly unfolding, and God designs that we shall be intelligent in regard to it, that we may be able to distinguish between right and wrong, between righteousness and unrighteousness.

The third angel's message, the great testing truth for this time, is to be taught in all our institutions. God designs that through them this special warning shall be given, and bright beams of light shall shine to the world. Time is short. The perils of the last days are upon us, and we should watch and pray, and study and heed the lessons that are given us in the books of Daniel and the Revelation.

When John was banished from those he loved to lonely Patmos, Christ knew where to find His faithful witness. John said: "I John, who also am your brother, and companion in tribulation, and in the kingdom and patience of Jesus Christ, was in the isle that is called Patmos, for the word of God, and for the testimony of Jesus Christ. I was in the Spirit on the Lord's day, and heard behind me a great voice, as of a trumpet." The Lord's day is the seventh day, the Sabbath of creation. On the day that God sanctified and blessed, Christ signified "by His angel unto His servant John" things which must come to pass before the close of the world's history, and He means that we should become intelligent with regard to them. It is not in vain that He declares: "Blessed is he that readeth, and they that hear the words of this prophecy, and keep those things which are written therein: for the time is at hand." Revelation 1:9, 10, 1-3. This is the education that is to be patiently given. Let our lessons be appropriate for the day in which we live, and let our religious instruction be given in accordance with the messages God sends.

We shall have to stand before magistrates to answer for our allegiance to the law of God, to make known the reasons of our faith. And the youth should understand these things. They should know the things that will come to pass before the closing up of the world's history. These things concern our eternal welfare, and teachers and students should give more attention to them. By pen and voice, knowledge should be imparted which will be meat in due season, not only to the young, but to those of mature years also.

We are living in the closing scenes of these perilous times. The Lord foresaw the unbelief that now prevails respecting His coming; and again and again He has given warning in His word that this event will be unexpected. The great day will come as a snare "on all them that dwell on the face of the whole earth." Luke 21:35. But there are two classes. To one the apostle gives these encouraging words: "Ye, brethren, are not in darkness, that that day should overtake you as a thief." 1 Thessalonians 5:4. Some will be ready when the Bridegroom comes, and will go in with Him to the marriage. How precious is this thought to those who are waiting and watching for His appearing! Christ "loved the church, and gave Himself for it; that He might sanctify and cleanse it with the washing of water by the word, that He might present it to Himself a glorious church, not having spot, or wrinkle, or any such thing; but that it should be holy and without blemish." Ephesians 5:25-27. Those whom God loves enjoy this favor because they are lovely in character.

The great, grand work of bringing out a people who will have Christlike characters, and who will be able to stand in the day of the Lord, is to be accomplished. As long as we sail with the current of the world we need neither canvas nor oar. It is when we turn squarely about to stem the current that our labors begin. Satan will bring in every kind of theory to pervert the truth. The work will go hard, for since the fall of Adam it has been the fashion of the world to sin. But Christ is on the field of action. The Holy Spirit is at work. Divine agencies are combining with the human in reshaping the character according to the perfect pattern, and man is to work out that which God works in. Will we as a people do this God-given work? Will we carefully heed all the light that has been given, keeping constantly before us the one object of fitting students for the kingdom of God? If by faith we advance step by step in the right way, following the Great Leader, light will shine along our pathway; and circumstances will occur to remove the difficulties. The approval of God will give hope, and ministering angels will co-operate with us, bringing light and grace, and courage and gladness.

Then let no more time be lost in dwelling on the many things which are not essential and which have no bearing upon the present necessities of God's people. Let no more time be lost in exalting men who know not the truth, "for the time is at hand." There is no time now to fill the mind with theories of what is popularly called "higher education." The time devoted to that which does not tend to assimilate the soul to the likeness of Christ is so much time lost for eternity. This we cannot afford, for every moment is freighted with eternal interests. Now, when the great work of judging the living is about to begin, shall we allow unsanctified ambition to take possession of the heart and lead us to neglect the education required to meet the needs in this day of peril?

In every case the great decision is to be made whether we shall receive the mark of the beast or his image, or the seal of the living God. And now, when we are on the borders of the eternal world, what can be of so much value to us as to be found loyal and true to the God of heaven? What is there that we should prize above His truth and His law? What education can be given to the students in our schools that is so necessary as a knowledge of "What saith the Scriptures?"

We know that there are many schools which afford opportunities for education in the sciences, but we desire something more than this. The science of true education is the truth, which is to be so deeply impressed on the soul that it cannot be obliterated by the error that everywhere abounds. The third angel's message is truth, and light, and power, and to present it so that right impressions will be made upon hearts should be the work of our schools as well as of our churches, of the teacher as well as of the minister. Those who accept positions as educators should prize more and more the revealed will of God so plainly and strikingly presented in Daniel and the Revelation.

BIBLE STUDY

The urgent necessities that are making themselves felt in this time demand a constant education in the word of God. This is present truth. Throughout the world there should be a reform in Bible study, for it is needed now as never before. As this reform progresses, a mighty work will be wrought; for when God declared that His word should not return unto Him void, He meant all that He said. A knowledge of God and of Jesus Christ "whom He has sent" is the highest education, and it will cover the earth with its wonderful enlightenment as the waters cover the sea.

Bible study is especially needed in the schools. Students should be rooted and grounded in divine truth. Their attention should be called, not to the assertions of men, but to the word of God. Above all other books, the word of God must be our study, the great textbook, the basis of all education; and our children are to be educated in the truths found therein, irrespective of previous habits and customs. In doing this, teachers and students will find the hidden treasure, the higher education.

Bible rules are to be the guide of the daily life. The cross of Christ is to be the theme, revealing the lessons we must learn and practice. Christ must be brought into all the studies, that students may drink in the knowledge of God and may represent Him in character. His excellence is to be our study in time as well as in eternity. The word of God, spoken by Christ in the Old and New Testaments, is the bread from heaven; but much that is called science is as dishes of human invention, adulterated food; it is not the true manna.

In God's word is found wisdom unquestionable, inexhaustible—wisdom that originated, not in the finite, but in the infinite mind. But much of that which God has revealed in His word is dark to men, because the jewels of truth are buried beneath the rubbish of human wisdom and tradition. To many the treasures of the word remain hidden, because they have not been searched for with earnest perseverance until the golden precepts were understood. The word must be searched in order to purify and prepare those who receive it to become members of the royal family, children of the heavenly King.

The study of God's word should take the place of the study of those books that have led minds into mysticism and away from the truth. Its living principles, woven into our lives, will be our safeguard in trials and temptations; its divine instruction is the only way to success. As the test comes to every soul, there will be apostasies. Some will prove to be traitors, heady, high-minded, and self-sufficient, and will turn away from the truth, making shipwreck of faith. Why? Because they did not live "by every word that proceedeth out of the mouth of God." They did not dig deep and make their foundation sure.

When the words of the Lord through His chosen messengers are brought to them, they murmur and think the way is made too strait. In the sixth chapter of John we read of some who were thought to be disciples of Christ, but who, when the plain truth was presented to them, were displeased and walked no more with Him. In like manner these superficial students also will turn away from Christ.

Everyone who has been converted to God is called upon to grow in capability by using his talents; every branch of the living Vine that does not grow is pruned off and cast away as rubbish. What, then, shall be the character of the education given in our schools? Shall it be according to the wisdom of this world or according to that wisdom that is from above? Will not teachers awake to their responsibility in this matter and see that the word of God has a larger place in the instruction given in our schools?

THE TRAINING OF WORKERS

One great object of our schools is the training of youth to engage in service in our institutions and in different lines of gospel work. The people everywhere are to have the Bible opened to them. The time has come, the important time when through God's messengers the scroll is being unrolled to the world. The truth comprised in the first, second, and third angels' messages must go to every nation, kindred, tongue, and people; it must lighten the darkness of every continent and extend to the islands of the sea. Nothing of human invention must be allowed to retard this work. That this may be accomplished, there is need of cultivated and consecrated talent; there is need of persons who can do excellent work in the meekness of Christ because self is hid in Christ. Novices cannot acceptably do the work of unfolding the hidden treasure to enrich souls in spiritual things. "Consider what I say; and the Lord give thee understanding in all things." "Study to show thyself approved unto God, a workman that needeth not to be ashamed, rightly dividing the word of truth." 2 Timothy 2:7, 15. This charge to Timothy is to be an educating power in every family and in every school.

Earnest efforts are called for on the part of all connected with our institutions, not only our schools, but our sanitariums and publishing houses also, to qualify men, women, and youth to become colaborers with God. Students are to be instructed to work intelligently in Christ's lines, to present a noble, elevated, Christian character to those with whom they associate. Those who have charge of training the youth connected with any line of our work should be men who have a deep sense of the value of souls. Unless they drink deeply of the Holy Spirit, there is an evil watcher who will create annoying circumstances. The educator should be wise to discern that while faithfulness and kindness will win souls, harshness never will. Arbitrary words and actions stir up the worst passions of the human heart. If men and women professing to be Christians have not learned to put away their own evil and childish tempers, how can they expect to be honored and respected?

Then what carefulness should be exercised in selecting proper persons as instructors, that they may not only be faithful in their work, but may manifest a right temper. If they are not trustworthy, they should be discharged. God will hold every institution responsible for any neglect to see that kindness and love are encouraged. It should never be forgotten that Christ Himself has charge of our institutions.

The best ministerial talent should be employed in teaching the Bible in our schools. Those selected for this work need to be thorough Bible students and to have a deep Christian experience, and their salary should be paid from the tithe. God designs that all our institutions shall become instrumentalities for educating and developing workers of whom He will not be ashamed, workers who can be sent out as well-qualified missionaries to do service for the Master; but this object has not been kept in view. In many respects we are far behind in this work, and the Lord requires that a zeal be shown in it infinitely greater than has hitherto been manifested. He has called us out from the world that we may be witnesses for His truth, and all through our ranks young men and women should be trained for positions of usefulness and influence.

There is an urgent demand for laborers in the gospel field. Young men are needed for this work; God calls for them. Their education is of primary importance in our colleges, and in no case should it be ignored or regarded as a secondary matter. It is entirely wrong for teachers, by suggesting other occupations, to discourage young men who might be qualified to do acceptable work in the ministry. Those who present hindrances to prevent young men from fitting themselves for this work are counterworking the plans of God, and they will have to give an account of their course. There is among us more than an average of men of ability. If their capabilities were brought into use, we should have twenty ministers where we now have one.

Young men who design to enter the ministry should not spend a number of years solely in obtaining an education. Teachers should be able to comprehend the situation and to adapt their instruction to the wants of this class, and special advantages should be given them for a brief yet comprehensive study of the branches most needed to fit them for their work. But this plan has not been followed. Too little attention has been given to the education of young men for the ministry. We have not many years to work, and teachers should be imbued with the Spirit of God and work in harmony with His revealed will, instead of carrying out their own plans. We are losing much every year because we do not heed the counsel of the Lord on these points.

In our schools missionary nurses should receive lessons from well-qualified physicians, and as a part of their education should learn how to battle with disease and to show the value of nature's remedies. This work is greatly needed. Cities and towns are steeped in sin and moral corruption, yet there are Lots in every Sodom. The poison of sin is at work at the heart of society, and God calls for reformers to stand in defense of the law which He has established to govern the physical system. They should at the same time maintain an elevated standard in the training of the mind and the culture of the heart, that the Great Physician may co-operate with the human helping hand in doing a work of mercy and necessity in the relief of suffering.

It is also the Lord's design that our schools shall give young people a training which will prepare them to teach in any department of the Sabbath school or to discharge the duties in any of its offices. We should see a different state of affairs if a number of consecrated young persons would devote themselves to the Sabbath school work, taking pains to educate themselves and then to instruct others as to the best methods to be employed in leading souls to Christ. This is a line of work that brings returns.

MISSIONARY TEACHERS

Teachers should be educated for missionary work. Everywhere there are openings for the missionary, and it will not be possible to supply laborers from any two or three countries to answer all the appeals for help. Besides the education of those who are to be sent out from our older conferences as missionaries, persons in various parts of the world should be trained to work for their own countrymen and their own neighbors; and as far as possible it is better and safer for them to receive their education in the field where they are to labor. It is seldom best, either for the worker or for the advancement of the work, that he should go to distant lands for his education. The Lord would have every possible provision made to meet these necessities; and if churches are awake to their responsibilities, they will know how to act in any emergency.

To supply the need of laborers, God desires that educational centers be established in different countries where students of promise may be educated in the practical branches of knowledge and in Bible truth. As these persons engage in labor, they will give character to the work of present truth in the new fields. They will awaken an interest among unbelievers and aid in rescuing souls from the bondage of sin. The very best teachers should be sent to the various countries where schools are to be established, to carry on the educational work.

It is possible to have too many educational facilities centered in one place. Smaller schools, conducted after the plan of the schools of the prophets, would be a far greater blessing. The money which was invested in enlarging Battle Creek College to accommodate the ministers' school would better have been invested in establishing schools in rural districts in America and in the regions beyond. No more buildings were needed in Battle Creek; ample facilities were already provided for the education of as many students as ought to congregate in one place. It was not best that so many students should attend this school, for there was talent and wisdom to manage only a certain number. The ministerial institutes could have been held in buildings already erected, and the money used in enlarging the college could have been invested to better advantage in erecting school buildings in other localities.

New buildings in Battle Creek meant encouragement for families to move there in order to educate their children in the college. But it would have been a far greater blessing to all concerned had the students been educated in some other locality and in much smaller numbers. The flocking of the people to Battle Creek is as much the fault of those who are in leading positions as of those who have moved to this place. There are better fields for missionary enterprise than Battle Creek, and yet those in responsible positions have been planning to have everything there of the most convenient character; and the large facilities are saying to the people: "Come to Battle Creek; move here with your families, and educate your children here."

If some of our large educational institutions were broken up into smaller ones, and schools established in various places, greater progress might be made in physical, mental, and moral culture. The Lord has not said that there should be fewer buildings, but that these buildings should not be centered too much in one place. The large amount of means invested in a few localities should be used in providing facilities for a wider field so that many more students could be accommodated.

The time has come for lifting the standard of truth in many places, for arousing an interest and extending the missionary field until it shall encompass the world. The time has come when many more should have the message of truth brought to their attention. Much can be done in this direction that is not done. While the churches are responsible for keeping their own lamps trimmed and burning, devoted young people must be educated in their own countries to carry forward this work. Schools should be established, not such elaborate schools as those at Battle Creek and College View, but more simple schools with more humble buildings, and with teachers who will adopt the same plans that were followed in the schools of the prophets. Instead of concentrating the light in one place, where many do not appreciate or improve on that which is given them, the light should be carried into many places of the earth. If devoted, God-fearing teachers of well-balanced minds and practical ideas would go into missionary fields and work in a humble way, imparting that which they have received, God would give His Holy Spirit to many who are destitute of His grace.

ELEMENTS OF SUCCESS

In the work of reform, teachers and students should co-operate, each working to the best advantage to make our schools such as God can approve. Unity of action is necessary to success. An army in battle would become confused and be defeated if the individual soldiers should move according to their own impulses instead of acting in harmony under the direction of a competent general. The soldiers of Christ also must act in harmony. A few converted souls, uniting for one grand purpose under one head, will achieve victories in every encounter.

If there is disunion among those who claim to believe the truth, the world will conclude that this people cannot be of God, because they are working against one another. When we are one with Christ, we shall be united among ourselves. Those who are not yoked up with Christ always pull the wrong way. They possess a temperament that belongs to man's carnal nature, and at the least excuse passion is wide awake to meet passion. This causes a collision; and loud voices are heard in committee meetings, in board meetings, and in public assemblies, opposing reform methods.

Obedience to every word of God is another condition of success. Victories are not gained by ceremonies or display, but by simple obedience to the highest General, the Lord God of heaven. He who trusts in this Leader will never know defeat. Defeat comes in depending on human methods, human inventions, and placing the divine secondary. Obedience was the lesson that the Captain of the Lord's host sought to teach the vast armies of Israel — obedience in things in which they could see no success. When there is obedience to the voice of our Leader, Christ will conduct His battles in ways that will surprise the greatest powers of earth.

We are soldiers of Christ; and those who enlist in His army are expected to do difficult work, work which will tax their energies to the utmost. We must understand that a soldier's life is one of aggressive warfare, of perseverance and endurance. For Christ's sake we are to endure trials. We are not engaged in mimic battles. We have to meet most powerful adversaries; for "we wrestle not against flesh and blood, but against principalities, against powers, against the rulers of the darkness of this world, against spiritual wickedness in high places." Ephesians 6:12. We are to find our strength just where the early disciples found their strength: "These all continued with one accord in prayer and supplication." "And they were all filled with the Holy Ghost, and they spake the word of God with boldness. And the multitude of them that believed were of one heart and of one soul." Acts 1:14; 4:31, 32.

HINDRANCES TO REFORM

To some extent the Bible has been introduced into our schools, and some efforts have been made in the direction of reform; but it is most difficult to adopt right principles after having been so long accustomed to popular methods. The first attempts to change the old customs brought severe trials upon those who would walk in the way which God has pointed out. Mistakes have been made, and great loss has resulted. There have been hindrances which have tended to keep us in common, worldly lines, and to prevent us from grasping true educational principles. To the unconverted, who view matters from the lowlands of human selfishness, unbelief, and indifference, right principles and methods have appeared wrong.

Some teachers and managers who are only half converted are stumbling blocks to others. They concede some things and make half reforms; but when greater knowledge comes, they refuse to advance, preferring to work according to their own ideas. In doing this they pluck and eat of that tree of knowledge which places the human above the divine. "Now therefore fear the Lord, and serve Him in sincerity and in truth: and put away the gods which your fathers served on the other side of the flood, and in Egypt; and serve ye the Lord. And if it seem evil unto you to serve the Lord, choose you this day whom ye will serve." "If the Lord be God, follow Him: but if Baal, then follow him." Joshua 24:14, 15; 1 Kings 18:21. We should have been far in advance of our present spiritual condition had we moved forward as the light came to us.

When new methods have been advocated, so many doubtful questions have been introduced, so many councils held that every difficulty might be discerned, that reformers have been handicapped, and some have ceased to urge reforms. They seem unable to stem the current of doubt and criticism. Comparatively few received the gospel in Athens because the people cherished pride of intellect and worldly wisdom, and counted the gospel of Christ foolishness. But "the foolishness of God is wiser than men; and the weakness of God is stronger than men." Therefore "we preach Christ crucified, unto the Jews a stumbling block, and unto the Greeks foolishness; but unto them which are called, both Jews and Greeks, Christ the power of God, and the wisdom of God." 1 Corinthians 1:25, 23, 24.

We need now to begin over again. Reforms must be entered into with heart and soul and will. Errors may be hoary with age; but age does not make error truth, nor truth error. Altogether too long have the old customs and habits been followed. The Lord would now have every idea that is false put away from teachers and students. We are not at liberty to teach that which shall meet the world's standard or the standard of the church, simply because it is the custom to do so. The lessons which Christ taught are to be the standard. That which the Lord has spoken concerning the instruction to be given in our schools is to be strictly regarded; for if there is not in some respects an education of an altogether different character from that which has been carried on in some of our schools, we need not have gone to the expense of purchasing lands and erecting school buildings.

Some will urge that if religious teaching is to be made prominent our schools will become unpopular; that those who are not of our faith will not patronize them. Very well; then let them go to other schools, where they will find a system of education that suits their taste. It is Satan's purpose by these considerations to prevent the attainment of the object for which our schools were established. Hindered by his devices, the managers reason after the manner of the world and copy its plans and imitate its customs. Many have so far shown their lack of wisdom from above as to join with the enemies of God and the truth in providing worldly entertainments for the students. In doing this they bring upon themselves the frown of God, for they mislead the youth and do a work for Satan. This work, with all its results, they must meet at the bar of God.

Those who pursue such a course show that they cannot be trusted. After the evil has been done, they may confess their error; but can they undo the influence they have exerted? Will the "well done" be spoken to those who have been false to their trust? These unfaithful workmen have not built upon the eternal Rock, and their foundation will prove to be sliding sand. When the Lord requires us to be distinct and peculiar, how can we crave popularity or seek to imitate the customs and practices of the world? "Know ye not that the friendship of the world is enmity with God? whosoever therefore will be a friend of the world is the enemy of God." James 4:4.

To lower the standard in order to secure popularity and an increase of numbers, and then to make this increase a cause of rejoicing, shows great blindness. If numbers were an evidence of success, Satan might claim the pre-eminence; for in this world his followers are largely in the majority. It is the degree of moral power pervading a school that is a test of its prosperity. It is the virtue, intelligence, and piety of the people composing our schools, not their numbers, that should be a source of joy and thankfulness. Then shall our schools become converted to the world and follow its customs and fashions? "I beseech you therefore, brethren, by the mercies of God, that ye

. . . be not conformed to this world: but be ye transformed by the renewing of your mind, that ye may prove what is that good, and acceptable, and perfect, will of God." Romans 12:1, 2.

Men will employ every means to make less prominent the difference between Seventh-day Adventists and observers of the first day of the week. A company was presented before me under the name of Seventh-day Adventists, who were advising that the banner, or sign, which makes us a distinct people should not be held out so strikingly; for they claimed that this was not the best policy in order to secure success to our institutions. But this is not a time to haul down our colors, to be ashamed of our faith. This distinctive banner, described in the words, "Here is the patience of the saints: here are they that keep the commandments of God, and the faith of Jesus," is to be borne through the world to the close of probation. While efforts should be increased to advance in different localities, there must be no cloaking of our faith to secure patronage. Truth must come to souls ready to perish; and if it is in any way hidden, God is dishonored, and the blood of souls will be upon our garments.

Just as long as those in connection with our institutions walk humbly with God, heavenly intelligences will co-operate with them; but let all bear in mind the fact that God has said: "Them that honor Me I will honor." 1 Samuel 2:30. Never for one moment should the impression be given to anyone that it would be for his profit to hide his faith and doctrines from the unbelieving people of the world, fearing that he may not be so highly esteemed if his principles are known. Christ requires from all His followers open, manly confession of faith. Each must take his position and be what God designed he should be, a spectacle to the world, to angels, and to men. The whole universe is looking with inexpressible interest to see the closing work of the great controversy between Christ and Satan. Every Christian is to be a light, not hid under a bushel or under a bed, but put on a candlestick, that light may be given to all who are in the house. Never, from cowardice or worldly policy, let the truth of God be placed in the background.

Though in many respects our institutions of learning have swung into worldly conformity, though step by step they have advanced toward the world, they are prisoners of hope. Fate has not so woven its meshes about their workings that they need to remain helpless and in uncertainty. If they will listen to His voice and follow in His ways, God will correct and enlighten them, and bring them back to their upright position of distinction from the world. When the advantage of working upon Christian principles is discerned, when self is hid in Christ, much greater progress will be made; for each worker will feel his own human weakness; he will supplicate for the wisdom and grace of God, and will receive the divine help that is pledged for every emergency.

Opposing circumstances should create a firm determination to overcome them. One barrier broken down will give greater ability and courage to go forward. Press in the right direction, and make a change, solidly, intelligently. Then circumstances will be your helpers and not your hindrances. Make a beginning. The oak is in the acorn.

TO TEACHERS AND MANAGERS

I call upon our school faculties to use sound judgment and to work on a higher plane. Our educational facilities must be purified from all dross. Our institutions must be conducted on Christian principles if they would triumph over opposing obstacles. If they are conducted on worldly-policy plans, there will be a want of solidity in the work, a want of farseeing spiritual discernment. The condition of the world previous to the first appearing of Christ is a picture of the condition of the world just previous to His second advent. The Jewish people were destroyed because they rejected the message of salvation sent down from heaven. Shall those in this generation to whom God has given great light and wonderful opportunities follow in the trend of those who rejected light to their ruin?

Many today have veils upon their faces. These veils are sympathy with the customs and practices of the world, which hide from them the glory of the Lord. God desires us to keep our eyes fixed upon Him, that we may lose sight of the things of this world.

As the truth is brought into practical life, the standard is to be elevated higher and higher to meet the requirements of the Bible. This will necessitate opposition to the fashions, customs, practices, and maxims of the world. Worldly influences, like the waves of the sea, beat against the followers of Christ to sweep them away from the true principles of His meekness and grace; but we are to stand as firm as a rock to principle. It will require moral courage to do this, and those whose souls are not riveted to the eternal Rock will be swept away by the worldly current. We can stand firm only as our life is hid with Christ in God. Moral independence is wholly in place when opposing the world. By conforming entirely to the will of God, we shall be placed upon vantage ground, and shall see the necessity of decided separation from the customs and practices of the world.

We are not to elevate our standard just a little above the world's standard, but we are to make the distinction decidedly apparent. The reason we have had so little influence upon unbelieving relatives and associates is that there has been so little decided difference between our practices and those of the world.

Many teachers permit their minds to take too narrow and low a range. They do not keep the divine plan ever in view, but are fixing their eyes upon worldly models. Look up, "where Christ sitteth on the right hand of God," and then labor that your pupils may be conformed to His perfect character. Point the youth to Peter's ladder of eight rounds, and place their feet, not on the highest round, but on the lowest, and with earnest solicitation urge them to climb to the very top.

Christ, who connects earth with heaven, is the ladder. The base is planted firmly on the earth in His humanity; the topmost round reaches to the throne of God in His divinity. The humanity of Christ embraces fallen humanity, while His divinity lays hold upon the throne of God. We are saved by climbing round after round of the ladder, looking to Christ, clinging to Christ, mounting step by step to the height of Christ, so that He is made unto us wisdom and righteousness and sanctification and redemption. Faith, virtue, knowledge, temperance, patience, godliness, brotherly kindness, and charity are the rounds of this ladder. All these graces are to be manifested in the Christian character; and "if ye do these things, ye shall never fall: for so an entrance shall be ministered unto you abundantly into the everlasting kingdom of our Lord and Saviour Jesus Christ." 2 Peter 1:10, 11.

It is no easy matter to gain the priceless treasure of eternal life. No one can do this and drift with the current of the world. He must come out from the world and be separate and touch not the unclean. No one can act like a worldling without being carried down by the current of the world. No one will make any upward progress without persevering effort. He who would overcome must hold fast to Christ. He must not look back, but keep the eye ever upward, gaining one grace after another. Individual vigilance is the price of safety. Satan is playing the game of life for your soul. Swerve not to his side a single inch, lest he gain advantage over you.

If we ever reach heaven, it will be by linking our souls to Christ, leaning upon Him, and cutting loose from the world, its follies and enchantments. There must be on our part a spiritual co-operation with the heavenly intelligences. We must believe and work and pray and watch and wait. As the purchase of the Son of God, we are His property, and everyone should have an education in the school of Christ. Both teachers and pupils are to make diligent work for eternity. The end of all things is at hand. There is need now of men armed and equipped to battle for God.

It is not men whom we are to exalt, but God, the only true and living God. The unselfish life, the generous, self-sacrificing spirit, the sympathy and love of those who hold positions of trust in our institutions, should have a purifying, ennobling influence which would be eloquent for good. Their words in counsel would not then come from a self-sufficient, self-exalted spirit; but their unobtrusive virtues would be of more value than gold. If man lays hold of the divine nature, working upon the plan of addition, adding grace to grace in perfecting a Christian character, God will work upon the plan of multiplication. He says in His word: "Grace and peace be multiplied unto you through the knowledge of God, and of Jesus our Lord." 2 Peter 1:2.

"Thus saith the Lord, Let not the wise man glory in his wisdom, neither let the mighty man glory in his might, let not the rich man glory in his riches: but let him that glorieth glory in this, that he understandeth and knoweth Me, that I am the Lord which exercise loving-kindness, judgment, and righteousness, in the earth: for in these things I delight, saith the Lord." Jeremiah 9:23, 24. "He hath showed thee, O man, what is good; and what doth the Lord require of thee, but to do justly, and to love mercy, and to walk humbly with thy God?" "Who is a God like unto Thee, that pardoneth iniquity, and passeth by the transgression of the remnant of His heritage? He retaineth not His anger forever, because He delighteth in mercy." Micah 6:8; 7:18. "Wash you, make you clean; put away the evil of your doings from before Mine eyes; cease to do evil; learn to do well." Isaiah 1:16, 17.

These are the words of God to us. The past is contained in the book where all things are written. We cannot blot out the record; but if we choose to learn them, the past will teach us its lessons. As we make it our monitor, we may also make it our friend. As we call to mind that in the past which is disagreeable, let it teach us not to repeat the same error. In the future let nothing be recorded which will cause regret in the by and by.

We may now avoid a bad showing. Every day we are making our history. Yesterday is beyond our amendment or control; today only is ours. Then let us not grieve the Spirit of God today, for tomorrow we shall not be able to recall what we have done. Today will then be yesterday.

Let us seek to follow the counsel of God in all things, for He is infinite in wisdom. Though in the past we have come short of doing what we might have done for our children and youth, let us now repent and redeem the time. The Lord says: "Though your sins be as scarlet, they shall be as white as snow; though they be red like crimson, they shall be as wool. If ye be willing and obedient, ye shall eat the good of the land: but if ye refuse and rebel, ye shall be devoured with the sword." Isaiah 1:18-20. The message, "Go forward," is still to be heard and repeated. The varying circumstances taking place in our world call for labor that will meet these peculiar developments. The Lord has need of men who are spiritually sharp and clear-sighted, men who are certainly receiving manna fresh from heaven. The Holy Spirit works upon the hearts of such men, and God's word flashes light into the mind, revealing to them more than ever before the true wisdom.

The education given to the young molds the whole social fabric. Throughout the world society is in disorder, and a thorough transformation is needed. Many suppose that better educational facilities, greater skill, and more recent methods will set things right. They profess to believe and receive the living oracles, and yet they give the word of God an inferior position in the great framework of education. That which should stand first is made subordinate to human inventions.

It is so easy to drift into worldly plans, methods, and customs and have no more thought of the time in which we live, or of the great work to be accomplished, than had the people in Noah's day. There is constant danger that our educators will travel over the same ground as did the Jews, conforming to customs, practices, and traditions which God has not given. With tenacity and firmness some cling to old habits and a love of various studies which are not essential, as if their salvation depended upon these things. In doing this they turn away from the special work of God and give to the students a deficient, a wrong education. Minds are directed from a plain "Thus saith the Lord," which involves eternal interests, to human theories and teachings. Infinite, eternal truth, the revelation of God, is explained in the light of human interpretations, when only the Holy Spirit's power can unfold spiritual things. Human wisdom is foolishness; for it misses the whole of God's providences, which look into eternity.

———

Reformers are not destroyers. They will never seek to ruin those who do not harmonize with their plans and assimilate to them. Reformers must advance, not retreat. They must be decided, firm, resolute, unflinching; but firmness must not degenerate into a domineering spirit. God desires to have all who serve Him firm as a rock where principle is concerned, but meek and lowly of heart, as was Christ. Then, abiding in Christ, they can do the work He would do were He in their place. A rude, condemnatory spirit is not essential to heroism in the reforms for this time. All selfish methods in the service of God are an abomination in His sight.

———

Satan works to make the prayer of Christ of none effect. He makes continual efforts to create bitterness and discord; for where there is unity there is strength, a oneness which all the powers of hell cannot break. All who shall aid the enemies of God by bringing weakness and sorrow and discouragement upon any of God's people, through their own perverse ways and tempers, are working directly against the prayer of Christ.

CHARACTER AND WORK OF TEACHERS

THE work done in our schools is not to be like that done in the colleges and seminaries of the world. In the grand work of education, instruction in the sciences is not to be of an inferior character, but that knowledge must be considered of first importance which will fit a people to stand in the great day of God's preparation. Our schools must be more like the schools of the prophets. They should be training schools, where the students may be brought under the discipline of Christ and learn of the Great Teacher. They should be family schools, where every student will receive special help from his teachers as the members of the family should receive help in the home. Tenderness, sympathy, unity, and love are to be cherished. There should be unselfish, devoted, faithful teachers, teachers who are constrained by the love of God and who, with hearts full of tenderness, will have a care for the health and happiness of the students. It should be their aim to advance the students in every essential branch of knowledge.

Wise teachers should be chosen for our schools, those who will feel responsible to God to impress upon minds the necessity of knowing Christ as a personal Saviour. From the highest to the lowest grade they should show special care for the salvation of the students and through personal effort seek to lead their feet into straight paths. They should look with pity upon those who have been badly trained in childhood, and seek to remedy defects, which, if retained, will greatly mar the character. No one can do this work who has not first learned in the school of Christ how to teach.

All who teach in our schools should have a close connection with God and a thorough understanding of His word, that they may be able to bring divine wisdom and knowledge into the work of educating the youth for usefulness in this life and for the future, immortal life. They should be men and women who not only have a knowledge of the truth, but who are doers of the word of God. "It is written" should be expressed in their words and by their lives. By their own practice they should teach simplicity and correct habits in everything. No man or woman should be connected with our schools as an educator who has not had an experience in obeying the word of the Lord.

Principal and teachers need to be baptized with the Holy Spirit. The earnest prayer of contrite souls will be lodged by the throne, and God will answer these prayers in His own time if we cling to His arm by faith. Let self be merged in Christ, and Christ in God, and there will be such a display of His power as will melt and subdue hearts. Christ taught in a way altogether different from ordinary methods, and we are to be laborers together with Him.

Teaching means much more than many suppose. It requires great skill to make the truth understood. For this reason every teacher should strive to have an increased knowledge of spiritual truth, but he cannot gain this knowledge while divorcing himself from the word of God. If he would have his powers and capabilities daily improved he must study; he must eat and digest the word, and work in Christ's lines. The soul that is nourished by the bread of life will have every faculty vitalized by the Spirit of God. This is the meat which endureth unto everlasting life.

Teachers who will learn from the Great Teacher will

realize the help of God as did Daniel and his fellows. They need to climb heavenward instead of remaining on the plain. Christian experience should be combined with all true education. "Ye also, as lively stones, are built up a spiritual house, an holy priesthood, to offer up spiritual sacrifices, acceptable to God by Jesus Christ." 1 Peter 2:5. Teachers and students should study this representation and see if they are of that class who, through the abundant grace given, are obtaining the experience that every child of God must have before he can enter the higher grade. In all their instruction teachers should impart light from the throne of God; for education is a work the effect of which will be seen throughout the ceaseless ages of eternity.

Teachers should lead students to think, and clearly to understand the truth for themselves. It is not enough for the teacher to explain or for the student to believe; inquiry must be awakened, and the student must be drawn out to state the truth in his own language, thus making it evident that he sees its force and makes the application. By painstaking effort the vital truths should thus be impressed upon the mind. This may be a slow process; but it is of more value than rushing over important subjects without due consideration. God expects His institutions to excel those of the world; for they are His representatives. Men truly connected with God will show to the world that a more than human agent is standing at the helm.

Our teachers need to be constant learners. The reformers need to be themselves reformed, not only in their methods of labor, but in their own hearts. They need to be transformed by the grace of God. When Nicodemus, a great teacher in Israel, came to Jesus, the Master laid before him the conditions of divine life, teaching him the very alphabet of conversion. Nicodemus asked: "How can these things be?" "Art thou a master of Israel," Christ answered, "and knowest not these things?" This question might be addressed to many who are now holding positions as teachers, but who have neglected the preparation essential to qualify them for this work. If Christ's words were received into the soul there would be a much higher intelligence and a much deeper spiritual knowledge of what constitutes a disciple, a sincere follower of Christ, and an educator whom He can approve.

DEFICIENCIES OF TEACHERS

Many of our teachers have much to unlearn and much of a different character to learn. Unless they are willing to do this,—unless they become thoroughly familiar with the word of God and their minds are absorbed in studying the glorious truths concerning the life of the Great Teacher,—they will encourage the very errors the Lord is seeking to correct. Plans and opinions that should not be entertained will imprint themselves on the mind, and in all honesty they will come to wrong and dangerous conclusions. Thus seed will be sown that is not true grain. Many customs and practices common in school work, and which may be regarded as little things, cannot now be brought into our schools. It may be difficult for teachers to give up long-cherished ideas and methods; but if they will honestly and humbly inquire at every step, "Is this the way of the Lord?" and will yield to His guidance, He will lead them in safe paths, and their views will change by experience.

The teachers in our schools need to search the Scriptures until they understand them for their individual selves, opening their hearts to the precious rays of light which God has given, and walking therein. They will then be taught of God and will labor in entirely different lines, bringing into their instruction less of the theories and sentiments of men who have never had a connection with God. They will honor finite wisdom far less, and will feel a deep soul hunger for that wisdom which comes from God.

To the question Christ put to the twelve, "Will ye also go away?" Peter answered: "Lord, to whom shall we go? Thou hast the words of eternal life. And we believe and are sure that Thou art that Christ, the Son of the living God." John 6:67-69. When teachers bring these words into the work of their classrooms, the Holy Spirit will be present to do its work upon minds and hearts.

THE TEACHER'S WORK

Teachers are to be laborers together with God in promoting and carrying forward the work which Christ by His own example has taught them to do. They are to be indeed the light of the world, because they manifest those gracious attributes revealed in the character and work of Christ, attributes which will enrich and beautify their own lives as Christ's disciples.

What a solemn, sacred, important work is the endeavor to represent Christ's character and His Spirit to our world! This is the privilege of every principal and of every teacher connected with him in the work of educating, training, and disciplining the minds of youth. All need to be under the inspiring, assuring conviction that they are indeed wearing the yoke of Christ and carrying His burden.

Trials will be met in this work; discouragements will press in upon the soul as teachers see that their labors are not always appreciated. Satan will exercise his power over them in temptations, in discouragements, in afflictions of bodily infirmities, hoping that he can cause them to murmur against God and close their understanding to His goodness, mercy, and love, and the exceeding weight of glory that is to be the reward of the overcomer. But God is leading these souls to more perfect confidence in their heavenly Father. His eye is upon them every moment; and if they lift their cry to Him in faith, if they will stay their souls upon Him in their perplexities, the Lord will bring them forth as gold purified. The Lord Jesus has said: "I will never leave thee, nor forsake thee." Hebrews 13:5. God may permit a train of circumstances to come that will lead them to flee to the Stronghold, by faith pressing to the throne of God amid thick clouds of darkness; for even here His presence is concealed. But He is ever ready to deliver all that trust in Him. Gained in such a way, the victory will be more complete, the triumph more sure; for the tried, sore-pressed, and afflicted one can say: "Though He slay me, yet will I trust in Him." Job 13:15. "Although the fig tree shall not blossom, neither shall fruit be in the vines; the labor of the olive shall fail, and the fields shall yield no meat; the flock shall be cut off from the fold, and there shall be no herd in the stalls: yet I will rejoice in the Lord, I will joy in the God of my salvation." Habakkuk 3:17, 18.

A PERSONAL APPEAL

I appeal to the teachers in our educational institutions not to let religious earnestness and zeal retrograde. Make no backward movements, but let your watchword be: "Advance." Our schools must rise to a much higher plane of action; broader views must be held; stronger faith and deeper piety must exist; the word of God must be made the root and branch of all wisdom and intellectual attainments. When the converting power of God takes hold of them, they will see that a knowledge of God covers a much broader field than the so-called "advance methods" of education. In all the education given, they should remem-

ber the words of Christ: "Ye are the light of the world."
Matthew 5:14. Then they will not experience so great
hindrance in preparing missionaries to go out and give
their knowledge to others.

We have every endowment of capability every facility
provided for discharging the duties devolving upon us;
and we should be grateful to God that by His mercy we
have these advantages, and that we possess the knowledge
of His grace and of present truth and duty. Are you,
then, as teachers, trying to maintain the false education
you have received? Are you losing the precious opportunities granted you to become better acquainted with
God's plans and methods? Do you believe the word of
God? Are you every day becoming better able to understand, to give yourselves to the Lord, and to be used in
His service? Are you missionaries to do God's will? Do
you believe the Bible and heed what it says? Do you believe that we are living in the last days of this earth's history? And have you hearts that can feel? We have a
large work before us; we are to be bearers of the sacred
light of the word, which is to illume all nations. We are
Christians, and what are we doing?

Take your position, teachers, as true educators, and by
words and expressions of interest for their souls pour into
the hearts of the students the living stream of redeeming
love. Counsel with them before their minds are preoccu-
pied with their literary work. Entreat them to seek Christ
and His righteousness. Show them the changes that will
surely take place if the heart is given to Christ. Fasten
their attention on Him; this will close the door to the
foolish aspirations that naturally arise, and will prepare
the mind for the reception of divine truth. The youth
must be taught that time is golden, that it is perilous for
them to think they can sow "wild oats" and not reap a
harvest of woe and ruin. They must be taught to be

sober-minded, and to admire the good in the character of others. They must be trained to place the will on the side of God's will, that they may be able to sing the new song and blend with the harmonies of heaven.

Put off all manifestations of self-importance, for this can be no help to you in your work; and yet I beseech you to place a high estimate upon your own character, for you are bought with an infinite price. Be careful, be prayerful, be serious. Do not feel that you can mingle the common with the sacred. This has been done so continually in the past that the spiritual discernment of teachers has been obscured, and they cannot distinguish between the sacred and the common. They have taken common fire and have exalted and praised and cherished it, and the Lord has turned away in displeasure. Teachers, will it not be better to make a full consecration of yourselves to God? Will you imperil your souls by a divided service?

By pen and voice give due honor to God. Sanctify the Lord God in your hearts and be ready always to give to every man that asks you a reason of the hope that is in you with meekness and fear. Will the teachers in our schools understand this? Will they take the word of God as the lessonbook able to make them wise unto salvation? Will they impart this higher wisdom to students, giving them clear and accurate ideas of truth, that they may be able to present these ideas to others? It may seem that the teaching of God's word has but little effect upon many minds and hearts; but if the teacher's work has been wrought in God, some lessons of divine truth will linger in the memory of even the most careless. The Holy Spirit will water the seed sown, and often it will spring up after many days and bear fruit to the glory of God.

The Great Teacher who came down from heaven has not directed teachers to study any of the reputedly great

authors. He says: "Come unto Me. . . . Learn of Me;
. . . and ye shall find rest unto your souls." Matthew
11:28, 29. Christ has promised, and in learning lessons
of Him we shall find rest. All the treasures of heaven
were committed to Him that He might give these gifts
to the diligent, persevering seeker. He is of God made
unto us "wisdom, and righteousness, and sanctification,
and redemption." 1 Corinthians 1:30.

Teachers must understand what lessons to impart, or
they cannot prepare students to be transferred to the
higher grade. They must study Christ's lessons and the
character of His teaching. They must see its freedom
from formalism and tradition, and appreciate the origi-
nality, the authority, the spirituality, the tenderness, the
benevolence, and the practicability of His teaching. Those
who make the word of God their study, those who dig
for the treasures of truth, will themselves become imbued
with the Spirit of Christ, and by beholding they will become changed into His likeness. Those who appreciate
the word will teach as disciples who have been sitting at
the feet of Jesus and have accustomed themselves to learn
of Him. In the place of bringing into our schools books
containing the suppositions of the world's great authors,
they will say: Tempt me not to disregard the greatest
Author and the greatest Teacher, through whom I have
everlasting life. He never mistakes. He is the great Fountainhead whence all wisdom flows. Then let every teacher
sow the seed of truth in the minds of students. Christ is
the standard Teacher.

The word of the eternal God is our guide. Through
this word we have been made wise unto salvation. This
word is ever to be in our hearts and on our lips. "It is

written" is to be our anchor. Those who make God's word their counselor realize the weakness of the human heart and the power of the grace of God to subdue every unsanctified, unholy impulse. Their hearts are ever prayerful, and they have the guardianship of holy angels. When the enemy comes in like a flood, the Spirit of God lifts up for them a standard against him. There is harmony in the heart; for the precious, powerful influences of truth bear sway. There is a revelation of the faith that works by love and purifies the soul.

Pray that you may be born again. If you have this new birth you will delight yourself, not in the crooked ways of your own desires, but in the Lord. You will desire to be under His authority. You will strive constantly to reach a higher standard. Be not only Bible readers, but earnest Bible students, that you may know what God requires of you. You need an experimental knowledge of how to do His will. Christ is our Teacher.

Let every teacher in our schools and every manager in our institutions study what it is essential for them to do in order to work in His lines and carry with them a sense of pardon, comfort, and hope.

Heavenly messengers are sent to minister unto those who shall be heirs of salvation; and these would converse with the teachers if they were not so satisfied with the well-trodden path of tradition, if they were not so fearful of getting away from the shadow of the world. Teachers should beware lest they close the gates so that the Lord can find no entrance into the hearts of the youth.

WORDS FROM A HEAVENLY INSTRUCTOR

In the night season I was in a large company where the subject of education was agitating the minds of all present. Many were bringing up objections to changing the character of the education which has long been in vogue. One who has long been our instructor was speaking to the people. He said: "The subject of education should interest the whole Seventh-day Adventist body. The decisions regarding the character of our schoolwork should not be left wholly to principals and teachers."

Some were strenuously urging the study of infidel authors and were recommending the very books which the Lord has condemned, and which, therefore, should not in any way be sanctioned. After much earnest conversation and discussion our instructor stepped forward, and, taking in his hand books that had been earnestly advocated as essential to a higher education, he said: "Do you find in these authors sentiments and principles that make it altogether safe to place them in the hands of students? Human minds are easily charmed by Satan's lies; and these works produce a distaste for the contemplation of the word of God, which, if received and appreciated, will ensure eternal life to the receiver. You are creatures of habit and should remember that right habits are blessings both in their effect on your own character and in their influence for good over others; but wrong habits, when once established, exercise a despotic power and bring minds into bondage. If you had never read one word in these books you would today be far better able to comprehend that Book which, above all other books, is worthy to be studied, and which gives the only correct ideas regarding higher education.

"The fact that it has been customary to include these

authors among your lessonbooks, and that this custom is hoary with age, is no argument in its favor. Long use does not necessarily recommend these books as safe or essential. They have led thousands where Satan led Adam and Eve—to the tree of knowledge of which God has forbidden us to eat. They have led students to forsake the study of the Scriptures for a line of study that is not essential. If students thus educated are ever fitted to work for souls, they will have to unlearn much that they have learned. They will find the unlearning a difficult work; for objectionable ideas have taken root in their minds like weeds in a garden, and as a result some will never be able to distinguish between right and wrong. The good and the evil have been mingled in their education. The faces of men have been uplifted for them to behold, and the theories of men have been exalted; so that as they attempt to teach others, the little truth which they are able to repeat is interwoven with the opinions and sayings and doings of men. The words of men who give evidence that they have not a practical knowledge of Christ should find no place in our schools. They will be hindrances to proper education.

"You have the word of the living God, and for the asking you may have the gift of the Holy Spirit to make that word a power to those who believe and obey. The Holy Spirit's work is to guide into all truth. When you depend on the word of the living God with heart and mind and soul, the channel of communication will be unobstructed. Deep, earnest study of the word under the guidance of the Holy Spirit will give you fresh manna, and the same Spirit will make its use effectual. The exertion made by the youth to discipline the mind for high and holy aspirations will be rewarded. Those who make persevering efforts in this direction, putting the mind to the task of comprehending God's word, are prepared to be laborers together with God.

"The world acknowledges as teachers some whom God cannot endorse as safe instructors. By these the Bible is discarded, and the productions of infidel authors are recommended as if they contained those sentiments which should be woven into the character. What can you expect from the sowing of this kind of seed? In the study of these objectionable books the minds of teachers as well as of students become corrupted, and the enemy sows his tares. It cannot be otherwise. By drinking of an impure fountain, poison is introduced into the system. Inexperienced youth taken over this line of study receive impressions which lead their thoughts into channels that are fatal to piety. Youth who have been sent to our schools have learned from books which were thought to be safe because they were used and encouraged in the schools of the world. But from the worldly schools thus followed many students have gone forth infidels because of the study of these very books.

"Why have you not extolled the word of God above every human production? Is it not enough to keep close to the Author of all truth? Are you not satisfied to draw water fresh from the streams of Lebanon? God has living fountains from which to refresh the thirsty soul, and stores of precious food with which to strengthen the spirituality. Learn of Him, and He will enable you to give to those who ask a reason of the hope that is within you. Have you thought that a better knowledge of what the Lord has said would have a deleterious effect upon teachers and students?"

There was a hush in the assembly, and conviction came upon each heart. Men who had thought themselves wise and strong saw that they were weak and lacking in the knowledge of that Book which concerns the eternal destiny of the human soul.

The messenger of God then took from the hands of several teachers those books which they had been making their study, some of which had been written by infidel authors and contained infidel sentiments, and laid them aside, saying: "There never has been a time in your lives when the study of these books was for your present good and advancement, or for your future, eternal good. Why will you fill your shelves with books that divert the mind from Christ? Why do you spend money for that which is not bread? Christ calls you: 'Learn of Me; for I am meek and lowly in heart.' You need to eat of the Bread of life which came down from heaven. You need to be more diligent students of the Holy Scriptures and to drink from the living Fountain. Draw, draw from Christ in earnest prayer. Obtain a daily experience in eating the flesh and drinking the blood of the Son of God. Human authors can never supply your great need for this time; but by beholding Christ, the Author and Finisher of your faith, you will be changed into His likeness."

Placing the Bible in their hands, he continued: "You have little knowledge of this book. You know not the Scriptures nor the power of God, nor do you understand the deep importance of the message to be borne to a perishing world. The time past has shown that both teachers and students know very little in regard to the awful truths which are living issues for this time. Should the third angel's message be proclaimed in all lines to many who stand as educators, it would not be understood by them. Had you the knowledge which comes from God, your whole being would proclaim the truth of the living God to a world dead in trespasses and sins. But books and papers that contain little of present truth are exalted, and men are becoming too wise to follow a 'Thus saith the Lord.'

"By every teacher in our schools the only true God is to be uplifted, but many of the watchmen are asleep. They are as the blind leading the blind. Yet the day of the Lord is right upon us. As a thief it is coming with stealthy tread, and it will take unawares all who are not watching. Who among our teachers are awake and as faithful stewards of the grace of God are giving the trumpet a certain sound? Who are proclaiming the message of the third angel, calling the world to make ready for the great day of God? The message we bear has the seal of the living God."

Pointing to the Bible he said: "The Scriptures of the Old and New Testaments are to be combined in the work of fitting a people to stand in the day of the Lord. Earnestly improve your present opportunities. Make the word of the living God your lessonbook. If this had always been done, students lost to the cause of God would now be missionaries. Jehovah is the only true God, and He is to be reverenced and worshiped. Those who respect the words of infidel authors and lead students to look upon these books as essential in their education lessen their faith in God. The tone, the spirit, the influence of these books is deleterious to those who depend on them for knowledge. Influences have been brought to bear upon the students that have led them to look away from Christ, the Light of the world, and evil angels rejoice that those who profess to know God deny Him as He has been thus denied in our schools. The Sun of Righteousness has been shining upon the church to dispel the darkness and to call the attention of God's people to the preparation essential for those who would shine as lights in the world. Those who receive this light will comprehend it; those who do not receive it will walk in darkness, knowing not at what they stumble. The soul is never safe unless it is under the divine guidance. Then it will be led into all truth. The word of Christ will fall with living power upon obedient hearts; and through the application of divine truth the perfect image of God will be reproduced, and in heaven it will be said: 'Ye are complete in Him.' " Colossians 2:10.

———

In no case should students be allowed to take so many studies that they will be prevented from attending religious exercises.

———

None but He who has created man can effect a change in the human heart. God alone can give the increase. Every teacher is to realize that he is to be moved by divine agencies. The human judgment and ideas of the most experienced are liable to be imperfect and faulty, and the frail instrument, subject to his own hereditary traits of character, has need to submit to the sanctification of the Holy Spirit every day, else self will gather the reins and want to drive. In the meek and lowly spirit of the learner all human methods and plans and ideas must be brought to God for His correction and endorsement; otherwise the restless energy of Paul or the skillful logic of Apollos will be powerless to effect the conversion of souls.

SCHOOL HOMES

In attending our colleges many of the youth are separated from the softening, subduing influences of the home circle. At the very time of life when they need vigilant supervision they are withdrawn from the restraints of parental influence and authority, and are thrown into the society of a large number of their own age, of varied characters and habits of life. Some of these have in childhood received too little discipline and are superficial and frivolous; others have been governed too much and have felt, when away from the hands that held the reins of control perhaps too tightly, that they were free to do as they pleased. They despise the very thought of restraint. By these associations the dangers of the young are greatly increased.

Our school homes have been established that our youth may not be left to drift hither and thither, and be exposed to the evil influences which everywhere abound; but that, as far as possible, a home atmosphere may be provided that they may be preserved from temptations to immorality and be led to Jesus. The family of heaven represents that which the family on earth should be; and our school homes, where are gathered youth who are seeking a preparation for the service of God, should approach as nearly as possible to the divine model.

Teachers who are placed in charge of these homes bear grave responsibilities; for they are to act as fathers and mothers, showing an interest in the students, one and all, such as parents show in their children. The varying elements in the characters of the youth with whom they are called to deal bring upon them care and many heavy burdens, and great tact as well as much patience is required to balance in the right direction minds that have been warped by bad management. The teachers need great managing ability; they must be true to principle and yet wise and tender, linking love and Christlike sympathy with discipline. They should be men and women of faith, of wisdom, and of prayer. They should not manifest stern, unbending dignity, but should mingle with the youth, becoming one with them in their joys and sorrows as well as in their daily routine of work. Cheerful, loving obedience will generally be the fruit of such effort.

DOMESTIC DUTIES

The education which the young men and women who attend our colleges should receive in the home life is deserving of special attention. It is of great importance in the work of character building that students who attend our colleges be taught to take up the work that is appointed them, throwing off all inclination to sloth. They need to become familiar with the duties of daily life. They should be taught to do their domestic duties thoroughly and well, with as little noise and confusion as possible. Everything should be done decently and in order. The kitchen and all other parts of the building should be kept sweet and clean. Books should be laid aside till their proper season, and no more study should be taken than can be attended to without neglecting the household duties. The study of books is not to engross the mind to the neglect of home duties upon which the comfort of the family depends.

In the performance of these duties careless, neglectful, disorderly habits should be overcome; for unless corrected, these habits will be carried into every phase of life, and the life will be spoiled for usefulness, spoiled for true missionary work. Unless corrected with perseverance and resolution they will overcome the student for time and for eternity. The young should be encouraged to form correct habits in dress, that their appearance may be neat and attractive; they should be taught to keep their garments clean and neatly mended. All their habits should be such as to make them a help and a comfort to others.

Special directions were given to the armies of the children of Israel that in and around their tents everything should be clean and orderly lest the angel of God should pass through their encampment and see their uncleanness. Would the Lord be particular to notice these things? He would; for the fact is stated, lest in viewing their uncleanness He could not go forth with their armies to battle against their enemies. In like manner all our actions are noticed by God. That God who was so particular that the children of Israel should grow up with habits of cleanliness will not sanction any impurity in the home today.

God has given to parents and teachers the work of educating the children and youth in these lines, and from every act of their lives they may be taught spiritual lessons. While training them in habits of physical cleanliness we should teach them that God desires them to be clean in heart as well as in body. While sweeping a room they may learn how the Lord purifies the heart. They would not close the doors and windows and leave in the room some purifying substance, but would open the doors and throw wide the windows, and with diligent effort expel all the dust. So the windows of impulse and feeling must be opened toward heaven, and the dust of selfishness and earthliness must be expelled. The grace of God must sweep through the chambers of the mind, and every element of the nature must be purified and vitalized by the Spirit of God. Disorder and untidiness in daily duties will lead to forgetfulness of God and to keeping the form of godliness in a profession of faith, having lost the reality. We are to watch and pray, else we shall grasp the shadow and lose the substance.

A living faith like threads of gold should run through the daily experience in the performance of little duties. Then students will be led to understand the pure principles which God designs shall prompt every act of their lives. Then all the daily work will be of such a character as to promote Christian growth. Then the vital principles of faith, trust, and love for Jesus will penetrate into the most minute details of daily life. There will be a looking unto Jesus, and love for Him will be the continual motive, giving vital force to every duty that is undertaken. There will be a striving after righteousness, a hope that "maketh not ashamed." Whatever is done will be done to the glory of God.

To each student in the home I would say, Be true to home duties. Be faithful in the discharge of little responsibilities. Be a real living Christian in the home. Let Christian principles rule your heart and control your conduct. Heed every suggestion made by the teacher, but do not make it a necessity always to be told what to do. Discern for yourself. Notice for yourself if all things in your own room are spotless and in order, that nothing there may be an offense to God, but that when holy angels shall pass through your room, they may be led to linger because attracted by the prevailing order and cleanliness. In doing your duties promptly, neatly, faithfully, you are missionaries. You are bearing witness for Christ. You are showing that the religion of Christ does not, in principle or in practice, make you untidy, coarse, disrespectful to your teachers, giving little heed to their counsel and instruction. Bible religion, practiced, will make you kind, thoughtful, faithful. You will not neglect the little things that should be done. Adopt as your motto the words of Christ: "He that is faithful in that which is least is faithful also in much."

CHRISTIAN SOCIABILITY AND COURTESY

Christian sociability is altogether too little cultivated by God's people. This branch of education should not be neglected or lost sight of in our schools.

Students should be taught that they are not independent atoms, but that each one is a thread which is to unite with other threads in composing a fabric. In no department can this instruction be more effectually given than in the school home. Here students are daily surrounded by opportunities which, if improved, will greatly aid in developing the social traits of their characters. It lies in their own power so to improve their time and opportunities as to develop a character that will make them happy and useful. Those who shut themselves up within themselves, who are unwilling to be drawn upon to bless others by friendly associations, lose many blessings; for by mutual contact minds receive polish and refinement; by social intercourse, acquaintances are formed and friendships contracted which result in a unity of heart and an atmosphere of love which is pleasing in the sight of heaven.

Especially should those who have tasted the love of Christ develop their social powers, for in this way they may win souls to the Saviour. Christ should not be hid away in their hearts, shut in as a coveted treasure, sacred and sweet, to be enjoyed solely by themselves; nor should the love of Christ be manifested toward those only who please their fancy. Students are to be taught the Christlikeness of exhibiting a kindly interest, a social disposition, toward those who are in the greatest need, even though these may not be their own chosen companions. At all times and in all places Jesus manifested a loving interest in the human family and shed about Him the light of a cheerful piety. Students should be taught to follow in His steps. They should be taught to manifest Christian interest, sympathy, and love for their youthful companions, and endeavor to draw them to Jesus; Christ should be in their hearts as a well of water springing up into everlasting life, refreshing all with whom they come in contact.

It is this willing, loving ministry for others in times of necessity that is accounted precious with God. Thus even while attending school, students may, if true to their profession, be living missionaries for God. All this will take time; but the time thus employed is profitably spent, for in this way the student is learning how to present Christianity to the world.

Christ did not refuse to mingle with others in friendly intercourse. When invited to a feast by Pharisee or publican, He accepted the invitation. On such occasions every word that He uttered was a savor of life unto life to His hearers; for He made the dinner hour an occasion of imparting many precious lessons adapted to their needs. Christ thus taught His disciples how to conduct themselves when in the company of those who were not religious as well as of those who were. By His own example He taught them that, when attending any public gathering, their conversation need not be of the same character as that usually indulged in on such occasions.

When students sit at the table, if Christ is abiding in the soul there will come forth from the treasure house of the heart words which are pure and uplifting; if Christ is not abiding there, a satisfaction will be found in frivolity, in jesting and joking, which is a hindrance to spiritual growth and a cause of grief to the angels of God. The tongue is an unruly member, but it should not be so. It should be converted; for the talent of speech is a very precious talent. Christ is ever ready to impart of His riches, and we should gather the jewels that come from Him, that, when we speak, these jewels may drop from our lips.

The temper, the personal peculiarities, the habits from which character is developed—everything practiced in the home will reveal itself in all the associations of life. The inclinations followed will work out in thoughts, in words, in acts of the same character. If every student composing the school family would make an effort to restrain all unkind and uncourteous words, and speak with respect to all; if he would bear in mind that he is preparing to become a member of the heavenly family; if he would guard his influence by sacred sentinels, that it should not scatter away from Christ; if he would endeavor to have every act of his life show forth the praises of Him who has called him out of darkness into His marvelous light, what a reformatory influence would go forth from every school home!

RELIGIOUS EXERCISES

Of all the features of an education to be given in our school homes the religious exercises are the most important. They should be treated with the greatest solemnity and reverence, yet all the pleasantness possible should be brought into them. They should not be prolonged till they become wearisome, for the impression thus made upon the minds of the youth will cause them to associate religion with all that is dry and uninteresting; and many will be led to cast their influence on the side of the enemy, who, if properly taught, would become a blessing to the world and to the church. The Sabbath meetings, the morning and evening service in the home and in the chapel, unless wisely planned and vitalized by the Spirit of God, may become the most formal, unpleasant, unattractive, and to the youth the most burdensome, of all the school exercises. The social meetings and all other religious exercises should be so planned and managed that they will be not only profitable, but so pleasant as to be positively attractive. Praying together will bind hearts to God in bonds that will endure; confessing Christ openly and bravely, exhibiting in our characters His meekness, humility, and love, will charm others with the beauty of holiness.

On all these occasions Christ should be set forth as "the chiefest among ten thousand," the One "altogether lovely." Song of Solomon 5:10, 16. He should be presented as the Source of all true pleasure and satisfaction, the Giver of every good and perfect gift, the Author of every blessing, the One in whom all our hopes of eternal life are centered. In every religious exercise let the love of God and the joy of the Christian experience appear in their true beauty. Present the Saviour as the restorer from every effect of sin.

To accomplish this result all narrowness must be avoided. Sincere, earnest, heartfelt devotion will be needed. Ardent, active piety in the teachers will be essential. But there is power for us if we will have it. There is grace for us if we will appreciate it. The Holy Spirit is waiting our demand if we will only demand it with that intensity of purpose which is proportionate to the value of the object we seek. Angels of heaven are taking notice of all our work and are watching to see how they can so minister to each one that he will reflect the likeness of Christ in character and become conformed to the divine image. When those in charge of our school homes appreciate the privileges and opportunities placed within their reach, they will do a work for God of which heaven will approve.

INDUSTRIAL REFORM

Because difficulties arise, we are not to drop the industries that have been taken hold of as branches of education. While attending school the youth should have an opportunity for learning the use of tools. Under the guidance of experienced workmen, carpenters who are apt to teach, patient, and kind, the students themselves should erect buildings on the school grounds and make needed improvements, thus by practical lessons learning how to build economically. The students should also be trained to manage all the different kinds of work connected with printing, such as typesetting, presswork, and bookbinding, together with tentmaking and other useful lines of work. Small fruits should be planted, and vegetables and flowers cultivated, and this work the lady students may be called out of doors to do. Thus, while exercising brain, bone, and muscle, they will also be gaining a knowledge of practical life.

Culture on all these points will make our youth useful in carrying the truth to foreign countries. They will not then have to depend upon the people among whom they are living to cook and sew and build for them, nor will it be necessary to spend money to transport men thousands of miles to plan schoolhouses, meetinghouses, and cottages. Missionaries will be much more influential among the people if they are able to teach the inexperienced how to labor according to the best methods and to produce the best results. They will thus be able to demonstrate that missionaries can become industrial educators, and this kind of instruction will be appreciated especially where means are limited. A much smaller fund will be required to sustain such missionaries, because, combined with their studies, they have put to the very best use their physical powers in practical labor; and wherever they may go all they have gained in this line will give them vantage ground. Students in the industrial departments, whether they are employed in domestic work, in cultivating the ground, or in other ways, should have time and opportunity given them to tell the practical, spiritual lessons they have learned in connection with the work. In all the practical duties of life, comparisons should be made with the teachings of nature and of the Bible.

The reasons that have led us in a few places to turn away from cities and locate our schools in the country, hold good with the schools in other places. To expend money in additional buildings when a school is already deeply in debt is not in accordance with God's plan. Had the money which our larger schools have used in expensive buildings been invested in procuring land where students could receive a proper education, so large a number of students would not now be struggling under the weight of increasing debt, and the work of these institutions would be in a more prosperous condition. Had this course been followed, there would have been some grumbling from students, and many objections would have been raised by parents; but the students would have secured an all-round education, which would have prepared them, not only for practical work in various trades, but for a place on the Lord's farm in the earth made new.

Had all our schools encouraged work in agricultural lines, they would now have an altogether different showing. There would not be so great discouragements. Opposing influences would have been overcome; financial conditions would have changed. With the students, labor would have been equalized; and as all the human machinery was proportionately taxed, greater physical and mental strength would have been developed. But the instruction which the Lord has been pleased to give has been taken hold of so feebly that obstacles have not been overcome.

It reveals cowardice to move so slowly and uncertainly in the labor line—that line which will give the very best kind of education. Look at nature. There is room within her vast boundaries for schools to be established where grounds can be cleared and land cultivated. This work is essential to the education most favorable to spiritual advancement; for nature's voice is the voice of Christ, teaching us innumerable lessons of love and power and submission and perseverance. Some do not appreciate the value of agricultural work. These should not plan for our schools, for they will hold everything from advancing in right lines. In the past their influence has been a hindrance.

If the land is cultivated, it will, with the blessing of God, supply our necessities. We are not to be discouraged about temporal things because of apparent failures, nor should we be disheartened by delay. We should work the soil cheerfully, hopefully, gratefully, believing that the earth holds in her bosom rich stores for the faithful worker to garner, stores richer than gold or silver. The niggardliness laid to her charge is false witness. With proper, intelligent cultivation the earth will yield its treasures for the benefit of man. The mountains and hills are changing; the earth is waxing old like a garment; but the blessing of God, which spreads a table for His people in the wilderness, will never cease.

Serious times are before us, and there is great need for families to get out of the cities into the country, that the truth may be carried into the byways as well as the highways of the earth. Much depends upon laying our plans according to the word of the Lord and with persevering energy carrying them out. More depends upon consecrated activity and perseverance than upon genius and book learning. All the talents and ability given to human agents, if unused, are of little value.

A return to simpler methods will be appreciated by the children and youth. Work in the garden and field will be an agreeable change from the wearisome routine of abstract lessons, to which their young minds should never be confined. To the nervous child, who finds lessons from books exhausting and hard to remember, it will be especially valuable. There is health and happiness for him in the study of nature; and the impressions made will not fade out of his mind, for they will be associated with objects that are continually before his eyes.

Working the soil is one of the best kinds of employment, calling the muscles into action and resting the mind. Study in agricultural lines should be the A, B, and C of the education given in our schools. This is the very first work that should be entered upon. Our schools should not depend upon imported produce, for grain and vegetables, and the fruits so essential to health. Our youth need an education in felling trees and tilling the soil as well as in literary lines. Different teachers should be appointed to oversee a number of students in their work and should work with them. Thus the teachers themselves will learn to carry responsibilities as burden bearers. Proper students also should in this way be educated to bear responsibilities and to be laborers together with the teachers. All should counsel together as to the very best methods of carrying on the work.

Time is too short now to accomplish that which might have been done in past generations. But even in these last days we can do much to correct the existing evils in the education of youth. And because time is short, we should be in earnest and work zealously to give the young an education consistent with our faith. We are reformers. We desire that our children should study to the best advantage. In order to do this, employment should be given them which will call into exercise the muscles. Daily, systematic labor should constitute a part of the education of youth even at this late period. Much can now be gained in this way. In following this plan the students will realize elasticity of spirit and vigor of thought, and in a given time can accomplish more mental labor than they could by study alone. And thus they can leave school with constitutions unimpaired and with strength and courage to persevere in any position where the providence of God may place them.

―――――――

The exercise that teaches the hand to be useful and trains the young to bear their share of life's burdens, gives physical strength and develops every faculty. All should find something to do that will be beneficial to themselves and helpful to others. God appointed work as a blessing, and only the diligent worker finds the true glory and joy of life.

―――――――

Brain and muscle must be taxed proportionately if health and vigor are to be maintained. The youth can then bring to the study of the word of God healthy perception and well-balanced nerves. They will have wholesome thoughts and can retain the precious things that are brought from the word. They will digest its truths and as a result will have brain power to discern what is truth. Then, as occasion demands, they can give to every man that asks a reason of the hope that is in them with meekness and fear.

THE AVONDALE SCHOOL FARM

THERE are some things regarding the disposition and use of the lands near our school and church which have been opened before me and which I am instructed to present to you. Until recently I have not felt at liberty to speak of them, and even now I do not feel free to reveal all things because our people are not yet prepared to understand all that in the providence of God will be developed at Avondale.

In the visions of the night some things were clearly presented before me. Persons were selecting allotments of land near the school, on which they proposed to build houses and establish homes. But One stood in our midst who said: "You are making a great mistake which you will have cause to regret. This land is not to be occupied with buildings except to provide the facilities essential for the teachers and students of the school. This land about the school is to be reserved as the school farm. It is to become a living parable to the students. The students are not to regard the school land as a common thing, but are to look upon it as a lessonbook open before them which the Lord would have them study. Its lessons will impart knowledge in the culture of the soul.

"If you should allow the land near the school to be occupied with private houses and then be driven to select for cultivation other land at a distance from the school, it would be a great mistake and one always to be regretted. All the land near the building is to be regarded as the school farm, where the youth can be educated under well-qualified superintendents. The youth who shall attend our schools need all the land near by. They are to plant it with ornamental and fruit trees, and to cultivate garden produce.

"The school farm is to be regarded as a lessonbook in

nature from which the teachers may draw their object lessons. Our students are to be taught that Christ, who created the world and all things that are therein, is the life and light of every living thing. The life of every child and youth who is willing to grasp the opportunities of receiving a proper education will be made thankful and happy while at school by the things upon which his eyes shall rest."

THE WORK BEFORE US

We need more teachers and more talent to educate the students in various lines, that many persons may go from this place willing and able to carry to others the knowledge which they have received. Orphan boys and girls are to find a home here. Buildings should be erected for a hospital, and boats should be provided to accomodate the school. A competent farm manager should be employed, also wise, energetic men to act as superintendents of the several industrial enterprises, men who will use their undivided talents in teaching the students how to work.

Many young people will come to school who desire a training in industrial lines. The industrial instruction should include the keeping of accounts, carpentry, and everything that is comprehended in farming. Preparation should also be made for teaching blacksmithing, painting, shoemaking, cooking, baking, laundering, mending, typewriting, and printing. Every power at our command is to be brought into this training work, that students may go out equipped for the duties of practical life.

Cottages and buildings essential to the schoolwork are to be erected by the students themselves. These should not be crowded close together, nor located near the school buildings proper. In the management of this work small companies should be formed who, under competent leaders, should be taught to carry a full sense of their responsibility. All these things cannot be accomplished at once, but we are to begin to work in faith.

THE LAND TO BE RESERVED

The Lord would have the grounds about the school dedicated to Him as His own schoolroom. We are located where there is plenty of land, and the grounds near the school and the church should not be occupied with private dwellings. Those who believe the truth for this time are not all transformed in character. They are not all proper object lessons, for they do not represent the character of Christ. There are many who would be pleased to get close to the church and the school who would not be helps, but hindrances. They feel that they should be helped and favored. They do not appreciate either the character or the situation of the work in which we are engaged. They do not understand that all that has been done at Avondale has been accomplished with the hardest labor and through the use of money given with sacrifice or which must be paid back to those from whom it was borrowed.

Among those who will desire to settle near our schools there will be some who are filled with self-importance and anxiety about their own reputation. They are sensitive and factious. These need to be converted, for they are far from standing where they can receive the blessing of the Lord. Satan tempts them to ask favors which, if granted, will only injure them, and thus they bring anxiety to their brethren. The living principles of the word of God need to be brought into the lives of many who now find no room for these principles. Those who are learning in the school of Christ will count every favor from God as too good for them. They will realize that they do not deserve all the good things they receive, and they will count themselves happy. Their faces will express peace and rest in the Lord, for they have the word of God that He cares for them.

"Thus saith the Lord, The heaven is My throne, and the earth is My footstool: where is the house that ye build unto Me? and where is the place of My rest? For all those things hath Mine hand made, and all those things have been, saith the Lord: but to this man will I look, even to him that is poor and of a contrite spirit, and trembleth at My word." Isaiah 66:1, 2. During the closing days of 1898 we had many experiences to teach us what these words mean. My heart was greatly burdened, and matters were then opened before me in regard to the evils that would arise from disposing of the land near the school to be occupied with dwelling houses. We seemed to be in a meeting for counsel, and there stood among us One who was expected to help us out of our difficulties. The words He spoke were plain and decided:

"This land, by the appointment of God, is for the benefit of the school. You have had evidences of the working of human nature and what it will reveal under temptation. The greater the number of families that settle around the school buildings, the more difficulties there will be in the way of teachers and students. The natural selfishness of the children of men is ready to spring into life if everything is not convenient for them. This land about the school is to be the school farm, and this farm is to occupy much more space than you have thought it would. Work in connection with study is to be done here according to the counsels given. Avondale is to be a philanthropic center. God's people in Australasia are to be moved upon by the Spirit of the Lord to give sympathy and means for the support and encouragement of many charitable and benevolent enterprises, which shall be the means of teaching the poor, the helpless, and the ignorant how to help themselves."

A PANORAMA

On several occasions the light has come to me that the land around our school is to be used as the Lord's farm. In a special sense portions of this farm should be highly cultivated. Spread out before me I saw land planted with every kind of fruit tree that will bear fruit in this locality; there were also vegetable gardens, where seeds were sown and cultivated.

If the managers of this farm and the teachers in the school will receive the Holy Spirit to work with them, they will have wisdom in their management, and God will bless their labors. The care of the trees, the planting and the sowing, and the gathering of the harvest are to be wonderful lessons for all the students. The invisible links which connect the sowing and the reaping are to be studied, and the goodness of God is to be pointed out and appreciated. It is the Lord that gives the virtue and the power to the soil and to the seed. Were it not for the divine agency, combined with human tact and ability, the seed sown would be useless. There is an unseen power constantly at work in man's behalf to feed and to clothe him. The parable of the seed as studied in the daily experience of teacher and student is to reveal that God is at work in nature, and it is to make plain the things of the kingdom of heaven.

GOD AND NATURE

Next to the Bible, nature is to be our great lessonbook. But there is no virtue in deifying nature, for this is exalting the thing made above the great Master Builder who designed the work, and who every hour keeps it operating according to His appointment. As we sow the seed and cultivate the plant, we are to remember that God created the seed, and He gives it to the earth. By His divine power He cares for that seed. It is by His appointment that the seed in dying gives its life to the blade and to the ear which contains in itself other seeds to be treasured and again put into the earth to yield their harvest. We may also study how the co-operation of man acts a part. The human agent has his part to act, his work to do. This is one of the lessons which nature teaches, and we shall see in it a solemn, a beautiful work.

There is much talk about God in nature, as if the Lord were bound by the laws of nature to be nature's servant. Many theories would lead minds to suppose that nature is a self-sustaining agency apart from the Deity, having its own inherent power with which to work. In this men do not know what they are talking about. Do they suppose that nature has a self-existing power without the continual agency of Jehovah? The Lord does not work through His laws to supersede the laws of nature. He does His work through the laws and properties of His instruments, and nature obeys a "Thus saith the Lord."

The God of nature is perpetually at work. His infinite power works unseen, but manifestations appear in the effects which the work produces. The same God who guides the planets works in the fruit orchard and in the vegetable garden. He never made a thorn, a thistle, or a tare. These are Satan's work, the result of degeneration, introduced by him among the precious things; but it is through God's immediate agency that every bud bursts into blossom. When He was in the world in the form of humanity, Christ said: "My Father worketh hitherto, and I work." John 5:17. So when the students employ their time and strength in agricultural work, in heaven it is said of them, Ye "are laborers together with God." 1 Corinthians 3:9.

Let the lands near the school and the church be retained. Those who come to settle in Cooranbong can, if they choose, find for themselves homes near by, or on portions of, the Avondale estate. But the light given me is that all that section of land from the school orchard to the Maitland road, and extending on both sides of the road from the meetinghouse to the school, should become a farm and a park, beautified with fragrant flowers and ornamental trees. There should be orchards, and every kind of produce should be cultivated that is adapted to the soil, that this place may become an object lesson to those living close by and afar off.

Then let everything not essential to the work of the school be kept at a distance, that the sacredness of the place may not be disturbed through the proximity of families and buildings. Let the school stand alone. It will be better for private families, however devoted they may be in the service of the Lord, to be located at some distance from the school buildings. The school is the Lord's property, and the grounds about it are His farm, where the Great Sower can make His garden a lessonbook. The results of the labors will be seen, "first the blade, then the ear, after that the full corn in the ear." Mark 4:28. The land will yield its treasures, bringing the joyousness of an abundant harvest; and the produce gathered through the blessing of God is to be used as nature's lessonbook, from which spiritual lessons can be made plain and applied to the necessities of the soul.

AN OBJECT LESSON

There are great things before us which we see must be done, and as fast as the means can be obtained we must go forward. Patient, painstaking effort needs to be made for the encouragement and uplifting of the surrounding communities, and for their education in industrial and sanitary lines. The school and all its surroundings should be object lessons, teaching the ways of improvement, and appealing to the people for reform, so that taste, industry, and refinement may take the place of coarseness, uncleanness, disorder, ignorance, and sin. Even the poorest can improve their surroundings by rising early and working diligently. By our lives and example we can help others to discern that which is repulsive in their character or about their premises, and with Christian courtesy we may encourage improvement.

The question will often arise: What can be done where poverty prevails and is to be contended with at every step? Under these circumstances how can we impress minds with correct ideas of improvement? Certainly the work is difficult; and unless the teachers, the thinking men, and the men who have means will exercise their talents and will lift just as Christ would lift were He in their place, an important work will be left undone. The necessary reformation will never be made unless men and women are helped by a power outside of themselves. Those who have talents and capabilities must use these gifts to bless their fellow men, laboring to place them upon a footing where they can help themselves. It is thus that the education gained at our schools should be put to the very best use.

God's entrusted talents are not to be hid under a bushel or under a bed. "Ye are the light of the world," Christ said. Matthew 5:14. As you see families living in hovels, with scant furniture and clothing, without tools, without books or other marks of refinement about their homes, will you become interested in them, and endeavor to teach them how to put their energies to the very best use, that there may be improvement, and that their work may move forward? It is by diligent labor, by putting to the wisest use every capability, by learning to waste no time, that they will become successful in improving their premises and cultivating their land.

Physical effort and moral power are to be united in our endeavors to regenerate and reform. We are to seek to gain knowledge in both temporal and spiritual lines, that we may communicate it to others. We are to seek to live out the gospel in all its bearings, that its temporal and spiritual blessings may be felt all around us.

MISSIONARY LABOR THE HIGHEST TRAINING

The Lord will surely bless all who seek to bless others. The school is to be so conducted that teachers and students will be continually gaining in power through the faithful use of the talents given them. By putting to a practical use that which they have learned, they will constantly increase in wisdom and knowledge. We are to learn from the Book of books the principles upon which we are to live and labor. By consecrating all our God-given abilities to Him who has the first right to them, we may make precious advances in everything that is worthy of our attention.

When entered upon with this spirit, the missionary work becomes elevating and uplifting both to the laborer and to the person helped. Let everyone who claims to be a child of the heavenly King seek constantly to represent the principles of the kingdom of God. Let each remember that in spirit, in word, and in works he is to be loyal and true to all the precepts and commandments of the Lord. We are to be faithful, trustworthy subjects of the kingdom of Christ, that those who are worldly-wise may have a true representation of the riches, the goodness, the mercy, the tenderness, and the courtesy of the citizens of the kingdom of God.

The students who will get the most good out of life are those who will live the word of God in their connections and dealings with their fellow men. Those who receive to give will feel the greatest satisfaction in this life. Those members of the human family who live for themselves are always in want, for they are never satisfied. There is no Christianity in shutting up our sympathies to our own selfish hearts. The Lord has ordained channels through which He lets flow His goodness, mercy, and truth; and we are to be co-workers with Christ in communicating to others practical wisdom and benevolence. We are to bring brightness and blessing into their lives, thus doing a good and holy work.

If the Avondale school ever becomes what the Lord is seeking to make it, the missionary effort of teachers and students will bear fruit. Both in the school and outside, willing subjects will be brought to allegiance to God. The rebellion which took place in heaven under the power of a lie, and the deception which led Adam and Eve to disobey the law of God, opened the floodgates of woe upon our world; but all who believe in Christ may become sons and daughters of God. Through the power of the truth they may be restored, and fallen man may become loyal to his Maker. The truth, peculiar in its working power, is adapted to the minds and hearts of wandering sinners. Through its influence the lost sheep may be brought back to the fold.

Whatever may be the position or possessions of any individual who has a knowledge of the truth, the word of God teaches him that all he has is held by him in trust. It is lent him to test his character. His worldly business, his talents, his income, his opportunities, are all to be accounted for to Him to whom by creation and redemption he belongs. When he uses every precious talent in carrying forward God's great work of education, when he strives to obtain the very best knowledge of how to be useful, how to labor for the salvation of souls ready to perish, God's blessing will surely attend his efforts. God bestows His gifts upon us that we may minister to others, and thus become like Him. Those who receive His gifts that they may impart to others, become like Christ. It is in helping and uplifting others that we become ennobled and purified. This is the work that causes glory to flow back to God. We must become intelligent upon these points. Our souls must be purified from all selfishness; for God desires to use His people as representatives of the heavenly kingdom.

Our schools must be conducted under the supervision of God. There is a work to be done for young men and women that is not yet accomplished. There are much larger numbers of young people who need to have the advantages of our training schools. They need the manual training course, that will teach them how to lead an active, energetic life. All kinds of labor must be connected with our schools. Under wise, judicious, God-fearing directors the students are to be taught. Every branch of the work is to be conducted in the most thorough and systematic ways that long experience and wisdom can enable us to plan and execute.

Let the teachers wake up to the importance of this subject and teach agriculture and other industries that it is essential for the students to understand. Seek in every department of labor to reach the very best results.

Let the science of the word of God be brought into the work, that the students may understand correct principles and may reach the highest possible standard. Exert your God-given abilities, and bring all your energies into the development of the Lord's farm. Study and labor, that the best results and the greatest returns may come from the seed sowing, that there may be an abundant supply of food, both temporal and spiritual, for the increased number of students that shall be gathered in to be trained as Christian workers.

We have seen the giant trees felled and uprooted; we have seen the plowshare pressed into the earth, turning deep furrows for the planting of trees and the sowing of seed. The students are learning what plowing means and that the hoe and the shovel, the rake and the harrow, are all implements of honorable and profitable industry. Mistakes will often be made, but every error lies close beside the truth. Wisdom will be learned by failures, and the energy that will make a beginning gives hope of success in the end. Hesitation will keep things back, precipitancy will alike retard; but all will serve as lessons if the human agent will have it so.

The impression that work is degrading has laid thousands in the grave. Those who perform only manual labor frequently work to excess, while brain workers suffer for want of the healthful vigor physical labor gives. If the intellectual would share the burden of the laboring class to such a degree that the muscles would be strengthened, the laborers might devote a portion of their time to mental and moral culture. Those of sedentary and literary habits should take physical exercise. Health should be a sufficient inducement to lead them to unite physical with their mental labor.

CHURCH SCHOOLS

THE WORK OF CHURCH SCHOOLS

THE church has a special work to do in educating and training its children that they may not, in attending school, or in any other association, be influenced by those of corrupt habits. The world is full of iniquity and disregard of the requirements of God. The cities have become as Sodom, and our children are daily being exposed to many evils. Those who attend the public schools often associate with others more neglected than they, those who, aside from the time spent in the schoolroom, are left to obtain a street education. The hearts of the young are easily impressed; and unless their surroundings are of the right character, Satan will use these neglected children to influence those who are more carefully trained. Thus before Sabbathkeeping parents know what evil is being done, the lessons of depravity are learned, and the souls of their little ones are corrupted.

The Protestant churches have accepted the spurious sabbath, the child of the papacy, and have exalted it above God's holy, sanctified day. It is our work to make plain to our children that the first day of the week is not the true Sabbath, and that its observance, after light has come to us as to what is the true Sabbath, is a plain contradiction of the law of God. Do our children receive from the teachers in the public schools ideas that are in harmony with the word of God? Is sin presented as an offense against God? Is obedience to all the commandments of God taught as the beginning of all wisdom? We send our children to the Sabbath school that they may be instructed in regard to the truth, and then as they go to the day school, lessons containing falsehood are given them to learn. These things confuse the mind, and should not be; for if the young receive ideas that pervert the truth, how will the influence of this education be counteracted?

Can we wonder that under such circumstances some of the youth among us do not appreciate religious advantages? Can we wonder that they drift into temptation? Can we wonder that, neglected as they have been, their energies are devoted to amusements which do them no good, that their religious aspirations are weakened and their spiritual life darkened? The mind will be of the same character as that upon which it feeds, the harvest of the same nature as the seed sown. Do not these facts sufficiently show the necessity of guarding from the earliest years the education of the youth? Would it not be better for the youth to grow up in a degree of ignorance as to what is commonly accepted as education than for them to become careless in regard to the truth of God?

SEPARATION FROM THE WORLD

When the children of Israel were gathered out from among the Egyptians, the Lord said: "For I will pass through the land of Egypt this night, and will smite all the first-born in the land of Egypt, both man and beast; and against all the gods of Egypt I will execute judgment: I am the Lord." "And ye shall take a bunch of hyssop, and dip it in the blood that is in the basin, and strike the lintel and the two side posts with the blood that is in the basin; and none of you shall go out at the door of his house until the morning. For the Lord will pass through to smite the Egyptians; and when He seeth the blood upon the lintel, and on the two side posts, the Lord will pass over the door, and will not suffer the destroyer to come in unto your houses to smite you. And ye shall observe this thing for an ordinance to thee and to thy sons forever." Exodus 12:12, 22-24. The blood upon the lintel of the door symbolized the blood of Christ, who alone saved the first-born of the Hebrews from the curse. Any one of the children of the Hebrews who was found in an Egyptian habitation was destroyed.

This experience of the Israelites was written for the instruction of those who should live in the last days. Before the overflowing scourge shall come upon the dwellers of the earth, the Lord calls upon all who are Israelites indeed to prepare for that event. To parents He sends the warning cry: Gather your children into your own houses; gather them away from those who are disregarding the commandments of God, who are teaching and practicing evil. Get out of the large cities as fast as possible. Establish church schools. Give your children the word of God as the foundation of all their education. This is full of beautiful lessons, and if pupils make it their study in the primary grade below, they will be prepared for the higher grade above.

The word of God comes to us at this time: "Be ye not unequally yoked together with unbelievers: for what fellowship hath righteousness with unrighteousness? and what communion hath light with darkness? and what concord hath Christ with Belial? or what part hath he that believeth with an infidel? and what agreement hath the temple of God with idols? for ye are the temple of the living God; as God hath said, I will dwell in them, and walk in them; and I will be their God, and they shall be My people. Wherefore come out from among them, and be ye separate, saith the Lord, and touch not the unclean thing; and I will receive you, and will be a Father unto you, and ye shall be My sons and daughters, saith the Lord Almighty." 2 Corinthians 6:14-18. Where are your children? Are you educating them to discern and to escape the corruptions that are in the world through lust? Are you seeking to save their souls, or are you by your neglect aiding in their destruction?

THE CHILDREN NEGLECTED

Altogether too little attention has been given our children and youth. The older members of the church have not looked upon them with tenderness and sympathy, desiring that they might be advanced in the divine life, and the children have therefore failed to develop in the Christian life as they should have done. Some church members who have loved and feared God in the past are allowing their business to be all-absorbing, and are hiding their light under a bushel. They have forgotten to serve God and are making their business the grave of their religion.

Shall the youth be left to drift hither and thither, to become discouraged and to fall into temptations that are everywhere lurking to catch their unwary feet? The work that lies nearest to our church members is to become interested in our youth, with kindness, patience, and tenderness giving them line upon line, precept upon precept. Oh, where are the fathers and mothers in Israel? There ought to be a large number who, as stewards of the grace of Christ, would feel not merely a casual interest but a special interest in the young. There ought to be many whose hearts are touched by the pitiable situation in which our youth are placed, who realize that Satan is working by every conceivable device to draw them into his net. God requires the church to arouse from its lethargy and see what manner of service is demanded in this time of peril.

The eyes of our brethren and sisters should be anointed

with the heavenly eyesalve, that they may discern the necessities of this time. The lambs of the flock must be fed, and the Lord of heaven is looking on to see who is doing the work He desires to have done for the children and youth. The church is asleep and does not realize the magnitude of this matter. "Why," says one, "what is the need of being so particular thoroughly to educate our youth? It seems to me that if a few who have decided to follow some literary calling, or some other calling that requires a certain discipline, receive special attention, this is all that is necessary. It is not necessary that all our young people should be so well trained. Will not the thorough education of a few answer every essential requirement?"

No, I answer, most decidedly not. What selection would we be able to make from our youth? How could we tell who would be the most promising, who would render the best service to God? In our human judgment we might do as did Samuel, who, when sent to find the anointed of the Lord, looked upon the outward appearance. But the Lord said to Samuel: "Look not on his countenance, or on the height of his stature; because I have refused him: for the Lord seeth not as man seeth; for man looketh on the outward appearance, but the Lord looketh on the heart." 1 Samuel 16:7. Not one of the noble-looking sons of Jesse would the Lord accept; but when David, the youngest son, a mere youth and the shepherd of the sheep, was called from the field and passed before Samuel, the Lord said: "Arise, anoint him: for this is he." Verse 12. Who can determine which one of a family will prove to be efficient in the work of God? All the youth should be permitted to have the blessings and privileges of an education at our schools, that they may be inspired to become laborers together with God.

CHURCH SCHOOLS NEEDED

Many families who, for the purpose of educating their children, move to places where our large schools are established, would do better service for the Master by remaining where they are. They should encourage the church of which they are members to establish a church school where the children within their borders could receive an all-round, practical Christian education. It would be vastly better for their children, for themselves, and for the cause of God if they would remain in the smaller churches, where their help is needed, instead of going to the larger churches, where, because they are not needed, there is a constant temptation to fall into spiritual inactivity.

Wherever there are a few Sabbathkeepers, the parents should unite in providing a place for a day school where their children and youth can be instructed. They should employ a Christian teacher who, as a consecrated missionary, shall educate the children in such a way as to lead them to become missionaries. Let teachers be employed who will give a thorough education in the common branches, the Bible being made the foundation and the life of all study. Parents should gird on the armor and by their own example teach their children to be missionaries. They should work while it is day, for "the night cometh, when no man can work." John 9:4. If they will put forth unselfish efforts, perseveringly teaching their children to bear responsibilities, the Lord will work with them.

Some families of Sabbathkeepers live alone or far separated from others of like faith. These have sometimes sent their children to our boarding schools, where they have received help and have returned to be a blessing in their own home. But some cannot send their children away from home to be educated. In such cases parents should endeavor to employ an exemplary religious teacher who will feel it a pleasure to work for the Master in any capacity and be willing to cultivate any part of the Lord's vineyard. Fathers and mothers should co-operate with the teacher, laboring earnestly for the conversion of their children. Let them strive to keep the spiritual interest fresh and wholesome in the home and to bring up their children in the nurture and admonition of the Lord. Let them devote a portion of each day to study and become learners with their children. Thus they may make the educational hour one of pleasure and profit, and their confidence will increase in this method of seeking for the salvation of their children. Parents will find that their own growth will be more rapid as they learn to work for their children. As they thus work in a humble way unbelief will disappear. Faith and activity will impart assurance and satisfaction that will increase day by day as they follow on to know the Lord and to make Him known. Their prayers will become earnest, for they will have some definite object for which to pray.

In some countries parents are compelled by law to send their children to school. In these countries, in localities where there is a church, schools should be established if there are no more than six children to attend. Work as if you were working for your life to save the children from being drowned in the polluting, corrupting influences of the world.

We are far behind our duty in this important matter. In many places schools should have been in operation years ago. Many localities would thus have had representatives of the truth who would have given character to the work of the Lord. Instead of centering so many large buildings in a few places, schools should have been established in many localities.

Let these schools now be started under wise direction,

that the children and youth may be educated in their own churches. It is a grievous offense to God that there has been so great neglect in this line when Providence has so abundantly supplied us with facilities with which to work. But though in the past we have come short of doing what we might have done for the youth and children, let us now repent and redeem the time. The Lord says: "Though your sins be as scarlet, they shall be as white as snow; though they be red like crimson, they shall be as wool. If ye be willing and obedient, ye shall eat the good of the land." Isaiah 1:18, 19.

THE CHARACTER OF CHURCH SCHOOLS AND OF THEIR TEACHERS

The character of the work done in our church schools should be of the very highest order. Jesus Christ, the Restorer, is the only remedy for a wrong education, and the lessons taught in His word should ever be kept before the youth in the most attractive form. The school discipline should supplement the home training, and both at home and at school simplicity and godliness should be maintained. Men and women will be found who have talent to work in these small schools, but who cannot work to advantage in the larger ones. As they practice the Bible lessons they will themselves receive an education of the highest value.

In selecting teachers we should use every precaution, knowing that this is as solemn a matter as the selecting of persons for the ministry. Wise men who can discern character should make the selection, for the very best talent that can be secured is needed to educate and mold the minds of the young and to carry on successfully the many lines of work that will need to be done by the teacher in our church schools. No person of an inferior or narrow cast of mind should be placed in charge of one of these schools. Do not place over the children young and inexperienced teachers who have no managing ability, for their efforts will tend to disorganization. Order is heaven's first law, and every school should in this respect be a model of heaven.

To place over young children teachers who are proud and unloving is wicked. A teacher of this stamp will do great harm to those who are rapidly developing character. If teachers are not submissive to God, if they have no love for the children over whom they preside, or if they show partiality for those who please their fancy and manifest indifference to those who are less attractive or to those who are restless and nervous, they should not be employed; for the result of their work will be a loss of souls for Christ.

Teachers are needed, especially for the children, who are calm and kind, manifesting forbearance and love for the very ones who most need it. Jesus loved the children; He regarded them as younger members of the Lord's family. He always treated them with kindness and respect, and teachers are to follow His example. They should have the true missionary spirit, for the children are to be trained to become missionaries. They should feel that the Lord has committed to them as a solemn trust the souls of the children and youth. Our church schools need teachers who have high moral qualities, those who can be trusted, those who are sound in the faith and who have tact and patience, those who walk with God and abstain from the very appearance of evil. In their work they will find clouds. There will be clouds and darkness, storms and tempests, prejudice to meet from parents who have incorrect ideas of the characters which their children should form; for there are many who claim to believe the Bible, while they fail to bring its principles into the home life. But if the teachers are constant learners in the school of Christ, these circumstances will never conquer them.

Let parents seek the Lord with intense earnestness, that they may not be stumbling blocks in the way of their children. Let envy and jealousy be banished from the heart, and let the peace of Christ come in to unite the members of the church in true Christian fellowship. Let the windows of the soul be closed against the poisonous malaria of earth, and let them be opened heavenward to receive the healing rays of the sunshine of Christ's righteousness. Until the spirit of criticism and suspicion is banished from the heart, the Lord cannot do for the church that which He longs to do in opening the way for the establishment of schools; until there is unity, He will not move upon those to whom He has entrusted means and ability for the carrying forward of this work. Parents must reach a higher standard, keeping the way of the Lord and practicing righteousness, that they may be light bearers. There must be an entire transformation of mind and character. A spirit of disunion cherished in the hearts of a few will communicate itself to others and undo the influence for good that would be exerted by the school. Unless parents are ready and anxious to co-operate with the teacher for the salvation of their children, they are not prepared to have a school established among them.

RESULTS OF CHURCH SCHOOL WORK

When properly conducted, church schools will be the means of lifting the standard of truth in the places where they are established; for children who are receiving a Christian education will be witnesses for Christ. As Jesus in the temple solved the mysteries which priests and rulers had not discerned, so in the closing work of this earth children who have been rightly educated will in their simplicity speak words which will be an astonishment to men who now talk of "higher education." As the children sang in the temple courts, "Hosanna; Blessed is He that cometh in the name of the Lord," so in these last days children's voices will be raised to give the last message of warning to a perishing world. When heavenly intelligences see that men are no longer permitted to present the truth, the Spirit of God will come upon the children, and they will do a work in the proclamation of the truth which the older workers cannot do, because their way will be hedged up.

Our church schools are ordained by God to prepare the children for this great work. Here children are to be instructed in the special truths for this time and in practical missionary work. They are to enlist in the army of workers to help the sick and the suffering. Children can take part in the medical missionary work and by their jots and tittles can help to carry it forward. Their investments may be small, but every little helps, and by their efforts many souls will be won to the truth. By them God's message will be made known and His saving health to all nations. Then let the church carry a burden for the lambs of the flock. Let the children be educated and trained to do service for God, for they are the Lord's heritage.

———

Years ago school buildings suitable for church schools should have been erected in which the children and youth could receive a true education.

———

The lessonbooks used in our church schools should be of a character to bring the law of God to the attention. Thus the light and strength and power of the truth will be magnified. Youth from the world, some even whose minds have been depraved, will connect with these schools, and there they will be converted. Their witness for the truth may be stopped for a while by the false theories entertained by the parents, but in the end, truth will triumph. I am instructed to say that this kind of missionary work will have a telling influence in diffusing light and knowledge.

How important that families who settle where a school is located should be good representatives of our holy faith!

Churches where schools are established may well tremble as they see themselves entrusted with moral responsibilities too great for words to express. Shall this work that has been nobly begun fail or languish for want of consecrated workers? Shall selfish projects and ambitions find room in this enterprise? Will the workers permit the love of gain, the love of ease, the lack of piety, to banish Christ from their hearts and exclude Him from the school? God forbid! The work is already far advanced. In educational lines everything is arranged for an earnest reform, for a truer, more effective education. Will our people accept this holy trust? Will they humble themselves at the cross of Calvary, ready for every sacrifice and every service?

Parents and teachers should seek most earnestly for that wisdom which Jesus is ever ready to give; for they are dealing with human minds at the most interesting and impressible period of their development. They should aim so to cultivate the tendencies of the youth that at each stage of their life they may represent the natural beauty appropriate to that period, unfolding gradually, as do the plants and flowers in the garden.

The management and instruction of children is the noblest missionary work that any man or woman can undertake. By the proper use of objects the lessons should be made very plain, that their minds may be led from nature up to nature's God. We must have in our schools those who possess the tact and skill to carry forward this line of work, thus sowing seeds of truth. The great day of God alone can reveal the good this work will do.

———

Special talent should be given to the education of the little ones. Many can put the crib high and give food to the sheep, but it is a more difficult matter to put the crib low and feed the lambs. This is a lesson which primary teachers need to learn.

———

The eye of the mind needs to be educated, or the child will find pleasure in beholding evil.

———

Teachers should sometimes enter into the sports and plays of the little children and teach them how to play. In this way they may be able to check unkind feelings and actions without seeming to criticize or find fault. This companionship will bind together the hearts of teachers and pupils, and school will be a delight to all.

———

Teachers must love the children because they are the younger members of the Lord's family. The Lord will inquire of them as of the parents: "Where is the flock that was given thee, thy beautiful flock?" Jeremiah 13:20.

SCHOOL MANAGEMENT AND FINANCE

I wish that I could command language to express clearly the importance of the proper management of our schools. All should feel that our schools are the Lord's instrumentalities, through which He would make Himself known to man. Everywhere men and women are needed to act as channels of light. The truth of God is to be carried to all lands, that men may be enlightened by it.

As a people having advanced light, we should devise means by which to develop an army of educated missionaries to enter the various departments of the work of God. We need well-disciplined, cultivated young men and women in our schools, in our sanitariums, in the medical missionary work, in the offices of publication, in the conferences of different states, and in the field at large. We need young men and women, who, having high intellectual culture, are fitted to do the best work for the Lord. We have done something toward reaching this standard, but still we are far behind that which the Lord has designed. As a church, as individuals, if we would stand clear in the judgment we must make more liberal efforts for the training of our young people, that they may be better fitted for the various branches of the great work committed to our hands. As a people who have great light, we should lay wise plans in order that the ingenious minds of those who have talent may be strengthened and disciplined and polished, that the work of Christ may not be hindered by lack of skillful laborers who will do their work with earnestness and fidelity.

Some would be content with the thorough education

of a few of the most promising of our youth; but they all need an education that they may be fitted for usefulness in this life, qualified for places of responsibility in both private and public life. There is great necessity for making plans that there may be a large number of competent workers, and many should fit themselves as teachers, that others may be trained and disciplined for the great work of the future. The church should take in the situation and by their influence and means seek to bring about this much-desired end.

FREEDOM FROM DEBT

That our schools may nobly accomplish the purpose for which they are established, they should be free from debt. They should not be left to bear the burden of paying interest. In the establishment of training schools for workers, and especially in new fields where the brethren are few and their means limited, rather than delay the work it may be better to hire some money from the friends of the enterprise; but whenever it is possible, let our institutions be dedicated free from debt.

The Lord has means for His work in the hands of His stewards; and as long as our schools have debts which were incurred in their establishment, in the erection of necessary buildings, and in providing necessary facilities, it is our duty to present the case to our brethren and ask them to lessen these debts. Our ministers should feel a burden for this work. They should encourage all to labor harmoniously and to lift in proportion to their ability. If this work had been taken hold of with fidelity and diligence in past years, the debts on our older schools could have been lifted long ago.

ECONOMY

In the erection of school buildings, in their furnishing, and in every feature of their management the strictest economy must be practiced. Our schools are not to be conducted on any narrow or selfish plans. They should be as homelike as possible, and in every feature they are to teach correct lessons of simplicity, usefulness, thrift, and economy.

The students are in our schools for a special training to become acquainted with all lines of work that should they go out as missionaries they could be self-reliant and able, through their educated ability, to furnish themselves with necessary conveniences and facilities. Whether men or women, they should learn to mend, wash, and keep their own clothes in order. They should be able to cook their own meals. They should be familiar with agriculture and with mechanical pursuits. Thus they can lighten their own expenses, and, by their example, inculcate principles of thrift and economy. These lessons can best be taught where economy in all things is conscientiously practiced.

Not only for the financial welfare of the schools, but also as an education to the students, economy should be faithfully studied and conscientiously and diligently practiced. The managers must guard carefully every point, that there may be no needless expense, to bring a burden of debt upon the school. Every student who loves God supremely will help to bear the responsibility in this matter. Those who have been educated to do this can demonstrate by precept and example to those with whom they come in contact the principles taught by our self-denying Redeemer. Self-indulgence is a great evil and must be overcome.

Some have felt reluctant to let the students know of

the financial embarrassment of the schools; but it will be far better for the students to see and understand our lack of means, for they will thus be able to help in the practice of economy. Many who come to our schools leave homes that are unadorned and where they have been accustomed to eat simple food without a number of courses. What influence will our example have on these? Let us teach them that while we have so many ways in which to use our means; while thousands are starving, dying of the plague, of famine, of bloodshed, and of fire, it becomes every one of us to consider carefully, to get nothing that is needless, simply to gratify appetite or to make an appearance.

If our schools are conducted on right lines, debts will not be piling up, and still the students will be made comfortable, and the table will be supplied with plenty of good, substantial food. Our economy must never be of that kind which would lead to providing meager meals. Students should have an abundance of wholesome food. But let those in charge of the cooking gather up the fragments that nothing be lost.

Students should be taught to guard carefully their own property and that of the school. They should be made to understand the duty to bind about every needless expense at the school and while traveling to and from their homes. Self-denial is essential. We must heed the instruction given, for we are nearing the end of time. More and more shall we be obliged to plan, and devise, and economize. We cannot manage as if we had a bank on which to draw in case of emergency; therefore we must not get into straitened places. As individuals and as managers of the Lord's institutions we shall necessarily have to cut away everything intended for display and bring our expenses within the narrow compass of our income.

GOOD MANAGEMENT

The financial management in some of our schools can be greatly improved. More wisdom, more brain power, must be brought to bear upon the work. More practical methods must be brought in to stop the increase of expenditure, which would result in indebtedness. In Battle Creek and College View altogether too much money has been invested in buildings, and more than was necessary has been spent in furnishing the school homes.

When the managers of a school find that it is not meeting running expenses, and debts are heaping up, they should act like levelheaded businessmen and change their methods and plans. When one year has proved that the financial management has been wrong, let wisdom's voice be heard. Let there be a decided reformation. Teachers may manifest a Christlike excellence in serious, solid thinking and planning to improve the state of things. They should enter heartily into the plans of the managers and share their burdens.

LOW TUITIONS

In some of our schools the price of tuitions has been too low. This has in many ways been detrimental to the educational work. It has brought discouraging debt; it has thrown upon the management a continual suspicion of miscalculation, want of economy, and wrong planning; it has been very discouraging to the teachers; and it leads the people to demand correspondingly low prices in other schools. Whatever may have been the object in placing the tuition at less than a living rate, the fact that a school has been running behind heavily is sufficient reason for reconsidering the plans and arranging its charges so that in the future its showing may be different. The amount charged for tuition, board, and residence should be sufficient to pay the salaries of the faculty, to supply the table with an abundance of healthful, nourishing food, to maintain the furnishing of the rooms, to keep the buildings in repair, and to meet other necessary running expenses. This is an important matter and calls for no narrow calculation, but for a thorough investigation. The counsel of the Lord is needed. The school should have a sufficient income not only to pay the necessary running expenses, but to be able to furnish the students during the school term with some things essential for their work.

Debts must not be allowed to accumulate term after term. The very highest kind of education that could be given is to shun the incurring of debt as you would shun disease. When one year after another passes, and there is no sign of diminishing the debt, but it is rather increased, a halt should be called. Let the managers say: "We refuse to run the school any longer unless some sure system is devised." It would be better, far better, to close the school until the managers learn the science of conducting it on a paying basis. For Christ's sake, as the chosen people of God, call yourselves to task and inaugurate a sound financial system in our schools.

Whenever it becomes necessary to raise the prices at any school, let the matter first be laid before the patrons of the institution, showing them that the fees have been placed at too low a figure and that, as a result, debts are accumulating upon the school, thus crippling and hindering its work. Properly increasing the tuitions may cause a decrease in the attendance, but a large attendance should not be so much a matter of rejoicing as freedom from debt.

One of the results of low tuition at Battle Creek has been the gathering together in one place of a larger number of students and a larger number of families than was wise. If two thirds of the people in Battle Creek were plants of the Lord in other localities, they would have room to grow. Greater results would have appeared if a portion of the time and energy bestowed on the large school in Battle Creek to keep it in a healthy condition had been used for schools in other localities where there is room for agricultural pursuits to be carried on as a part of the education. Had there been a willingness to follow the Lord's ways and His plans, many plants would now be growing in other places. Over and over again the word of the Lord has come to us that plants both of churches and of schools should be made in other localities, that there were too many weighty responsibilities in one place. Get the people out of the large centers and establish interests in other places, is the instruction given. Had this instruction been heeded, had there been a distribution of means and facilities, the money expended on the extra college buildings at Battle Creek would have abundantly provided for two new plants in other localities, and the tree would have grown and borne such fruit as has not been seen, because men choose to follow their own wisdom.

Our brethren say the plea comes from ministers and parents that there are scores of young people in our ranks who need the advantages of our training schools, who cannot attend unless tuitions are less. But those who plead for low tuitions should carefully weigh matters on all sides. If students cannot of themselves command sufficient means to pay the actual expense of good and faithful work in their education, is it not better that their parents, their friends, the churches to which they belong, or largehearted, benevolent brethren in their conference, should assist them than that a burden of debt should be brought upon the school? It would be far better to let the many patrons of the institution share the expense than for the school to run in debt.

Methods must be devised to prevent the accumulation of debt upon our institutions. The whole cause must not be made to suffer because of debt which will never be lifted unless there is an entire change and the work is carried forward on some different basis. Let all who have acted a part in allowing this cloud of debt to cover them now feel it their duty to do what they can to remove it.

ASSISTING WORTHY STUDENTS

The churches in different localities should feel that a solemn responsibility rests upon them to train youth and educate talent to engage in missionary work. When they see those in the church who give promise of making useful workers, but who are not able to support themselves in the school, they should assume the responsibility of sending them to one of our training schools. There is excellent ability in the churches that needs to be brought into service. There are persons who would do good service in the Lord's vineyard, but many are too poor to obtain without assistance the education that they require. The churches should feel it a privilege to take a part in defraying the expenses of such.

Those who have the truth in their hearts are always openhearted, helping where it is necessary. They lead out, and others imitate their example. If there are some who should have the benefit of the school, but who cannot pay full price for their tuition, let the churches show their liberality by helping them.

Besides this, in each conference a fund should be raised to lend to worthy poor students who desire to give themselves to the missionary work; and in some cases they should even receive donations. When the Battle Creek College was first started, there was a fund placed in the Review and Herald office for the benefit of those who wished to obtain an education but had not the means. This was used by several students until they could get a good start; then from their earnings they would replace what they had drawn, so that others might be benefited by the fund. The youth should have it plainly set before them that they must work their own way as far as possible and thus partly defray their expenses. That which costs little will be appreciated little. But that which costs a price somewhere near its real value will be estimated accordingly.

TEACHING SELF-RELIANCE

By precept and example, teach self-denial, economy, largeheartedness, and self-reliance. Everyone who has a true character will be qualified to cope with difficulties and will be prompt in following a "Thus saith the Lord." Men are not prepared to understand their obligation to God until they have learned in Christ's school to wear His yoke of restraint and obedience. Sacrifice is the very beginning of our work in advancing the truth and in establishing institutions. It is an essential part of education. Sacrifice must become habitual in all our character building in this life if we would have a building not made with hands, eternal in the heavens.

Through erroneous ideas regarding the use of money the youth are exposed to many dangers. They are not to be carried along and supplied with money as if there were an inexhaustible supply from which they could draw to gratify every supposed need. Money is to be regarded as a gift entrusted to us of God to do His work, to build up His kingdom, and the youth should learn to restrict their desires. Teach that none may prostitute their powers in self-pleasing and self-gratification. Those whom God has endowed with ability to acquire means are under obligation to Him to use that means, through heaven's imparted wisdom, to His name's glory. Every shilling wasted on self-indulgence, or given to special friends who will spend it to indulge pride and selfishness, is robbing God's treasury. The money expended for garments to make a pleasing show is so much that might have been used to advance the cause of God in new places. Oh, that God would give all a true sense of what it means to be a Christian! It is to be Christlike, and Christ lived not to please Himself.

DUTY OF OUR CONFERENCES

Our conferences look to the schools for educated and well-trained laborers, and they should give the schools a most hearty and intelligent support. Light has been plainly given that those who minister in our schools, teaching the word of God, explaining the Scriptures, educating the students in the things of God, should be supported by the tithe money. This instruction was given long ago, and more recently it has been repeated again and again.

Wherever schools are established, wise managers must be provided, "able men, such as fear God, men of truth, hating covetousness," men who will do their very best in the various responsibilities of their positions. Business ability they should have, but it is of still greater importance that they walk humbly with God and are guided by the Holy Spirit. Such men will be taught of God, and they will seek counsel of their brethren who are men of prayer.

The managers of our schools must labor with pure motives. In their unselfishness they will remember that other parts of the great harvest field will require the same facilities that are provided for the school under their care. In every plan they will remember that equality and unity are to be preserved. They will carefully estimate the expense of every undertaking and will endeavor not to absorb so large an amount of money as to deprive other fields of necessary facilities.

Too often ministers have been brought in to carry responsibilities which they were in no way fitted to bear. Lay these responsibilities upon men who have business tact, men who can give themselves to business, who can visit the schools and keep an account of the financial condition, and who can also give instruction regarding the keeping of the accounts. The work of the school should be inspected several times each year. Let the ministers act as counselors, but lay not on them the financial responsibilities.

INSPECTION BY GENERAL CONFERENCE AUDITOR

The light given me by the Lord is that wise men, men of financial ability, should visit our schools in every country and keep an account of their financial standing. This matter should not be left to ministers or committeemen, who have no time to take this burden. The teachers are not to be left with this responsibility. These matters of school business call for talent which has not been provided.

If the leaders had exercised clear-sighted judgment in past years, the discouraging financial conditions that have so hindered the cause in recent years would never have been permitted to exist.

If our educational work had been carried on in accordance with the instruction given for our guidance, the dark shadow of heavy debt would not today be hanging over our institutions.

THE CHURCH SCHOOLS

The same principles which, if followed, will bring success and blessing to our training schools and colleges, should govern our plans and work for the church schools. Let all share the expense. Let the church see that those who ought to receive its benefits are attending the school. Poor families should be assisted. We cannot call ourselves true missionaries if we neglect those at our very doors who are at the most critical age and who need our aid to secure knowledge and experience that will fit them for the service of God.

The Lord would have painstaking efforts made in the education of our children. True missionary work done by teachers who are daily taught of God would bring many souls to a knowledge of the truth as it is in Jesus, and children thus educated will impart to others the light and knowledge received. Shall the members of the church give means to advance the cause of Christ among others and leave their own children to carry on the work and service of Satan?

As church schools are established, the people of God will find it a valuable education for themselves to learn how to conduct the school on a basis of financial success. If this cannot be done, close the school until, with the help of God, plans can be devised to carry it on without the blot of debt upon it. Men of financial ability should look over the accounts once, twice, or thrice a year, to ascertain the true standing of the school and see that enormous expenses, which will result in the accumulation of indebtedness, do not exist. We should shun debt as we should shun the leprosy.

———

Many of our youth who desire to obtain an education feel too unconcerned in regard to becoming involved in debt. They look upon a study of books as the principal means of an education. They do not realize the value of a practical business education and are content to be carried through years of study on the means of others rather than to work their own way. They do not look critically at the outcome of this. They do not study from cause to effect.

Often the result of such a course is a disproportionate development of the faculties. The student does not understand the weak points of his character; he does not realize his own deficiencies. By depending on others he loses an experience of practical life that it will be difficult for him to recover. He does not learn self-reliance. He does not learn how to exercise faith. True faith will enable the soul to rise out of an imperfect, undeveloped state and understand what true wisdom is. If students will develop brain, bone, and muscle harmoniously, they will be better able to study and better qualified to cope with the realities of life. But if they follow their own erroneous ideas as to what constitutes education, they will not become self-made, all-round men and women.

―――――

"Happy is the man that findeth wisdom, and the man that getteth understanding. For the merchandise of it is better than the merchandise of silver, and the gain thereof than fine gold. She is more precious than rubies: and all the things thou canst desire are not to be compared unto her. Length of days is in her right hand; and in her left hand riches and honor. Her ways are ways of pleasantness, and all her paths are peace. She is a tree of life to them that lay hold upon her: and happy is everyone that retaineth her." Proverbs 3:13-18.

MEDICAL MISSIONARY WORK

"Everything . . . whithersoever
the rivers shall come, shall live."
"Their waters they issued out of
the sanctuary."

GOD'S DESIGN IN OUR SANITARIUMS

Every institution established by Seventh-day Adventists is to be to the world what Joseph was in Egypt and what Daniel and his fellows were in Babylon. As in the providence of God these chosen ones were taken captive, it was to carry to heathen nations the blessings that come to humanity through a knowledge of God. They were to be representatives of Jehovah. They were never to compromise with idolaters; their religious faith and their name as worshipers of the living God they were to bear as a special honor.

And this they did. In prosperity and adversity they honored God, and God honored them.

Called from a dungeon, a servant of captives, a prey of ingratitude and malice, Joseph proved true to his allegiance to the God of heaven. And all Egypt marveled at the wisdom of the man whom God instructed. Pharaoh "made him lord of his house, and ruler of all his substance: to bind his princes at his pleasure; and teach his senators wisdom." Psalm 105:21, 22. Not to the people of Egypt alone, but to all the nations connected with that powerful kingdom, God manifested Himself through Joseph. He desired to make him a light bearer to all peoples, and He placed him next the throne of the world's greatest empire, that the heavenly illumination might extend far and near. By his wisdom and justice, by the purity and benevolence of his daily life, by his devotion to the interests of the people,—and that people a nation of idolaters,—Joseph was a representative of Christ. In their benefactor, to whom all Egypt turned with gratitude and praise, that heathen people, and through them all the nations with which they were connected, were to behold the love of their Creator and Redeemer.

So in Daniel God placed a light beside the throne of the world's greatest kingdom, that all who would might learn of the true and living God. At the court of Babylon were gathered representatives from all lands, men of the choicest talents, men the most richly endowed with natural gifts and possessed of the highest culture this world could bestow; yet amid them all the Hebrew captives were without a peer. In physical strength and beauty, in mental vigor and literary attainments, and in spiritual power and insight they stood unrivaled. "In all matters of wisdom and understanding, that the king inquired of them, he found them ten times better than all the magicians and astrologers that were in all his realm." Daniel 1:20. While faithful to his duties in the king's court, Daniel so faithfully maintained his loyalty to God that God could honor him as His messenger to the Babylonian monarch. Through him the mysteries of the future were unfolded, and Nebuchadnezzar himself was constrained to acknowledge the God of Daniel as "a God of gods, and a Lord of kings, and a revealer of secrets." Daniel 2:47.

So the institutions established by God's people today are to glorify His name. The only way in which we can fulfill His expectation is by being representatives of the truth for this time. God is to be recognized in the institutions established by Seventh-day Adventists. By them the truth for this time is to be represented before the world with convincing power.

We are called to represent to the world the character of God as it was revealed to Moses. In answer to the prayer of Moses, "Show me Thy glory," the Lord promised, "I will make all My goodness pass before thee." "And the Lord passed by before him, and proclaimed, The Lord, The Lord God, merciful and gracious, long-suffering, and abundant in goodness and truth, keeping mercy for thousands, forgiving iniquity and transgression and sin." Exodus 33:18, 19; 34:6, 7. This is the fruit that God desires from His people. In the purity of their characters, in the holiness of their lives, in their mercy and loving-kindness and compassion, they are to demonstrate that "the law of the Lord is perfect, converting the soul." Psalm 19:7.

God's purpose for His institutions today may also be read in the purpose which He sought to accomplish through the Jewish nation. Through Israel it was His design to impart rich blessings to all peoples. Through them the way was to be prepared for the diffusion of His light to the whole world. The nations of the world, through following corrupt practices, had lost a knowledge of God. Yet in His mercy God did not blot them out of existence. He purposed to give them opportunity for becoming acquainted with Him through His church. He designed that the principles revealed through His people should be the means of restoring in man the moral image of God.

Christ was their instructor. As He was with them in the wilderness, so after their establishment in the Promised Land He was still their Teacher and Guide. In the tabernacle and the temple His glory dwelt in the holy Shekinah above the mercy seat. In their behalf He constantly manifested the riches of His love and patience.

God desired to make of His people Israel a praise and a glory. Every spiritual advantage was given them. God withheld from them nothing favorable to the formation of character that would make them representatives of Himself.

Their obedience to the laws of God would make them marvels of prosperity before the nations of the world. He who could give them wisdom and skill in all cunning work would continue to be their teacher and would ennoble and elevate them through obedience to His laws. If obedient, they would be preserved from the diseases that afflicted other nations and would be blessed with vigor of intellect. The glory of God, His majesty and power, were to be revealed in all their prosperity. They were to be a kingdom of priests and princes. God furnished them with every facility for becoming the greatest nation on the earth.

In the most definite manner, God through Moses set before them His purpose and made plain the terms of their prosperity. "Thou art an holy people unto the Lord thy God," He said; "the Lord thy God hath chosen thee to be a special people unto Himself, above all people that are upon the face of the earth. . . . Know therefore that the Lord thy God, He is God, the faithful God, which keepeth covenant and mercy with them that love Him and keep His commandments to a thousand generations. . . . It shall come to pass, if ye hearken to these judgments, and keep, and do them, that the Lord thy God shall keep unto thee the covenant and the mercy which He sware unto thy fathers: and He will love thee, and bless thee, and multiply thee. . . . Thou shalt be blessed above all people." Deuteronomy 7:6-14.

"Thou hast avouched the Lord this day to be thy God, and to walk in His ways, and to keep His statutes, and His commandments, and His judgments, and to hearken unto His voice: and the Lord hath avouched thee this day to be His peculiar people, as He hath promised thee, and that thou shouldest keep all His commandments; and to make thee high above all nations which He hath made, in praise, and in name, and in honor; and that thou mayest be an holy people unto the Lord thy God, as He hath spoken." Deuteronomy 26:17-19.

In these words are set forth the conditions of all true prosperity, conditions with which, if they fulfill the purpose of their establishment, all our institutions must comply.

The Lord years ago gave me special light in regard to the establishment of a health institution where the sick could be treated on altogether different lines from those followed in any other institution in our world. It was to be founded and conducted upon Bible principles, as the Lord's instrumentality, and it was to be in His hands one of the most effective agencies for giving light to the world. It was God's purpose that it should stand forth with scientific ability, with moral and spiritual power, and as a faithful sentinel of reform in all its bearings. All who should act a part in it were to be reformers, having respect to its principles, and heeding the light of health reform shining upon us as a people.

God designed that the institution which He should establish should stand forth as a beacon of light, of warning and reproof. He would prove to the world that an institution conducted on religious principles, as an asylum for the sick, could be sustained without sacrificing its peculiar, holy character; that it could be kept free from the objectionable features found in other health institutions. It was to be an instrumentality for bringing about great reforms.

The Lord revealed that the prosperity of the Sanitarium was not to be dependent alone upon the knowledge and skill of its physicians, but upon the favor of God. It was to be known as an institution where God was acknowledged as the Monarch of the universe, an institution that was under His special supervision. Its managers were to make God first and last and best in everything. And in this was to be its strength. If conducted in a manner that God could approve, it would be highly successful, and would stand in advance of all other institutions of the kind in the world. Great light, great knowledge, and superior privileges were given. And in accordance with the light received would be the responsibility of those to whom the carrying forward of the institution was entrusted.

As our work has extended and institutions have multiplied, God's purpose in their establishment remains the same. The conditions of prosperity are unchanged.

The human family is suffering because of transgression of the laws of God. The Lord desires that men shall be led to understand the cause of their suffering and the only way to find relief. He desires them to see that their well-being—physical, mental, and moral—depends upon their obedience to His law. It is His purpose that our institutions shall be as object lessons showing the results of obedience to right principles.

In the preparation of a people for the Lord's second coming a great work is to be accomplished through the promulgation of health principles. The people are to be instructed in regard to the needs of the physical organism and the value of healthful living as taught in the Scriptures, that the bodies which God has created may be presented to Him a living sacrifice, fitted to render Him acceptable service. There is a great work to be done for suffering humanity in relieving their sufferings by the use of the natural agencies that God has provided and in teaching them how to prevent sickness by the regulation of the appetites and passions. The people should be taught that transgression of the laws of nature is transgression of the laws of God. They should be taught the truth in physical as well as in spiritual lines that "the fear of the Lord tendeth to life." Proverbs 19:23. "If thou wilt enter into life," Christ says, "keep the commandments." Matthew 19:17. Live out "My law as the apple of thine eye." Proverbs 7:2. God's commandments, obeyed, are "life unto those that find them, and health to all their flesh." Proverbs 4:22.

Our sanitariums are an educating power to teach the people in these lines. Those who are taught can in turn impart to others a knowledge of health-restoring and health-preserving principles. Thus our sanitariums are to be an instrumentality for reaching the people, an agency for showing them the evil of disregarding the laws of life and health, and for teaching them how to preserve the body in the best condition. Sanitariums are to be established in different countries that are entered by our missionaries and are to be centers from which a work of healing, restoring, and educating shall be carried on.

We are to labor both for the health of the body and for the saving of the soul. Our mission is the same as that of our Master, of whom it is written that He went about doing good and healing all who were oppressed by Satan. Acts 10:38. Of His own work He says: "The Spirit of the Lord God is upon Me; because the Lord hath anointed Me to preach good tidings unto the meek." "He hath sent Me to heal the brokenhearted, to preach deliverance to the captives, and recovering of sight to the blind, to set at liberty them that are bruised." Isaiah 61:1; Luke 4:18. As we follow Christ's example of labor for the good of others we shall awaken their interest in the God whom we love and serve.

Our sanitariums in all their departments should be

memorials for God, His instrumentalities for sowing the seeds of truth in human hearts. This they will be if rightly conducted.

The living truth of God is to be made known in our medical institutions. Many persons who come to them are hungering and thirsting for truth, and when it is rightly presented they will receive it with gladness. Our sanitariums have been the means of elevating the truth for this time and bringing it before thousands. The religious influence that pervades these institutions inspires the guests with confidence. The assurance that the Lord presides there, and the many prayers offered for the sick, make an impression upon their hearts. Many who have never before thought of the value of the soul are convicted by the Spirit of God, and not a few are led to change their whole course of life. Impressions that will never be effaced are made upon many who have been self-satisfied, who have thought their own standard of character to be sufficient, and who have felt no need of the righteousness of Christ. When the future test comes, when enlightenment comes to them, not a few of these will take their stand with God's remnant people.

God is honored by institutions conducted in this way. In His mercy He has made the sanitariums such a power in the relief of physical suffering that thousands have been drawn to them to be cured of their maladies. And with many, physical healing is accompanied by the healing of the soul. From the Saviour they receive the forgiveness of their sins. They receive the grace of Christ and identify themselves with Him, with His interests, His honor. Many go away from our sanitariums with new hearts. The change is decided. These, returning to their homes, are as lights in the world. The Lord makes them His witnesses. Their testimony is: "I have seen His greatness, I have tasted His goodness. 'Come and hear, all ye that fear God, and I will declare what He hath done for my soul.'" Psalm 66:16.

Thus through the prospering hand of our God upon them our sanitariums have been the means of accomplishing great good. And they are to rise still higher. God will work with the people who will honor Him.

Wonderful is the work which God designs to accomplish through His servants, that His name may be glorified. God made Joseph a fountain of life to the Egyptian nation. Through Joseph the life of that whole people was preserved. Through Daniel God saved the life of all the wise men of Babylon. And these deliverances were as object lessons; they illustrated to the people the spiritual blessings offered them through connection with the God whom Joseph and Daniel worshiped. So through His people today God desires to bring blessings to the world. Every worker in whose heart Christ abides, everyone who will show forth His love to the world, is a worker together with God for the blessing of humanity. As he receives from the Saviour grace to impart to others, from his whole being flows forth the tide of spiritual life. Christ came as the Great Physician to heal the wounds that sin has made in the human family; and His Spirit, working through His servants, imparts to sin-sick, suffering human beings a mighty healing power that is efficacious for the body and the soul. "In that day," says the Scriptures, "there shall be a fountain opened to the house of David and to the inhabitants of Jerusalem for sin and for uncleanness." Zechariah 13:1. The waters of this fountain contain medicinal properties that will heal both physical and spiritual infirmities.

From this fountain flows the mighty river seen in Ezekiel's vision. "These waters issue out toward the east country, and go down into the desert, and go into the sea: which being brought forth into the sea, the waters shall be healed. And it shall come to pass, that everything that liveth, which moveth, whithersoever the rivers shall come, shall live. . . . And by the river upon the bank thereof, on this side and on that side, shall grow all trees for meat, whose leaf shall not fade, neither shall the fruit thereof be consumed: it shall bring forth new fruit according to his months, because their waters they issued out of the sanctuary: and the fruit thereof shall be for meat, and the leaf thereof for medicine." Ezekiel 47:8-12.

Such a river of life and healing God designs that, by His power working through them, our sanitariums shall be. ⸺

Our sanitariums are to show forth to the world the benevolence of heaven; and though Christ's visible presence is not discerned in the building, yet the workers may claim the promise: "Lo, I am with you alway, even unto the end of the world."

⸺

The promises of God to Israel are also for the institutions established today for the glory of His name: "Thus saith the Lord the maker thereof, the Lord that formed it, to establish it; the Lord is His name; Call unto Me, and I will answer thee, and show thee great and mighty things, which thou knowest not. For thus saith the Lord, the God of Israel, concerning . . . this city. Behold, I will bring it health and cure, and I will cure them, and will reveal unto them the abundance of peace and truth. . . . And I will cleanse them from all their iniquity. . . . And it shall be to Me a name of joy, a praise and an honor before all the nations of the earth, which shall hear all the good that I do unto them." "In those days shall Judah be saved, and Jerusalem shall dwell safely: and this is the name wherewith she shall be called, The Lord our Righteousness." Jeremiah 33:2-9, 16.

THE PHYSICIAN'S WORK FOR SOULS

Every medical practitioner may through faith in Christ have in his possession a cure of the highest value, a remedy for the sin-sick soul. The physician who is converted and sanctified through the truth is registered in heaven as a laborer together with God, a follower of Jesus Christ. Through the sanctification of the truth God gives to physicians and nurses wisdom and skill in treating the sick, and this work is opening the fast-closed door to many hearts. Men and women are led to understand the truth which is needed to save the soul as well as the body.

This is an element that gives character to the work for this time. The medical missionary work is as the right arm to the third angel's message which must be proclaimed to a fallen world; and physicians, managers, and workers in any line, in acting faithfully their part, are doing the work of the message. Thus the sound of the truth will go forth to every nation and kindred and tongue and people. In this work the heavenly angels bear a part. They awaken spiritual joy and melody in the hearts of those who have been freed from suffering, and thanksgiving to God arises from the lips of many who have received the precious truth.

Every physician in our ranks should be a Christian. Only those physicians who are genuine Bible Christians can discharge aright the high duties of their profession.

The physician who understands the responsibility and accountability of his position will feel the necessity of Christ's presence with him in his work for those for whom such a sacrifice has been made. He will subordinate everything to the higher interests which concern the life that may be saved unto life eternal. He will do all in his power to save both the body and the soul. He

(229)

will try to do the very work that Christ would do were He in his place. The physician who loves Christ and the souls for whom Christ died will seek earnestly to bring into the sickroom a leaf from the tree of life. He will try to break the bread of life to the sufferer. Notwithstanding the obstacles and difficulties to be met, this is the solemn, sacred work of the medical profession.

True missionary work is that in which the Saviour's work is best represented, His methods most closely copied, His glory best promoted. Missionary work that falls short of this standard is recorded in heaven as defective. It is weighed in the balances of the sanctuary and found wanting.

Physicians should seek to direct the minds of their patients to Christ, the Physician of soul and body. That which physicians can only attempt to do, Christ accomplishes. The human agent strives to prolong life. Christ is life itself. He who passed through death to destroy him that had the power of death is the Source of all vitality. There is balm in Gilead, and a Physician there. Christ endured an agonizing death under the most humiliating circumstances that we might have life. He gave up His precious life that He might vanquish death. But He rose from the tomb, and the myriads of angels who came to behold Him take up the life He had laid down heard His words of triumphant joy as He stood above Joseph's rent sepulcher proclaiming: "I am the resurrection, and the life."

The question, "If a man die, shall he live again?" has been answered. By bearing the penalty of sin, by going down into the grave, Christ has brightened the tomb for all who die in faith. God in human form has brought life and immortality to light through the gospel. In dying, Christ secured eternal life for all who believe in

Him. In dying, He condemned the originator of sin and disloyalty to suffer the penalty of sin — eternal death.

The possessor and giver of eternal life, Christ was the only one who could conquer death. He is our Redeemer; and blessed is every physician who is in a true sense of the word a missionary, a savior of souls for whom Christ gave His life. Such a physician learns day by day from the Great Physician how to watch and work for the saving of the souls and bodies of men and women. The Saviour is present in the sickroom, in the operating room; and His power for His name's glory accomplishes great things.

The physician can do a noble work if he is connected with the Great Physician. To the relatives of the sick, whose hearts are full of sympathy for the sufferer, he may find opportunity to speak the words of life; and he can soothe and uplift the mind of the sufferer by leading him to look to the One who can save to the uttermost all who come to Him for salvation.

When the Spirit of God works on the mind of the afflicted one, leading him to inquire for truth, let the physician work for the precious soul as Christ would work for it. Do not urge upon him any special doctrine, but point him to Jesus as the sin-pardoning Saviour. Angels of God will impress the mind. Some will refuse to be illuminated by the light which God would let shine into the chambers of the mind and into the soul-temple; but many will respond to the light, and from these minds deception and error in its various forms will be swept away.

Every opportunity of working as Christ worked should be carefully improved. The physician should talk of the works of healing wrought by Christ, of His tenderness and love. He should believe that Jesus is his companion, close by his side. "We are laborers together with God." 1 Corinthians 3:9. Never should the physician neglect to direct the minds of his patients to Christ, the Chief Physician. If he has the Saviour abiding in his own heart, his thoughts will ever be directed to the Healer of soul and body. He will lead the minds of sufferers to Him who can restore, who when on earth restored the sick to health and healed the soul as well as the body, saying: "Son, thy sins be forgiven thee." Mark 2:5.

Never should familiarity with suffering cause the physician to become careless or unsympathetic. In cases of dangerous illness the afflicted one feels that he is at the mercy of the physician. He looks to that physician as his only earthly hope, and the physician should ever point the trembling soul to One who is greater than himself, even the Son of God, who gave His life to save him from death, who pities the sufferer, and who by His divine power will give skill and wisdom to all who ask Him.

When the patient knows not how his case will turn, is the time for the physician to impress the mind. He should not do this with a desire to distinguish himself, but that he may point the soul to Christ as a personal Saviour. If the life is spared, there is a soul for that physician to watch for. The patient feels that the physician is the very life of his life. And to what purpose should this great confidence be employed? Always to win a soul to Christ and magnify the power of God.

When the crisis has passed and success is apparent, be the patient a believer or an unbeliever, let a few moments be spent with him in prayer. Give expression to your thankfulness for the life that has been spared. The physician who follows such a course carries his patient to the One upon whom he is dependent for life. Words of gratitude may flow from the patient to the physician, for through God he has bound this life up with his own;

but let the praise and thanksgiving be given to God as to One who is present though invisible.

On the sickbed Christ is often accepted and confessed; and this will be done oftener in the future than it has been in the past, for a quick work will the Lord do in our world. Words of wisdom are to be on the lips of the physician, and Christ will water the seed sown, causing it to bring forth fruit unto eternal life.

We lose the most precious opportunities by neglecting to speak a word in season. Too often a precious talent that ought to produce a thousandfold is left unused. If the golden privilege is not watched for, it will pass. Something was allowed to prevent the physician from doing his appointed work as a minister of righteousness.

There are none too many godly physicians to minister in their profession. There is much work to be done, and ministers and doctors are to work in perfect union. Luke, the writer of the Gospel that bears his name, is called "the beloved physician," and those who do a work similar to that which he did are living out the gospel.

Countless are the opportunities of the physician for warning the impenitent, cheering the disconsolate and hopeless, and prescribing for the health of mind and body. As he thus instructs the people in the principles of true temperance, and as a guardian of souls gives advice to those who are mentally and physically diseased, the physician is acting his part in the great work of making ready a people prepared for the Lord. This is what medical missionary work is to accomplish in its relation to the third angel's message.

Ministers and physicians are to work harmoniously with earnestness to save souls that are becoming entangled in Satan's snares. They are to point men and women to Jesus, their righteousness, their strength, and the health of their countenance. Continually they are to watch for souls. There are those who are struggling with strong temptations, in danger of being overcome in the fight with satanic agencies. Will you pass these by without offering them assistance? If you see a soul in need of help, engage in conversation with him even though you do not know him. Pray with him. Point him to Jesus.

This work belongs just as surely to the doctor as to the minister. By public and private effort the physician should seek to win souls to Christ.

In all our enterprises and in all our institutions God is to be acknowledged as the Master Worker. The physicians are to stand as His representatives. The medical fraternity have made many reforms, and they are still to advance. Those who hold the lives of human beings in their hands should be educated, refined, sanctified. Then will the Lord work through them in mighty power to glorify His name.

————

Christ's work for the paralytic is an illustration of the way we are to work. Through his friends this man had heard of Jesus and requested to be brought into the presence of the mighty Healer. The Saviour knew that the paralytic had been tortured by the suggestions of the priests that because of his sins God had cast him off. Therefore His first work was to give him peace of mind. "Son," He said, "thy sins be forgiven thee." This assurance filled his heart with peace and joy. But some who were present began to murmur, saying in their hearts, "Who can forgive sins but God only?" Then that they might know that the Son of man had power to forgive sins, Christ said to the sick man: "Arise, and take up thy bed, and go thy way into thine house." This shows how the Saviour bound together the work of preaching the truth and healing the sick.

UNITY IN OUR WORK

As the medical missionary work becomes more extended, there will be a temptation to make it independent of our conferences. But it has been presented to me that this plan is not right. The different lines of our work are but parts of one great whole. They have one center.

In Colossians we read: "The body is of Christ. Let no man beguile you of your reward in a voluntary humility and worshiping of angels, intruding into those things which he hath not seen, vainly puffed up by his fleshly mind, and not holding the Head, from which all the body by joints and bands having nourishment ministered, and knit together, increaseth with the increase of God." Colossians 2:17-19. Our work in all its lines is to demonstrate the influence of the cross. The work of God in the plan of salvation is not to be done in any disjointed way. It is not to operate at random. The plan that provided the influence of the cross provided also the methods of its diffusion. This method is simple in its principles and comprehensive in its plain, distinct lines. Part is connected with part in perfect order and relation.

God has brought His people together in church capacity in order that they may reveal to the world the wisdom of Him who formed this organization. He knew what plans to outline for the efficiency and success of His people. Adherence to these plans will enable them to testify of the divine authorship of God's great plan for the restoration of the world.

Those who take part in God's work are to be led and guided by Him. Every human ambition is to be merged in Christ, who is the head over all the institutions that God has established. He knows how to set in operation and keep in operation His own agencies. He knows that the cross must occupy the central place because it is the means of man's atonement and because of the influence it exerts on every part of the divine government. The Lord Jesus, who has been through all the history of our world, understands the methods that should be invested with power over human minds. He knows the importance of every agency and understands how the varied agencies should be related one to another.

"None of us liveth to himself." Romans 14:7. This is a law of God in heaven and on earth. God is the great center. From Him all life proceeds. To Him all service, homage, and allegiance belong. For all created beings there is the one great principle of life—dependence upon and co-operation with God. The relationship existing in the pure family of God in heaven was to exist in the family of God on earth. Under God, Adam was to stand at the head of the earthly family to maintain the principles of the heavenly family. This would have brought peace and happiness. But the law that none "liveth to himself" Satan was determined to oppose. He desired to live for self. He sought to make himself a center of influence. It was this that incited rebellion in heaven, and it was man's acceptance of this principle that brought sin on earth. When Adam sinned, man broke away from the heaven-ordained center. A demon became the central power in the world. Where God's throne should have been, Satan had placed his throne. The world laid its homage, as a willing offering, at the feet of the enemy.

Who could bring in the principles ordained by God in His rule and government to counterwork the plans of Satan and bring the world back to its loyalty? God said: I will send My Son. "God so loved the world, that He gave His only-begotten Son, that whosoever believeth in Him should not perish, but have everlasting life."

John 3:16. This is the remedy for sin. Christ says: "Where Satan has set his throne, there shall stand My cross. Satan shall be cast out, and I will be lifted up to draw all men unto Me. I will become the center of the redeemed world. The Lord God shall be exalted. Those who are now controlled by human ambition, human passions, shall become workers for Me. Evil influences have conspired to counterwork all good. They have confederated to make men think it righteous to oppose the law of Jehovah. But My army shall meet in conflict with the satanic force. My Spirit shall combine with every heavenly agency to oppose them. I will engage every sanctified human agency in the universe. None of My agencies are to be absent. I have work for all who love Me, employment for every soul who will work under My direction. The activity of Satan's army, the danger that surrounds the human soul, calls for the energies of every worker. But no compulsion shall be exercised. Man's depravity is to be met by the love, the patience, the longsuffering of God. My work shall be to save those who are under Satan's rule."

Through Christ, God works to bring man back to his first relation to his Creator and to correct the disorganizing influences brought in by Satan. Christ alone stood unpolluted in a world of selfishness, where men would destroy a friend or a brother in ordei to accomplish a scheme put into their hands by Satan. Christ came to our world, clothing His divinity with humanity, that humanity might touch humanity and divinity grasp divinity. Amid the din of selfishness He could say to men: Return to your center—God. He Himself made it possible for man to do this by carrying out in this world the principles of heaven. In humanity He lived the law of God. To men in every nation, every country, every clime, He will impart heaven's choicest gifts if they will accept God as their Creator and Christ as their Redeemer.

Christ alone can do this. His gospel in the hearts and hands of His followers is the power which is to accomplish this great work. "O the depth of the riches both of the wisdom and knowledge of God!" By Himself becoming subject to Satan's misrepresentations, Christ made it possible for the work of redemption to be accomplished. Thus was Satan to show himself to be the cause of disloyalty in God's universe. Thus was to be forever settled the great controversy between Christ and Satan.

Satan strengthens the destructive tendencies of man's nature. He brings in envy, jealousy, selfishness, covetousness, emulation, and strife for the highest place. Evil agencies act their part through the devising of Satan. Thus the enemy's plans, with their destructive tendencies, have been brought into the church. Christ comes with His own redeeming influence, proposing through the agency of His Spirit to impart His efficiency to men, and to employ them as His instrumentalities, laborers together with Him in seeking to draw the world back to its loyalty.

Men are bound in fellowship, in dependence, to one another. By the golden links of the chain of love they are to be bound fast to the throne of God. This can be done only by Christ's imparting to finite man the attributes which man would ever have possessed had he remained loyal and true to God.

Those who, through an intelligent understanding of the Scriptures, view the cross aright, those who truly believe in Jesus, have a sure foundation for their faith. They have that faith which works by love and purifies the soul from all its hereditary and cultivated imperfections.

God has united believers in church capacity in order

that one may strengthen another in good and righteous endeavor. The church on earth would indeed be a symbol of the church in heaven if the members were of one mind and of one faith. It is those who are not moved by the Holy Spirit that mar God's plan. Another spirit takes possession of them, and they help to strengthen the forces of darkness. Those who are sanctified by the precious blood of Christ will not become the means of counterworking the great plan which God has devised. They will not bring human depravity into things small or great. They will do nothing to perpetuate division in the church.

It is true there are tares among the wheat; in the body of Sabbathkeepers evils are seen; but because of this shall we disparage the church? Shall not the managers of every institution, the leaders of every church, take up the work of purification in such a way that the transformation in the church shall make it a bright light in a dark place?

What may not even one believer do in the exercise of pure, heavenly principles if he refuses to be contaminated, if he will stand as firm as a rock to a "Thus saith the Lord"? Angels of God will come to his help, preparing the way before him.

Paul wrote to the Romans: "I beseech you therefore, brethren, by the mercies of God, that ye present your bodies a living sacrifice, holy, acceptable unto God, which is your reasonable service. And be not conformed to this world: but be ye transformed by the renewing of your mind, that ye may prove what is that good, and acceptable, and perfect, will of God." Romans 12:1, 2. This entire chapter is a lesson which I entreat all who claim to be members of the body of Christ to study. Again Paul wrote: "If the first fruit be holy, the lump is also holy: and if the root be holy, so are the branches. And if some of the branches be broken off, and thou, being a wild olive tree, wert grafted in among them, and with them partakest of the root and fatness of the olive tree; boast not against the branches. But if thou boast, thou bearest not the root, but the root thee. Thou wilt say then, The branches were broken off, that I might be grafted in. Well; because of unbelief they were broken off, and thou standest by faith. Be not high-minded, but fear: for if God spared not the natural branches, take heed lest He also spare not thee. Behold therefore the goodness and severity of God: on them which fell, severity; but toward thee, goodness, if thou continue in His goodness: otherwise thou also shalt be cut off." Romans 11:16-22. Very plainly these words show that there is to be no disparaging of the agencies which God has placed in the church.

Sanctified ministry calls for self-denial. The cross must be uplifted and its place in the gospel work shown. Human influence is to draw its efficacy from the One who is able to save and to keep saved all who recognize their dependence on Him. By the union of church members with Christ and with one another the transforming power of the gospel is to be diffused throughout the world.

In the work of the gospel the Lord uses different instrumentalities, and nothing is to be allowed to separate these instrumentalities. Never should a sanitarium be established as an enterprise independent of the church. Our physicians are to unite with the work of the ministers of the gospel. Through their labors souls are to be saved, that the name cf God may be magnified.

Medical missionary work is in no case to be divorced from the gospel ministry. The Lord has specified that the two shall be as closely connected as the arm is with the body. Without this union neither part of the work is complete. The medical missionary work is the gospel in illustration.

But God did not design that the medical missionary work should eclipse the work of the third angel's message. The arm is not to become the body. The third angel's message is the gospel message for these last days, and in no case is it to be overshadowed by other interests and made to appear an unessential consideration. When in our institutions anything is placed above the third angel's message, the gospel is not there the great leading power.

The cross is the center of all religious institutions. These institutions are to be under the control of the Spirit of God; in no institution is any one man to be the sole head. The divine mind has men for every place.

Through the power of the Holy Spirit, every work of God's appointment is to be elevated and ennobled, and made to witness for the Lord. Man must place himself under the control of the eternal mind, whose dictates he is to obey in every particular.

Let us seek to understand our privilege of walking and working with God. The gospel, though it contains God's expressed will, is of no value to men, high or low, rich or poor, unless they place themselves in subjection to God. He who bears to his fellow men the remedy for sin must himself first be moved by the Spirit of God. He must not ply the oars unless he is under divine direction. He cannot work effectually, he cannot carry out the will of God in harmony with the divine mind, unless he finds out, not from human sources, but from infinite wisdom, that God is pleased with his plans.

God's benevolent design embraces every branch of His

work. The law of reciprocal dependence and influence is to be recognized and obeyed. "None of us liveth to himself." The enemy has used the chain of dependence to draw men together. They have united to destroy God's image in man, to counterwork the gospel by perverting its principles. They are represented in God's word as being bound in bundles to be burned. Satan is uniting his forces for perdition. The unity of God's chosen people has been terribly shaken. God presents a remedy. This remedy is not one influence among many influences and on the same level with them; it is an influence above all influences upon the face of the earth, corrective, uplifting, and ennobling. Those who work in the gospel should be elevated and sanctified, for they are dealing with God's great principles. Yoked up with Christ, they are laborers together with God. Thus the Lord desires to bind His followers together, that they may be a power for good, each acting his part, yet all cherishing the sacred principle of dependence on the Head.

———

Christ was bound up in all branches of the work of God. He made no division. He did not feel that He was infringing on the work of the physician when He healed the sick. He proclaimed the truth, and when the sick came to Him to be healed, He was just as ready to lay His hands on them as He was to preach the gospel. He was just as much at home in this work as in proclaiming the truth.

RESPONSIBILITIES OF MEDICAL WORKERS

THE fourth chapter of the Epistle to the Ephesians contains lessons given us by God. In this chapter one speaks under the inspiration of God, one to whom in holy vision God had given instruction. He describes the distribution of God's gifts to His workers, saying: "He gave some, apostles; and some, prophets; and some, evangelists; and some, pastors and teachers; for the perfecting of the saints, for the work of the ministry, for the edifying of the body of Christ: till we all come in the unity of the faith, and of the knowledge of the Son of God, unto a perfect man, unto the measure of the stature of the fullness of Christ." Ephesians 4:11-13. Here we are shown that God gives to every man his work, and in doing this work man is fulfilling his part of God's great plan.

This lesson should be carefully considered by our physicians and medical missionaries. God established His instrumentalities among a people who recognize the laws of the divine government. The sick are to be healed through the combined effort of the human and the divine. Every gift, every power, that Christ promised His disciples He bestows upon those who will serve Him faithfully. And He who gives mental capabilities, and who entrusts talents to the men and women who are His by creation and redemption, expects that these talents and capabilities will be increased by use. Every talent must be employed in blessing others and thus bringing honor to God. But physicians have been led to suppose that their capabilities were their individual property. The powers given them for God's work they have used in branching out into lines of work to which God has not appointed them.

Satan works every moment to find an opportunity for

stealing in. He tells the physician that his talents are too valuable to be bound up among Seventh-day Adventists, that if he were free he could do a very large work. The physician is tempted to feel that he has methods which he can carry independent of the people for whom God has wrought that He might place them above every other people on the face of the earth. But let not the physician feel that his influence would increase if he should separate himself from this work. Should he attempt to carry out his plans he would not meet with success.

Selfishness introduced in any degree into ministerial or medical work is an infraction of the law of God. When men glory in their capabilities and cause the praise of men to flow to finite beings, they dishonor God, and He will remove that in which they glory. The physicians connected with our sanitariums and medical missionary work have by God's providence been bound to this people, whom He has commanded to be a light in the world. Their work is to give all that the Lord has given them —to give, not as one influence among many, but as the influence through God to make effective the truth for this time.

God has committed to us a special work, a work that no other people can do. He has promised us the aid of His Holy Spirit. The heavenly current is flowing earthward for the accomplishment of the very work appointed us. Let not this heavenly current be turned aside by our deviations from the straightforward path marked out by Christ.

Physicians are not to suppose that they can compass the world by their plans and efforts. God has not set them to embrace so much with their own labors merely. The man who invests his powers in many lines of work cannot take in hand the management of a health institution and do it justice.

If the Lord's workers take up lines of labor which crowd out that which should be done by them in communicating light to the world, God does not receive through their labors the glory that should accrue to His holy name. When God calls a man to do a certain work in His cause, He does not also lay upon him burdens that other men can and should bear. These may be essential, but according to His own wisdom God apportions to every man his work. He does not want the minds of His responsible men strained to the utmost point of endurance by taking up many lines of labor. If the worker does not take up his appointed task, that which the Lord sees is the very thing he is fitted to do, he is neglecting duties which, if properly executed, would result in the promulgation of the truth and would prepare men for the great crisis before us.

God cannot give in greatest measure either physical or mental power to those who gather to themselves burdens which He has not appointed. When men take upon themselves such responsibilities, however good the work may be, their physical strength is overtaxed, and their minds become confused, and they cannot attain the highest success.

Physicians in our institutions should not engage in numerous enterprises and thus allow their work to flag when it should stand upon right principles and exert a world-wide influence. God has not set His colaborers to embrace so many things, to make such large plans, that they fail in their allotted place of accomplishing the great good He expects them to do in diffusing light to the world, in drawing men and women as He is leading by His supreme wisdom.

The enemy has determined to counterwork the designs of God to benefit humanity in revealing to them what constitutes true medical missionary work. So many interests have been brought in that the workers cannot do all things according to the pattern shown in the mount. I have been instructed that the work appointed to the physicians in our institutions is enough for them to do, and what the Lord requires of them is to link up closely with the gospel missionaries and do their work with faithfulness. He has not asked our physicians to embrace so large and varied a work as some have undertaken. He has not made it the special work of our physicians to labor for those in the dens of iniquity in our large cities. The Lord does not require impossibilities of His servants. The work which He gave to our physicians was to symbolize to the world the ministry of the gospel in medical missionary work.

The Lord does not lay upon His people all the burden of laboring for a class so hardened by sin that many of them will neither be benefited themselves nor benefit others. If there are men who can take up the work for the most degraded, if God lays upon them a burden to labor for the masses in various ways, let these go forth and gather from the world the means required for doing this work. Let them not depend on the means which God intends shall sustain the work of the third angel's message.

Our sanitariums need the power of brain and heart of which they are being robbed by another line of work. Everything that Satan can do he will do to multiply the responsibilities of our physicians, for he knows that this means weakness instead of strength to the institutions with which they are connected.

Great consideration must be exercised in the work that we undertake. We are not to assume large burdens in the care of infant children. This work is being done by others. We have a special work in caring for and educating the children more advanced in years. Let families who can do so adopt the little ones, and they will receive a blessing in so doing. But there is a higher and more special work to engage the attention of our physicians in educating those who have grown up with deformed characters. The principles of health reform must be brought before parents. They must be converted, that they may act as missionaries in their own homes. This work our physicians have done, and can still do, if they will not sacrifice themselves by carrying so many and varied responsibilities.

The head physician in any institution holds a difficult position, and he should keep himself free from minor responsibilities; for these will give him no time for rest. He should have sufficient trustworthy help, for he has trying work to perform. He must bow in prayer with the suffering ones and lead his patients to the Great Physician. If as a humble suppliant he seeks God for wisdom to deal with each case, his strength and influence will be greatly increased.

Of himself, what can man accomplish in the great work set forth by the infinite God? Christ says: "Without Me ye can do nothing." John 15:5. He came to our world to show men how to do the work given them by God, and He says to us: "Come unto Me, all ye that labor and are heavy-laden, and I will give you rest. Take My yoke upon you, and learn of Me; for I am meek and lowly in heart: and ye shall find rest unto your souls. For My yoke is easy, and My burden is light." Matthew 11:28-30. Why is Christ's yoke easy and His burden light? Because He bore the weight of it upon the cross of Calvary.

Personal religion is essential for every physician if he is to be successful in caring for the sick. He needs a power greater than his own intuition and skill. God desires physicians to link up with Him and know that every soul is precious in His sight. He who depends upon

God, realizing that He alone who made man knows how to direct, will not fail in his appointed work as a healer of bodily infirmities or as a physician of the souls for whom Christ died.

One who bears the heavy responsibilities of the physician needs the prayers of the gospel minister, and he should be linked, soul, mind, and body, with the truth of God. Then he can speak a word in season to the afflicted. He can watch for souls as one who must give an account. He can present Christ as the way, the truth, and the life. The Scriptures come clearly to his mind, and he speaks as one who knows the value of the souls with whom he is dealing.

CONFORMITY TO THE WORLD

The Lord Jesus has said: "If any man will come after Me, let him deny himself, and take up his cross daily, and follow Me." Luke 9:23. Christ's words made an impression on the minds of His hearers. Many of them, though not clearly comprehending His instruction, were moved by deep conviction to say decidedly: "Never man spake like this Man." John 7:46. The disciples did not always understand the lessons which Christ wished to convey by parables, and when the multitude had gone away, they would ask Him to explain His words. He was ever ready to lead them to a perfect understanding of His word and His will; for from them, in clear, distinct lines, truth was to go forth to the world.

At times Christ reproached His disciples with the slowness of their comprehension. He placed in their possession truths of which they little suspected the value. He had been with them a long time, giving them lessons in divine truth; but their previous religious education, the erroneous interpretation which they had heard the Jewish teachers place on the Scriptures, kept their minds clouded. Christ promised them that He would send them His Spirit, who would recall His words to their minds as forgotten truths. "He shall teach you all things," Christ said, "and bring all things to your remembrance, whatsoever I have said unto you." John 14:26.

The way the Jewish teachers explained the Scriptures, their endless repetitions of maxims and fiction, called forth from Christ the words: "This people draweth nigh unto Me with their mouth, and honoreth Me with their lips; but their heart is far from Me." They performed in the temple courts their round of service. They offered sacrifices typifying the great Sacrifice, saying by their ceremonies, "Come, my Saviour;" yet Christ, the One whom all these ceremonies represented, was among them, and they would not recognize nor receive Him. The Saviour declared: "In vain they do worship Me, teaching for doctrines the commandments of men." Matthew 15:8, 9.

Christ is saying to His servants today, as He said to His disciples: "If any man will come after Me, let him deny himself, and take up his cross daily, and follow Me." But men are as slow now to learn the lesson as in Christ's day. God has given His people warning after warning; but the customs, habits, and practices of the world have had so great power on the minds of His professed people that His warnings have been disregarded.

Those who act a part in God's great cause are not to follow the example of worldlings. The voice of God is to be heeded. He who depends on men for strength and influence leans on a broken reed.

Depending on men has been the great weakness of the church. Men have dishonored God by failing to appreciate His sufficiency, by coveting the influence of men. Thus Israel became weak. The people wanted to be like the other nations of the world, and they asked for a king. They desired to be guided by human power which they could see, rather than by the divine, invisible power that till that time had led and guided them, and had given them victory in battle. They made their own choice, and the result was seen in the destruction of Jerusalem and the dispersion of the nation.

We cannot put confidence in any man, however learned, however elevated he may be, unless he holds the beginning of his confidence in God firm unto the end. What must have been the power of the enemy upon Solomon, a man whom Inspiration has thrice called the beloved of God, and to whom was committed the great work of building the temple! In that very work Solomon made an alliance with idolatrous nations, and through his marriages he bound himself up with heathen women through whose influence he in his later years forsook the temple of God to worship in the groves he had prepared for their idols.

So now, men set God aside as not sufficient for them. They resort to worldly men for recognition and think that by means of the influence gained from the world they can do some great thing. But they mistake. By leaning on the arm of the world instead of the arm of God, they turn aside the work which God desires to accomplish through His chosen people.

When brought in contact with the higher classes of society, let not the physician feel that he must conceal the peculiar characteristics which sanctification through the truth gives him. The physicians who unite with the work of God are to co-operate with God as His appointed instrumentalities; they are to give all their powers and efficiency to magnifying the work of God's commandment-keeping people. Those who in their human wisdom try to conceal the peculiar characteristics that distinguish God's people from the world will lose their spiritual life and will no longer be upheld by His power.

Our medical workers should never entertain the idea that it is essential to make an appearance of being wealthy. There will be a strong temptation to do this with the thought that it will give influence. But I am instructed to say that it will have the opposite effect.

All who seek to uplift themselves by conforming to the world set an example that is misleading. God recognizes as His those only who practice the self-denial and sacrifice which He has enjoined. Physicians are to understand that their power lies in their meekness and lowliness of heart. God will honor those who make Him their dependence.

The style of a physician's dress, his equipage, his furniture, count not one jot with God. He cannot work by His Holy Spirit with those who try to compete with the world in dress and display. He who follows Christ must deny himself and take up the cross.

The physician who loves and fears God will need to make no outward display in order to distinguish himself; for the Sun of Righteousness is shining in his heart and is revealed in his life, and this gives him distinction. Those who work in Christ's lines will be living epistles, known and read of all men. Through their example and influence men of wealth and talent will be turned from the cheapness of material things to lay hold on eternal realities. The greatest respect will ever be shown to the physician who reveals that he receives his directions from God. Nothing will work so powerfully for the advancement of God's instrumentality as for those connected with it to stand steadfast as His faithful servants.

The physician will find that it is for his present and eternal good to follow the Lord's ways of working. The mind that God has made He can mold without the power of man, but He honors men by asking them to co-operate with Him in His great work.

Many regard their own wisdom as sufficient, and they arrange things according to their judgment, thinking to bring about wonderful results. But if they would depend on God, and not on themselves, they would receive heavenly wisdom. Those who are so engrossed with their work that they cannot find time to press their way to the throne of grace and obtain counsel from God will turn the work into wrong channels. Our strength lies in our union with God through His only-begotten Son and in our union with one another.

The surgeon most truly successful is he who loves God, who sees God in His created work and worships Him as he traces His wise arrangement in the human organism. The most successful physician is he who fears God from his youth, as did Timothy, who feels that Christ is his constant companion, a friend with whom he can always commune. Such a physician would not exchange his position for the highest office the world could give. He is more anxious to honor God and secure His approval than to secure patronage and honor from the great men of the world.

PRAYER

Every sanitarium established among Seventh-day Adventists should be made a Bethel. All who are connected with this branch of the work should be consecrated to God. Those who minister to the sick, who perform delicate, grave operations, should remember that one slip of the knife, one nervous tremor, may cause a soul to be launched into eternity. They should not be allowed to take so many responsibilities that they have no time for special seasons of prayer. By earnest prayer they should acknowledge their dependence upon God. Only through a sense of God's pure truth working in the mind and heart, only through the calmness and strength that He alone can impart, are they qualified to perform those critical operations which mean life or death to the afflicted ones.

The physician who is truly converted will not gather to himself responsibilities that interfere with his work for souls. Since without Christ we can do nothing, how can a physician or a medical missionary engage successfully in his important work without earnestly seeking the Lord in prayer? Prayer and a study of the word bring life and health to the soul.

The Lord is waiting to manifest through His people His grace and power. But He requires that those who engage in His service shall keep their minds ever directed to Him. Every day they should have time for reading the word of God and for prayer. Every officer and every soldier under the command of the God of Israel needs time in which to consult with God and seek His blessing. If the worker allows himself to be drawn away from this, he will lose his spiritual power. Individually we are to walk and talk with God; then the sacred influence of the gospel of Christ in all its preciousness will appear in our lives.

A work of reformation is to be carried on in our institutions. Physicians, workers, nurses, are to realize that they are on probation, on trial for their present life, and for that life which measures with the life of God. We are to put every faculty to the stretch in order to bring saving truths to the attention of suffering human beings. This must be done in connection with the work of healing the sick. Then the cause of truth will stand before the world in the strength which God designs it to have. Through the influence of sanctified workers the truth will be magnified. It will go forth "as a lamp that burneth."

THE WORLD'S NEED

WHEN Christ saw the multitudes that gathered about Him, "He was moved with compassion on them, because they fainted, and were scattered abroad, as sheep having no shepherd." Christ saw the sickness, the sorrow, the want and degradation of the multitudes that thronged His steps. To Him were presented the needs and woes of humanity throughout the world. Among the high and the low, the most honored and the most degraded, He beheld souls who were longing for the very blessings He had come to bring, souls who needed only a knowledge of His grace to become subjects of His kingdom. "Then saith He unto His disciples, The harvest truly is plenteous, but the laborers are few; pray ye therefore the Lord of the harvest, that He will send forth laborers into His harvest." Matthew 9:36-38.

Today the same needs exist. The world is in need of workers who will labor as Christ did for the suffering and the sinful. There is indeed a multitude to be reached. The world is full of sickness, suffering, distress, and sin. It is full of those who need to be ministered unto—the weak, the helpless, the ignorant, the degraded.

Many of the youth of this generation, in the midst of churches, religious institutions, and professedly Christian homes, are choosing the path to destruction. Through intemperate habits they bring upon themselves disease, and through greed to obtain money for sinful indulgences they fall into dishonest practices. Health and character are ruined. Aliens from God and outcasts from society, these poor souls feel that they are without hope either for this life or for the life to come. The hearts of parents are broken. Men speak of these erring ones as

(254)

hopeless, but God looks upon them with pitying tenderness. He understands all the circumstances that have led them to fall under temptation. This is a class that demands labor.

Nigh and afar off are souls, not only the youth but those of all ages, who are in poverty and distress, sunken in sin, and weighed down with a sense of guilt. It is the work of God's servants to seek for these souls, to pray with them and for them, and lead them step by step to the Saviour.

But those who do not recognize the claims of God are not the only ones who are in distress and in need of help. In the world today, where selfishness, greed, and oppression rule, many of the Lord's true children are in need and affliction. In lowly, miserable places, surrounded with poverty, disease, and guilt, many are patiently bearing their own burden of suffering, and trying to comfort the hopeless and sin-stricken about them. Many of them are almost unknown to the churches or to the ministers; but they are the Lord's lights, shining amid the darkness. For these the Lord has a special care, and He calls upon His people to be His helping hand in relieving their wants. Wherever there is a church, special attention should be given to searching out this class and ministering to them.

And while working for the poor, we should give attention also to the rich, whose souls are equally precious in the sight of God. Christ worked for all who would hear His word. He sought not only the publican and the outcast, but the rich and cultured Pharisee, the Jewish nobleman, and the Roman ruler. The wealthy man needs to be labored for in the love and fear of God. Too often he trusts in his riches and feels not his danger. The worldly possessions which the Lord has entrusted to men are often a source of great temptation. Thousands are thus led into sinful indulgences that confirm them in habits of intemperance and vice. Among the wretched victims of want and sin are found many who were once in possession of wealth. Men of different vocations and different stations in life have been overcome by the pollutions of the world, by the use of strong drink, by indulgence in the lusts of the flesh, and have fallen under temptation. While these fallen ones excite our pity and demand our help, should not some attention be given also to those who have not yet descended to these depths, but who are setting their feet in the same path? There are thousands occupying positions of honor and usefulness who are indulging habits that mean ruin to soul and body. Should not the most earnest effort be made to enlighten them?

Ministers of the gospel, statesmen, authors, men of wealth and talent, men of vast business capacity and power for usefulness, are in deadly peril because they do not see the necessity of strict temperance in all things. They need to have their attention called to the principles of temperance, not in a narrow or arbitrary way, but in the light of God's great purpose for humanity. Could the principles of true temperance be thus brought before them, there are very many of the higher classes who would recognize their value and give them a hearty acceptance.

There is another danger to which the wealthy classes are especially exposed, and here also is a field for the work of the medical missionary. Multitudes who are prosperous in the world and who never stoop to the common forms of vice, are yet brought to destruction through the love of riches. Absorbed in their worldly treasures, they are insensible to the claims of God and the needs of their fellow men. Instead of regarding their wealth as a talent to be used for the glory of God and the uplifting of humanity, they look upon it as a means of indulging and glorifying themselves. They add house to house and land to land, they fill their homes with luxuries, while want stalks the streets, and all about them are human beings in misery and crime, in disease and death. Those who thus give their lives to self-serving are developing in themselves, not the attributes of God, but the attributes of Satan.

These men are in need of the gospel. They need to have their eyes turned from the vanity of material things to behold the preciousness of the enduring riches. They need to learn the joy of giving, the blessedness of being co-workers with God.

Persons of this class are often the most difficult of access, but Christ will open ways whereby they may be reached. Let the wisest, the most trustful, the most hopeful, laborers seek for these souls. With the wisdom and tact born of divine love, with the refinement and courtesy that result alone from the presence of Christ in the soul, let them work for those who, dazzled by the glitter of earthly riches, see not the glory of the heavenly treasure. Let the workers study the Bible with them, pressing sacred truth home to their hearts. Read to them the words of God: "But of Him are ye in Christ Jesus, who of God is made unto us wisdom, and righteousness, and sanctification, and redemption." "Thus saith the Lord, Let not the wise man glory in his wisdom, neither let the mighty man glory in his might, let not the rich man glory in his riches: but let him that glorieth glory in this, that he understandeth and knoweth Me, that I am the Lord which exercise loving-kindness, judgment, and righteousness, in the earth: for in these things I delight, saith the Lord." "In whom we have redemption through His blood, the forgiveness of sins, according to the riches of His grace." "But my God shall supply all your need according to His riches in glory by Christ Jesus." 1 Corinthians 1:30; Jeremiah 9:23, 24; Ephesians 1:7; Philippians 4:19.

Such an appeal, made in the spirit of Christ, will not be thought impertinent. It will impress the minds of many in the higher classes.

By efforts put forth in wisdom and love, many a rich man may be awakened to a sense of his responsibility and his accountability to God. When it is made plain that the Lord expects them as His representatives to relieve suffering humanity, many will respond and will give of their means and their sympathy for the benefit of the poor. When their minds are thus drawn away from their own selfish interests, many will be led to surrender themselves to Christ. With their talents of influence and means they will gladly unite in the work of beneficence with the humble missionary who was God's agent in their conversion. By a right use of their earthly treasure they will lay up "a treasure in the heavens that faileth not, where no thief approacheth, neither moth corrupteth." They will secure for themselves the treasure that wisdom offers, even "durable riches and righteousness."

Through observing our lives, the people of the world form their opinion of God and of the religion of Christ. All who do not know Christ need to have the high, noble principles of His character kept constantly before them in the lives of those who do know Him. To meet this need, to carry the light of Christ's love into the homes of the great and the lowly, the rich and the poor, is the high duty and precious privilege of the medical missionary.

"Ye are the salt of the earth," Christ said to His disciples; and in these words He was speaking to His workers of today. If you are salt, saving properties are in you, and the virtue of your character will have a saving influence.

Although a man may have sunk to the very depths of sin, there is a possibility of saving him. Many have lost the sense of eternal realities, lost the similitude of God, and they hardly know whether they have souls to be saved or not. They have neither faith in God nor confidence in man. But they can understand and appreciate acts of practical sympathy and helpfulness. As they see one with no inducement of earthly praise or compensation come into their wretched homes, ministering to the sick, feeding the hungry, clothing the naked, and tenderly pointing all to Him of whose love and pity the human worker is but the messenger—as they see this, their hearts are touched. Gratitude springs up. Faith is kindled. They see that God cares for them, and they are prepared to listen as His word is opened.

In this work of restoration much painstaking effort will be required. No startling communications of strange doctrines should be made to these souls; but as they are helped physically, the truth for this time should be presented. Men and women and youth need to see the law of God with its far-reaching requirements. It is not hardship, toil, or poverty that degrades humanity; it is sin, the transgression of God's law. The efforts put forth to rescue the outcast and degraded will be of no avail unless the claims of the law of God and the need of loyalty to Him are impressed on mind and heart. God has enjoined nothing that is not necessary to bind up humanity with Him. "The law of the Lord is perfect, converting the soul. . . . The commandment of the Lord is pure, enlightening the eyes." "By the word of Thy lips," says the psalmist, "I have kept me from the paths of the destroyer." Psalms 19:7, 8; 17:4.

Angels are helping in this work to restore the fallen and bring them back to the One who has given His life to redeem them, and the Holy Spirit is co-operating with the ministry of human agencies to arouse the moral powers by working on the heart, reproving of sin, of righteousness, and of judgment.

As God's children devote themselves to this work, many will lay hold of the hand stretched out to save them. They are constrained to turn from their evil ways. Some of the rescued ones may, through faith in Christ, rise to high places of service and be entrusted with responsibilities in the work of saving souls. They know by experience the necessities of those for whom they labor, and they know how to help them; they know what means can best be used to recover the perishing. They are filled with gratitude to God for the blessings they have received; their hearts are quickened by love, and their energies are strengthened to lift up others who can never rise without help. Taking the Bible as their guide and the Holy Spirit as their helper and comforter, they find a new career opening before them. Every one of these souls that is added to the force of workers, provided with facilities and instruction as to how to save souls for Christ, becomes a colaborer with those who brought him the light of truth. Thus God is honored and His truth advanced.

————

The world will be convinced not so much by what the pulpit teaches as by what the church lives. The preacher announces the theory of the gospel, but the practical piety of the church demonstrates its power.

THE CHURCH'S NEED

WHILE the world needs sympathy, while it needs the prayers and assistance of God's people, while it needs to see Christ in the lives of His followers, the people of God are equally in need of opportunities that draw out their sympathies, give efficiency to their prayers, and develop in them a character like that of the divine pattern.

It is to provide these opportunities that God has placed among us the poor, the unfortunate, the sick, and the suffering. They are Christ's legacy to His church, and they are to be cared for as He would care for them. In this way God takes away the dross and purifies the gold, giving us that culture of heart and character which we need.

The Lord could carry forward His work without our co-operation. He is not dependent on us for our money, our time, or our labor. But the church is very precious in His sight. It is the case which contains His jewels, the fold which encloses His flock, and He longs to see it without spot or blemish or any such thing. He yearns after it with unspeakable love. This is why He has given us opportunities to work for Him, and He accepts our labors as tokens of our love and loyalty.

In placing among us the poor and the suffering, the Lord is testing us to reveal to us what is in our hearts. We cannot with safety swerve from principle, we cannot violate justice, we cannot neglect mercy. When we see a brother falling into decay we are not to pass him by on the other side, but are to make decided and immediate efforts to fulfill the word of God by helping him. We cannot work contrary to God's special directions without having the result of our work reflect upon us. It should be firmly settled, rooted, and grounded in the conscience, that whatever dishonors God in our course of action cannot benefit us.

It should be written upon the conscience as with a pen of iron upon a rock, that he who disregards mercy, compassion, and righteousness, he who neglects the poor, who ignores the needs of suffering humanity, who is not kind and courteous, is so conducting himself that God cannot co-operate with him in the development of character. The culture of the mind and heart is more easily accomplished when we feel such tender sympathy for others that we bestow our benefits and privileges to relieve their necessities. Getting and holding all that we can for ourselves tends to poverty of soul. But all the attributes of Christ await the reception of those who will do the very work that God has appointed them to do, working in Christ's lines.

Our Redeemer sends His messengers to bear a testimony to His people. He says: "Behold, I stand at the door, and knock: if any man hear My voice, and open the door, I will come in to him, and will sup with him, and he with Me." Revelation 3:20. But many refuse to receive Him. The Holy Spirit waits to soften and subdue hearts; but they are not willing to open the door and let the Saviour in, for fear that He will require something of them. And so Jesus of Nazareth passes by. He longs to bestow on them the rich blessings of His grace, but they refuse to accept them. What a terrible thing it is to exclude Christ from His own temple! What a loss to the church!

———

Good works cost us a sacrifice, but it is in this very sacrifice that they provide discipline. These obligations bring us into conflict with natural feelings and propensities, and in fulfilling them we gain victory after victory over the objectionable traits of our characters. The warfare goes on, and thus we grow in grace. Thus we reflect the likeness of Christ and are prepared for a place among the blessed in the kingdom of God.

————

Blessings, both temporal and spiritual, will accompany those who impart to the needy that which they receive from the Master. Jesus worked a miracle to feed the five thousand, a tired, hungry multitude. He chose a pleasant place in which to accommodate the people and commanded them to sit down. Then He took the five loaves and the two small fishes. No doubt many remarks were made as to the impossibility of satisfying five thousand hungry men, besides women and children, from that scanty store. But Jesus gave thanks and placed the food in the hands of the disciples to be distributed. They gave to the multitude, the food increasing in their hands. And when the multitude had been fed, the disciples themselves sat down and ate with Christ of the heaven-imparted store. This is a precious lesson for every one of Christ's followers.

————

Pure and undefiled religion is "to visit the fatherless and widows in their affliction, and to keep himself unspotted from the world." James 1:27. Our church members are greatly in need of a knowledge of practical godliness. They need to practice self-denial and self-sacrifice. They need to give evidence to the world that they are Christlike. Therefore the work that Christ requires of them is not to be done by proxy, placing on some committee or some institution the burden that they themselves should bear. They are to become Christlike in character by giving of their means and time, their sympathy, their personal effort, to help the sick, to comfort the sorrowing, to relieve the poor, to encourage the desponding, to enlighten souls in darkness, to point sinners to Christ, to bring home to hearts the obligation of God's law.

People are watching and weighing those who claim to believe the special truths for this time. They are watching to see wherein their life and conduct represent Christ. By humbly and earnestly engaging in the work of doing good to all, God's people will exert an influence that will tell in every town and city where the truth has entered. If all who know the truth will take hold of this work as opportunities are presented, day by day doing little acts of love in the neighborhood where they live, Christ will be manifest to their neighbors. The gospel will be revealed as a living power and not as cunningly devised fables or idle speculations. It will be revealed as a reality, not the result of imagination or enthusiasm. This will be of more consequence than sermons or professions or creeds.

Satan is playing the game of life for every soul. He knows that practical sympathy is a test of the purity and unselfishness of the heart, and he will make every possible effort to close our hearts to the needs of others, that we may finally be unmoved by the sight of suffering. He will bring in many things to prevent the expression of love and sympathy. It is thus that he ruined Judas. Judas was constantly planning to benefit self. In this he represents a large class of professed Christians of today. Therefore we need to study his case. We are as near to Christ as he was. Yet if, as with Judas, association with Christ does not make us one with Him, if it does not cultivate within our hearts a sincere sympathy for those for whom

Christ gave His life, we are in the same danger as was Judas of being outside of Christ, the sport of Satan's temptations.

We need to guard against the first deviation from righteousness; for one transgression, one neglect to manifest the spirit of Christ, opens the way for another and still another, until the mind is overmastered by the principles of the enemy. If cultivated, the spirit of selfishness becomes a devouring passion which nothing but the power of Christ can subdue.

THE MESSAGE OF ISAIAH FIFTY-EIGHT

I cannot too strongly urge all our church members, all who are true missionaries, all who believe the third angel's message, all who turn away their feet from the Sabbath, to consider the message of the fifty-eighth chapter of Isaiah. The work of beneficence enjoined in this chapter is the work that God requires His people to do at this time. It is a work of His own appointment. We are not left in doubt as to where the message applies, and the time of its marked fulfillment, for we read: "They that shall be of thee shall build the old waste places: thou shalt raise up the foundations of many generations; and thou shalt be called, The repairer of the breach, The restorer of paths to dwell in." Verse 12. God's memorial, the seventh-day Sabbath, the sign of His work in creating the world, has been displaced by the man of sin. God's people have a special work to do in repairing the breach that has been made in His law; and the nearer we approach the end, the more urgent this work becomes. All who love God will show that they bear His sign by keeping His commandments. They are the restorers of paths to dwell in. The Lord says: "If thou turn away thy foot from the Sabbath, from doing thy pleasure on My holy day; and call the Sabbath a delight,

. . . then shalt thou delight thyself in the Lord; and I will cause thee to ride upon the high places of the earth." Verses 13, 14. Thus genuine medical missionary work is bound up inseparably with the keeping of God's commandments, of which the Sabbath is especially mentioned, since it is the great memorial of God's creative work. Its observance is bound up with the work of restoring the moral image of God in man. This is the ministry which God's people are to carry forward at this time. This ministry, rightly performed, will bring rich blessings to the church.

As believers in Christ we need greater faith. We need to be more fervent in prayer. Many wonder why their prayers are so lifeless, their faith so feeble and wavering, their Christian experience so dark and uncertain. Have we not fasted, they say, and "walked mournfully before the Lord of hosts?" In the fifty-eighth chapter of Isaiah Christ has shown how this condition of things may be changed. He says: "Is not this the fast that I have chosen? to loose the bands of wickedness, to undo the heavy burdens, and to let the oppressed go free, and that ye break every yoke? Is it not to deal thy bread to the hungry, and that thou bring the poor that are cast out to thy house? when thou seest the naked, that thou cover him; and that thou hide not thyself from thine own flesh?" Verses 6, 7. This is the recipe that Christ has prescribed for the fainthearted, doubting, trembling soul. Let the sorrowful ones, who walk mournfully before the Lord, arise and help someone who needs help.

Every church is in need of the controlling power of the Holy Spirit, and now is the time to pray for it. But in all God's work for man He plans that man shall cooperate with Him. To this end the Lord calls upon the church to have a higher piety, a more just sense of duty, a clearer realization of their obligations to their Creator.

He calls upon them to be a pure, sanctified, working people. And the Christian help work is one means of bringing this about, for the Holy Spirit communicates with all who are doing God's service.

To those who have been engaged in this work I would say: Continue to work with tact and ability. Arouse your associates to work under some name whereby they may be organized to co-operate in harmonious action. Get the young men and women in the churches to work. Combine medical missionary work with the proclamation of the third angel's message. Make regular, organized efforts to lift the church members out of the dead level in which they have been for years. Send out into the churches workers who will live the principles of health reform. Let those be sent who can see the necessity of self-denial in appetite, or they will be a snare to the church. See if the breath of life will not then come into our churches. A new element needs to be brought into the work. God's people must realize their great need and peril, and take up the work that lies nearest them.

With those who engage in this work, speaking words in season and out of season, helping the needy, telling them of the wonderful love of Christ for them, the Saviour is always present, impressing the hearts of the poor and miserable and wretched. When the church accepts its God-given work, the promise is: "Then shall thy light break forth as the morning, and thine health shall spring forth speedily: and thy righteousness shall go before thee; the glory of the Lord shall be thy rearward." Christ is our righteousness; He goes before us in this work, and the glory of the Lord follows.

All that heaven contains is awaiting the draft of every soul who will labor in Christ's lines. As the members of our churches individually take up their appointed work, they will be surrounded with an entirely different atmosphere. A blessing and a power will attend their labors. They will experience a higher culture of mind and heart. The selfishness that has bound up their souls will be overcome. Their faith will be a living principle. Their prayers will be more fervent. The quickening, sanctifying influence of the Holy Spirit will be poured out upon them, and they will be brought nearer to the kingdom of heaven.

————

The Saviour ignores both rank and caste, worldly honor and riches. It is character and devotedness of purpose that are of high value with Him. He does not take sides with the strong and worldly favored. He, the Son of the living God, stoops to uplift the fallen. By pledges and words of assurance He seeks to win to Himself the lost, perishing soul. Angels of God are watching to see who of His followers will exercise tender pity and sympathy. They are watching to see who of God's people will manifest the love of Jesus.

Those who realize the wretchedness of sin, and the divine compassion of Christ in His infinite sacrifice for fallen man, will have communion with Christ. Their hearts will be full of tenderness; the expression of the countenance and the tone of the voice will show forth sympathy; their efforts will be characterized by earnest solicitude, love, and energy; and they will be a power through God to win souls to Christ.

We all need to sow a crop of patience, compassion, and love. We shall reap the harvest we are sowing. Our characters are now forming for eternity. Here on earth we are training for heaven. We owe everything to grace, free grace, sovereign grace. Grace in the covenant ordained our adoption. Grace in the Saviour effected our redemption, our regeneration, and our adoption to heirship with Christ. Let this grace be revealed to others.

OUR DUTY TO THE HOUSEHOLD OF FAITH

NEW SABBATHKEEPERS

THERE are two classes of poor whom we have always within our borders—those who ruin themselves by their own independent course of action and continue in their transgression, and those who for the truth's sake have been brought into straitened circumstances. We are to love our neighbor as ourselves, and then toward both these classes we shall do the right thing under the guidance and counsel of sound wisdom.

There is no question in regard to the Lord's poor. They are to be helped in every case where it will be for their benefit.

God wants His people to reveal to a sinful world that He has not left them to perish. Special pains should be taken to help those who for the truth's sake are cast out from their homes and are obliged to suffer. More and more there will be need of large, open, generous hearts, those who will deny self and will take hold of the cases of these very ones whom the Lord loves. The poor among God's people must not be left without provision for their wants. Some way must be found whereby they may obtain a livelihood. Some will need to be taught to work. Others who work hard and are taxed to the utmost of their ability to support their families will need special assistance. We should take an interest in these cases and help them to secure employment. There should be a fund to aid such worthy poor families who love God and keep His commandments.

Care must be taken that the means needed for this work shall not be diverted into other channels. It makes a difference whether we help the poor who through keeping God's commandments are reduced to want and suffering, or whether we neglect these in order to help blasphemers who tread underfoot the commandments of God. And God regards the difference. Sabbathkeepers should not pass by the Lord's suffering, needy ones to take upon themselves the burden of supporting those who continue in transgression of God's law, those who are educated to look for help to anyone who will sustain them. This is not the right kind of missionary work. It is not in harmony with the Lord's plan.

Wherever a church is established, its members are to do a faithful work for the needy believers. But they are not to stop here. They are also to aid others, irrespective of their faith. As the result of such effort, some of these will receive the special truths for this time.

THE POOR, THE SICK, AND THE AGED

"If there be among you a poor man of one of thy brethren within any of thy gates in thy land which the Lord thy God giveth thee, thou shalt not harden thine heart, nor shut thine hand from thy poor brother: but thou shalt open thine hand wide unto him, and shalt surely lend him sufficient for his need, in that which he wanteth. Beware that there be not a thought in thy wicked heart, saying, The seventh year, the year of release, is at hand; and thine eye be evil against thy poor brother, and thou givest him nought; and he cry unto the Lord against thee, and it be sin unto thee. Thou shalt surely give him, and thine heart shall not be grieved when thou givest unto him: because that for this thing the Lord thy God shall bless thee in all thy works, and in all that thou puttest thine hand unto. For the poor shall never cease out of the land: therefore I command thee, saying, Thou shalt open thine hand wide unto thy brother, to thy poor, and to thy needy, in thy land." Deuteronomy 15:7-11.

Through circumstances some who love and obey God become poor. Some are not careful; they do not know how to manage. Others are poor through sickness and misfortune. Whatever the cause, they are in need, and to help them is an important line of missionary work.

All our churches should have a care for their own poor. Our love for God is to be expressed in doing good to the needy and suffering of the household of faith whose necessities come to our knowledge and require our care. Every soul is under special obligation to God to notice His worthy poor with particular compassion. Under no consideration are these to be passed by.

Paul wrote to the Corinthian church: "Moreover, brethren, we do you to wit of the grace of God bestowed on the churches of Macedonia; how that in a great trial of affliction the abundance of their joy and their deep poverty abounded unto the riches of their liberality. For to their power, I bear record, yea, and beyond their power they were willing of themselves; praying us with much entreaty that we would receive the gift, and take upon us the fellowship of the ministering to the saints. And this they did, not as we hoped, but first gave their own selves to the Lord, and unto us by the will of God. Insomuch that we desired Titus, that as he had begun, so he would also finish in you the same grace also."

There had been a famine at Jerusalem, and Paul knew that many of the Christians had been scattered abroad and that those who remained would be likely to be deprived of human sympathy and exposed to religious enmity. Therefore he exhorted the churches to send pecuniary assistance to their brethren in Jerusalem. The amount raised by the churches exceeded the expectation of the apostles. Constrained by the love of Christ, the believers gave liberally, and they were filled with joy because they should thus express their gratitude to the

Redeemer and their love for the brethren. This is the true basis of charity according to God's word.

The matter of caring for our aged brethren and sisters who have no homes is constantly being urged. What can be done for them? The light which the Lord has given me has been repeated: It is not best to establish institutions for the care of the aged, that they may be in a company together. Nor should they be sent away from home to receive care. Let the members of every family minister to their own relatives. When this is not possible, the work belongs to the church, and it should be accepted both as a duty and as a privilege. All who have Christ's spirit will regard the feeble and aged with special respect and tenderness.

God suffers His poor to be in the borders of every church. They are always to be among us, and the Lord places upon the members of every church a personal responsibility to care for them. We are not to lay our responsibility upon others. Toward those within our own borders we are to manifest the same love and sympathy that Christ would manifest were He in our place. Thus we are to be disciplined, that we may be prepared to work in Christ's lines.

The minister should educate the various families and strengthen the church to care for its own sick and poor. He should set at work the God-given faculties of the people, and if one church is overtaxed in this line, other churches should come to its assistance. Let the church members exercise tact and ingenuity in caring for these, the Lord's people. Let them deny themselves luxuries and needless ornaments, that they may make the suffering needy ones comfortable. In doing this they practice the instruction given in the fifty-eighth chapter of Isaiah, and the blessing there pronounced will be theirs.

OUR DUTY TO THE WORLD

"God so loved the world, that He gave His only-begotten Son." He "sent not His Son into the world to condemn the world; but that the world through Him might be saved." John 3:16, 17. The love of God embraces all mankind. Christ, in giving the commission to the disciples, said: "Go ye into all the world, and preach the gospel to every creature." Mark 16:15.

Christ intended that a greater work should be done in behalf of men than we have yet seen. He did not intend that such large numbers should choose to stand under the banner of Satan and be enrolled as rebels against the government of God. The world's Redeemer did not design that His purchased inheritance should live and die in their sins. Why, then, are so few reached and saved? It is because so many of those who profess to be Christians are working in the same lines as the great apostate. Thousands who know not God might today be rejoicing in His love if those who claim to serve Him would work as Christ worked.

The blessings of salvation, temporal as well as spiritual, are for all mankind. There are many who complain of God because the world is so full of want and suffering; but God never meant that this misery should exist. He never meant that one man should have an abundance of the luxuries of life, while the children of others cry for bread. The Lord is a God of benevolence. He has made ample provision for the wants of all, and through His representatives, to whom He has entrusted His goods, He designs that the needs of all His creatures shall be supplied.

Let those who believe the word of the Lord read the instruction contained in Leviticus and Deuteronomy.

There they will learn what kind of education was given to the families of Israel. While God's chosen people were to stand forth distinct and holy, separate from the nations that knew Him not, they were to treat the stranger kindly. He was not to be looked down upon because he was not of Israel. The Israelites were to love the stranger because Christ died as verily to save him as He did to save Israel. At their feasts of thanksgiving, when they recounted the mercies of God, the stranger was to be made welcome. At the time of harvest they were to leave in the field a portion for the stranger and the poor. So the strangers were to share also in God's spiritual blessings. The Lord God of Israel commanded that they should be received if they chose the society of those who knew and acknowledged Him. In this way they would learn the law of Jehovah and glorify Him by their obedience.

So today God desires His children, both in spiritual and in temporal things, to impart blessings to the world. For every disciple of Christ in every age were spoken those precious words of the Saviour: Out of him "shall flow rivers of living water."

But instead of imparting the gifts of God, many who profess to be Christians are wrapped up in their own narrow interests, and they selfishly withhold God's blessings from their fellow men.

While God in His providence has laden the earth with His bounties and filled its storehouses with the comforts of life, want and misery are on every hand. A liberal Providence has placed in the hands of His human agents an abundance to supply the necessities of all, but the stewards of God are unfaithful. In the professed Christian world there is enough expended in extravagant display to supply the wants of all the hungry and to clothe the naked. Many who have taken upon themselves the name of Christ are spending His money for selfish pleasure, for the gratification of appetite, for strong drink and rich dainties, for extravagant houses and furniture and dress, while to suffering human beings they give scarcely a look of pity or a word of sympathy.

What misery exists in the very heart of our so-called Christian countries! Think of the condition of the poor in our large cities. In these cities there are multitudes of human beings who do not receive as much care and consideration as are given to the brutes. There are thousands of wretched children, ragged and half starved, with vice and depravity written on their faces. Families are herded together in miserable tenements, many of them dark cellars reeking with dampness and filth. Children are born in these terrible places. Infancy and youth behold nothing attractive, nothing of the beauty of natural things that God has created to delight the senses. These children are left to grow up molded and fashioned in character by the low precepts, the wretchedness, and the wicked example around them. They hear the name of God only in profanity. Impure words, the fumes of liquor and tobacco, moral degradation of every kind, meets the eye and perverts the senses. And from these abodes of wretchedness piteous cries for food and clothing are sent out by many who know nothing about prayer.

By our churches there is a work to be done of which many have little idea, a work as yet almost untouched. "I was anhungered," Christ says, "and ye gave Me meat: I was thirsty, and ye gave Me drink: I was a stranger, and ye took Me in: naked, and ye clothed Me: I was sick, and ye visited Me; I was in prison, and ye came unto Me." Matthew 25:35, 36. Some think that if they give money to this work, it is all they are required to do; but this is an error. Donations of money cannot take the place of personal ministry. It is right to give our means, and many more should do this; but according to their strength and opportunities, personal service is required of all.

The work of gathering in the needy, the oppressed, the suffering, the destitute, is the very work which every church that believes the truth for this time should long since have been doing. We are to show the tender sympathy of the Samaritan in supplying physical necessities, feeding the hungry, bringing the poor that are cast out to our homes, gathering from God every day grace and strength that will enable us to reach to the very depths of human misery and help those who cannot possibly help themselves. In doing this work we have a favorable opportunity to set forth Christ the crucified One.

Every church member should feel it his special duty to labor for those living in his neighborhood. Study how you can best help those who take no interest in religious things. As you visit your friends and neighbors, show an interest in their spiritual as well as in their temporal welfare. Present Christ as a sin-pardoning Saviour. Invite your neighbors to your home, and read with them from the precious Bible and from books that explain its truths. This, united with simple songs and fervent prayers, will touch their hearts. Let church members educate themselves to do this work. This is just as essential as to save the benighted souls in foreign countries. While some feel the burden of souls afar off, let the many who are at home feel the burden of precious souls around them and work just as diligently for their salvation.

The hours so often spent in amusement that refreshes neither body nor soul should be spent in visiting the poor, the sick, and the suffering, or in seeking to help someone who is in need.

In trying to help the poor, the despised, the forsaken, do not work for them mounted on the stilts of your dignity and superiority, for in this way you will accomplish nothing. Become truly converted, and learn of Him who is meek and lowly in heart. We must set the Lord always before us. As servants of Christ, keep saying, lest you forget it: "I am bought with a price."

God calls not only for your benevolence, but for your cheerful countenance, your hopeful words, the grasp of your hand. As you visit the Lord's afflicted ones, you will find some from whom hope has departed; bring back the sunshine to them. There are those who need the bread of life; read to them from the word of God. Upon others there is a soul sickness that no earthly balm can reach or physician heal; pray for these, and bring them to Jesus.

On special occasions some indulge in sentimental feelings which lead to impulsive movements. They may think that in this way they are doing great service for Christ, but they are not. Their zeal soon dies, and then Christ's service is neglected. It is not fitful service that God accepts; it is not by emotional spasms of activity that we can do good to our fellow men. Spasmodic efforts to do good often result in more injury than benefit.

Methods of helping the needy should be carefully and prayerfully considered. We are to seek God for wisdom, for He knows better than shortsighted mortals how to care for the creatures He has made. There are some who give indiscriminately to everyone who solicits their aid. In this they err. In trying to help the needy, we should be careful to give them the right kind of help. There are those who when helped will continue to make themselves special objects of need. They will be dependent as long as they see anything on which to depend. By giving undue time and attention to these, we may encourage idleness, helplessness, extravagance, and intemperance.

When we give to the poor we should consider: "Am I encouraging prodigality? Am I helping or injuring them?" No man who can earn his own livelihood has a right to depend on others.

The proverb, "The world owes me a living," has in it the essence of falsehood, fraud, and robbery. The world owes no man a living who is able to work and gain a living for himself. But if one comes to our door and asks for food, we should not turn him away hungry. His poverty may be the result of misfortune.

We should help those who with large families to support have constantly to battle with feebleness and poverty. Many a widowed mother with her fatherless children is working far beyond her strength in order to keep her little ones with her, and provide them with food and clothing. Many such mothers have died from over-exertion. Every widow needs the comfort of hopeful, encouraging words, and there are very many who should have substantial aid.

Men and women of God, persons of discernment and wisdom, should be appointed to look after the poor and needy, the household of faith first. These should report to the church and counsel as to what should be done.

Instead of encouraging the poor to think that they can have their eating and drinking provided free or nearly so, we should place them where they can help themselves. We should endeavor to provide them with work, and if necessary teach them how to work. Let the members of poor households be taught how to cook, how to make and mend their own clothing, how to care properly for the home. Let boys and girls be thoroughly taught some useful trade or occupation. We are to educate the poor to become self-reliant. This will be true help, for it will not only make them self-sustaining, but will enable them to help others.

It is God's purpose that the rich and the poor shall be closely bound together by the ties of sympathy and helpfulness. He bids us interest ourselves in every case of suffering and need that shall come to our knowledge.

Think it not lowering to your dignity to minister to suffering humanity. Look not with indifference and contempt upon those who have laid the temple of the soul in ruins. These are objects of divine compassion. He who created all, cares for all. Even those who have fallen the lowest are not beyond the reach of His love and pity. If we are truly His disciples, we shall manifest the same spirit. The love that is inspired by our love for Jesus will see in every soul, rich or poor, a value that cannot be measured by human estimate. Let your life reveal a love that is higher than you can possibly express in words.

Often the hearts of men will harden under rebuke, but they cannot withstand the love expressed toward them in Christ. We should bid the sinner not to feel himself an outcast from God. Bid the sinner look to Christ, who alone can heal the soul leprous with sin. Reveal to the desperate, discouraged sufferer that he is a prisoner of hope. Let your message be: "Behold the Lamb of God, which taketh away the sin of the world."

I have been instructed that the medical missionary work will discover, in the very depths of degradation, men who, though they have given themselves up to intemperate, dissolute habits, will respond to the right kind of labor. But they need to be recognized and encouraged. Firm, patient, earnest effort will be required in order to lift them up. They cannot restore themselves. They may hear Christ's call, but their ears are too dull to take in its meaning; their eyes are too blind to see anything good in store for them. They are dead in trespasses and sins. Yet even these are not to be excluded from the gospel feast. They are to receive the invitation: "Come." Though they may feel unworthy, the Lord says: "Compel them to come in." Listen to no excuse. By love and kindness lay right hold of them. "Ye, beloved, building up yourselves on your most holy faith, praying in the Holy Ghost, keep yourselves in the love of God, looking for the mercy of our Lord Jesus Christ unto eternal life. And of some have compassion, making a difference: and others save with fear, pulling them out of the fire." Jude 20-23. Press home upon the conscience the terrible results of the transgression of God's law. Show that it is not God who causes pain and suffering, but that man through his own ignorance and sin has brought this condition upon himself.

This work, properly conducted, will save many a poor sinner who has been neglected by the churches. Many not of our faith are longing for the very help that Christians are in duty bound to give. If God's people would show a genuine interest in their neighbors, many would be reached by the special truths for this time. Nothing will or ever can give character to the work like helping the people just where they are. Thousands might today be rejoicing in the message if those who claim to love God and keep His commandments would work as Christ worked.

When the medical missionary work thus wins men and women to a saving knowledge of Christ and His truth, money and earnest labor may safely be invested in it, for it is a work that will endure.

THE CARE OF ORPHANS

AMONG all whose needs demand our interest, the widow and the fatherless have the strongest claims upon our tender sympathy. They are the objects of the Lord's special care. They are lent to Christians in trust for God. "Pure religion and undefiled before God and the Father is this, To visit the fatherless and widows in their affliction, and to keep himself unspotted from the world." James 1:27.

Many a father who has died in the faith, resting upon the eternal promise of God, has left his loved ones in full trust that the Lord would care for them. And how does the Lord provide for these bereaved ones? He does not work a miracle in sending manna from heaven; He does not send ravens to bring them food; but He works a miracle upon human hearts, expelling selfishness from the soul and unsealing the fountains of benevolence. He tests the love of His professed followers by committing to their tender mercies the afflicted and bereaved ones.

Let those who have the love of God open their hearts and homes to take in these children. It is not the best plan to care for the orphans in large institutions. If they have no relatives able to provide for them, the members of our churches should either adopt these little ones into their families or find suitable homes for them in other households.

These children are in a special sense the ones whom Christ looks upon, whom it is an offense to Him to neglect. Every kind act done to them in the name of Jesus is accepted by Him as done to Himself.

Those who in any way rob them of the means they should have, those who regard their wants with indifference, will be dealt with by the Judge of all the earth. "Shall not God avenge His own elect, which cry day and night unto Him, though He bear long with them? I tell you that He will avenge them speedily." "He shall have judgment without mercy, that hath showed no mercy." Luke 18:7, 8; James 2:13. The Lord bids us: "Bring the poor that are cast out to thy house." Isaiah 58:7. Christianity must supply fathers and mothers and homes for these destitute ones. Compassion for the widow and orphan, manifested in prayers and corresponding deeds, will come up in remembrance before God, to be rewarded by and by.

There is a wide field of usefulness before all who will work for the Master in caring for these children and youth who have been deprived of the watchful guidance of parents and the subduing influence of a Christian home. Many of them have inherited evil traits of character; and if left to grow up in ignorance, they will drift into associations that lead to vice and crime. These unpromising children need to be placed in a position favorable for the formation of a right character, that they may become children of God.

Are you who profess to be children of God acting your part in teaching these, who so much need to be patiently taught how to come to the Saviour? Are you acting your part as faithful servants of Christ? Are these unformed, perhaps ill-balanced, minds cared for with that love which Christ has manifested for us? The souls of children and youth are in deadly peril if left to themselves. They need patient instruction, love, and tender Christian care.

Were there no revelation to point out our duty, the very sight of our eyes, and what we know of the inevitable working of cause and effect, should arouse us to rescue these unfortunate ones. If the members of the church would bring into this work the same energy and tact and skill that they employ in the common business relations of life, if they would seek wisdom from God and earnestly study how to mold these undisciplined minds, many souls that are ready to perish might be rescued.

If parents would feel the solicitude for the salvation of their own children that they should feel, if they would bear them in their prayers to the throne of grace and live out their prayers, knowing that God would co-operate with them, they might become successful workers for children outside of their own family, and especially for those who do not have parental counsel and guidance. The Lord calls upon every member of the church to do his duty to these orphans.

A CHRISTLIKE WORK

In caring for the children we should not work from the standpoint of duty merely, but from love, because Christ died for their salvation. Christ has purchased these souls who need our care, and He expects us to love them as He has loved us in our sins and waywardness. Love is the agency through which God works to draw the heart to Him, for "God is love." In every enterprise of mercy this principle alone can give efficiency; the finite must unite with the Infinite.

This work for others will require effort, self-denial, and self-sacrifice. But what is the little sacrifice that we can make in comparison with the sacrifice which God has made for us in the gift of His only-begotten Son?

God imparts His blessing to us that we may impart to others. When we ask Him for our daily bread, He looks into our hearts to see if we will share the same with those more needy than ourselves. When we pray, "God be merciful to me a sinner," He watches to see if we will manifest compassion toward those with whom we associate. This is the evidence of our connection with God, that we are merciful even as our Father in heaven is merciful.

God is always giving; and upon whom are His gifts bestowed? Upon those who are faultless in character? "He maketh His sun to rise on the evil and on the good, and sendeth rain on the just and on the unjust." Matthew 5:45. Notwithstanding the sinfulness of humanity, notwithstanding that we so often grieve the heart of Christ and prove ourselves most undeserving, yet when we ask His forgiveness, He does not turn us away. His love is freely extended to us, and He bids us: Love one another as I have loved you. John 13:34.

Brethren and sisters, I ask you to consider this matter carefully. Think of the wants of the fatherless and motherless. Are not your hearts stirred as you witness their sufferings? See if something cannot be done for the care of these helpless ones. As far as lies in your power, make a home for the homeless. Let everyone stand ready to act a part in helping forward this work. The Lord said to Peter: "Feed My lambs." This command is to us, and by opening our homes for the orphans we aid in its fulfillment. Let not Jesus be disappointed in you.

Take these children and present them to God as a fragrant offering. Ask His blessing upon them, and then mold and fashion them according to Christ's order. Will our people accept this holy trust? Because of our shallow piety and worldly ambition, shall those for whom Christ has died be left to suffer, to go in wrong paths?

The word of God abounds with instruction as to how we should treat the widow, the fatherless, and the needy, suffering poor. If all would obey this instruction, the widow's heart would sing for joy; hungry little children would be fed; the destitute would be clothed; and those ready to perish would be revived. Heavenly intelligences are looking on, and when, imbued with zeal for Christ's honor, we place ourselves in the channel of God's providence, these heavenly messengers will impart to us a new spiritual power so that we shall be able to combat difficulties and triumph over obstacles.

And what a blessing would reward the workers! To many who are now indolent, selfish, and self-centered, it would be as life from the dead. There would be among us a revival of heavenly charity and wisdom and zeal.

MINISTERS' WIVES ADOPTING ORPHANS

The question has been asked whether a minister's wife should adopt infant children. I answer: if she has no inclination or fitness to engage in missionary work outside her home, and feels it her duty to take orphan children and care for them, she may do a good work. But let the choice of children be first made from among those who have been left orphans by Sabbathkeeping parents. God will bless men and women as they with willing hearts share their homes with these homeless ones. But if the minister's wife can herself act a part in the work of educating others, she should consecrate her powers to God as a Christian worker. She should be a true helper to her husband, assisting him in his work, improving her intellect, and helping to give the message. The way is open for humble, consecrated women, dignified by the grace of Christ, to visit those in need of help, and shed light into discouraged souls. They can lift up the bowed down by praying with them and pointing them to Christ. Such should not devote their time and strength to one helpless little mortal that requires constant care and attention. They should not thus voluntarily tie their hands.

ORPHANS' HOMES

When all is done that can be done in providing for orphans in our own homes, there will still be many needy ones in the world who should be cared for. They may be ragged, uncouth, and seemingly in every way unattractive; but they are bought with a price, and are just as precious in the sight of God as are our own little ones. They are God's property, for whom Christians are responsible. Their souls, God says, "will I require at thine hand."

To care for these needy ones is a good work; yet in this age of the world the Lord does not give us as a people directions to establish large and expensive institutions for this purpose. If, however, there are among us individuals who feel called of God to establish institutions for the care of orphan children, let them follow out their convictions of duty. But in caring for the world's poor they should appeal to the world for support. They are not to draw upon the people to whom the Lord has given the most important work ever given to men, the work of bringing the last message of mercy before all nations, kindreds, tongues, and people. The Lord's treasury must have a surplus to sustain the work of the gospel in "regions beyond."

Let those who feel the burden of establishing these institutions have wise solicitors to present their necessities and raise funds. Let the people of the world be aroused, let the denominational churches be canvassed by men who feel the necessity that something be done in behalf of the poor and orphans. In every church there are those who fear God. Let these be appealed to, for to them God has given this work.

The institutions that have been established by our people to care for orphans and the infirm and aged among us, should be sustained. Let not these be left to languish and bring a reproach upon the cause of God. To aid in the support of these institutions should be looked upon not merely as a duty, but as a precious privilege. Instead of making needless gifts to one another, let us bestow our gifts upon the poor and helpless. When the Lord sees that we are doing our best for the relief of these needy ones, He will move upon others to aid in this good work.

The design of an orphans' home should be not merely to provide the children with food and clothing, but to place them under the care of Christian teachers who will educate them in the knowledge of God and His Son. Those who work in this line should be men and women who are largehearted and inspired with enthusiasm at the cross of Calvary. They should be men and women who are cultured and self-sacrificing, who will work as Christ worked, for the cause of God and the cause of humanity.

As these homeless ones are placed where they can obtain knowledge and happiness and virtue, and become sons and daughters of the heavenly King, they will be prepared to act a Christlike part in society. They are to be so educated that they in their turn will help others. Thus the good work will be extended and perpetuated.

What mother ever loved her child as Jesus loves His children? He looks upon the marred character with grief deeper, keener than any mother's. He sees the future retribution of an evil course of action. Then let everything be done that can be done for the neglected soul.

THE MEDICAL MISSIONARY WORK AND THE THIRD ANGEL'S MESSAGE

AGAIN and again I have been instructed that the medical missionary work is to bear the same relation to the work of the third angel's message that the arm and hand bear to the body. Under the direction of the divine Head they are to work unitedly in preparing the way for the coming of Christ. The right arm of the body of truth is to be constantly active, constantly at work, and God will strengthen it. But it is not to be made the body. At the same time the body is not to say to the arm: "I have no need of thee." The body has need of the arm in order to do active, aggressive work. Both have their appointed work, and each will suffer great loss if worked independently of the other.

The work of preaching the third angel's message has not been regarded by some as God designs it should be. It has been treated as an inferior work, while it should occupy an important place among the human agencies in the salvation of man. The minds of men must be called to the Scriptures as the most effective agency in the salvation of souls, and the ministry of the word is the great educational force to produce this result. Those who disparage the ministry and try to conduct the medical missionary work independently are trying to separate the arm from the body. What would be the result should they succeed? We should see hands and arms flying about, dispensing means without the direction of the head. The work would become disproportionate and unbalanced. That which God designed should be the hand and arm would take the place of the whole body, and the ministry would be belittled or altogether ignored.

This would unsettle minds and bring in confusion, and many portions of the Lord's vineyard would be left unworked.

The medical missionary work should be a part of the work of every church in our land. Disconnected from the church it would soon become a strange medley of disorganized atoms. It would consume, but not produce. Instead of acting as God's helping hand to forward His truth, it would sap the life and force from the church and weaken the message. Conducted independently, it would not only consume talent and means needed in other lines, but in the very work of helping the helpless apart from the ministry of the word, it would place men where they would scoff at Bible truth.

The gospel ministry is needed to give permanence and stability to the medical missionary work; and the ministry needs the medical missionary work to demonstrate the practical working of the gospel. Neither part of the work is complete without the other.

The message of the soon coming of the Saviour must be given in all parts of the world, and a solemn dignity should characterize it in every branch. A large vineyard is to be worked, and the wise husbandman will work it so that every part will produce fruit. If in the medical missionary work the living principles of truth are kept pure, uncontaminated by anything that would dim their luster, the Lord will preside over the work. If those who bear the heavy burdens will stand true and steadfast to the principles of truth, the Lord will uphold and sustain them.

The union that should exist between the medical missionary work and the ministry is clearly set forth in the fifty-eighth chapter of Isaiah. There is wisdom and blessing for those who will engage in the work as here presented. This chapter is explicit, and there is in it enough to enlighten anyone who wishes to do the will of God. It presents abundant opportunity to minister to suffering humanity, and at the same time to be an instrument in God's hands of bringing the light of truth before a perishing world. If the work of the third angel's message is carried on in right lines, the ministry will not be given an inferior place, nor will the poor and sick be neglected. In His word God has united these two lines of work, and no man should divorce them.

There may be and there is danger of losing sight of the great principles of truth when doing the work for the poor that it is right to do, but we are ever to bear in mind that in carrying forward this work the spiritual necessities of the soul are to be kept prominent. In our efforts to relieve temporal necessities we are in danger of separating from the last gospel message its leading and most urgent features. As it has been carried on in some places, the medical missionary work has absorbed talent and means that belong to other lines of the work, and the effort in lines more directly spiritual has been neglected. Because of the ever-increasing opportunities for ministering to the temporal needs of all classes, there is danger that this work will eclipse the message that God has given us to bear in every city—the proclamation of the soon coming of Christ, the necessity of obedience to the commandments of God and the testimony of Jesus. This message is the burden of our work. It is to be proclaimed with a loud cry and is to go to the whole world. In both home and foreign fields the presentation of health principles must be united with it, but not be independent of it or in any way take its place; neither should this work absorb so much attention as to belittle other branches. The Lord has instructed us to consider the work in all its bearings, that it may have a proportionate, symmetrical, well-balanced development.

The truth for this time embraces the whole gospel. Rightly presented it will work in man the very changes that will make evident the power of God's grace upon the heart. It will do a complete work and develop a complete man. Then let no line be drawn between the genuine medical missionary work and the gospel ministry. Let these two blend in giving the invitation: "Come; for all things are now ready." Let them be joined in an inseparable union, even as the arm is joined to the body.

MEDICAL MISSIONARY WORKERS

The Lord has need of all kinds of skillful workmen. "He gave some, apostles; and some, prophets; and some, evangelists; and some, pastors and teachers; for the perfecting of the saints, for the work of the ministry, for the edifying of the body of Christ: till we all come in the unity of the faith, and of the knowledge of the Son of God, unto a perfect man, unto the measure of the stature of the fullness of Christ." Ephesians 4:11-13.

Every child of God should have sanctified judgment to consider the cause as a whole and the relation of each part to every other part, that none may lack. The field is large, and there is a great work of reform to be carried forward, not in one or two lines, but in every line. The medical missionary work is a part of this work of reform, but it should never become the means of separating the workers in the ministry from their field of labor. The education of students in medical missionary lines is not complete unless they are trained to work in connection with the church and the ministry, and the usefulness of those who are preparing for the ministry would be greatly increased if they would become intelligent on the great and important subject of health. The influence of the Holy Spirit is needed that the work may be properly balanced and that it may move forward solidly in every line.

"PRESS TOGETHER"

The Lord's work is one, and His people are to be one. He has not directed that any one feature of the message should be carried on independently or become all-absorbing. In all His labors He united the medical missionary work with the ministry of the word. He sent out the twelve apostles, and afterward the seventy, to preach the gospel to the people, and He gave them power also to heal the sick and to cast out devils in His name. Thus should the Lord's messengers enter His work today. Today the message comes to us: "As My Father hath sent Me, even so send I you. And when He had said this, He breathed on them, and saith unto them, Receive ye the Holy Ghost." John 20:21, 22.

Satan will invent every possible scheme to separate those whom God is seeking to make one. But we must not be misled by his devices. If the medical missionary work is carried on as a part of the gospel, worldlings will see the good that is being done; they will be convicted of its genuineness and will give it their support.

We are nearing the end of this earth's history, and God calls upon all to lift the standard bearing the inscription: "Here are they that keep the commandments of God, and the faith of Jesus." He calls upon His people to work in perfect harmony. He calls upon those engaged in our medical work to unite with the ministry; He calls upon the ministry to co-operate with the medical missionary workers; and He calls upon the church to take up their appointed duty, holding up the standard of true reform in their own territory, leaving the trained and experienced workers to press on into new fields. No word is to be spoken to discourage any, for this grieves the heart of Christ and greatly pleases the adversary. All need to be baptized with the Holy Spirit; all should refrain from censuring and disparaging remarks, and draw near to Christ, that they may appreciate the heavy responsibilities which the co-workers with Him are carrying. "Press together; press together," are the words of our divine Instructor. Unity is strength; disunion is weakness and defeat.

———

In our work for the poor and unfortunate, we shall need to be guarded, lest we gather responsibilities which we shall not be able to carry. Before adopting plans and methods that require a large outlay of means, we are to consider whether they bear the divine signature. God does not sanction the pushing forward of one line of work without regard to other lines. He designs that the medical missionary work shall prepare the way for the presentation of the saving truth for this time, the proclamation of the third angel's message. If this design is met, the message will not be eclipsed nor its progress hindered.

———

It is not numerous institutions, large buildings, or great display that God requires, but the harmonious action of a peculiar people, a people chosen by God and precious. Every man is to stand in his lot and place, thinking, speaking, and acting in harmony with the Spirit of God. Then, and not till then, will the work be a complete, symmetrical whole.

NEGLECT BY THE CHURCH AND
THE MINISTRY

IN the invitation to the gospel supper the Lord Jesus has specified the work to be done—the work that the churches in every locality, north, south, east, and west, should do.

The churches need to have their eyes anointed with the heavenly eyesalve, that they may see the many opportunities all about them to minister for God. Repeatedly God has called upon His people to go out into the highways and hedges, and compel men to come in, that His house may be full; yet even within the shadow of our own doors are families in which we have not shown sufficient interest to lead them to think that we cared for their souls. It is this work lying nearest us that the Lord now calls upon the church to undertake. We are not to stand, saying: "Who is my neighbor?" We are to remember that our neighbor is the one who most needs our sympathy and help. Our neighbor is every soul who is wounded and bruised by the adversary. Our neighbor is everyone who is the property of God. In Christ the distinctions made by the Jews as to who was their neighbor are swept away. There are no territorial lines, no artificial distinctions, no caste, no aristocracy.

OPPORTUNITIES SLIGHTED

The spirit of the good Samaritan has not been largely represented in our churches. Many in need of help have been passed by, as the priest and Levite passed by the wounded and bruised stranger who had been left to die by the wayside. The very ones who needed the power of the divine Healer to cure their wounds have been left

(294)

uncared for and unnoticed. Many have acted as if it were enough to know that Satan had his trap all set for a soul, and they could go home and care not for the lost sheep. It is evident that those who manifest such a spirit have not been partakers of the divine nature, but of the attributes of the enemy of God.

Someone must fulfill the commission of Christ; someone must carry on the work which He began to do on earth; and the church has been given this privilege. For this purpose it has been organized. Why, then, have not church members accepted the responsibility? There are those who have seen this great neglect; they have seen the needs of many who are in suffering and want; they have recognized in these poor souls those for whom Christ gave His life, and their hearts have been stirred with pity, every energy has been roused to action. They have entered upon a work of organizing those who will co-operate with them in bringing the truth of the gospel before many who are now in vice and iniquity, that they may be redeemed from a life of dissipation and sin. Those who have been engaged in this Christian help work have been doing what the Lord desires to have done, and He has accepted their labors. That which has been done in this line is a work which every Seventh-day Adventist should heartily sympathize with and indorse, and take hold of earnestly. In neglecting this work which is within their own borders, in refusing to bear these burdens, the church is meeting with great loss. Had the church taken up this work as they should have done, they would have been the means of saving many souls.

Because of their neglect the Lord has looked with disfavor upon the church. A love of ease and selfish indulgence has been shown by many. Some who have had the privilege of knowing Bible truth have not brought it into the inner sanctuary of the soul. God holds all these accountable for the talents which they have not returned to Him in honest, faithful service in making every effort possible to seek and to save those who were lost. These slothful servants are represented as coming to the wedding supper without the wedding garment, the robe of the righteousness of Christ. They have nominally accepted the truth, but they do not practice it. Professedly circumcised, they are in reality among the uncircumcised.

Why do we not become enthused with the Spirit of Christ? Why are we so little moved by the pitiful cries of a suffering world? Do we consider our exalted privilege of adding a star to Christ's crown—a soul cut loose from the chains with which Satan has bound him, a soul saved in the kingdom of God? The church must realize its obligation to carry the gospel of present truth to every creature. I entreat of you to read the third and fourth chapters of Zechariah. If these chapters are understood, if they are received, a work will be done for those who are hungering and thirsting for righteousness, a work that means to the church: "Go forward and upward."

RESULTS OF NEGLECT

Wherever a church is established, all the members should engage actively in missionary work. They should visit every family in the neighborhood and know their spiritual condition. If professed Christians had engaged in this work from the time when their names were first placed on the church books, there would not now be such widespread unbelief, such depths of iniquity, such unparalleled wickedness, as is seen in the world at the present time. If every church member had sought to enlighten others, thousands upon thousands would today stand with God's commandment-keeping people.

And not only in the world do we see the result of the

church's neglect to work in Christ's lines. By this neglect a condition of things has been brought into the church that has eclipsed the high and holy interests of the work of God. A spirit of criticism and bitterness has come into the church, and the spiritual discernment of many has been dimmed. Because of this the cause of Christ has suffered great loss. Heavenly intelligences have been waiting to co-operate with human agencies, but we have not discerned their presence.

NEED OF REPENTANCE

It is now high time that we repent. All the people of God should interest themselves in the work of doing good. They should unite heart and soul in earnest endeavor to uplift and enlighten their fellow men. They should put on the wedding garment that Christ has provided, that they may be prepared to work in His lines. They should not receive the grace of God in vain. With humble, devoted reverence they should labor on the right hand and on the left, consecrating to God their entire service and all their capabilities.

There must be an awakening among the people of God. The entire church is to be tested. The worldly-wise man, who meditates and plans, and whose business is ever in his mind, should seek to become wise in matters of eternal interest. If he would put forth as much energy to secure the heavenly treasure and the life which measures with the life of God as he does to secure worldly gain, what could he not accomplish?

The unfaithful steward did not enrich himself with his master's goods; he merely wasted them. He let idleness take the place of sincere, wholehearted labor. He was unfaithful in the appropriation of his lord's goods. Unfaithful steward, do you not see that you will lose your soul if you do not co-operate with God and make the most of your talents for the Master? Your mind was given that you might understand how to work. Your eyes were given that you might be keen to discern your God-given opportunities. Your ears are to listen for the commands of God. Your knees are to bow three times a day in heartfelt prayer. Your feet are to run in the way of God's commandments. Thought, effort, talent, should be put into exercise, that you may be prepared to graduate into the school above and hear from the lips of One who has overcome all temptations in our behalf the words: "To him that overcometh will I grant to sit with Me in My throne, even as I also overcame, and am set down with My Father in His throne." "Thus saith the Lord of hosts; If thou wilt walk in My ways, and if thou wilt keep My charge, then thou shalt also judge My house, and shalt also keep My courts, and I will give thee places to walk among these that stand by." Revelation 3:21; Zechariah 3:7. If you do not co-operate with the Lord by giving yourself to Him and doing His service you will be judged unfit to be a subject of His pure, heavenly kingdom.

NEGLECT BY THE MINISTRY

While I have been commissioned to point out the danger of swaying things too heavily in the medical missionary line to the neglect of other lines of service, this does not excuse those who have held themselves aloof from the medical missionary work. Those who have not been in sympathy with this work should now be very careful how they speak, for they are not intelligent on this subject. Whatever their position in the conference, they should be very guarded in giving utterance to sentiments that will help no one. The indifference and opposition that some have manifested in reference to this question makes it inconsistent that their words should have a large influence. They are not clear-sighted.

Some are worried and perplexed because they see that the medical missionary work is becoming disproportionate, because in receiving so much talent and means, this work far exceeds the work being done in other lines. What is the matter? Is it that the leaders of the medical missionary work are doing too much, or that the leaders in other lines of work are doing too little? It is presented to me that in many lines of work we are doing but a small part of what ought to be done. Faith, zeal, and energy are not manifested as they should be in the work of the ministry. The efforts of many are tame and spiritless. It is evident that light given us by God regarding our duty and privileges has not been acted upon. Men have supplanted God's plans with their own plans. I am commissioned to say that the prosperity of the medical missionary work is in God's order. This work must be done; the truth must be carried into the highways and byways. And ministers and church members should awake and see the necessity of co-operating in this work.

With earnest, untiring energy those who have felt the burden of the Christian help work have testified by their works that they are not content to be mere theoretical believers. They have tried to walk in the light. They have put their belief into practice. They have combined faith and works. They have done the very work the Lord has specified should be done, and many souls have been enlightened, and convicted, and helped.

The indifference among our ministers in regard to health reform and the medical missionary work is surprising. Even those who do not profess to be Christians treat the subject with greater respect than do some of our own people, and these are going in advance of us.

Why, I inquire, are some of our ministerial brethren so far behind in proclaiming the exalted theme of temperance? My brethren, the word given to you is: "Take hold of the work of health reform; go forward." If you think that the medical missionary work is assuming undue proportions, take the men who have been working in these lines with you into your fields of labor, two here and two there. Receive these medical missionaries as you would receive Christ, and see what work they can do. You will not find them dwarfs in religious experience. See if in this way you cannot bring much of heaven's vital current into the churches. See if there are not some who will grasp the education they so much need, and bear the testimony: "God, who is rich in mercy, for His great love wherewith He loved us, even when we were dead in sins, hath quickened us together with Christ, (by grace ye are saved;) and hath raised us up together, and made us sit together in heavenly places in Christ Jesus." Ephesians 2:4-6. Our great need is unity, perfect oneness in God's work.

Those who cannot see the importance and bearing of the medical missionary work should not feel authorized to endeavor to control any phase of it. They need an increased knowledge in every line of health reform. They need to be purified, sanctified, and ennobled. They need to be molded and fashioned after the divine similitude. Then they will see that the medical missionary work is a part of the work of God. The reason why so many church members do not understand this branch of the work is that they are not following their Leader step by step in self-denial and self-sacrifice. The medical missionary work is God's work and bears His signature, and while means must not be absorbed in this one line so as to hinder or cripple the work that should be done in new fields, it should not be regarded as unimportant.

The gospel ministry is an organization for the proclamation of the truth to the sick and to the well. It combines the medical missionary work and the ministry of the word. By these combined agencies opportunities are given to communicate light and to present the gospel to all classes and all grades of society. God wants the ministers and the church members to take a decided, active interest in the medical missionary work.

To take people right where they are, whatever their position or condition, and help them in every way possible — this is gospel ministry. Those who are diseased in body are nearly always diseased in mind, and when the soul is sick, the body also is affected. Ministers should feel it a part of their work to minister to the sick and the afflicted whenever opportunity presents itself. The minister of the gospel is to present the message, which must be received if the people are to become sanctified and made ready for the coming of the Lord. This work is to embrace all that was embraced in Christ's ministry.

Then why do not all our ministers heartily co-operate with those who are carrying forward medical missionary work? Why do they not carefully study the life of Christ, that they may know how He labored, and then follow His example? Is it for you, the appointed ministers of Christ, who have His example before you, to stand off and criticize the very work that He came among men to do? The work now being done in medical missionary lines ought to have been done years ago, and would have been done if God's people had been soundly converted to the truth, if they had studied the word with humble hearts, if they had reverenced the God of the universe and studied His will instead of pleasing themselves. Had our people done this work, many persons of ability and influence would have been converted and joined us in giving the message of Christ's soon coming.

Those who understand physiology and hygiene will, in their ministerial labor, find it a means whereby they may enlighten others in regard to the proper and intelligent treatment of the physical, mental, and moral powers. Therefore those who are preparing for the ministry should make a diligent study of the human organism, that they may know how to care for the body, not by means of drugs, but from nature's own laboratory. The Lord will bless those who make every effort to keep themselves free from disease and lead others to regard as sacred the health of the body as well as of the soul.

The ambassadors of Christ, those to whom have been committed the living oracles of God, can be doubly useful if they know how to help the sick. A practical knowledge of health reform will better qualify men and women to proclaim the message of mercy and retribution to the world.

Ministers should be educators who understand and appreciate the needs of humanity. They should encourage the church members to obtain a practical knowledge of all lines of missionary work, that they may be a blessing to all classes of people. They should be quick to discern those who appreciate questions relating to spiritual life, who have tact and ability to watch for and care for souls as those who must give an account. They should assist these to organize the working forces of the church, so that men, women, and youth of various temperaments, in various callings and positions, will take hold of the work that must be done, bringing their God-given talents into most solemn service for the Master.

Our ideas of Christian benevolence must be worked out if we would have them enlarged. Practical work will accomplish far more than sermons. The ideas of our ministers must broaden, and from an earnest personal experience they should speak words that will arouse the dormant energies of the people. By a daily connection with God they should obtain a deeper insight into their own lives and the lives of others, thus enlarging the circle of their influence. In this way they will be co-workers with Christ, able to enlighten others because they are themselves channels of light.

————

As the members of the church dig deeper and make their foundation sure, riveting their souls to the eternal Rock, as they learn to love God supremely, they will learn to love their neighbor as themselves.

The power of the Lord is magnified when the human heart is tender, sensitive to another's woe, and pitiful for his suffering. Angels of God are ready to co-operate with human instrumentalities in ministering to souls. When the Holy Spirit works upon our hearts and minds, we shall not shun duty and responsibility, and pass by on the other side, leaving the wounded, helpless soul to its misery.

————

In consideration of the value Christ places upon the purchase of His blood, He adopts men as His children, makes them the objects of His tender care; and in order that they may have their temporal and spiritual necessities supplied, He commits them to His church, saying: Inasmuch as ye do it unto one of the least of these My brethren, ye do it unto Me.

This is to be our watchword: "Inasmuch as ye have done it unto one of the least of these My brethren, ye have done it unto Me." And if we faithfully carry it into our daily lives we shall hear the benediction: "Well done, thou good and faithful servant: . . . enter thou into the joy of thy Lord." Will it pay to endure as a Christian the tests and trials of God?

In the work of cleansing and purifying our own souls our intense desire to make our own calling and election sure will inspire us with a yearning for others who are in need. The same energy and careful thought which we once brought into worldly matters will be put into the service of Him to whom we owe everything. We shall do as Christ did, seizing every opportunity to work for those who without help will perish in their degradation. We shall extend to others a helping hand. Then with singing and praise and thanksgiving we shall rejoice with God and the heavenly angels as we see sin-sick souls uplifted and helped, as we see the deluded and insane clothed and in their right minds sitting at the feet of Jesus, learning of Him. As we do this work, receiving of God and rendering back to Him that which He has in confidence lent us to dispose of for His name's glory, His blessing will rest upon us. Then let poor, discouraged, sin-sick souls know that in keeping of His commandments "there is great reward," and by our own experience show to others that blessing and service are linked together.

Though precious time and talent have been spent in caring for and pleasing ourselves, the hand of the Lord is stretched out still; and if we will work today in His vineyard, scattering His invitation of mercy broadcast through the world, He will accept our service. How many will you work for, that they may reach the haven of rest and share the commendation: "Well done, thou good and faithful servant"? How many will you help to crown with glory and honor and eternal life? The Saviour calls for workers. Will you volunteer?

THE REWARD OF SERVICE

"WHEN thou makest a dinner or a supper," Christ said, "call not thy friends, nor thy brethren, neither thy kinsmen, nor thy rich neighbors; lest they also bid thee again, and a recompense be made thee. But when thou makest a feast, call the poor, the maimed, the lame, the blind: and thou shalt be blessed; for they cannot recompense thee; for thou shalt be recompensed at the resurrection of the just." Luke 14:12-14.

In these words Christ draws a contrast between the self-seeking practices of the world and the unselfish ministry of which He has given an example in His own life. For such ministry He offers no reward of worldly gain or recognition. "Thou shalt be recompensed," He says, "at the resurrection of the just." Then the results of every life will be made manifest, and everyone will reap that which he has sown.

To every worker for God this thought should be a stimulus and an encouragement. In this life our work for God often seems to be almost fruitless. Our efforts to do good may be earnest and persevering, yet we may not be permitted to witness their results. To us the effort may seem to be lost. But the Saviour assures us that our work is noted in heaven, and that the recompense cannot fail. The apostle Paul, writing by the Holy Spirit, says: "Let us not be weary in well-doing: for in due season we shall reap, if we faint not." And in the words of the psalmist we read: "He that goeth forth and weepeth, bearing precious seed, shall doubtless come again with rejoicing, bringing his sheaves with him." Galatians 6:9; Psalm 126:6.

And while the great final reward is given at Christ's

coming, truehearted service for God brings a reward, even in this life. Obstacles, opposition, and bitter heartbreaking discouragements the worker will have to meet. He may not see the fruit of his toil. But in face of all this he finds in his labor a blessed recompense. All who surrender themselves to God in unselfish service for humanity are in co-operation with the Lord of glory. This thought sweetens all toil, it braces the will, it nerves the spirit for whatever may befall. Working with unselfish heart, ennobled by being partakers of Christ's sufferings, sharing His sympathies, they help to swell the tide of His joy, and bring honor and praise to His exalted name.

In fellowship with God, with Christ, and with holy angels they are surrounded with a heavenly atmosphere, an atmosphere that brings health to the body, vigor to the intellect, and joy to the soul.

All who consecrate body, soul, and spirit to God's service will be constantly receiving a new endowment of physical, mental, and spiritual power. The inexhaustible supplies of heaven are at their command. Christ gives them the breath of His own spirit, the life of His own life. The Holy Spirit puts forth its highest energies to work in heart and mind.

"Then shall thy light break forth as the morning, and thine health shall spring forth speedily." Thou shalt "call, and the Lord shall answer; thou shalt cry, and He shall say, Here I am." Thy light shall "rise in obscurity, and thy darkness be as the noonday: and the Lord shall guide thee continually, and satisfy thy soul in drought, and make fat thy bones: and thou shalt be like a watered garden, and like a spring of water, whose waters fail not." Isaiah 58:8-11.

Many are God's promises to those who minister to His afflicted ones. He says: "Blessed is he that considereth the poor: the Lord will deliver him in time of trouble. The Lord will preserve him, and keep him alive; and he shall be blessed upon the earth: and Thou wilt not deliver him unto the will of his enemies. The Lord will strengthen him upon the bed of languishing: Thou wilt make all his bed in his sickness." "Trust in the Lord, and do good; so shalt thou dwell in the land, and verily thou shalt be fed." Psalms 41:1-3; 37:3. "Honor the Lord with thy substance, and with the first fruits of all thine increase: so shall thy barns be filled with plenty, and thy presses shall burst out with new wine." "There is that scattereth, and yet increaseth; and there is that withholdeth more than is meet, but it tendeth to poverty." "He that hath pity upon the poor lendeth unto the Lord; and that which he hath given will He pay him again." "The liberal soul shall be made fat: and he that watereth shall be watered also himself." Proverbs 3:9, 10; 11:24; 19:17; 11:25.

And while much of the fruit of their labor is not apparent in this life, God's workers have His sure promise of ultimate success. As the world's Redeemer, Christ was constantly confronted with apparent failure. He seemed to do little of the work which He longed to do in uplifting and saving. Satanic agencies were constantly working to obstruct His way. But He would not be discouraged. Ever before Him He saw the result of His mission. He knew that truth would finally triumph in the contest with evil, and to His disciples He said: "These things I have spoken unto you, that in Me ye might have peace. In the world ye shall have tribulation: but be of good cheer; I have overcome the world." John 16:33. The life of Christ's disciples is to be like His, a series of uninterrupted victories, not seen to be such here, but recognized as such in the great hereafter.

Those who labor for the good of others are working

in union with the heavenly angels. They have their constant companionship, their unceasing ministry. Angels of light and power are ever near to protect, to comfort, to heal, to instruct, to inspire. The highest education, the truest culture, and the most exalted service possible to human beings in this world are theirs.

And often our merciful Father encourages His children and strengthens their faith by permitting them here to see evidence of the power of His grace upon the hearts and lives of those for whom they labor. "My thoughts are not your thoughts, neither are your ways My ways, saith the Lord. For as the heavens are higher than the earth, so are My ways higher than your ways, and My thoughts than your thoughts. For as the rain cometh down, and the snow from heaven, and returneth not thither, but watereth the earth, and maketh it bring forth and bud, that it may give seed to the sower, and bread to the eater: so shall My word be that goeth forth out of My mouth: it shall not return unto Me void, but it shall accomplish that which I please, and it shall prosper in the thing whereto I sent it. For ye shall go out with joy, and be led forth with peace: the mountains and the hills shall break forth before you into singing, and all the trees of the field shall clap their hands. Instead of the thorn shall come up the fir tree, and instead of the brier shall come up the myrtle tree: and it shall be to the Lord for a name, for an everlasting sign that shall not be cut off." Isaiah 55:8-13.

In the transformation of character, the casting out of evil passions, the development of the sweet graces of God's Holy Spirit, we see the fulfillment of the promise, "Instead of the thorn shall come up the fir tree, and instead of the brier shall come up the myrtle tree." We behold life's desert "rejoice, and blossom as the rose."

Christ delights to take apparently hopeless material,

those whom Satan has debased and through whom he has worked, and make them the subjects of His grace. He rejoices to deliver them from suffering and from the wrath that is to fall upon the disobedient. He makes His children His agents in the accomplishment of this work, and in its success, even in this life, they find a precious reward.

But what is this compared with the joy that will be theirs in the great day of final revealing? "Now we see through a glass, darkly; but then face to face;" now we know in part, but then we shall know even as also we are known. 1 Corinthians 13:12.

It is the reward of Christ's workers to enter into His joy. That joy, to which Christ Himself looks forward with eager desire, is presented in His request to His Father: "I will that they also, whom Thou hast given Me, be with Me where I am." John 17:24.

The angels were waiting to welcome Jesus as He ascended after His resurrection. The heavenly host longed to greet again their loved Commander, returned to them from the prison house of death. Eagerly they pressed about Him as He entered the gates of heaven. But He waved them back. His heart was with the lonely, sorrowing band of disciples whom He had left upon Olivet. It is still with His struggling children on earth, who have the battle with the destroyer yet to wage. "Father," He says, "I will that they also, whom Thou hast given Me, be with Me where I am."

Christ's redeemed ones are His jewels, His precious and peculiar treasure. "They shall be as the stones of a crown"—"the riches of the glory of His inheritance in the saints." Zechariah 9:16; Ephesians 1:18. In them "He shall see of the travail of His soul, and shall be satisfied." Isaiah 53:11.

And will not His workers rejoice when they, too, behold the fruit of their labors? The apostle Paul, writing to the Thessalonian converts, says: "What is our hope, or joy, or crown of rejoicing? Are not even ye in the presence of our Lord Jesus Christ at His coming? for ye are our glory and joy." 1 Thessalonians 2:19, 20. And he exhorts the Philippian brethren to "be blameless and harmless," to "shine as lights in the world; holding forth the word of life; that I may rejoice in the day of Christ, that I have not run in vain, neither labored in vain." Philippians 2:15, 16.

Every impulse of the Holy Spirit leading men to goodness and to God is noted in the books of heaven, and in the day of God everyone who has given himself as an instrument for the Holy Spirit's working will be permitted to behold what his life has wrought.

The poor widow who cast her two mites into the Lord's treasury little knew what she was doing. Her example of self-sacrifice has acted and reacted upon thousands of hearts in every land and in every age. It has brought to the treasury of God gifts from the high and the low, the rich and the poor. It has helped to sustain missions, to establish hospitals, to feed the hungry, clothe the naked, heal the sick, and preach the gospel to the poor. Multitudes have been blessed through her unselfish deed. And the outworking of all these lines of influence she, in the day of God, will be permitted to see. So with Mary's precious gift to the Saviour. How many have been inspired to loving service by the memory of that broken alabaster box! And how she will rejoice as she beholds all this!

Wonderful will be the revealing as the lines of holy influence, with their precious results, are brought to view. What will be the gratitude of souls that will meet us in the heavenly courts as they understand the sympathetic, loving interest which has been taken in their salvation!

All praise, honor, and glory will be given to God and to the Lamb for our redemption; but it will not detract from the glory of God to express gratitude to the instrumentality He has employed in the salvation of souls ready to perish.

The redeemed will meet and recognize those whose attention they have directed to the uplifted Saviour. What blessed converse they have with these souls! "I was a sinner," it will be said, "without God and without hope in the world, and you came to me, and drew my attention to the precious Saviour as my only hope. And I believed in Him. I repented of my sins, and was made to sit together with His saints in heavenly places in Christ Jesus." Others will say: "I was a heathen in heathen lands. You left your friends and comfortable home, and came to teach me how to find Jesus and believe in Him as the only true God. I demolished my idols and worshiped God, and now I see Him face to face. I am saved, eternally saved, ever to behold Him whom I love. I then saw Him only with the eye of faith, but now I see Him as He is. I can now express my gratitude for His redeeming mercy to Him who loved me and washed me from my sins in His own blood."

Others will express their gratitude to those who fed the hungry and clothed the naked. "When despair bound my soul in unbelief, the Lord sent you to me," they say, "to speak words of hope and comfort. You brought me food for my physical necessities, and you opened to me the word of God, awakening me to my spiritual needs. You treated me as a brother. You sympathized with me in my sorrows and restored my bruised and wounded soul so that I could grasp the hand of Christ that was reached out to save me. In my ignorance you taught me patiently that I had a Father in heaven who cared for me. You read to me the precious promises of God's word.

You inspired in me faith that He would save me. My heart was softened, subdued, broken, as I contemplated the sacrifice which Christ had made for me. I became hungry for the bread of life, and the truth was precious to my soul. I am here, saved, eternally saved, ever to live in His presence, and to praise Him who gave His life for me."

What rejoicing there will be as these redeemed ones meet and greet those who have had a burden in their behalf! And those who have lived, not to please themselves, but to be a blessing to the unfortunate who have so few blessings—how their hearts will thrill with satisfaction! They will realize the promise: "Thou shalt be blessed; for they cannot recompense thee: for thou shalt be recompensed at the resurrection of the just."

"Thou shalt delight thyself in the Lord; and I will cause thee to ride upon the high places of the earth, and feed thee with the heritage of Jacob thy father: for the mouth of the Lord hath spoken it." Isaiah 58:14.

"Fear not: . . . I am thy shield, and thy exceeding great reward." Genesis 15:1.

"I am thy part and thine inheritance." Numbers 18:20.

"Where I am, there shall also My servant be." John 12:26.

SECTION FIVE

CANVASSING

"Blessed are ye that sow
beside all waters."

IMPORTANCE OF THE WORK

THE canvassing work, properly conducted, is missionary work of the highest order, and it is as good and successful a method as can be employed for placing before the people the important truths for this time. The importance of the work of the ministry is unmistakable; but many who are hungry for the bread of life have not the privilege of hearing the word from God's delegated preachers. For this reason it is essential that our publications be widely circulated. Thus the message will go where the living preacher cannot go, and the attention of many will be called to the important events connected with the closing scenes of this world's history.

God has ordained the canvassing work as a means of presenting before the people the light contained in our books, and canvassers should be impressed with the importance of bringing before the world as fast as possible the books necessary for their spiritual education and enlightenment. This is the very work the Lord would have His people do at this time. All who consecrate themselves to God to work as canvassers are assisting to give the last message of warning to the world. We cannot too highly estimate this work; for were it not for the efforts of the canvasser, many would never hear the warning.

It is true that some who buy the books will lay them on the shelf or place them on the parlor table and seldom

(313)

look at them. Still God has a care for His truth, and the time will come when these books will be sought for and read. Sickness or misfortune may enter the home, and through the truth contained in the books God sends to troubled hearts peace and hope and rest. His love is revealed to them, and they understand the preciousness of the forgiveness of their sins. Thus the Lord co-operates with His self-denying workers.

There are many, who, because of prejudice, will never know the truth unless it is brought to their homes. The canvasser may find these souls and minister to them. There is a line of work in house-to-house labor which he can accomplish more successfully than others. He can become acquainted with the people and understand their true necessities; he can pray with them and can point them to the Lamb of God that taketh away the sin of the world. Thus the way will be opened for the special message for this time to find access to their hearts.

Much responsibility rests upon the canvasser. He should go to his work prepared to explain the Scriptures. If he puts his trust in the Lord as he travels from place to place, angels of God will be round about him, giving him words to speak that will bring light and hope and courage to many souls.

Let the canvasser remember that he has an opportunity to sow beside all waters. Let him remember, as he sells the books which give a knowledge of the truth, that he is doing the work of God and that every talent is to be used to the glory of His name. God will be with everyone who seeks to understand the truth that he may set it before others in clear lines. God has spoken plainly and clearly. "The Spirit and the bride say, Come. And let him that heareth say, Come." Revelation 22:17. We are to make no delay in giving instruction to those who need it, that they may be brought to a knowledge of the truth as it is in Jesus.

The lost sheep of God's fold are scattered in every place, and the work that should be done for them is being neglected. From the light given me I know that where there is one canvasser in the field, there should be one hundred. Canvassers should be encouraged to take hold of this work, not to canvass for storybooks, but to bring before the world the books containing truth essential for this time.

Let canvassers go forth with the word of the Lord, remembering that those who obey the commandments and teach others to obey them will be rewarded by seeing souls converted, and one soul truly converted will bring others to Christ. Thus the work will advance into new territory.

The time has come when a large work should be done by the canvassers. The world is asleep, and as watchmen they are to ring the warning bell to awake the sleepers to their danger. The churches know not the time of their visitation. Often they can best learn the truth through the efforts of the canvasser. Those who go forth in the name of the Lord are His messengers to give to the multitudes who are in darkness and error the glad tidings of salvation through Christ in obeying the law of God.

I have been instructed that even where the people hear the message from the living preacher, the canvasser should carry on his work in co-operation with the minister; for though the minister may faithfully present the message, the people are not able to retain it all. The printed page is therefore essential, not only in awakening them to the importance of the truth for this time, but in rooting and grounding them in the truth and establishing them against deceptive error. Papers and books are the Lord's means of keeping the message for this time continually before the people. In enlightening and confirming souls in the truth the publications will do a far greater work than can be accomplished by the ministry of the word alone. The silent messengers that are placed in the homes of the people through the work of the canvasser will strengthen the gospel ministry in every way; for the Holy Spirit will impress minds as they read the books, just as He impresses the minds of those who listen to the preaching of the word. The same ministry of angels attends the books that contain the truth as attends the work of the minister.

The tidings of every successful effort on our part to dispel the darkness and to diffuse the light and knowledge of God and of Jesus Christ, whom He has sent, are borne upward. The act is presented before the heavenly intelligences and thrills through all the principalities and powers, enlisting the sympathy of all heavenly beings.

"Thanks be unto God, which always causeth us to triumph in Christ, and maketh manifest the savor of His knowledge by us in every place. For we are unto God a sweet savor of Christ, in them that are saved, and in them that perish: to the one we are the savor of death unto death; and to the other the savor of life unto life. And who is sufficient for these things?" 2 Corinthians 2:14-16.

QUALIFICATIONS OF THE CANVASSER

Since canvassing for our literature is a missionary work, it should be conducted from a missionary standpoint. Those selected as canvassers should be men and women who feel the burden of service, whose object is not to get gain, but to give light to the people. All our service is to be done to the glory of God, to give the light of truth to those who are in darkness. Selfish principles, love of gain, dignity, or position, should not be once named among us.

Canvassers need to be daily converted to God, that their words and deeds may be a savor of life unto life, that they may exert a saving influence. The reason why many have failed in the canvassing work is that they were not genuine Christians; they did not know the spirit of conversion. They had a theory as to how the work should be done, but they did not feel their dependence upon God.

Canvassers, remember that in the books you handle you are presenting, not the cup containing the wine of Babylon, doctrines of error dealt to the kings of the earth, but the cup full of the preciousness of the truths of redemption. Will you yourselves drink of it? Your minds can be brought into captivity to the will of Christ, and He can put upon you His own superscription. By beholding, you will become changed from glory to glory, from character to character. God wants you to come to the front, speaking the words He will give you. He wants you to show that you place a high estimate upon humanity, humanity that has been purchased by the precious blood of the Saviour. When you fall upon the Rock and are broken, you will experience the power of Christ, and others will recognize the power of the truth upon your hearts.

To those who are attending school that they may learn how to do the work of God more perfectly, I would say: Remember that it is only by a daily consecration to God that you can become soul winners. There have been those who were unable to go to school because they were too poor to pay their way. But when they became sons and daughters of God they took hold of the work where they were, laboring for those around them. Though destitute of the knowledge obtained in school, they consecrated themselves to God, and God worked through them. Like the disciples when called from their nets to follow Christ, they learned precious lessons from the Saviour. They linked themselves with the Great Teacher, and the knowledge they gained from the Scriptures qualified them to speak to others of Christ. Thus they became truly wise, because they were not too wise in their own estimation to receive instruction from above. The renewing power of the Holy Spirit gave them practical, saving energy.

The knowledge of the most learned man, if he has not learned in Christ's school, is foolishness so far as leading souls to Christ is concerned. God can work with those only who will accept the invitation: "Come unto Me, all ye that labor and are heavy-laden, and I will give you rest. Take My yoke upon you, and learn of Me; for I am meek and lowly in heart: and ye shall find rest unto your souls. For My yoke is easy, and My burden is light." Matthew 11:28-30.

By many of our canvassers there has been a departure from right principles. Through a desire to reap worldly advantage their minds have been drawn away from the real purpose and spirit of the work. Let none think that display will make a right impression upon the people. This will not secure the best or most permanent results.

Our work is to direct minds to the solemn truths for this time. It is only when our own hearts are imbued with the spirit of the truths contained in the book we are selling, and when in humility we call the attention of the people to these truths, that real success will attend our efforts; for it is only then that the Holy Spirit, who convinces of sin, of righteousness, and of judgment, will be present to impress hearts.

Our books should be handled by consecrated workers, whom the Holy Spirit can use as His instrumentalities. Christ is our sufficiency, and we are to present the truth in humble simplicity, letting it bear its own savor of life unto life.

Humble, fervent prayer would do more in behalf of the circulation of our books than all the expensive embellishments in the world. If the workers will turn their attention to that which is true and living and real; if they will pray for, believe for, and trust in the Holy Spirit, His power will be poured upon them in strong, heavenly currents, and right and lasting impressions will be made upon the human heart. Then pray and work, and work and pray, and the Lord will work with you.

Every canvasser has positive and constant need of the angelic ministration; for he has an important work to do, a work that he cannot do in his own strength. Those who are born again, who are willing to be guided by the Holy Spirit, doing in Christ's way that which they can do, those who will work as if they could see the heavenly universe watching them, will be accompanied and instructed by holy angels, who will go before them to the dwellings of the people, preparing the way for them. Such help is far above all the advantages which expensive embellishments are supposed to give.

When men realize the times in which we are living,

they will work as in the sight of heaven. The canvasser will handle those books that bring light and strength to the soul. He will drink in the spirit of those books and will put his whole soul into the work of presenting them to the people. His strength, his courage, his success, will depend on how fully the truth presented in the books is woven into his own experience and developed in his character. When his own life is thus molded, he can go forward, representing to others the sacred truth he is handling. Imbued with the Spirit of God he will gain a deep, rich experience, and heavenly angels will give him success in the work.

To our canvassers, to all whom God has entrusted with talents that they may co-operate with Him, I would say: Pray, oh, pray for a deeper experience. Go forth with your hearts softened and subdued by a study of the precious truths that God has given us for this time. Drink deeply of the water of salvation, that it may be in your hearts as a living spring, flowing forth to refresh souls ready to perish. God will then give wisdom to enable you to impart aright. He will make you channels for communicating His blessings. He will help you to reveal His attributes by imparting to others the wisdom and understanding that He has imparted to you.

I pray the Lord that you may understand this subject in its length and breadth and depth, and that you may feel your responsibility to represent the character of Christ by patience, by courage, and by steadfast integrity. "And the peace of God, which passeth all understanding, shall guard your hearts and your thoughts in Christ Jesus." Philippians 4: 7, R. V.

THE CANVASSER A GOSPEL WORKER

THE intelligent, God-fearing, truth-loving canvasser should be respected; for he occupies a position equal to that of the gospel minister. Many of our young ministers and those who are fitting for the ministry would, if truly converted, do much good by working in the canvassing field. And by meeting the people and presenting to them our publications they would gain an experience which they cannot gain by simply preaching. As they went from house to house they could converse with the people, carrying with them the fragrance of Christ's life. In thus endeavoring to bless others they would themselves be blessed; they would obtain an experience in faith; their knowledge of the Scriptures would greatly increase; and they would be constantly learning how to win souls for Christ.

All our ministers should feel free to carry with them books to dispose of wherever they go. Wherever a minister goes, he can leave a book in the family where he stays, either selling it or giving it to them. Much of this work was done in the early history of the message. Ministers acted as colporteurs, using the means obtained from the sale of the books to help in the advancement of the work in places where help was needed. These can speak intelligently in regard to this method of work; for they have had an experience in this line.

Let none think that it belittles a minister of the gospel to engage in canvassing as a means of carrying truth to the people. In doing this work he is laboring in the same manner as did the apostle Paul, who says: "Ye know, from the first day that I came into Asia, after what manner I have been with you at all seasons, serving the Lord with all humility of mind, and with many tears, and temptations, which befell me by the lying in wait of the Jews: and how I kept back nothing that was profitable unto you, but have showed you, and have taught you publicly, and from house to house, testifying both to the Jews, and also to the Greeks, repentance toward God, and faith toward our Lord Jesus Christ." Acts 20: 18-21. The eloquent Paul, to whom God manifested Himself in a wonderful manner, went from house to house in all humility of mind, and with many tears and temptations.

All who desire an opportunity for true ministry, and who will give themselves unreservedly to God, will find in the canvassing work opportunities to speak upon many things pertaining to the future, immortal life. The experience thus gained will be of the greatest value to those who are fitting themselves for the ministry. It is the accompaniment of the Holy Spirit of God that prepares workers, both men and women, to become pastors to the flock of God. As they cherish the thought that Christ is their Companion, a holy awe, a sacred joy, will be felt by them amid all their trying experiences and all their tests. They will learn how to pray as they work. They will be educated in patience, kindness, affability, and helpfulness. They will practice true Christian courtesy, bearing in mind that Christ, their Companion, cannot approve of harsh, unkind words or feelings. Their words will be purified. The power of speech will be regarded as a precious talent, lent them to do a high and holy work. The human agent will learn how to represent the divine Companion with whom he is associated. To that unseen Holy One he will show respect and reverence because he is wearing His yoke and is learning His pure, holy ways. Those who have faith in this divine Attendant will develop. They will be gifted with power to clothe the message of truth with a sacred beauty.

There are some who are adapted to the work of the colporteur and who can accomplish more in this line than by preaching. If the Spirit of Christ dwells in their hearts, they will find opportunity to present His word to others and to direct minds to the special truths for this time. Men suited to this work undertake it; but some injudicious minister flatters them that their gifts should be employed in preaching instead of in the work of the colporteur. Thus they are influenced to get a license to preach, and the very ones who might have been trained to make good missionaries to visit families at their homes, to talk and pray with them, are turned away from a work for which they are fitted, to make poor ministers, and the field where so much labor is needed and where so much good might be accomplished is neglected.

The preaching of the word is a means by which the Lord has ordained that His warning message shall be given to the world. In the Scriptures the faithful teacher is represented as a shepherd of the flock of God. He is to be respected and his work appreciated. Genuine medical missionary work is bound up with the ministry, and the canvassing work is to be a part both of the medical missionary work and of the ministry. To those who are engaged in this work I would say: As you visit the people, tell them that you are a gospel worker and that you love the Lord. Do not seek a home in a hotel, but stay at a private house and become acquainted with the family. Christ was sowing the seeds of truth wherever He was, and as His followers you can witness for the Master, doing a most precious work in fireside labor. In thus coming close to the people you will often find those who are sick and discouraged. If you are pressing close to the side of Christ, wearing His yoke, you will daily learn of Him how to carry messages of peace and comfort to the sorrowing and disappointed, the sad and broken-hearted. You can point the discouraged ones to the word of God and take the sick to the Lord in prayer. As you pray, speak to Christ as you would to a trusted, much-loved friend. Maintain a sweet, free, pleasant dignity, as a child of God. This will be recognized.

Canvassers should be able to give instruction in regard to the treatment of the sick. They should learn the simple methods of hygienic treatment. Thus they may work as medical missionaries, ministering to the souls and the bodies of the suffering. This work should now be going forward in all parts of the world. Thus multitudes might be blessed by the prayers and instruction of God's servants.

We need to realize the importance of the canvassing work as one great means of finding out those who are in peril and bringing them to Christ. Canvassers should never be prohibited from speaking of the love of Christ, from telling their experience in their service for the Master. They should be free to speak or to pray with those who are awakened. The simple story of Christ's love for man will open doors for them, even to the homes of unbelievers.

As the canvasser visits the people at their homes, he will often have opportunity to read to them from the Bible or from books that teach the truth. When he discovers those who are searching for truth he can hold Bible readings with them. These Bible readings are just what the people need. God will use in His service those who thus show a deep interest in perishing souls. Through them He will impart light to those who are ready to receive instruction.

Some who labor in the canvassing field have a zeal that is not according to knowledge. Because of their lack of wisdom, because they have been so much inclined to act the minister and theologian, it has been almost a necessity to place restrictions upon our canvassers. When the Lord's voice calls, "Whom shall I send, and who will go for Us?" the Divine Spirit puts it into hearts to respond: "Here am I; send me." Isaiah 6:8. But bear in mind that the live coal from the altar must first touch your lips. Then the words you speak will be wise and holy words. Then you will have wisdom to know what to say and what to leave unsaid. You will not try to reveal your smartness as theologians. You will be careful not to arouse a combative spirit or excite prejudice by introducing controverted points of doctrine. You will find enough to talk about that will not excite opposition, but that will open the heart to desire a deeper knowledge of God's word.

The Lord desires you to be soul winners; therefore, while you should not force doctrinal points upon the people, you should "be ready always to give an answer to every man that asketh you a reason of the hope that is in you with meekness and fear." 1 Peter 3:15. Why fear? Fear lest your words should savor of self-importance, lest unadvised words be spoken, lest the words and manner should not be after Christ's likeness. Connect firmly with Christ, and present the truth as it is in Him. Hearts cannot fail to be touched by the story of the atonement. As you learn the meekness and lowliness of Christ, you will know what you should say to the people; for the Holy Spirit will tell you what words to speak. Those who realize the necessity of keeping the heart under the control of the Holy Spirit will be enabled to sow seed that will spring up unto eternal life. This is the work of the evangelistic canvasser.

UNITED EFFORT IN CANVASSING

PERFECT unity should exist among the workers who handle the books that are to flood the world with light. Wherever the canvassing work is presented among our people, let both the health books and the religious books be presented together as parts of a united work. The relation of the religious and the health books is presented to me as illustrated by the union of the warp and the woof to form a beautiful pattern and a perfect piece of work.

In the past the health books have not been handled with the interest which their importance demands. Though by a large class they have been highly appreciated, yet many have not thought it essential that they should go to the world. But what can be a better preparation for the coming of the Lord and for the reception of other truths essential to prepare a people for His coming than to arouse the people to see the evils of this age and to stir them to reformation from self-indulgent and unhealthful habits? Is not the world in need of being aroused on the subject of health reform? Are not the people in need of the truths presented in the health books? A different sentiment from that which has heretofore prevailed regarding the health works should be entertained by many of our canvassers in the field.

Divisions and distinct parties should not be seen among our canvassers and general agents. All should be interested in the sale of the books treating upon the health question as well as in the sale of the distinctively religious works. The line is not to be drawn that certain books only are to occupy the attention of the canvassers. There must be perfect unity, a well-balanced, symmetrical development of the work in all its parts.

(326)

The indifference with which the health books have been treated by many is an offense to God. To separate the health work from the great body of the work is not in His order. Present truth lies in the work of health reform as verily as in other features of gospel work. No one branch when separated from others can be a perfect whole.

The gospel of health has able advocates, but their work has been made very hard because so many ministers, presidents of conferences, and others in positions of influence have failed to give the question of health reform its proper attention. They have not recognized it in its relation to the work of the message as the right arm of the body. While very little respect has been shown to this department by many of the people, and by some of the ministers, the Lord has shown His regard for it by giving it abundant prosperity. When properly conducted, the health work is an entering wedge, making a way for other truths to reach the heart. When the third angel's message is received in its fullness, health reform will be given its place in the councils of the conference, in the work of the church, in the home, at the table, and in all the household arrangements. Then the right arm will serve and protect the body.

But while the health work has its place in the promulgation of the third angel's message, its advocates must not in any way strive to make it take the place of the message. The health books should occupy their proper position, but the circulation of these books is only one of many lines in the great work to be done. The glowing impressions sometimes given to the canvasser in regard to the health books must not result in excluding from the field other important books that should come before the people. Those who have charge of the canvassing work should be men who can discern the relation of each part of the work to the great whole. Let them give due attention to the circulation of the health books, but not make this line so prominent as to draw men away from other lines of vital interest, thus excluding the books that bear the special message of truth to the world.

Just as much education is necessary for the handling of the religious books as for the handling of those treating upon the question of health and temperance. Just as much should be said in regard to the work of canvassing for books containing spiritual food, just as much effort should be made to encourage and educate workers to circulate the books containing the third angel's message, as is said and done to develop workers for the health books.

The one class of books will always make a place for the other. Both are essential, and both should occupy the field at the same time. Each is the complement of the other and can in nowise take its place. Both treat on subjects of highest value, and both must act their part in the preparation of the people of God for these last days. Both should stand as present truth to enlighten, to arouse, to convince. Both should blend in the work of sanctifying and purifying the churches that are looking and waiting for the coming of the Son of God in power and great glory.

Let each publisher and general agent work enthusiastically to encourage the agents now in the field and to hunt up and train new workers. Let each strengthen and build up the work as much as possible without weakening the work of others. Let all be done in brotherly love and without selfishness.

REVIVAL OF THE CANVASSING WORK

THE importance of the canvassing work is kept ever before me. This work has not of late had the life infused into it which was once given by the agents who made it their specialty. Canvassers have been called from their evangelistic work to engage in other labor. This is not as it should be. Many of our canvassers, if truly converted and consecrated, can accomplish more in this line than in any other in bringing the truth for this time before the people.

We have the word of God to show that the end is near. The world is to be warned, and as never before we are to be laborers with Christ. The work of warning has been entrusted to us. We are to be channels of light to the world, imparting to others the light we receive from the great Light Bearer. The words and works of all men are to be tried. Let us not be backward now. That which is to be done in warning the world must be done without delay. Let not the canvassing work be left to languish. Let the books containing the light on present truth be placed before as many as possible.

The presidents of our conferences and others in responsible positions have a duty to do in this matter, that the different branches of our work may receive equal attention. Canvassers are to be educated and trained to do the work required in selling the books upon present truth which the people need. There is need of men of deep Christian experience, men of well-balanced minds, strong, well-educated men, to engage in this work. The Lord desires those to take hold of the canvassing work who are capable of educating others, who can awaken in promising young men and women an interest in this line, leading them to take up the bookwork and handle it successfully. Some have the talent, education, and experience which would enable them to educate the youth for the canvassing work in such a way that much more would be accomplished than is now being done.

Those who have gained an experience in this work have a special duty to perform in teaching others. Educate, educate, educate young men and women to sell the books which the Lord by His Holy Spirit has stirred His servants to write. God desires us to be faithful in educating those who accept the truth, that they may believe to a purpose and work intelligently in the Lord's way. Let inexperienced persons be connected with experienced workers, that they may learn how to work. Let them seek God most earnestly. These may do a good work in canvassing if they will obey the words: "Take heed unto thyself, and unto the doctrine." 1 Timothy 4:16. Those who give evidence that they are truly converted, and who take up the canvassing work, will see that it is the best preparation for other lines of missionary labor.

If those who know the truth would practice it, methods would be devised for meeting the people where they are. It was the providence of God which in the beginning of the Christian church scattered the saints abroad, sending them out of Jerusalem into many parts of the world. The disciples of Christ did not stay in Jerusalem or in the cities near by, but they went beyond the limits of their own country into the great thoroughfares of travel, seeking for the lost that they might bring them to God. To-day the Lord desires to see His work carried forward in many places. We must not confine our labors to a few localities.

We must not discourage our brethren, weakening their hands so that the work which God desires to accomplish through them shall not be done. Let not too much time be occupied in fitting up men to do missionary work. Instruction is necessary, but let all remember that Christ is the Great Teacher and the Source of all true wisdom. Let young and old consecrate themselves to God, take up the work, and go forward, laboring in humility under the control of the Holy Spirit. Let those who have been in school go out into the field and put to a practical use the knowledge they have gained. If canvassers will do this, using the ability which God has given them, seeking counsel from Him, and combining the work of selling books with personal labor for the people, their talents will increase by exercise, and they will learn many practical lessons which they could not possibly learn in school. The education obtained in this practical way may properly be termed higher education.

There is no higher work than evangelistic canvassing, for it involves the performance of the highest moral duties. Those who engage in this work need always to be under the control of the Spirit of God. There must be no exalting of self. What have any of us that we did not receive from Christ? We must love as brethren, revealing our love by helping one another. We must be pitiful and courteous. We must press together, drawing in even cords. Only those who live the prayer of Christ, working it out in practical life, will stand the test that is to come upon all the world. Those who exalt self place themselves in Satan's power, preparing to receive his deceptions. The word of the Lord to His people is that we lift the standard higher and still higher. If we obey His voice, He will work with us, and our efforts will be crowned with success. In our work we shall receive rich blessings from on high and shall lay up treasure beside the throne of God.

If we only knew what is before us we would not be so

Now = SHAKING dilatory in the work of the Lord. We are in the shaking time, the time when everything that can be shaken will be shaken. The Lord will not excuse those who know the truth if they do not in word and deed obey His commands. If we make no effort to win souls to Christ we shall be held responsible for the work we might have done, but did not do because of our spiritual indolence. Those who belong to the Lord's kingdom must work earnestly for the saving of souls. They must do their part to bind up the law and seal it among the disciples.

The Lord designs that the light which He has given on the Scriptures shall shine forth in clear, bright rays; and it is the duty of our canvassers to put forth a strong, united effort that God's design may be accomplished. A great and important work is before us. The enemy of souls realizes this, and he is using every means in his power to lead the canvasser to take up some other line of work. This order of things should be changed. God calls the canvassers back to their work. He calls for volunteers who will put all their energies and enlightenment into the work, helping wherever there is opportunity. The Master calls for everyone to do the part given him according to his ability. Who will respond to the call? Who will go forth to labor in wisdom and grace and the love of Christ for those nigh and afar off? Who will sacrifice ease and pleasure, and enter the places of error, superstition, and darkness, working earnestly and perseveringly, speaking the truth in simplicity, praying in faith, doing house-to-house labor? Who at this time will go forth without the camp, imbued with the power of the Holy Spirit, bearing reproach for Christ's sake, opening the Scriptures to the people, and calling them to repentance?

God has His workmen in every age. The call of the hour is answered by the coming of the man. Thus when the divine Voice cries, "Whom shall I send, and who will go for Us?" the response will come, "Here am I; send me." Isaiah 6:8. Let all who labor effectually in the canvassing field feel in their hearts that they are doing the work of the Lord in ministering to souls who know not the truth for this time. They are sounding the note of warning in the highways and byways to prepare a people for the great day of the Lord, which is so soon to break upon the world. We have no time to lose. We must encourage this work. Who will go forth now with our publications? The Lord imparts a fitness for the work to every man and woman who will co-operate with divine power. All the requisite talent, courage, perseverance, faith, and tact will come as they put the armor on. A great work is to be done in our world, and human agencies will surely respond to the demand. The world must hear the warning. When the call comes, "Whom shall I send, and who will go for Us?" send back the answer clear and distinct, "Here am I; send me."

———

"In the morning sow thy seed, and in the evening withhold not thine hand: for thou knowest not whether shall prosper, either this or that, or whether they both shall be alike good." Ecclesiastes 11:6.

———

Selection of Canvassers. Some are better adapted than others for doing a certain work; therefore it is not correct to think that everyone can be a canvasser. Some have no special adaptability for this work; but they are not, because of this, to be regarded as faithless or unwilling. The Lord is not unreasonable in His requirements. The church is as a garden in which is a variety of flowers, each with its own peculiarities. Though in many respects all may differ, yet each has a value of its own.

God does not expect that with their different temperaments His people will each be prepared for any and every place. Let all remember that there are varied trusts. It is not the work of any man to prescribe the work of any other man contrary to his own convictions of duty. It is right to give counsel and suggest plans; but every man should be left free to seek direction from God, whose he is and whom he serves.

A Preparation for the Ministry. Some men whom God was calling to the work of the ministry have entered the field as canvassers. I have been instructed that this is an excellent preparation if their object is to disseminate light, to bring the truths of God's word directly to the home circle. In conversation the way will often be opened for them to speak of the religion of the Bible. If the work is entered upon as it should be, families will be visited, the workers will manifest Christian tenderness and love for souls, and great good will be the result. This will be an excellent experience for any who have the ministry in view.

Those who are fitting for the ministry can engage in no other occupation that will give them so large an experience as will the canvassing work.

Enduring Hardness. He who in his work meets with trials and temptations should profit by these experiences, learning to lean more decidedly upon God. He should feel his dependence every moment.

No complaint should be cherished in his heart or be

uttered by his lips. When successful, he should take no glory to himself, for his success is due to the working of God's angels upon the heart. And let him remember that both in the time of encouragement and the time of discouragement the heavenly messengers are always beside him. He should acknowledge the goodness of the Lord, praising Him with cheerfulness.

Christ laid aside His glory and came to this earth to suffer for sinners. If we meet with hardships in our work, let us look to Him who is the Author and Finisher of our faith. Then we shall not fail nor be discouraged. We shall endure hardness as good soldiers of Jesus Christ. Remember what He says of all true believers: "We are laborers together with God: ye are God's husbandry, ye are God's building." 1 Corinthians 3:9.

A Precious Experience. He who takes up the work of canvassing as he should must be both an educator and a student. While he tries to teach others he himself must learn to do the work of an evangelist. As canvassers go forth into the field with humble hearts, full of earnest activity, they will find many opportunities to speak a word in season to souls ready to die in discouragement. After laboring for these needy ones they will be able to say: "Ye were sometimes darkness, but now are ye light in the Lord." Ephesians 5:8. As they see the sinful course of others they can say: "Such were some of you: but ye are washed, but ye are sanctified, but ye are justified in the name of the Lord Jesus, and by the Spirit of our God." 1 Corinthians 6:11.

Those who work for God will meet with discouragement, but the promise is always theirs: "Lo, I am with you alway, even unto the end of the world." Matthew 28:20. God will give a most wonderful experience to those who will say: "I believe Thy promise; I will not fail nor become discouraged."

Reporting. Let those who gain such an experience in working for the Lord write an account of it for our papers, that others may be encouraged. Let the canvasser tell of the joy and blessing he has received in his ministry as an evangelist. These reports should find a place in our papers, for they are far-reaching in their influence. They will be as sweet fragrance in the church, a savor of life unto life. Thus it is seen that God works with those who co-operate with Him.

Example in Health Reform. In your association with unbelievers do not allow yourselves to be swerved from right principles. If you sit at their table, eat temperately and only of food that will not confuse the mind. Keep clear of intemperance. You cannot afford to weaken your mental or physical powers, lest you become unable to discern spiritual things. Keep your mind in such a condition that God can impress it with the precious truths of His word.

Thus you will have an influence upon others. Many try to correct the lives of others by attacking what they regard as wrong habits. They go to those whom they think in error, and point out defects, but do not put forth earnest, tactful effort in directing the mind to true principles. Such a course often fails of securing the desired results. In trying to correct others we too often arouse their combativeness, and thus do more harm than good. Do not watch others in order to point out their faults or errors. Teach by example. Let your self-denial and your victory over appetite be an illustration of obedience to right principles. Let your life bear witness to the sanctifying, ennobling influence of truth.

Of all the gifts that God has bestowed upon men, none is more precious than the gift of speech. If sanctified by the Holy Spirit, it is a power for good. It is with the tongue that we convince and persuade; with it we offer prayer and praise to God; and with it we convey rich thoughts of the Redeemer's love. By a right use of the gift of speech the canvasser can sow the precious seeds of truth in many hearts.

Integrity in Business. The work is halting because gospel principles are not obeyed by those who claim to be following Christ. The loose way in which some canvassers, both old and young, have performed their work shows that they have important lessons to learn. Much haphazard work has been presented before me. Some have trained themselves in deficient habits, and this deficiency has been brought into the work of God. The tract and missionary societies have been deeply involved in debt through the failure of canvassers to meet their indebtedness. Canvassers have felt that they were ill-treated if required to pay promptly for the books received from the publishing houses. Yet to require prompt remittal is the only way to carry on business.

Matters should be so arranged that canvassers shall have enough to live on without overdrawing. This door of temptation must be closed and barred. However honest a canvasser may be, circumstances will arise in his work which will be to him a sore temptation.

Laziness and indolence are not the fruit borne upon the Christian tree. No soul can practice prevarication or dishonesty in handling the Lord's goods and stand guiltless before God. All who do this are in action denying Christ. While they profess to keep and teach God's law, they fail to maintain its principles.

The Lord's goods should be handled with faithfulness. The Lord has entrusted men with life and health and reasoning powers, He has given them physical and mental strength to be exercised; and should not these gifts be faithfully and diligently employed to His name's glory? Have our brethren considered that they must give an account for all the talents placed in their possession? Have they traded wisely with their Lord's goods, or have they spent His substance recklessly, and are they written in heaven as unfaithful servants? Many are spending their Lord's money in riotous enjoyment, so called; they are not gaining an experience in self-denial, but spending money on vanities, and are failing to bear the cross after Jesus. Many who were privileged with precious, God-given opportunities have wasted their lives and are now found in suffering and want.

God calls for decided improvement to be made in the various branches of the work. The business done in connection with the cause of God must be marked with greater precision and exactness. There has not been firm, decided effort to bring about essential reform.

A Knowledge of Their Book. Canvassers should thoroughly acquaint themselves with the book they are handling and be able readily to call attention to the important chapters.

Colporteur Work. The canvasser should carry with him tracts, pamphlets, and small books to give to those who cannot buy. In this way the truth can be introduced into many homes.

Diligence. When the canvasser enters upon his work, he should not allow himself to be diverted, but should intelligently keep to the point with all diligence. And yet, while he is doing his canvassing, he should not be heedless of opportunities to help souls who are seeking for light and who need the consolation of the Scriptures. If the canvasser walks with God, if he prays for heavenly wisdom that he may do good and only good in his labor, he will be quick to discern his opportunities and the needs of the souls with whom he comes in contact. He will make the most of every opportunity for drawing souls to Christ. In the spirit of Christ he will be ready to speak a word to him that is weary.

———

By diligence in canvassing, by faithfully presenting to the people the cross of Calvary, the canvasser doubles his powers of usefulness. But while we present methods of work we cannot lay out an undeviating line in which everyone shall move, for circumstances alter cases. God will impress those whose hearts are open to truth and who are longing for guidance. He will say to His human agent: "Speak to this one or to that one of the love of Jesus." No sooner is the name of Jesus mentioned in love and tenderness than angels of God draw near to soften and subdue the heart.

Let canvassers be faithful students, learning how to make their work successful; and while thus employed, let them keep their eyes and ears and understanding open to receive wisdom from God, that they may know how to help those who are perishing for lack of a knowledge of Christ. Let every worker concentrate his energies and use his powers for the highest of all service, to recover men from the snare of Satan and bind them to God, making the chain of dependence through Jesus Christ fast to the throne encircled with the rainbow of promise.

Assurance of Success. A great and good work may be done by evangelistic canvassing. The Lord has given men tact and capabilities. Those who use these entrusted talents to His glory, weaving Bible principles into the web, will be given success. We are to work and pray, putting our trust in Him who will never fail.

Let canvassing evangelists give themselves up to be worked by the Holy Spirit. Let them by persevering prayer take hold of the power which comes from God, trusting in Him in living faith. His great and effectual influence will be with every true, faithful worker.

As God blesses the minister and the evangelist in their earnest efforts to place the truth before the people, so He will bless the faithful canvasser.

The humble, efficient worker who obediently responds to the call of God may be sure of receiving divine assistance. To feel so great and holy a responsibility is of itself elevating to the character. It calls into action the highest mental qualities, and their continued exercise strengthens and purifies mind and heart. The influence upon one's own life, as well as upon the life of others, is incalculable.

Careless spectators may not appreciate your work or see its importance. They may think it a losing business, a life of thankless labor and self-sacrifice. But the servant of Jesus sees it in the light shining from the cross. His sacrifices appear small in comparison with those of the blessed Master, and he is glad to follow in His steps. The success of his labor affords him the purest joy and is the richest recompense for a life of patient toil.

CAUTIONS AND COUNSELS

"Thine ears shall hear a word
behind thee, saying, This is
the way, walk ye in it."

SHOWING HOSPITALITY

THE Bible lays much stress upon the practice of hospitality. Not only does it enjoin hospitality as a duty, but it presents many beautiful pictures of the exercise of this grace and the blessings which it brings. Foremost among these is the experience of Abraham.

In the records of Genesis we see the patriarch at the hot summer noontide resting in his tent door under the shadow of the oaks of Mamre. Three travelers are passing near. They make no appeal for hospitality, solicit no favor; but Abraham does not permit them to go on their way unrefreshed. He is a man full of years, a man of dignity and wealth, one highly honored, and accustomed to command; yet on seeing these strangers he "ran to meet them from the tent door, and bowed himself toward the ground." Addressing the leader he said: "My Lord, if now I have found favor in Thy sight, pass not away, I pray Thee, from Thy servant." Genesis 18:2, 3. With his own hands he brought water that they might wash the dust of travel from their feet. He himself selected their food; while they were at rest under the cooling shade, Sarah his wife made ready for their entertainment, and Abraham stood respectfully beside them while they partook of his hospitality. This kindness he showed them simply as wayfarers, passing strangers, who might never come his way again. But, the entertainment over, his guests stood revealed. He had ministered not only to heavenly angels, but to their glorious Commander, his Creator, Redeemer, and King. And to Abraham the counsels of heaven were opened, and he was called "the friend of God."

Lot, Abraham's nephew, though he had made his home in Sodom, was imbued with the patriarch's spirit of kindness and hospitality. Seeing at nightfall two strangers at the city gate, and knowing the dangers sure to beset them in that wicked city, Lot insisted on bringing them to his home. To the peril that might result to himself and his household he gave no thought. It was a part of his lifework to protect the imperiled and to care for the homeless, and the deed performed in kindness to two unknown travelers brought angels to his home. Those whom he sought to protect, protected him. At nightfall he had led them for safety to his door; at the dawn they led him and his household forth in safety from the gate of the doomed city.

These acts of courtesy God thought of sufficient importance to record in His word; and more than a thousand years later they were referred to by an inspired apostle: "Be not forgetful to entertain strangers: for thereby some have entertained angels unawares." Hebrews 13:2.

The privilege granted Abraham and Lot is not denied to us. By showing hospitality to God's children we, too, may receive His angels into our dwellings. Even in our day, angels in human form enter the homes of men and are entertained by them. And Christians who live in the light of God's countenance are always accompanied by unseen angels, and these holy beings leave behind them a blessing in our homes.

"A lover of hospitality" is among the specifications given by the Holy Spirit as marking one who is to bear responsibility in the church. And to the whole church is given the injunction: "Use hospitality one to another without grudging. As every man hath received the gift, even so minister the same one to another, as good stewards of the manifold grace of God." 1 Peter 4:9, 10.

These admonitions have been strangely neglected. Even among those who profess to be Christians, true hospitality is little exercised. Among our own people the opportunity of showing hospitality is not regarded as it should be, as a privilege and blessing. There is altogether too little sociability, too little of a disposition to make room for two or three more at the family board, without embarrassment or parade. Some plead that "it is too much trouble." It would not be if you would say: "We have made no special preparation, but you are welcome to what we have." By the unexpected guest a welcome is appreciated far more than is the most elaborate preparation.

It is a denial of Christ to make preparation for visitors which requires time that rightly belongs to the Lord. In this we commit robbery of God. And we wrong others as well. In preparing an elaborate entertainment, many deprive their own families of needed attention, and their example leads others to follow the same course.

Needless worries and burdens are created by the desire to make a display in entertaining visitors. In order to prepare a great variety for the table, the housewife overworks; because of the many dishes prepared, the guests overeat; and disease and suffering, from overwork on the one hand and overeating on the other, are the result. These elaborate feasts are a burden and an injury.

But the Lord designs that we shall care for the interests of our brethren and sisters. The apostle Paul has given an illustration of this. To the church at Rome he says: "I commend unto you Phebe our sister, which is a servant of the church which is at Cenchrea: that ye receive her in the Lord, as becometh saints, and that ye assist her in whatsoever business she hath need of you: for she hath been a succorer of many, and of myself also." Romans 16:1, 2. Phebe entertained the apostle, and she was in a marked manner an entertainer of strangers who needed care. Her example should be followed by the churches of today.

God is displeased with the selfish interest so often manifested for "me and my family." Every family that cherishes this spirit needs to be converted by the pure principles exemplified in the life of Christ. Those who shut themselves up within themselves, who are unwilling to be drawn upon to entertain visitors, lose many blessings.

Some of our workers occupy positions where it is necessary for them often to entertain visitors, either their own brethren or strangers. It is urged by some that the conference should make an account of this, and that in addition to their regular wages they should be allowed a sufficient amount to cover this extra expense. But the Lord has given the work of entertaining to all His people. It is not in God's order for one or two to do the entertaining for a conference or a church, or for workers to be paid for entertaining their brethren. This is an invention born of selfishness, and angels of God make account of these things.

Those who travel from place to place as evangelists or missionaries in any line should receive hospitality from the members of the churches among whom they may labor. Brethren and sisters, make a home for these workers, even if it be at considerable personal sacrifice.

Christ keeps an account of every expense incurred in entertaining for His sake. He supplies all that is necessary for this work. Those who for Christ's sake entertain their brethren, doing their best to make the visit profitable both to their guests and to themselves, are recorded in heaven as worthy of special blessings.

Christ has given in His own life a lesson of hospitality. When surrounded by the hungry multitude beside the sea, He did not send them unrefreshed to their homes. He said to His disciples: "Give ye them to eat." Matthew 14: 16. And by an act of creative power He supplied food sufficient to satisfy their need. Yet how simple was the food provided! There were no luxuries. He who had all the resources of heaven at His command could have spread for the people a rich repast. But He supplied only that which would suffice for their need, that which was the daily food of the fisherfolk about the sea.

If men were today simple in their habits, living in harmony with nature's laws, there would be an abundant supply for all the needs of the human family. There would be fewer imaginary wants and more opportunity to work in God's ways.

Christ did not seek to attract men to Him by gratifying the desire for luxury. The simple fare He provided was an assurance not only of His power but of His love, of His tender care for them in the common needs of life. And while He fed them with the barley loaves, He gave them also to eat of the bread of life. Here is our example. Our fare may be plain and even scanty. Our lot may be shut in with poverty. Our resources may be no greater than were those of the disciples with the five loaves and the two fishes. Yet as we come in contact with those in need, Christ bids us: "Give ye them to eat." We are to impart of that which we have; and as we give, Christ will see that our lack is supplied.

In this connection read the story of the widow of Sarepta. To this woman in a heathen land God sent His servant in time of famine to ask for food. "And she said, As the Lord thy God liveth, I have not a cake, but an handful of meal in a barrel, and a little oil in a cruse: and, behold, I am gathering two sticks, that I may go in and dress it for me and my son, that we may eat it, and die. And Elijah said unto her, Fear not; go and do as thou hast said: but make me thereof a little cake first, and bring it unto me, and after make for thee and for thy son. For thus saith the Lord God of Israel, The barrel of meal shall not waste, neither shall the cruse of oil fail, until the day that the Lord sendeth rain upon the earth. And she went and did according to the saying of Elijah." 1 Kings 17: 12-15.

Wonderful was the hospitality shown to God's prophet by this Phoenician woman, and wonderfully were her faith and generosity rewarded. "She, and he, and her house, did eat many days. And the barrel of meal wasted not, neither did the cruse of oil fail, according to the word of the Lord, which He spake by Elijah. And it came to pass after these things, that the son of the woman, the mistress of the house, fell sick; and his sickness was so sore that there was no breath left in him. And she said unto Elijah, What have I to do with thee, O thou man of God? art thou come unto me to call my sin to remembrance, and to slay my son? And he said unto her, Give me thy son. And he took him out of her bosom, and carried him up into a loft, where he abode, and laid him upon his own bed. . . . And he stretched himself upon the child three times, and cried unto the Lord. . . . And the Lord heard the voice of Elijah; and the soul of the child came into him again, and he revived. And Elijah took the child, and brought him down out of the chamber into the house, and delivered him unto his mother: and Elijah said, See, thy son liveth. And the woman said to Elijah, Now by this I know that thou art a man of God, and that the word of the Lord in thy mouth is truth." Verses 15-24.

God has not changed. His power is no less now than in the days of Elijah. And no less sure now than when spoken by our Saviour is the promise that Christ has given: "He that receiveth a prophet in the name of a prophet shall receive a prophet's reward." Matthew 10:41.

To His faithful servants today as well as to His first disciples Christ's words apply: "He that receiveth you receiveth Me, and he that receiveth Me receiveth Him that sent Me." Verse 40. No act of kindness shown in His name will fail to be recognized and rewarded. And in the same tender recognition Christ includes even the feeblest and lowliest of the family of God. "Whosoever shall give to drink," He says, "unto one of these little ones"—those who are as children in their faith and their knowledge of Christ—"a cup of cold water only in the name of a disciple, verily I say unto you, he shall in nowise lose his reward." Verse 42.

Poverty need not shut us out from showing hospitality. We are to impart what we have. There are those who struggle for a livelihood and who have great difficulty in making their income meet their necessities; but they love Jesus in the person of His saints and are ready to show hospitality to believers and unbelievers, trying to make their visits profitable. At the family board and the family altar the guests are made welcome. The season of prayer makes its impression on those who receive entertainment, and even one visit may mean the saving of a soul from death. For this work the Lord makes a reckoning, saying: "I will repay."

Brethren and sisters, invite to your homes those who are in need of entertainment and kindly attention. Make no parade; but, as you see their necessity, take them in and show them genuine Christian hospitality. There are precious privileges in social intercourse.

"Man doth not live by bread only," and as we impart to others our temporal food, so we are to impart hope and courage and Christlike love. We are "to comfort them which are in any trouble, by the comfort wherewith we ourselves are comforted of God." 2 Corinthians 1:4. And the assurance is ours: "God is able to make all grace abound toward you; that ye, always having all sufficiency in all things, may abound to every good work."

We are in a world of sin and temptation; all around us are souls perishing out of Christ, and God wants us to labor for them in every way possible. If you have a pleasant home, invite to it the youth who have no home, those who are in need of help, who long for sympathy and kind words, for respect and courtesy. If you desire to bring them to Christ, you must show your love and respect for them as the purchase of His blood.

In the providence of God we are associated with those who are inexperienced, with many who need pity and compassion. They need succor, for they are weak. Young men need help. In the strength of Him whose loving-kindness is exercised toward the helpless, the ignorant, and those counted as the least of His little ones, we must labor for their future welfare, for the shaping of Christian character. The very ones who need help the most will at times try our patience sorely. "Take heed that ye despise not one of these little ones," Christ says, "for I say unto you, That in heaven their angels do always behold the face of My Father which is in heaven." Matthew 18:10. And to those who minister to these souls, the Saviour declares: "Inasmuch as ye have done it unto one of the least of these My brethren, ye have done it unto Me." Matthew 25:40.

The brows of those who do this work will wear the crown of sacrifice. But they will receive their reward. In heaven we shall see the youth whom we helped, those whom we invited to our homes, whom we led from temptation. We shall see their faces reflecting the radiance of the glory of God. "They shall see His face; and His name shall be in their foreheads." Revelation 22:4.

THE OBSERVANCE OF THE SABBATH

GREAT blessings are enfolded in the observance of the Sabbath, and God desires that the Sabbath day shall be to us a day of joy. There was joy at the institution of the Sabbath. God looked with satisfaction upon the work of His hands. All things that He had made He pronounced "very good." Genesis 1:31. Heaven and earth were filled with rejoicing. "The morning stars sang together, and all the sons of God shouted for joy." Job 38:7. Though sin has entered the world to mar His perfect work, God still gives to us the Sabbath as a witness that One omnipotent, infinite in goodness and mercy, created all things. Our heavenly Father desires through the observance of the Sabbath to preserve among men a knowledge of Himself. He desires that the Sabbath shall direct our minds to Him as the true and living God, and that through knowing Him we may have life and peace.

When the Lord delivered His people Israel from Egypt and committed to them His law, He taught them that by the observance of the Sabbath they were to be distinguished from idolaters. It was this that made the distinction between those who acknowledge the sovereignty of God and those who refuse to accept Him as their Creator and King. "It is a sign between Me and the children of Israel forever," the Lord said. "Wherefore the children of Israel shall keep the Sabbath, to observe the Sabbath throughout their generations, for a perpetual covenant." Exodus 31:17, 16.

As the Sabbath was the sign that distinguished Israel when they came out of Egypt to enter the earthly Canaan, so it is the sign that now distinguishes God's people as they come out from the world to enter the heavenly rest. The Sabbath is a sign of the relationship existing between God and His people, a sign that they honor His law. It distinguishes between His loyal subjects and transgressors.

From the pillar of cloud Christ declared concerning the Sabbath: "Verily My Sabbaths ye shall keep: for it is a sign between Me and you throughout your generations; that ye may know that I am the Lord that doth sanctify you." Exodus 31:13. The Sabbath given to the world as the sign of God as the Creator is also the sign of Him as the Sanctifier. The power that created all things is the power that re-creates the soul in His own likeness. To those who keep holy the Sabbath day it is the sign of sanctification. True sanctification is harmony with God, oneness with Him in character. It is received through obedience to those principles that are the transcript of His character. And the Sabbath is the sign of obedience. He who from the heart obeys the fourth commandment will obey the whole law. He is sanctified through obedience.

To us as to Israel the Sabbath is given "for a perpetual covenant." To those who reverence His holy day the Sabbath is a sign that God recognizes them as His chosen people. It is a pledge that He will fulfill to them His covenant. Every soul who accepts the sign of God's government places himself under the divine, everlasting covenant. He fastens himself to the golden chain of obedience, every link of which is a promise.

The fourth commandment alone of all the ten contains the seal of the great Lawgiver, the Creator of the heavens and the earth. Those who obey this commandment take upon themselves His name, and all the blessings it involves are theirs. "The Lord spake unto Moses, saying, Speak unto Aaron and unto his sons, saying, On this wise ye shall bless the children of Israel saying unto them,

"The Lord bless thee, and keep thee:
 The Lord make His face shine upon thee, and be gracious unto thee:
 The Lord lift up His countenance upon thee, and give thee peace.
 And they shall put My Name upon the children of Israel;
 And I will bless them." Numbers 6:22-27.

Through Moses was given also the promise: "The Lord shall establish thee an holy people unto Himself, as He hath sworn unto thee, if thou shalt keep the commandments of the Lord thy God, and walk in His ways. And all people of the earth shall see that thou art called by the name of the Lord. . . . And the Lord shall make thee the head, and not the tail; and thou shalt be above only, and thou shalt not be beneath; if that thou hearken unto the commandments of the Lord thy God, which I command thee this day, to observe and to do them." Deuteronomy 28:9-13.

The psalmist, speaking by the Holy Spirit, says:

"O come, let us sing unto the Lord:
 Let us make a joyful noise to the Rock of our salvation. . . .
 For the Lord is a great God,
 And a great King above all gods.
 In His hand are the deep places of the earth:
 The strength of the hills is His also.
 The sea is His, and He made it:
 And His hands formed the dry land.
 O come, let us worship and bow down:
 Let us kneel before the Lord our Maker.
 For He is our God."
"It is He that hath made us, and we are His;
 We are His people, and the sheep of His pasture."
                      Psalms 95:1-7; 100:3, R. V.

These promises given to Israel are also for God's people today. They are the messages which the Sabbath brings to us.

REFORM IN SABBATH OBSERVANCE

The Sabbath is a golden clasp that unites God and His people. But the Sabbath command has been broken. God's holy day has been desecrated. The Sabbath has been torn from its place by the man of sin, and a common working day has been exalted in its stead. A breach has been made in the law, and this breach is to be repaired. The true Sabbath is to be exalted to its rightful position as God's rest day. In the fifty-eighth chapter of Isaiah is outlined the work which God's people are to do. They are to magnify the law and make it honorable, to build up the old waste places, and to raise up the foundations of many generations. To those who do this work God says: "Thou shalt be called, The repairer of the breach, The restorer of paths to dwell in. If thou turn away thy foot from the Sabbath, from doing thy pleasure on My holy day; and call the Sabbath a delight, the holy of the Lord, honorable; and shalt honor Him, not doing thine own ways, nor finding thine own pleasure, nor speaking thine own words: then shalt thou delight thyself in the Lord; and I will cause thee to ride upon the high places of the earth, and feed thee with the heritage of Jacob thy father: for the mouth of the Lord hath spoken it." Verses 12-14.

The Sabbath question is to be the issue in the great final conflict in which all the world will act a part. Men have honored Satan's principles above the principles that rule in the heavens. They have accepted the spurious sabbath, which Satan has exalted as the sign of his authority. But God has set His seal upon His royal requirement. Each sabbath institution bears the name of its author, an ineffaceable mark that shows the authority of each. It is our work to lead the people to understand this. We are to show them that it is of vital consequence whether they bear the mark of God's kingdom or the mark of the kingdom of rebellion, for they acknowledge themselves subjects of the kingdom whose mark they bear. God has called us to uplift the standard of His downtrodden Sabbath. How important, then, that our example in Sabbathkeeping should be right.

In establishing new churches, ministers should give careful instruction as to the proper observance of the Sabbath. We must be guarded, lest the lax practices that prevail among Sundaykeepers shall be followed by those who profess to observe God's holy rest day. The line of demarcation is to be made clear and distinct between those who bear the mark of God's kingdom and those who bear the sign of the kingdom of rebellion.

Far more sacredness is attached to the Sabbath than is given it by many professed Sabbathkeepers. The Lord has been greatly dishonored by those who have not kept the Sabbath according to the commandment, either in the letter or in the spirit. He calls for a reform in the observance of the Sabbath.

PREPARATION FOR THE SABBATH

At the very beginning of the fourth commandment the Lord said, "Remember." He knew that amid the multitude of cares and perplexities man would be tempted to excuse himself from meeting the full requirement of the law, or would forget its sacred importance. Therefore He said: "Remember the Sabbath day, to keep it holy." Exodus 20:8.

All through the week we are to have the Sabbath in mind and be making preparation to keep it according to the commandment. We are not merely to observe the Sabbath as a legal matter. We are to understand its spiritual bearing upon all the transactions of life. All who regard the Sabbath as a sign between them and God, showing that He is the God who sanctifies them, will represent the principles of His government. They will bring into daily practice the laws of His kingdom. Daily it will be their prayer that the sanctification of the Sabbath may rest upon them. Every day they will have the companionship of Christ and will exemplify the perfection of His character. Every day their light will shine forth to others in good works.

In all that pertains to the success of God's work, the very first victories are to be won in the home life. Here the preparation for the Sabbath must begin. Throughout the week let parents remember that their home is to be a school in which their children shall be prepared for the courts above. Let their words be right words. No words which their children should not hear are to escape their lips. Let the spirit be kept free from irritation. Parents, during the week live as in the sight of a holy God, who has given you children to train for Him. Train for Him the little church in your home, that on the Sabbath all may be prepared to worship in the Lord's sanctuary. Each morning and evening present your children to God as His blood-bought heritage. Teach them that it is their highest duty and privilege to love and serve God.

Parents should be particular to make the worship of God an object lesson for their children. Passages of Scripture should be more often on their lips, especially those passages that prepare the heart for religious service. The precious words might well be often repeated: "My soul, wait thou only upon God; for my expectation is from Him." Psalm 62:5.

When the Sabbath is thus remembered, the temporal will not be allowed to encroach upon the spiritual. No duty pertaining to the six working days will be left for the Sabbath. During the week our energies will not be so exhausted in temporal labor that on the day when the Lord rested and was refreshed we shall be too weary to engage in His service.

While preparation for the Sabbath is to be made all through the week, Friday is to be the special preparation day. Through Moses the Lord said to the children of

Israel: "Tomorrow is the rest of the holy Sabbath unto the Lord: bake that which ye will bake today, and seethe that ye will seethe; and that which remaineth over lay up for you to be kept until the morning." "And the people went about, and gathered it [the manna], and ground it in mills, or beat it in a mortar, and baked it in pans, and made cakes of it." Exodus 16:23; Numbers 11:8. There was something to be done in preparing the heaven-sent bread for the children of Israel. The Lord told them that this work must be done on Friday, the preparation day. This was a test to them. God desired to see whether or not they would keep the Sabbath holy.

This direction from the lips of Jehovah is for our instruction. The Bible is a perfect guide, and if its pages are prayerfully studied by hearts willing to understand, none need err upon this question.

Many need instruction as to how they should appear in the assembly for worship on the Sabbath. They are not to enter the presence of God in the common clothing worn during the week. All should have a special Sabbath suit, to be worn when attending service in God's house. While we should not conform to worldly fashions, we are not to be indifferent in regard to our outward appearance. We are to be neat and trim, though without adornment. The children of God should be pure within and without.

On Friday let the preparation for the Sabbath be completed. See that all the clothing is in readiness and that all the cooking is done. Let the boots be blacked and the baths be taken. It is possible to do this. If you make it a rule you can do it. The Sabbath is not to be given to the repairing of garments, to the cooking of food, to pleasure seeking, or to any other worldly employment. Before the setting of the sun let all secular work be laid aside and all secular papers be put out of sight. Parents,

explain your work and its purpose to your children, and
let them share in your preparation to keep the Sabbath
according to the commandment.

We should jealously guard the edges of the Sabbath.
Remember that every moment is consecrated, holy time.
Whenever it is possible, employers should give their
workers the hours from Friday noon until the beginning
of the Sabbath. Give them time for preparation, that
they may welcome the Lord's day with quietness of
mind. By such a course you will suffer no loss even in
temporal things.

There is another work that should receive attention
on the preparation day. On this day all differences between brethren, whether in the family or in the church,
should be put away. Let all bitterness and wrath and
malice be expelled from the soul. In a humble spirit,
"confess your faults one to another, and pray one for
another, that ye may be healed." James 5:16.

Before the Sabbath begins, the mind as well as the
body should be withdrawn from worldly business. God
has set His Sabbath at the end of the six working days,
that men may stop and consider what they have gained
during the week in preparation for the pure kingdom
which admits no transgressor. We should each Sabbath
reckon with our souls to see whether the week that has
ended has brought spiritual gain or loss.

It means eternal salvation to keep the Sabbath holy
unto the Lord. God says: "Them that honor Me I will
honor." 1 Samuel 2:30.

THE SABBATH IN THE HOME

Before the setting of the sun let the members of the
family assemble to read God's word, to sing and pray.
There is need of reform here, for many have been remiss. We need to confess to God and to one another.

We should begin anew to make special arrangements that every member of the family may be prepared to honor the day which God has blessed and sanctified.

Let not the precious hours of the Sabbath be wasted in bed. On Sabbath morning the family should be astir early. If they rise late, there is confusion and bustle in preparing for breakfast and Sabbath school. There is hurrying, jostling, and impatience. Thus unholy feelings come into the home. The Sabbath, thus desecrated, becomes a weariness, and its coming is dreaded rather than loved.

We should not provide for the Sabbath a more liberal supply or a greater variety of food than for other days. Instead of this the food should be more simple, and less should be eaten, in order that the mind may be clear and vigorous to comprehend spiritual things. Overeating befogs the brain. The most precious words may be heard and not appreciated, because the mind is confused by an improper diet. By overeating on the Sabbath, many have done more than they think to dishonor God.

While cooking upon the Sabbath should be avoided, it is not necessary to eat cold food. In cold weather let the food prepared the day before be heated. And let the meals, though simple, be palatable and attractive. Provide something that will be regarded as a treat, something the family do not have every day.

At family worship let the children take a part. Let all bring their Bibles and each read a verse or two. Then let some familiar hymn be sung, followed by prayer. For this, Christ has given a model. The Lord's Prayer was not intended to be repeated merely as a form, but it is an illustration of what our prayers should be—simple, earnest, and comprehensive. In a simple petition tell the Lord your needs and express gratitude for His mercies. Thus you invite Jesus as a welcome guest into your home and heart. In the family long prayers concerning remote objects are not in place. They make the hour of prayer a weariness, when it should be regarded as a privilege and blessing. Make the season one of interest and joy.

The Sabbath school and the meeting for worship occupy only a part of the Sabbath. The portion remaining to the family may be made the most sacred and precious season of all the Sabbath hours. Much of this time parents should spend with their children. In many families the younger children are left to themselves to find entertainment as best they can. Left alone, the children soon become restless and begin to play or engage in some kind of mischief. Thus the Sabbath has to them no sacred significance.

In pleasant weather let parents walk with their children in the fields and groves. Amid the beautiful things of nature tell them the reason for the institution of the Sabbath. Describe to them God's great work of creation. Tell them that when the earth came from His hand, it was holy and beautiful. Every flower, every shrub, every tree, answered the purpose of its Creator. Everything upon which the eye rested was lovely and filled the mind with thoughts of the love of God. Every sound was music in harmony with the voice of God. Show that it was sin which marred God's perfect work; that thorns and thistles, sorrow and pain and death, are all the result of disobedience to God. Bid them see how the earth, though marred with the curse of sin, still reveals God's goodness. The green fields, the lofty trees, the glad sunshine, the clouds, the dew, the solemn stillness of the night, the glory of the starry heavens, and the moon in its beauty all bear witness of the Creator. Not a drop of rain falls, not a ray of light is shed on our unthankful world, but it testifies to the forbearance and love of God.

Tell them of the way of salvation; how "God so loved

the world, that He gave His only-begotten Son, that whosoever believeth in Him should not perish, but have everlasting life." John 3:16. Let the sweet story of Bethlehem be repeated. Present before the children Jesus, as a child obedient to His parents, as a youth faithful and industrious, helping to support the family. Thus you can teach them that the Saviour knows the trials, perplexities, and temptations, the hopes and joys, of the young, and that He can give them sympathy and help. From time to time read with them the interesting stories in Bible history. Question as to what they have learned in the Sabbath school, and study with them the next Sabbath's lesson.

As the sun goes down, let the voice of prayer and the hymn of praise mark the close of the sacred hours and invite God's presence through the cares of the week of labor.

Thus parents can make the Sabbath, as it should be, the most joyful day of the week. They can lead their children to regard it as a delight, the day of days, the holy of the Lord, honorable.

I counsel you, my brethren and sisters: "Remember the Sabbath day, to keep it holy." If you desire your children to observe the Sabbath according to the commandment, you must teach them by both precept and example. The deep engraving of truth in the heart is never wholly effaced. It may be obscured, but can never be obliterated. The impressions made in early life will be seen in afteryears. Circumstances may occur to separate the children from their parents and their home, but as long as they live the instruction given in childhood and youth will be a blessing.

TRAVELING ON THE SABBATH

If we desire the blessing promised to the obedient, we must observe the Sabbath more strictly. I fear that we often travel on this day when it might be avoided. In harmony with the light which the Lord has given in regard to the observance of the Sabbath, we should be more careful about traveling on the boats or cars on this day. In these matters we should set a right example before our children and youth. In order to reach the churches that need our help, and to give them the message that God desires them to hear, it may be necessary for us to travel on the Sabbath; but so far as possible we should secure our tickets and make all necessary arrangements on some other day. When starting on a journey we should make every possible effort to plan so as to avoid reaching our destination on the Sabbath.

When compelled to travel on the Sabbath we should try to avoid the company of those who would draw our attention to worldly things. We should keep our minds stayed upon God and commune with Him. Whenever there is opportunity we should speak to others in regard to the truth. We should always be ready to relieve suffering and to help those in need. In such cases God desires that the knowledge and wisdom He has given us should be put to use. But we should not talk about matters of business or engage in any common, worldly conversation. At all times and in all places God requires us to prove our loyalty to Him by honoring the Sabbath.

SABBATH MEETINGS

Christ has said: "Where two or three are gathered together in My name, there am I in the midst of them." Matthew 18: 20. Wherever there are as many as two or three believers, let them meet together on the Sabbath to claim the Lord's promise.

The little companies assembled to worship God on His holy day have a right to claim the rich blessing of Jehovah. They should believe that the Lord Jesus is

an honored guest in their assemblies. Every true wor-
shiper who keeps holy the Sabbath should claim the
promise: "That ye may know that I am the Lord that
doth sanctify you." Exodus 31:13.

The preaching at our Sabbath meetings should generally be short. Opportunity should be given for those who
love God to express their gratitude and adoration.

When the church is without a minister, someone
should be appointed as leader of the meeting. But it is
not necessary for him to preach a sermon or to occupy
a large part of the time of service. A short, interesting
Bible reading will often be of greater benefit than a
sermon. And this can be followed by a meeting for
prayer and testimony.

Those who occupy a leading position in the church
should not exhaust their physical and mental strength
through the week so that on the Sabbath they are unable
to bring the vivifying influence of the gospel of Christ
into the meeting. Do less temporal, everyday labor, but
do not rob God by giving Him, on the Sabbath, service
which He cannot accept. You should not be as men who
have no spiritual life. The people need your help on the
Sabbath. Give them food from the word. Bring your
choicest gifts to God on His holy day. Let the precious
life of the soul be given to Him in consecrated service.

Let none come to the place of worship to take a nap.
There should be no sleeping in the house of God. You
do not fall asleep when engaged in your temporal business, because you have an interest in your work. Shall
we allow the service which involves eternal interests to
be placed on a lower level than the temporal affairs of
life?

When we do this we miss the blessing which the Lord
designs us to have. The Sabbath is not to be a day of
useless idleness. Both in the home and in the church

a spirit of service is to be manifested. He who gave us six days for our temporal work has blessed and sanctified the seventh day and set it apart for Himself. On this day He will in a special manner bless all who consecrate themselves to His service.

All heaven is keeping the Sabbath, but not in a listless, do-nothing way. On this day every energy of the soul should be awake, for are we not to meet with God and with Christ our Saviour? We may behold Him by faith. He is longing to refresh and bless every soul.

Everyone should feel that he has a part to act in making the Sabbath meetings interesting. You are not to come together simply as a matter of form, but for the interchange of thought, for the relation of your daily experiences, for the expression of thanksgiving, for the utterance of your sincere desire for divine enlightenment, that you may know God, and Jesus Christ, whom He has sent. Communing together in regard to Christ will strengthen the soul for life's trials and conflicts. Never think that you can be Christians and yet withdraw yourselves within yourselves. Each one is a part of the great web of humanity, and the experience of each will be largely determined by the experience of his associates.

We do not obtain a hundredth part of the blessing we should obtain from assembling together to worship God. Our perceptive faculties need sharpening. Fellowship with one another should make us glad. With such a hope as we have, why are not our hearts all aglow with the love of God?

We must carry to every religious gathering a quickened spiritual consciousness that God and His angels are there, co-operating with all true worshipers. As you enter the place of worship, ask the Lord to remove all evil from your heart. Bring to His house only that which He can bless. Kneel before God in His temple, and consecrate to

Him His own, which He has purchased with the blood of Christ. Pray for the speaker or the leader of the meeting. Pray that great blessing may come through the one who is to hold forth the word of life. Strive earnestly to lay hold of a blessing for yourself.

God will bless all who thus prepare themselves for His service. They will understand what it means to have the assurance of the Spirit because they have received Christ by faith.

The place of worship may be very humble, but it is no less acknowledged by God. To those who worship God in spirit and in truth and in the beauty of holiness it will be as the gate of heaven. The company of believers may be few in number, but in God's sight they are very precious. By the cleaver of truth they have been taken as rough stones from the quarry of the world and have been brought into the workshop of God to be hewed and shaped. But even in the rough they are precious in the sight of God. The ax, the hammer, and the chisel of trial are in the hands of One who is skillful; they are used, not to destroy, but to work out the perfection of every soul. As precious stones, polished after the similitude of a palace, God designs us to find a place in the heavenly temple.

God's appointments and grants in our behalf are without limit. The throne of grace is itself the highest attraction because occupied by One who permits us to call Him Father. But God did not deem the principle of salvation complete while invested only with His own love. By His appointment He has placed at His altar an Advocate clothed with our nature. As our Intercessor, His office work is to introduce us to God as His sons and daughters. Christ intercedes in behalf of those who have received Him. To them He gives power, by virtue of His own merits, to become members of the royal family, children of the heavenly King. And the Father demonstrates His infinite love for Christ, who paid our ransom with His blood, by receiving and welcoming Christ's friends as His friends. He is satisfied with the atonement made. He is glorified by the incarnation, the life, death, and mediation of His Son.

No sooner does the child of God approach the mercy seat than he becomes the client of the great Advocate. At his first utterance of penitence and appeal for pardon Christ espouses his case and makes it His own, presenting the supplication before the Father as His own request.

As Christ intercedes in our behalf, the Father lays open all the treasures of His grace for our appropriation, to be enjoyed and to be communicated to others. "Ask in My name," Christ says; "I do not say that I will pray the Father for you; for the Father Himself loveth you, because you have loved Me. Make use of My name. This will give your prayers efficiency, and the Father will give you the riches of His grace; wherefore, 'ask, and ye shall receive, that your joy may be full.'" John 16: 24.

God desires His obedient children to claim His blessing and to come before Him with praise and thanksgiving. God is the Fountain of life and power. He can make the wilderness a fruitful field for the people that keep His commandments, for this is for the glory of His name. He has done for His chosen people that which should inspire every heart with thanksgiving, and it grieves Him that so little praise is offered. He desires to have a stronger expression from His people, showing that they know they have reason for joy and gladness.

The dealings of God with His people should be often repeated. How frequently were the waymarks set up by the Lord in His dealings with ancient Israel! Lest they should forget the history of the past, He commanded Moses to frame these events into song, that parents might teach them to their children. They were to gather up memorials and to lay them up in sight. Special pains were taken to preserve them, that when the children should inquire concerning these things, the whole story might be repeated. Thus the providential dealings and the marked goodness and mercy of God in His care and deliverance of His people were kept in mind. We are exhorted to "call to remembrance the former days, in which, after ye were illuminated, ye endured a great fight of afflictions." Hebrews 10:32. For His people in this generation the Lord has wrought as a wonder-working God. The past history of the cause of God needs to be often brought before the people, young and old. We need often to recount God's goodness and to praise Him for His wonderful works.

While we are exhorted not to forsake the assembling of ourselves together, these assemblies are not to be merely for our own refreshing. We are to be inspired with greater zeal to impart the consolation we have received. It is our duty to be very jealous for the glory of God and to bring no evil report, even by the sadness of the countenance or by ill-advised words, as if the requirements of God were a restriction upon our liberty. Even in this world of sorrow, disappointment, and sin the Lord desires us to be cheerful, and strong in His strength. The whole person is privileged to bear a decided testimony in every line. In features, in temper, in words, in character, we are to witness that the service of God is good. Thus we proclaim that "the law of the Lord is perfect, converting the soul." Psalm 19:7.

The bright and cheerful side of our religion will be represented by all who are daily consecrated to God. We should not dishonor God by the mournful relation of trials that appear grievous. All trials that are received as educators will produce joy. The whole religious life will be uplifting, elevating, ennobling, fragrant with good words and works. The enemy is well pleased to have souls depressed, downcast, mourning and groaning; he wants just such impressions made as to the effect of our faith. But God designs that the mind shall take no low level. He desires every soul to triumph in the keeping power of the Redeemer. The psalmist says: "Give unto the Lord, O ye mighty, give unto the Lord glory and strength. Give unto the Lord the glory due unto His name; worship the Lord in the beauty of holiness." "I will extol Thee, O Lord; for Thou hast lifted me up, and hast not made my foes to rejoice over me. O Lord my God, I cried unto Thee, and Thou hast healed me. . . . Sing unto the Lord, O ye saints of His, and give thanks at the remembrance of His holiness." Psalms 29:1, 2; 30:1-4.

The church of God below is one with the church of God above. Believers on the earth and the beings in heaven who have never fallen constitute one church. Every heavenly intelligence is interested in the assemblies of the saints who on earth meet to worship God. In the inner court of heaven they listen to the testimony of the witnesses for Christ in the outer court on earth, and the praise and thanksgiving from the worshipers below is taken up in the heavenly anthem, and praise and rejoicing sound through the heavenly courts because Christ has not died in vain for the fallen sons of Adam. While angels drink from the fountainhead, the saints on earth drink of the pure streams flowing from the throne, the streams that make glad the city of our God. Oh, that we could all realize the nearness of heaven to earth! When the earthborn children know it not, they have angels of light as their companions. A silent witness guards every soul that lives, seeking to draw that soul to Christ. As long as there is hope, until men resist the Holy Spirit to their eternal ruin, they are guarded by heavenly intelligences. Let us all bear in mind that in every assembly of the saints below are angels of God, listening to the testimonies, songs, and prayers. Let us remember that our praises are supplemented by the choirs of the angelic host above.

Then as you meet from Sabbath to Sabbath, sing praises to Him who has called you out of darkness into His marvelous light. "Unto Him that loved us, and washed us from our sins in His own blood" let the heart's adoration be given. Let the love of Christ be the burden of the speaker's utterance. Let it be expressed in simple language in every song of praise. Let the inspiration of the Spirit of God dictate your prayers. As the word of life is spoken, let your heartfelt response testify that you receive the message as from heaven. This is very old-fashioned, I know; but it will be a thank offering to God for the bread of life given to the hungry soul. This response to the inspiration of the Holy Spirit will be a strength to your own soul and an encouragement to others. It will give some evidence that there are in God's building living stones that emit light.

While we review, not the dark chapters in our experience, but the manifestations of God's great mercy and unfailing love, we shall praise far more than complain. We shall talk of the loving faithfulness of God as the true, tender, compassionate shepherd of His flock, which He has declared that none shall pluck out of His hand. The language of the heart will not be selfish murmuring and repining. Praise, like clear-flowing streams, will come from God's truly believing ones. "Goodness and mercy shall follow me all the days of my life: and I will dwell in the house of the Lord forever." "Thou shalt guide me with Thy counsel, and afterward receive me to glory. Whom have I in heaven but Thee? and there is none upon earth that I desire beside Thee." Psalms 23:6; 73:24, 25.

Why not awake the voice of our spiritual songs in the travels of our pilgrimage? Why not come back to our simplicity and life of fervor? The reason why we are not more joyful is that we have lost our first love. Let us then be zealous and repent, lest the candlestick be moved out of its place.

The temple of God is opened in heaven, and the threshold is flushed with the glory which is for every church that will love God and keep His commandments. We need to study, to meditate, and to pray. Then we shall have spiritual eyesight to discern the inner courts of the celestial temple. We shall catch the themes of song and thanksgiving of the heavenly choir round about the throne. When Zion shall arise and shine, her light will be most penetrating, and precious songs of praise and thanksgiving will be heard in the assemblies of the saints. Murmuring and complaining over little disappointments and difficulties will cease. As we apply the golden eyesalve we shall see the glories beyond. Faith will cut through the heavy shadow of Satan, and we shall see our Advocate offering up the incense of His own merits in our behalf. When we see this as it is, as the Lord desires us to see it, we shall be filled with a sense of the immensity and diversity of the love of God.

God teaches that we should assemble in His house to cultivate the attributes of perfect love. This will fit the dwellers of earth for the mansions that Christ has gone to prepare for all who love Him. There they will assemble in the sanctuary from Sabbath to Sabbath, from one new moon to another, to unite in loftiest strains of song, in praise and thanksgiving to Him who sits upon the throne, and to the Lamb for ever and ever.

A REVIVAL IN HEALTH REFORM

OBEDIENCE TO PHYSICAL LAW

Since the laws of nature are the laws of God, it is plainly our duty to give these laws careful study. We should study their requirements in regard to our own bodies and conform to them. Ignorance in these things is sin.

"Know ye not that your bodies are the members of Christ?" "What? know ye not that your body is the temple of the Holy Ghost which is in you, which ye have of God, and ye are not your own? For ye are bought with a price: therefore glorify God in your body, and in your spirit, which are God's." 1 Corinthians 6: 15, 19, 20. Our bodies are Christ's purchased property, and we are not at liberty to do with them as we please. Man has done this. He has treated his body as if its laws had no penalty. Through perverted appetite its organs and powers have become enfeebled, diseased, and crippled. And these results which Satan has brought about by his own specious temptations he uses to taunt God with. He presents before God the human body that Christ has purchased as His property, and what an unsightly representation of his Maker man is! Because man has sinned against his body and has corrupted his ways, God is dishonored.

When men and women are truly converted, they will conscientiously regard the laws of life that God has established in their being, thus seeking to avoid physical, mental, and moral feebleness. Obedience to these laws must be made a matter of personal duty. We ourselves must suffer the ills of violated law. We must answer to God for our habits and practices. Therefore the question for us is not, "What will the world say?" but, "How shall I, claiming to be a Christian, treat the habitation God has given me? Shall I work for my highest temporal and spiritual good by keeping my body as a temple for the indwelling of the Holy Spirit, or shall I sacrifice myself to the world's ideas and practices?"

Healthful living must be made a family matter. Parents should awake to their God-given responsibilities. Let them study the principles of health reform and teach their children that the path of self-denial is the only path of safety. The mass of the inhabitants of the world by their disregard of physical law are destroying their power of self-control and unfitting themselves to appreciate eternal realities. Willingly ignorant of their own structure, they lead their children in the path of self-indulgence, thus preparing the way for them to suffer the penalty of the transgression of nature's laws. This is not taking a wise interest in the welfare of their families.

THE CHURCH AND HEALTH REFORM

There is a message regarding health reform to be borne in every church. There is a work to be done in every school. Neither principal nor teachers should be entrusted with the education of the youth until they have a practical knowledge of this subject. Some have felt at liberty to criticize and question and find fault with health reform principles of which they knew little by experience. They should stand shoulder to shoulder, heart to heart, with those who are working in right lines.

The subject of health reform has been presented in the churches; but the light has not been heartily received. The selfish, health-destroying indulgences of men and women have counteracted the influence of the message that is to prepare a people for the great day of God. If the churches expect strength, they must live the truth which God has given them. If the members of our churches disregard the light on this subject, they will reap the sure result in both spiritual and physical degeneracy. And the influence of these older church members will leaven those newly come to the faith. The Lord does not now work to bring many souls into the truth, because of the church members who have never been converted and those who were once converted but who have backslidden. What influence would these unconsecrated members have on new converts? Would they not make of no effect the God-given message which His people are to bear?

Let all examine their own practices to see if they are not indulging in that which is a positive injury to them. Let them dispense with every unhealthful gratification in eating and drinking. Some go to distant countries to seek a better climate; but wherever they may be, the stomach creates for them a malarious atmosphere. They bring upon themselves suffering that no one can alleviate. Let them bring their daily practice into harmony with nature's laws; and by doing as well as believing, an atmosphere may be created about both soul and body that will be a savor of life unto life.

Brethren, we are far behind. Many of the things which the church should do in order to be a living church are not done. Through the indulgence of perverted appetite many place themselves in such a condition of health that there is a constant warring against the soul's highest interests. The truth, though presented in clear lines, is not accepted. I wish to set this matter before every member of our churches. Our habits must be brought into conformity to the will of God. We are assured, "It is God which worketh in you," but man must do his part in controlling appetite and passion. The religious life requires the action of mind and heart in harmony with the divine forces. No man can of himself work out his own salvation, and God cannot do this work for him without his co-operation. But when man works earnestly, God works with him, giving him power to become a son of God.

———

When persons are spoken to on the subject of health, they often say: "We know a great deal better than we do." They do not realize that they are accountable for every ray of light in regard to their physical well-being, and that their every habit is open to the inspection of God. Physical life is not to be treated in a haphazard manner. Every organ, every fiber of the being, is to be sacredly guarded from harmful practices.

DIET

Our habits of eating and drinking show whether we are of the world or among the number whom the Lord by His mighty cleaver of truth has separated from the world. These are His peculiar people, zealous of good works. God has spoken in His word. In the case of Daniel and his three companions there are sermons upon health reform. God has spoken in the history of the children of Israel, from whom for their good He sought to withhold a flesh diet. He fed them with bread from heaven; "man did eat angels' food." But they encouraged their earthly appetite; and the more they centered their thoughts upon the fleshpots of Egypt, the more they hated the food which God gave them to keep them in health physically, mentally, and morally. They longed for the fleshpots, and in this they did just as many in our own time have done.

Many are suffering, and many are going into the grave, because of the indulgence of appetite. They eat what suits their perverted taste, thus weakening the digestive organs and injuring their power to assimilate the food that is to sustain life. This brings on acute disease, and too often death follows. The delicate organism of the body is worn out by the suicidal practices of those who ought to know better.

The churches should be stanch and true to the light which God has given. Each member should work intelligently to put away from his life practice every perverted appetite.

EXTREMES IN DIET

I know that many of our brethren are in heart and practice opposed to health reform. I advocate no extremes. But as I have been looking over my manuscripts I have seen the decided testimonies borne and the warnings of dangers that come to our people through imitating the customs and practices of the world in self-indulgence, gratification of appetite, and pride of apparel. My heart is sick and sad over the existing state of things. Some say that some of our brethren have pressed these questions too strongly. But because some may have acted indiscreetly in pressing their sentiments concerning health reform on all occasions, will any dare to keep back the truth on this subject? The people of the world are generally far in the opposite extreme of indulgence and intemperance in eating and drinking; and, as the result, lustful practices abound.

There are many now under the shadow of death who have prepared to do a work for the Master, but who have not felt that a sacred obligation rested upon them to observe the laws of health. The laws of the physical system are indeed the laws of God, but this fact seems to have been forgotten. Some have limited themselves to a diet that cannot sustain them in health. They have not provided nourishing food to take the place of injurious articles; and they have not considered that tact and ingenuity must be exercised in preparing food in the most healthful manner. The system must be properly nourished in order to perform its work. It is contrary to health reform, after cutting off the great variety of unwholesome dishes, to go to the opposite extreme, reducing the quantity and quality of the food to a low standard. Instead of health reform this is health deform.

TRUE TEMPERANCE

The apostle Paul writes: "Know ye not that they which run in a race run all, but one receiveth the prize? So run, that ye may obtain. And every man that striveth for the mastery is temperate in all things. Now they do it to obtain a corruptible crown; but we an incorruptible. I therefore so run, not as uncertainly; so fight I, not as one that beateth the air: but I keep under my body, and bring it into subjection: lest that by any means, when I have preached to others, I myself should be a castaway." 1 Corinthians 9:24-27.

There are many in the world who indulge pernicious habits. Appetite is the law that governs them, and because of their wrong habits the moral sense is clouded and the power to discern sacred things is to a great extent destroyed. But it is necessary for Christians to be strictly temperate. They should place their standard high. Temperance in eating, drinking, and dressing is essential. Principle should rule instead of appetite or fancy. Those who eat too much or whose food is of an objectionable quality are easily led into dissipation and into other "foolish and hurtful lusts, which drown men in destruction and perdition." 1 Timothy 6:9. The "laborers together with God" should use every jot of their influence to encourage the spread of true temperance principles.

It means much to be true to God. He has claims upon

all who are engaged in His service. He desires that mind and body be preserved in the best condition of health, every power and endowment under the divine control, and as vigorous as careful, strictly temperate habits can make them. We are under obligation to God to make an unreserved consecration of ourselves to Him, body and soul, with all the faculties appreciated as His entrusted gifts, to be employed in His service. All our energies and capabilities are to be constantly strengthened and improved during this probationary period. Only those who appreciate these principles, and have been trained to care for their bodies intelligently and in the fear of God, should be chosen to take responsibilities in this work. Those who have been long in the truth, yet who cannot distinguish between the pure principles of righteousness and the principles of evil, whose understanding in regard to justice, mercy, and the love of God is clouded, should be relieved of responsibilities. Every church needs a clear, sharp testimony, giving the trumpet a certain sound.

If we can arouse the moral sensibilities of our people on the subject of temperance, a great victory will be gained. Temperance in all things of this life is to be taught and practiced. Temperance in eating, drinking, sleeping, and dressing is one of the grand principles of the religious life. Truth brought into the sanctuary of the soul will guide in the treatment of the body. Nothing that concerns the health of the human agent is to be regarded with indifference. Our eternal welfare depends upon the use we make during this life of our time, strength, and influence.

David declared: "I am fearfully and wonderfully made." When God has given us such a habitation, why should not every apartment be carefully examined? The chambers of the mind and heart are the most important. Then, instead of living in the basement of the house, enjoying sensual and debasing pleasures, should we not open these beautiful chambers and invite the Lord Jesus to come in and dwell with us?

MINISTERS TO TEACH HEALTH REFORM

Our ministers should become intelligent on health reform. They need to become acquainted with physiology and hygiene; they should understand the laws that govern physical life and their bearing upon the health of mind and soul.

Thousands upon thousands know little of the wonderful body God has given them or of the care it should receive; and they consider it of more importance to study subjects of far less consequence. The ministers have a work to do here. When they take a right position on this subject, much will be gained. In their own lives and homes they should obey the laws of life, practicing right principles and living healthfully. Then they will be able to speak correctly on this subject, leading the people higher and still higher in the work of reform. Living in the light themselves, they can bear a message of great value to those who are in need of just such a testimony.

There are precious blessings and a rich experience to be gained if ministers will combine the presentation of the health question with all their labors in the churches. The people must have the light on health reform. This work has been neglected, and many are ready to die because they need the light which they ought to have and must have before they will give up selfish indulgences.

The presidents of our conferences need to realize that it is high time they were placing themselves on the right side of this question. Ministers and teachers are to give to others the light they have received. Their work in every line is needed. God will help them; He will strengthen His servants who stand firmly and will not be swayed from truth and righteousness in order to accommodate self-indulgence.

The work of educating in medical missionary lines is an advance step of great importance in awakening man to his moral responsibilities. Had the ministers taken hold of this work in its various departments in accordance with the light which God has given, there would have been a most decided reformation in eating, drinking, and dressing. But some have stood directly in the way of the advance of health reform. They have held the people back by their indifference or condemnatory remarks, or by pleasantries and jokes. They themselves and a large number of others have been sufferers unto death, but all have not yet learned wisdom.

It has been only by the most aggressive warfare that any advancement has been made. The people have been unwilling to deny self, unwilling to yield the mind and will to the will of God; and in their own sufferings, and in their influence on others, they have realized the sure result of such a course.

The church is making history. Every day is a battle and a march. On every side we are beset by invisible foes, and we either conquer through the grace given us by God or we are conquered. I urge that those who are taking a neutral position in regard to health reform be converted. This light is precious, and the Lord gives me the message to urge that all who bear responsibilities in any line in the work of God take heed that truth is in the ascendancy in the heart and life. Only thus can any meet the temptations they are sure to encounter in the world.

Why do some of our ministering brethren manifest so little interest in health reform? It is because instruction on temperance in all things is opposed to their practice of self-indulgence. In some places this has been the great stumbling block in the way of our bringing the people to investigate and practice and teach health reform. No man should be set apart as a teacher of the people while his own teaching or example contradicts the testimony God has given His servants to bear in regard to diet, for this will bring confusion. His disregard of health reform unfits him to stand as the Lord's messenger.

The light that the Lord has given on this subject in His word is plain, and men will be tested and tried in many ways to see if they will heed it. Every church, every family, needs to be instructed in regard to Christian temperance. All should know how to eat and drink in order to preserve health. We are amid the closing scenes of this world's history, and there should be harmonious action in the ranks of Sabbathkeepers. Those who stand aloof from the great work of instructing the people upon this question do not follow where the Great Physician leads the way. "If any man will come after Me," Christ said, "let him deny himself, and take up his cross, and follow Me." Matthew 16:24.

———

The Lord has presented before me that many, many will be rescued from physical, mental, and moral degeneracy through the practical influence of health reform.

Health talks will be given, publications will be multiplied. The principles of health reform will be received with favor, and many will be enlightened. The influences that are associated with health reform will commend it to the judgment of all who want light, and they will advance step by step to receive the special truths for this time. Thus truth and righteousness will meet together.

———

Life is a holy trust, which God alone can enable us to keep and to use to His glory. But He who formed the wonderful structure of the body will take special care to keep it in order if men do not work at cross-purposes with Him. Every talent entrusted to us He will help us to improve and use in accordance with the will of the Giver. Days, months, and years are added to our existence that we may improve our opportunities and advantages for working out our individual salvation, and by our unselfish life promoting the well-being of others. Thus may we build up the kingdom of Christ and make manifest the glory of God.

———

The gospel and the medical missionary work are to advance together. The gospel is to be bound up with the principles of true health reform. Christianity is to be brought into the practical life. Earnest, thorough reformatory work is to be done. True Bible religion is an outflowing of the love of God for fallen man. God's people are to advance in straightforward lines to impress the hearts of those who are seeking for truth, who desire to act their part aright in this intensely earnest age. We are to present the principles of health reform before the people, doing all in our power to lead men and women to see the necessity of these principles, and to practice them.

THE IMPORTANCE OF VOICE CULTURE

In all our work more attention should be given to the culture of the voice. We may have knowledge, but unless we know how to use the voice correctly, our work will be a failure. Unless we can clothe our ideas in appropriate language, of what avail is our education? Knowledge will be of little advantage to us unless we cultivate the talent of speech; but it is a wonderful power when combined with the ability to speak wise, helpful words, and to speak them in a way that will command attention.

Students who expect to become workers in the cause of God should be trained to speak in a clear, straightforward manner, else they will be shorn of half their influence for good. The ability to speak plainly and clearly, in full, round tones, is invaluable in any line of work. This qualification is indispensable in those who desire to become ministers, evangelists, Bible workers, or canvassers. Those who are planning to enter these lines of work should be taught to use the voice in such a way that when they speak to people about the truth, a decided impression for good will be made. The truth must not be marred by being communicated through defective utterance.

The canvasser who can speak clearly and distinctly about the merits of the book he wishes to sell will find this a great help in his work. He may have an opportunity to read a chapter of the book, and by the music of his voice and the emphasis placed on the words he can make the scene presented stand out as clearly before the mind of the listener as if it could actually be seen.

The one who gives Bible readings in the congregation or in the family should be able to read with a soft, musical cadence which will charm the hearers.

(380)

Ministers of the gospel should know how to speak with power and expression, making the words of eternal life so expressive and impressive that the hearers cannot but feel their weight. I am pained as I hear the defective voices of many of our ministers. Such ministers rob God of the glory He might have if they had trained themselves to speak the word with power.

No man should regard himself as qualified to enter the ministry until by persevering effort he has overcome every defect in his utterance. If he attempts to speak to the people without knowing how to use the talent of speech, half his influence is lost, for he has little power to hold the attention of a congregation.

Whatever his calling, every person should learn to control the voice, so that when something goes wrong, he will not speak in tones that stir the worst passions of the heart. Too often the speaker and the one addressed speak sharply and harshly. Sharp, dictatorial words, uttered in hard, rasping tones, have separated friends and resulted in the loss of souls.

Instruction in vocal culture should be given in the home. Parents should teach their children to speak so plainly that the listeners can understand every word. They should teach them to read the Bible with clear, distinct utterance in a way that will honor God. And let not those who kneel around the family altar put their faces in their hands close down to the chair when they address God. Let them lift up their heads and with holy awe speak to their heavenly Father, uttering their words in tones that can be heard.

Parents, train yourselves to speak in a way that will be a blessing to your children. Women need to be educated in this respect. Even the busy mothers, if they will, can cultivate the talent of speech and can teach their children to read and speak correctly. They can do this while they go about their work. It is never too late for us to improve. God calls upon parents to bring all the perfection possible into the home circle.

In the social meeting there is special need of clear, distinct utterance, that all may hear the testimonies borne and be benefited by them. Difficulties are removed and help is given as in social meeting God's people relate their experiences. But too often the testimonies are borne with faulty, indistinct utterance, and it is impossible to gain a correct idea of what is said. Thus the blessing is often lost.

Let those who pray and those who speak pronounce their words properly and speak in clear, distinct, even tones. Prayer, if properly offered, is a power for good. It is one of the means used by the Lord to communicate to the people the precious treasures of truth. But prayer is not what it should be, because of the defective voices of those who utter it. Satan rejoices when the prayers offered to God are almost inaudible. Let God's people learn how to speak and pray in a way that will properly represent the great truths they possess. Let the testimonies borne and the prayers offered be clear and distinct. Thus God will be glorified.

Let all make the most of the talent of speech. God calls for a higher, more perfect ministry. He is dishonored by the imperfect utterance of the one who by painstaking effort could become an acceptable mouthpiece for Him. The truth is too often marred by the channel through which it passes.

The Lord calls upon all who are connected with His service to give attention to the cultivation of the voice, that they may utter in an acceptable manner the great and solemn truths He has entrusted to them. Let none mar the truth by defective utterance. Let not those who have neglected to cultivate the talent of speech suppose that they are qualified to minister, for they have yet to obtain the power to communicate.

When you speak, let every word be full and well rounded, every sentence clear and distinct to the very last word. Many as they approach the end of a sentence lower the tone of the voice, speaking so indistinctly that the force of the thought is destroyed. Words that are worth speaking at all are worth speaking in a clear, distinct voice, with emphasis and expression. But never search for words that will give the impression that you are learned. The greater your simplicity, the better will your words be understood.

Young men and young women, has God placed in your hearts a desire to do service for Him? Then by all means cultivate the voice to the utmost of your ability so that you can make plain the precious truth to others. Do not fall into the habit of praying so indistinctly and in such a low tone that your prayers need an interpreter. Pray simply, but clearly and distinctly. To let the voice sink so low that it cannot be heard is no evidence of humility.

To those who are planning to enter God's work as ministers, I would say: Strive with determination to be perfect in speech. Ask God to help you to accomplish this great object. When in the congregation you offer prayer, remember that you are addressing God, and that He desires you to speak so that all who are present can hear and can blend their supplications with yours. A prayer uttered so hurriedly that the words are jumbled together is no honor to God and does the hearers no good. Let ministers and all who offer public prayer learn to pray in such a way that God will be glorified and the hearers will be blessed. Let them speak slowly and distinctly and in tones loud enough to be heard by all so that the people may unite in saying, Amen.

GIVING TO GOD HIS OWN

THE Lord has given His people a message for this time. It is presented in the third chapter of Malachi. How could the Lord present His requirements in a clearer or more forcible manner than He has done in this chapter?

All should remember that God's claims upon us underlie every other claim. He gives to us bountifully, and the contract which He has made with man is that a tenth of his possessions shall be returned to God. The Lord graciously entrusts to His stewards His treasures, but of the tenth He says: This is Mine. Just in proportion as God has given His property to man, so man is to return to God a faithful tithe of all his substance. This distinct arrangement was made by Jesus Christ Himself.

This work involves solemn and eternal results, and it is too sacred to be left to human impulse. We should not feel free to deal with this matter as we choose. In answer to the claims of God, regular reserves should be set apart as sacred to His work.

THE FIRST FRUITS

Besides the tithe the Lord demands the first fruits of all our increase. These He has reserved in order that His work in the earth may be amply sustained. The Lord's servants are not to be limited to a meager supply. His messengers should not be handicapped in their work of holding forth the word of life. As they teach the truth they should have means to invest for the advancement of the work, which must be done at the right time in order to have the best and most saving influence. Deeds of mercy must be done; the poor and suffering must be aided. Gifts and offerings should be appropriated for this purpose. Especially in new fields, where the standard of truth has never yet been uplifted, this work must be done. If all the professed people of God, both old and young, would do their duty, there would be no dearth in the treasury. If all would pay a faithful tithe and devote to the Lord the first fruits of their increase, there would be a full supply of funds for His work. But the law of God is not respected or obeyed, and this has brought a pressure of want.

REMEMBER THE POOR

Every extravagance should be cut out of our lives, for the time we have for work is short. All around us we see want and suffering. Families are in need of food; little ones are crying for bread. The houses of the poor lack proper furniture and bedding. Many live in mere hovels which are almost destitute of conveniences. The cry of the poor reaches to heaven. God sees; God hears. But many glorify themselves. While their fellow men are poor and hungry, suffering for want of food, they expend much on their tables and eat far more than they require. What an account men will by and by have to render for their selfish use of God's money! Those who disregard the provision God has made for the poor will find not only that they have robbed their fellow men, but that in robbing them they have robbed God and have embezzled His goods.

ALL THINGS BELONG TO GOD

All the good that man enjoys comes because of the mercy of God. He is the great and bountiful Giver. His love is manifest to all in the abundant provision made for man. He has given us probationary time in which to form characters for the courts above. And it is not because He needs anything that He asks us to reserve a part of our possessions for Him.

The Lord created every tree in Eden pleasant to the eyes and good for food, and He bade Adam and Eve freely enjoy His bounties. But He made one exception. Of the tree of knowledge of good and evil they were not to eat. This tree God reserved as a constant reminder of His ownership of all. Thus He gave them opportunity to demonstrate their faith and trust in Him by their perfect obedience to His requirements.

So it is with God's claims upon us. He places His treasures in the hands of men, but requires that one tenth shall be faithfully laid aside for His work. He requires this portion to be placed in His treasury. It is to be rendered to Him as His own; it is sacred and is to be used for sacred purposes, for the support of those who carry the message of salvation to all parts of the world. He reserves this portion, that means may ever be flowing into His treasure house and that the light of truth may be carried to those who are nigh and those who are afar off. By faithfully obeying this requirement we acknowledge that all belongs to God.

And has not the Lord a right to demand this of us? Did He not give His only-begotten Son because He loved us and desired to save us from death? And shall not our gratitude offerings flow into His treasury to be drawn therefrom to advance His kingdom in the earth? Since God is the owner of all our goods, shall not gratitude to Him prompt us to make freewill offerings and thank offerings, thus acknowledging His ownership of soul, body, spirit, and property? Had God's plan been followed, means would now be flowing into His treasury; and funds to enable ministers to enter new fields, and workers to unite with ministers in lifting up the standard of truth in the dark places of the earth, would be abundant.

WITHOUT EXCUSE

It is a heaven-appointed plan that men should return to the Lord His own; and this is so plainly stated that men and women have no excuse for misunderstanding or evading the duties and responsibilities God has laid upon them. Those who claim that they cannot see this to be their duty, reveal to the heavenly universe, to the church, and to the world that they do not want to see this plainly stated requirement. They think that by following the Lord's plan they would detract from their own possessions. In the covetousness of their selfish souls they desire to have the whole capital, both principal and interest, to use for their own benefit.

God lays His hand upon all man's possessions, saying: I am the owner of the universe, and these goods are Mine. The tithe you have withheld I reserve for the support of My servants in their work of opening the Scriptures to those who are in the regions of darkness, who do not understand My law. In using My reserve fund to gratify your own desires you have robbed souls of the light which I made provision for them to receive. You have had opportunity to show loyalty to Me, but you have not done this. You have robbed Me; you have stolen My reserve fund. "Ye are cursed with a curse." Malachi 3:9.

ANOTHER OPPORTUNITY

The Lord is long-suffering and gracious, and to those who have done this wickedness He gives another opportunity. "Return unto Me," He says, "and I will return unto you." But they say: "Wherein shall we return?" Verse 7. Their means have been made to flow in channels of self-service and self-glorification as if their goods were their own and not lent treasures. Their perverted consciences have become so hard and unimpressible that they do not see the great wickedness they have done in so hedging up the way that the cause of truth could not advance.

Man, finite man, though using for himself the talents which God has reserved to publish salvation, to send the glad news of a Saviour's love to perishing souls, though hedging up the way by his selfishness, inquires: "Wherein have we robbed Thee?" God answers: "In tithes and offerings. Ye are cursed with a curse: for ye have robbed Me, even this whole nation." Verses 8, 9. The whole world is engaged in robbing God. With the money He has lent them, men indulge in dissipation, in amusements, revelings, feasting, and disgraceful indulgences. But God says: "I will come near to you to judgment." Verse 5. The whole world will have an account to settle in that great day when everyone shall receive sentence according to his deeds.

THE BLESSING

God pledges Himself to bless those who obey His commandments. "Bring ye all the tithes into the store-house, that there may be meat in Mine house, and prove Me now herewith, saith the Lord of hosts, if I will not open you the windows of heaven, and pour you out a blessing, that there shall not be room enough to receive it. And I will rebuke the devourer for your sakes, and he shall not destroy the fruits of your ground; neither shall your vine cast her fruit before the time in the field, saith the Lord of hosts. And all nations shall call you blessed: for ye shall be a delightsome land, saith the Lord of hosts." Verses 10-12.

With these words of light and truth before them, how dare men neglect so plain a duty? How dare they disobey God when obedience to His requirements means His blessing in both temporal and spiritual things, and disobedience means the curse of God? Satan is the destroyer. God cannot bless those who refuse to be faithful stewards. All He can do is to permit Satan to accomplish his destroying work. We see calamities of every kind and in every degree coming upon the earth, and why? The Lord's restraining power is not exercised. The world has disregarded the word of God. They live as though there were no God. Like the inhabitants of the Noachic world, they refuse to have any thought of God. Wickedness prevails to an alarming extent, and the earth is ripe for the harvest.

THE COMPLAINERS

"Your words have been stout against Me, saith the Lord. Yet ye say, What have we spoken so much against Thee? Ye have said, It is vain to serve God: and what profit is it that we have kept His ordinance, and that we have walked mournfully before the Lord of hosts? And now we call the proud happy; yea, they that work wickedness are set up; yea, they that tempt God are even delivered." Verses 13-15. Those who withhold from God His own make these complaints. The Lord asks them to prove Him by bringing their tithe into His storehouse to see whether He will not pour them out a blessing. But they cherish rebellion in their hearts and complain of God; at the same time they rob Him and embezzle His goods. When their sin is presented before them, they say: I have had adversity; my crops have been poor; but the wicked are prospered; it does not pay to keep the ordinance of the Lord.

But God does not want any to walk mournfully before Him. Those who thus complain of God have brought their adversity on themselves. They have robbed God, and His cause has been hindered because the money that should have flowed into His treasury was used for selfish purposes. They showed their disloyalty to God by failing to carry out His prescribed plan. When God prospered them, and they were asked to give Him His portion, they shook their heads and could not see that it was their duty. They closed the eyes of their understanding, that they might not see. They withheld the Lord's money and hindered the work which He designed to have done. God was not honored by the use made of His entrusted goods. Therefore He let the curse fall upon them, permitting the spoiler to destroy their fruits and to bring calamities upon them.

"THEY THAT FEARED THE LORD"

In Malachi 3:16 an opposite class is brought to view, a class that meet together, not to find fault with God, but to speak of His glory and tell of His mercies. These have been faithful in their duty. They have given to the Lord His own. Testimonies are borne by them that make the heavenly angels sing and rejoice. These have no complaints to make against God. Those who walk in the light, who are faithful and true in doing their duty, are not heard complaining and finding fault. They speak words of courage, hope, and faith. It is those who serve themselves, who do not give God His own, that complain.

"They that feared the Lord spake often one to another: and the Lord hearkened, and heard it, and a book of remembrance was written before Him for them that feared the Lord, and that thought upon His name. And they shall be Mine, saith the Lord of hosts, in that day when I make up My jewels; and I will spare them, as a man spareth his own son that serveth him. Then shall ye return, and discern between the righteous and the wicked, between him that serveth God and him that serveth Him not." Verses 16-18.

————

The reward of whole-souled liberality is the leading of mind and heart to a closer fellowship with the Spirit.

The man who has been unfortunate, and finds himself in debt, should not take the Lord's portion to cancel his debts to his fellow men. He should consider that in these transactions he is being tested, and that in reserving the Lord's portion for his own use he is robbing the Giver. He is debtor to God for all that he has, but he becomes a double debtor when he uses the Lord's reserved fund in paying debts to human beings. "Unfaithfulness to God" is written against his name in the books of heaven. He has an account to settle with God for appropriating the Lord's means for his own convenience. And the want of principle shown in his misappropriation of God's means will be revealed in his management of other matters. It will be seen in all matters connected with his own business. The man who will rob God is cultivating traits of character that will cut him off from admittance into the family of God above.

A selfish use of riches proves one unfaithful to God, and unfits the steward of means for the higher trust of heaven.

There are channels everywhere through which benevolence may flow. Needs are constantly arising, missions are handicapped for want of means. These must be abandoned unless God's people awake to the true state of things. Wait not until your death to make your will, but dispose of your means while you live.

CHRIST IN ALL THE BIBLE

The power of Christ, the crucified Saviour, to give eternal life, should be presented to the people. We should show them that the Old Testament is as verily the gospel in types and shadows as the New Testament is in its unfolding power. The New Testament does not present a new religion; the Old Testament does not present a religion to be superseded by the New. The New Testament is only the advancement and unfolding of the Old. Abel was a believer in Christ, and was as verily saved by His power as was Peter or Paul. Enoch was a representative of Christ as surely as was the beloved disciple John. Enoch walked with God, and he was not, for God took him. To him was committed the message of the second coming of Christ. "And Enoch also, the seventh from Adam, prophesied of these, saying, Behold, the Lord cometh with ten thousands of His saints, to execute judgment upon all." Jude 14, 15. The message preached by Enoch and his translation to heaven were a convincing argument to all who lived in his time. These things were an argument that Methuselah and Noah could use with power to show that the righteous could be translated.

That God who walked with Enoch was our Lord and Saviour Jesus Christ. He was the light of the world then just as He is now. Those who lived then were not without teachers to instruct them in the path of life; for Noah and Enoch were Christians. The gospel is given in precept in Leviticus. Implicit obedience is required now, as then. How essential it is that we understand the importance of this word!

The question is asked: What is the cause of the dearth in the church? The answer is: We allow our minds to

(392)

be drawn away from the word. If the word of God were eaten as the food for the soul, if it were treated with respect and deference, there would be no necessity for the many and repeated testimonies that are borne. The simple declarations of Scripture would be received and acted upon.

Its living principles are as the leaves of the tree of life for the healing of the nations.

The word of the living God is not merely written, but spoken. The Bible is God's voice speaking to us, just as surely as though we could hear it with our ears. If we realized this, with what awe would we open God's word, and with what earnestness would we search its precepts! The reading and contemplation of the Scriptures would be regarded as an audience with the Infinite One.

When Satan presses his suggestions upon our minds, we may, if we cherish a "Thus saith the Lord," be drawn into the secret pavilion of the Most High.

Many fail of imitating our holy Pattern because they study so little the definite features of that character. So many are full of busy plans, always active; and there is no time or place for the precious Jesus to be a close, dear companion. They do not refer every thought and action to Him, inquiring: "Is this the way of the Lord?" If they did they would walk with God, as did Enoch.

OUR ATTITUDE TOWARD THE CIVIL AUTHORITIES

By some of our brethren many things have been spoken and written that are interpreted as expressing antagonism to government and law. It is a mistake thus to lay ourselves open to misunderstanding. It is not wise to find fault continually with what is done by the rulers of government. It is not our work to attack individuals or institutions. We should exercise great care lest we be understood as putting ourselves in opposition to the civil authorities. It is true that our warfare is aggressive, but our weapons are to be those found in a plain "Thus saith the Lord." Our work is to prepare a people to stand in the great day of God. We should not be turned aside to lines that will encourage controversy or arouse antagonism in those not of our faith.

We should not work in a manner that will mark us out as seeming to advocate treason. We should weed out from our writings and utterances every expression that, taken by itself, could be so misrepresented as to make it appear antagonistic to law and order. Everything should be carefully considered, lest we place ourselves on record as encouraging disloyalty to our country and its laws. We are not required to defy authorities. There will come a time when, because of our advocacy of Bible truth, we shall be treated as traitors; but let not this time be hastened by unadvised movements that stir up animosity and strife.

The time will come when unguarded expressions of a denunciatory character, that have been carelessly spoken or written by our brethren, will be used by our enemies to condemn us. These will not be used merely to condemn those who made the statements, but will be charged upon the whole body of Adventists. Our accusers will say that on such and such a day one of our responsible men said thus and so against the administration of the laws of this government. Many will be astonished to see how many things have been cherished and remembered that will give point to the arguments of our adversaries. Many will be surprised to hear their own words strained into a meaning that they did not intend them to have. Then let our workers be careful to speak guardedly at all times and under all circumstances. Let all beware lest by reckless expressions they bring on a time of trouble before the great crisis which is to try men's souls.

The less we make direct charges against authorities and powers, the greater work we shall be able to accomplish, both in America and in foreign countries. Foreign nations will follow the example of the United States. Though she leads out, yet the same crisis will come upon our people in all parts of the world.

It is our work to magnify and exalt the law of God. The truth of God's holy word is to be made manifest. We are to hold up the Scriptures as the rule of life. In all modesty, in the spirit of grace, and in the love of God we are to point men to the fact that the Lord God is the Creator of the heavens and the earth, and that the seventh day is the Sabbath of the Lord.

In the name of the Lord we are to go forward, unfurling His banner, advocating His word. When the authorities command us not to do this work, when they forbid us to proclaim the commandments of God and the faith of Jesus, then it will be necessary for us to say as did the apostles: "Whether it be right in the sight of God to hearken unto you more than unto God, judge ye. For we cannot but speak the things which we have seen and heard." Acts 4: 19, 20.

The truth is to be set forth in the power of the Holy Spirit. This alone can make our words effective. Only through the Spirit's power will victory be gained and held. The human agent must be worked by the Spirit of God. The workers must be kept by the power of God through faith unto salvation. They must have divine wisdom, that nothing may be uttered which would stir up men to close our way. Through the inculcation of spiritual truth we are to prepare a people who shall be able, in meekness and fear, to give a reason for their faith before the highest authorities in our world.

We need to present the truth in its simplicity, to advocate practical godliness; and we should do this in the spirit of Christ. The manifestation of such a spirit will have the best influence upon our own souls, and it will have a convincing power upon others. Give the Lord opportunity to work through His own agents. Do not imagine that it will be possible for you to lay out plans for the future; let God be acknowledged as standing at the helm at all times and under every circumstance. He will work by means that will be suitable, and will maintain, increase, and build up His own people.

The Lord's agents should have a sanctified zeal, a zeal that is wholly under His control. Stormy times will come rapidly enough upon us, and we should take no course of our own that will hasten them. Tribulation will come of a character that will drive to God all who wish to be His, and His alone. Until tested and proved in the furnace of trial, we do not know ourselves, and it is not proper for us to measure the characters of others and to condemn those who have not yet had the light of the third angel's message.

If we wish men to be convinced that the truth we believe sanctifies the soul and transforms the character, let us not be continually charging them with vehement accusations. In this way we shall force them to the conclusion that the doctrine we profess cannot be the Christian doctrine, since it does not make us kind, courteous, and respectful. Christianity is not manifested in pugilistic accusations and condemnation.

Many of our people are in danger of trying to exercise a controlling power upon others and of bringing oppression upon their fellow men. There is danger that those who are entrusted with responsibilities will acknowledge but one power, the power of an unsanctified will. Some have exercised this power unscrupulously and have caused great discomfiture to those whom the Lord is using. One of the greatest curses in our world (and it is seen in churches and in society everywhere) is the love of supremacy. Men become absorbed in seeking to secure power and popularity. This spirit has manifested itself in the ranks of Sabbathkeepers, to our grief and shame. But spiritual success comes only to those who have learned meekness and lowliness in the school of Christ.

We should remember that the world will judge us by what we appear to be. Let those who are seeking to represent Christ be careful not to exhibit inconsistent features of character. Before we come fully to the front, let us see to it that the Holy Spirit is poured upon us from on high. When this is the case, we shall give a decided message, but it will be of a far less condemnatory character than that which some have been giving; and all who believe will be far more earnest for the salvation of our opponents. Let God have the matter of condemning authorities and governments wholly in His own keeping. In meekness and love let us as faithful sentinels defend the principles of truth as it is in Jesus.

LOVE AMONG BRETHREN

The characteristics most needful to be cherished by God's commandment-keeping people are patience and long-suffering, peace and love. When love is lacking, irretrievable loss is sustained; for souls are driven away from the truth, even after they have been connected with the cause of God. Our brethren in responsible positions, who have strength of influence, should remember the words of the apostle Paul, spoken by the Holy Spirit: "We then that are strong ought to bear the infirmities of the weak, and not to please ourselves. Let every one of us please his neighbor for his good to edification. For even Christ pleased not Himself; but, as it is written, The reproaches of them that reproached Thee fell on Me." Romans 15: 1-3. Again he says: "Brethren, if a man be overtaken in a fault, ye which are spiritual, restore such an one in the spirit of meekness; considering thyself, lest thou also be tempted. Bear ye one another's burdens, and so fulfill the law of Christ." Galatians 6: 1, 2.

Bear in mind that the work of restoring is to be our burden. This work is not to be done in a proud, officious, masterly way. Do not say, by your manner, "I have the power, and I will use it," and pour out accusations upon the erring one. Do your restoring "in the spirit of meekness; considering thyself, lest thou also be tempted." The work set before us to do for our brethren is not to cast them aside, not to press them into discouragement or despair by saying: "You have disappointed me, and I will not try to help you." He who sets himself up as full of wisdom and strength, and bears down upon one who is oppressed and distressed and longing for help, manifests the spirit of the Pharisee, and wraps himself about with the robe of his own self-constituted dignity. In his spirit he thanks God that he is not as other men are, and supposes that his course is praiseworthy and that he is too strong to be tempted. But "if a man think himself to be something, when he is nothing, he deceiveth himself." Verse 3. He himself is in constant danger. He who ignores the grave necessities of his brother will in the providence of God be brought over the same ground that his brother has traveled in trial and sorrow, and by a bitter experience it will be proved to him that he is as helpless and needy as was the suffering one whom he repulsed. "Be not deceived; God is not mocked: for whatsoever a man soweth, that shall he also reap." Verse 7.

"If there be therefore any consolation in Christ, if any comfort of love, if any fellowship of the Spirit, if any bowels and mercies, fulfill ye My joy, that ye be likeminded, having the same love, being of one accord, of one mind. Let nothing be done through strife or vainglory; but in lowliness of mind let each esteem other better than themselves. Look not every man on his own things, but every man also on the things of others. Let this mind be in you, which was also in Christ Jesus." Philippians 2: 1-5.

The closer we keep to Christ, and the more meek and lowly and self-distrustful we are, the firmer will be our hold on Christ, and the greater will be our power, through Christ, to convert sinners; for it is not the human agent that moves the soul. Heavenly intelligences co-operate with the human agent and impress the truth upon the heart. Abiding in Christ we are able to exert an influence over others; but it is because of the presence of Him who says: "Lo, I am with you alway, even unto the end of the world." Matthew 28: 20. The power we have to overcome Satan is the result of Christ working in us to will and to do of His good pleasure.

PRESENT TRUTH WITH GENTLENESS

The truth should be presented with divine tact, gentleness, and tenderness. It should come from a heart that has been softened and made sympathetic. We need to have close communion with God, lest self rise up, as it did in Jehu, and we pour forth a torrent of words that are unbefitting, that are not as dew or as the still showers that revive the withering plants. Let our words be gentle as we seek to win souls. God will be wisdom to him who seeks for wisdom from a divine source. We are to seek opportunities on every hand, we are to watch unto prayer, and be ready always to give a reason for the hope that is in us, with meekness and fear. Lest we shall impress unfavorably one soul for whom Christ died we should keep our hearts uplifted to God, so that when the opportunity presents itself, we may have the right word to speak at the right time. If you thus undertake work for God, the Spirit of God will be your helper. The Holy Spirit will apply the word spoken in love for the soul. The truth will have quickening power when spoken under the influence of the grace of Christ.

God's plan is first to get at the heart. Speak the truth, and let Him carry forward the reformatory power and principle. Make no reference to what opponents say, but let the truth alone be advanced. The truth can cut to the quick. Plainly unfold the word in all its impressiveness.

As trials thicken around us, both separation and unity will be seen in our ranks. Some who are now ready to take up weapons of warfare will in times of real peril make it manifest that they have not built upon the solid rock; they will yield to temptation. Those who have had great light and precious privileges, but have not improved them, will, under one pretext or another, go out from us.

Not having received the love of the truth, they will be taken in the delusions of the enemy; they will give heed to seducing spirits and doctrines of devils, and will depart from the faith. But, on the other hand, when the storm of persecution really breaks upon us, the true sheep will hear the true Shepherd's voice. Self-denying efforts will be put forth to save the lost, and many who have strayed from the fold will come back to follow the great Shepherd. The people of God will draw together and present to the enemy a united front. In view of the common peril, strife for supremacy will cease; there will be no disputing as to who shall be accounted greatest. No one of the true believers will say: "I am of Paul; and I of Apollos; and I of Cephas." The testimony of one and all will be: "I cleave unto Christ; I rejoice in Him as my personal Saviour."

Thus will the truth be brought into practical life, and thus will be answered the prayer of Christ, uttered just before His humiliation and death: "That they all may be one; as Thou, Father, art in Me, and I in Thee, that they also may be one in Us: that the world may believe that Thou hast sent Me." John 17:21. The love of Christ, the love of our brethren, will testify to the world that we have been with Jesus and learned of Him. Then will the message of the third angel swell to a loud cry, and the whole earth will be lightened with the glory of the Lord.

———

Our convictions need daily to be reinforced by humble, sincere prayer and reading of the word. While we each have an individuality, while we each should hold our convictions firmly, we must hold them as God's truth and in the strength which God imparts. If we do not, they will be wrung from our grasp.

GOD'S WORD TO BE SUPREME

THE people of God will recognize human government as an ordinance of divine appointment and will teach obedience to it as a sacred duty within its legitimate sphere. But when its claims conflict with the claims of God, the word of God must be recognized as above all human legislation. "Thus saith the Lord" is not to be set aside for Thus saith the church or the state. The crown of Christ is to be uplifted above the diadems of earthly potentates.

The principle we are to uphold at this time is the same that was maintained by the adherents of the gospel in the great Reformation. When the princes assembled at the Diet of Spires in 1529, it seemed that the hope of the world was about to be crushed out. To this assembly was presented the emperor's decree restricting religious liberty and prohibiting all further dissemination of the reformed doctrines. Would the princes of Germany accept the decree? Should the light of the gospel be shut out from the multitudes that were still in darkness? Mighty issues for the world were at stake. Those who had accepted the reformed faith met together, and the unanimous decision was: "Let us reject the decree. In matters of conscience the majority has no power."

The banner of truth and religious liberty which these Reformers held aloft has in this last conflict been committed to us. The responsibility for this great gift rests with those whom God has blessed with a knowledge of His word. We are to receive God's word as supreme authority. We must accept its truths for ourselves. And we can appreciate these truths only as we search them out by personal study. Then, as we make God's word the guide of our lives, for us is answered the prayer of Christ:

"Sanctify them through Thy truth: Thy word is truth." John 17:17. The acknowledgment of the truth in word and deed is our confession of faith. Only thus can others know that we believe the Bible.

Those Reformers whose protest has given us the name Protestant felt that God had called them to give the gospel to the world, and in doing this they were ready to sacrifice their possessions, their liberty, and their lives. Are we in this last conflict of the great controversy as faithful to our trust as were the early Reformers to theirs?

In the face of persecution and death, the truth for that time was spread far and near. The word of God was carried to the people; all classes, high and low, rich and poor, learned and ignorant, studied it eagerly, and those who received the light became in their turn its messengers. In those days the truth was brought home to the people through the press. Luther's pen was a power, and his writings, scattered broadcast, stirred the world. The same agencies are at our command, with facilities multiplied a hundredfold. Bibles, publications in many languages, setting forth the truth for this time, are at our hand and can be swiftly carried to all the world. We are to give the last warning of God to men, and what should be our earnestness in studying the Bible, and our zeal in spreading the light!

PREPARATION FOR THE FINAL CRISIS

THE great crisis is just before us. To meet its trials and temptations, and to perform its duties, will require persevering faith. But we may triumph gloriously; not one watching, praying, believing soul will be ensnared by the enemy.

In the time of trial before us God's pledge of security will be placed upon those who have kept the word of His patience. Christ will say to His faithful ones: "Come, My people, enter thou into thy chambers, and shut thy doors about thee: hide thyself as it were for a little moment, until the indignation be overpast." Isaiah 26:20. The Lion of Judah, so terrible to the rejectors of His grace, will be the Lamb of God to the obedient and faithful. The pillar of cloud which speaks wrath and terror to the transgressor of God's law is light and mercy and deliverance to those who have kept His commandments. The arm strong to smite the rebellious will be strong to deliver the loyal. Every faithful one will surely be gathered. "He shall send His angels with a great sound of a trumpet, and they shall gather together His elect from the four winds, from one end of heaven to the other." Matthew 24:31.

Brethren, to whom the truths of God's word have been opened, what part will you act in the closing scenes of this world's history? Are you awake to these solemn realities? Do you realize the grand work of preparation that is going on in heaven and on earth? Let all who have received the light, who have had the opportunity of reading and hearing the prophecy, take heed to those things that are written therein; "for the time is at hand." Let none now tamper with sin, the source of every misery in our world. No longer remain in lethargy and stupid indifference. Let not the destiny of your soul hang upon an uncertainty. Know that you are fully on the Lord's side. Let the inquiry go forth from sincere hearts and trembling lips, "Who shall be able to stand?" Have you, in these last precious hours of probation, been putting the very best material into your character building? Have you been purifying your souls from every stain? Have you followed the light? Have you works corresponding to your profession of faith?

Is the softening, subduing influence of the grace of God working upon you? Have you hearts that can feel, eyes that can see, ears that can hear? Is it in vain that the declaration of eternal truth has been made concerning the nations of the earth? They are under condemnation, preparing for the judgments of God; and in this day which is big with eternal results, the people chosen to be the depositaries of momentous truth ought to be abiding in Christ. Are you letting your light shine to illumine the nations that are perishing in their sins? Do you realize that you are to stand in defense of God's commandments before those who are treading them underfoot?

It is possible to be a partial, formal believer, and yet be found wanting and lose eternal life. It is possible to practice some of the Bible injunctions and be regarded as a Christian, and yet perish because you lack qualifications essential to Christian character. If you neglect or treat with indifference the warnings that God has given, if you cherish or excuse sin, you are sealing your soul's destiny. You will be weighed in the balance and found wanting. Grace, peace, and pardon will be forever withdrawn; Jesus will have passed by, never again to come within reach of your prayers and entreaties. While mercy lingers, while the Saviour is making intercession, let us make thorough work for eternity.

The return of Christ to our world will not be long delayed. Let this be the keynote of every message.

The blessed hope of the second appearing of Christ, with its solemn realities, needs to be often presented to the people. Looking for the soon appearing of our Lord will lead us to regard earthly things as emptiness and nothingness.

The battle of Armageddon is soon to be fought. He on whose vesture is written the name, King of kings, and Lord of lords, is soon to lead forth the armies of heaven.

It cannot now be said by the Lord's servants, as it was by the prophet Daniel: "The time appointed was long." Daniel 10:1. It is now but a short time till the witnesses for God will have done their work in preparing the way of the Lord.

We are to throw aside our narrow, selfish plans, remembering that we have a work of the largest magnitude and highest importance. In doing this work we are sounding the first, second, and third angel's messages, and are thus being prepared for the coming of that other angel from heaven who is to lighten the earth with his glory.

The day of the Lord is approaching with stealthy tread; but the supposed great and wise men know not the signs of Christ's coming or of the end of the world. Iniquity abounds, and the love of many has waxed cold.

There are thousands upon thousands, millions upon millions, who are now making their decision for eternal life or eternal death. The man who is wholly absorbed in his counting room, the man who finds pleasure at the gaming table, the man who loves to indulge perverted appetite, the amusement lover, the frequenters of the theater and the ballroom, put eternity out of their reckoning. The whole burden of their life is: What shall we eat? what shall we drink? and wherewithal shall we be clothed? They are not in the procession that is moving heavenward. They are led by the great apostate, and with him will be destroyed.

Unless we understand the importance of the moments that are swiftly passing into eternity, and make ready to stand in the great day of God, we shall be unfaithful stewards. The watchman is to know the time of night. Everything is now clothed with a solemnity that all who believe the truth for this time should realize. They should act in reference to the day of God. The judgments of God are about to fall upon the world, and we need to be preparing for that great day.

Our time is precious. We have but few, very few days of probation in which to make ready for the future, immortal life. We have no time to spend in haphazard movements. We should fear to skim the surface of the word of God.

It is as true now as when Christ was upon the earth, that every inroad made by the gospel upon the enemy's dominion is met by fierce opposition from his vast armies. The conflict that is right upon us will be the most terrible ever witnessed. But though Satan is represented as being as strong as the strong man armed, his overthrow will be complete, and everyone who unites with him in choosing apostasy rather than loyalty will perish with him.

The restraining Spirit of God is even now being withdrawn from the world. Hurricanes, storms, tempests, fire and flood, disasters by sea and land, follow each other in quick succession. Science seeks to explain all these. The signs thickening around us, telling of the near approach of the Son of God, are attributed to any other than the true cause. Men cannot discern the sentinel angels restraining the four winds that they shall not blow until the servants of God are sealed; but when God shall bid His angels loose the winds, there will be such a scene of strife as no pen can picture.

To those who are indifferent at this time Christ's warning is: "Because thou art lukewarm, and neither cold nor hot, I will spew thee out of My mouth." Revelation 3:16. The figure of spewing out of His mouth means that He cannot offer up your prayers or your expressions of love to God. He cannot endorse your teaching of His word or your spiritual work in anywise. He cannot present your religious exercises with the request that grace be given you.

Could the curtain be rolled back, could you discern the purposes of God and the judgments that are about to fall upon a doomed world, could you see your own attitude, you would fear and tremble for your own souls and for the souls of your fellow men. Earnest prayers of heart-rending anguish would go up to heaven. You would weep between the porch and the altar, confessing your spiritual blindness and backsliding.

"Blow the trumpet in Zion, sanctify a fast, call a solemn assembly: gather the people, sanctify the congregation, assemble the elders, gather the children: . . . let the bridegroom go forth of his chamber, and the bride out of her closet. Let the priests, the ministers of the Lord, weep between the porch and the altar, and let them say, Spare Thy people, O Lord, and give not Thine heritage to reproach." Joel 2: 15-17.

"Turn ye even to Me with all your heart, and with fasting, and with weeping, and with mourning: and rend your heart, and not your garments, and turn unto the Lord your God: for He is gracious and merciful, slow to anger, and of great kindness, and repenteth Him of the evil. Who knoweth if He will return and repent, and leave a blessing behind Him?" Verses 12-14.

After Israel's apostasy and bitter retribution, God's message of grace for the repentant people was: "Behold, I will allure her, and bring her into the wilderness, and speak comfortably unto her. And I will give her her vineyards from thence, and the valley of Achor for a door of hope: and she shall sing there, as in the days of her youth, and as in the day when she came up out of the land of Egypt." Hosea 2: 14, 15.

"And it shall be at that day, saith the Lord, that thou shalt call Me my husband; and shalt call Me no more my lord. . . . And I will betroth thee unto Me forever; yea, I will betroth thee unto Me in righteousness, and in judgment, and in loving-kindness, and in mercies. I will even betroth thee unto Me in faithfulness: and thou shalt know the Lord." Verses 16-20, margin.

"And ye shall know that I am in the midst of Israel, and that I am the Lord your God, and none else: and My people shall never be ashamed." Joel 2: 27.

Warning, admonition, promise, all are for us, upon whom the ends of the world are come. "Therefore let us not sleep, as do others; but let us watch and be sober." 1 Thessalonians 5:6.

———

"Take heed to yourselves, lest at any time your hearts be overcharged with surfeiting, and drunkenness, and cares of this life, and so that day come upon you unawares." Luke 21:34.

———

"Watch ye and pray, lest ye enter into temptation." Mark 14:38. Watch against the stealthy approach of the enemy, watch against old habits and natural inclinations, lest they assert themselves; force them back, and watch. Watch the thoughts, watch the plans, lest they become self-centered. Watch over the souls whom Christ has purchased with His own blood. Watch for opportunities to do them good.

———

Watch, "lest coming suddenly He find you sleeping." Mark 13:36.

CALLS TO SERVICE

> "I heard the voice of the Lord,
> saying, Whom shall I send, and
> who will go for us? Then said
> I, Here am I; send me."

YOUNG MEN IN THE MINISTRY

THERE must be no belittling of the gospel ministry. No enterprise should be so conducted as to cause the ministry of the word to be looked upon as an inferior matter. It is not so. Those who belittle the ministry are belittling Christ. The highest of all work is ministry in its various lines, and it should be kept before the youth that there is no work more blessed of God than that of the gospel minister.

Let not our young men be deterred from entering the ministry. There is danger that through glowing representations some will be drawn away from the path where God bids them walk. Some have been encouraged to take a course of study in medical lines who ought to be preparing themselves to enter the ministry. The Lord calls for more ministers to labor in His vineyard. The words were spoken: "Strengthen the outposts; have faithful sentinels in every part of the world." God calls for you, young men. He calls for whole armies of young men who are largehearted and large-minded, and who have a deep love for Christ and the truth.

The measure of capacity or learning is of far less consequence than is the spirit with which you engage in the work. It is not great and learned men that the ministry needs; it is not eloquent sermonizers. God calls for men who will give themselves to Him to be imbued with His Spirit. The cause of Christ and humanity demands sanctified, self-sacrificing men, those who can go forth without the camp, bearing the reproach. Let them be strong, valiant men, fit for worthy enterprises, and let them make a covenant with God by sacrifice.

The ministry is no place for idlers. God's servants are to make full proof of their ministry. They will not be sluggards, but as expositors of His word they will put forth their utmost energies to be faithful. They should never cease to be learners. They are to keep their own souls alive to the sacredness of the work and to the great responsibilities of their calling, that they may at no time or place bring to God a maimed sacrifice, an offering which has cost them neither study nor prayer. The Lord has need of men of intense spiritual life. Every worker may receive an endowment of strength from on high, and may go forward with faith and hope in the path where God bids him walk. The word of God abides in the young, consecrated laborer. He is quick, earnest, powerful, having in the counsel of God an unfailing source of supply.

God has called this people to give to the world the message of Christ's soon coming. We are to give to men the last call to the gospel feast, the last invitation to the marriage supper of the Lamb. Thousands of places that have not heard the call are yet to hear it. Many who have not given the message are yet to proclaim it. Again I appeal to our young men: Has not God called upon you to sound this message?

———

How many of our young men will enter the service of God, not to be served, but to serve? In times past there were those who fastened their minds upon one soul after another, saying: "Lord, help me to save this soul." But now such instances are rare. How many act as if they realized the peril of sinners? How many take those whom they know to be in peril, presenting them to God in prayer and supplicating Him to save them?

The apostle Paul could say of the early church: "They glorified God in me." Galatians 1:24. Shall we not strive to live so that the same words can be said of us? The Lord will provide ways and means for those who will seek Him with the whole heart. He desires us to acknowledge the divine superintendence shown in preparing fields of labor and preparing the way for these fields to be occupied successfully.

Let ministers and evangelists have more seasons of earnest prayer with those who are convicted by the truth. Remember that Christ is always with you. The Lord has in readiness the most precious exhibitions of His grace to strengthen and encourage the sincere, humble worker. Then reflect to others the light which God has caused to shine upon you. Those who do this bring to the Lord the most precious offering. The hearts of those who bear the good tidings of salvation are aglow with the spirit of praise.

"These things saith He that holdeth the seven stars in His right hand." Revelation 2:1.

The sweet influences that are to be abundant in the church are bound up with God's ministers, who are to represent the precious love of Christ. The stars of heaven are under the control of Christ. He fills them with light. He directs their movements. If He did not do this, they would become fallen stars. So with His ministers. They are but instruments in His hand, and all the good they accomplish is done through His power. Through them His light is to shine forth. It is to the honor of Christ that

He makes His ministers greater blessings to the church, through the workings of the Holy Spirit, than are the stars to the world. The Saviour is to be their sufficiency. If they will look to Him as He looked to His Father, they will do His works. As they make God their dependence, He will give them His brightness to reflect to the world.

Let those who are as stars in the hand of Christ remember that they are ever to preserve a sacred, holy dignity. They are Christ's representatives. Simplicity in Christ is the pure, sacred dignity of the truth.

God's servants are to preach His word to the people. Under the Holy Spirit's working they will come into order as stars in the hand of Christ, to shine forth with His brightness. Let those who claim to be Christ's ministers arise and shine; for their light has come, and the glory of the Lord has risen upon them. Let them understand that Christ expects them to do the same work as He has done. Let them leave the churches that know the truth, and go forth to establish new churches, to present the word of truth to those who are in ignorance of God's warning message.

The number of workers in the ministry is not to be lessened, but greatly increased. Where there is now one minister in the field, twenty are to be added; and if the Spirit of God controls them, these twenty will so present the truth that twenty more will be added.

Christ's dignity and officework are in imposing such conditions as He pleases. His followers are to become more and more a power in the proclamation of the truth as they draw nearer to the perfection of faith and of love for their brethren. God has provided divine assistance for all emergencies to which our human resources are unequal. He gives the Holy Spirit to help in every strait, to strengthen our hope and assurance, to illuminate our minds and purify our hearts. He means that sufficient facilities shall be provided for the working out of his plans. I bid you seek counsel from God. Seek Him with the whole heart, and "whatsoever He saith unto you, do." John 2:5.

————

The Lord has not called young men to work among the churches. They are not called to speak to an audience that does not need their immature labors, that is well aware of the fact, and feels, under their ministration, no drawing of the Spirit. Let young men of ability connect with experienced laborers in the great harvest field. Very many will succeed best by beginning with the canvassing work and improving the opportunities afforded them for gospel ministry.

But let none become shadows of some other man. Let them not become mere machines, to grind out certain subjects by human dictation. No sermon is to be planned out for them to preach where they go. Let them seek to be taught by God through the Holy Spirit. Let them seek help through prayer and the diligent study of God's word. If they do this, He who calls them to labor in the gospel will make it evident that they are chosen vessels. He will give them words to speak to the people.

Their first duty is to learn lessons in various lines from the Great Teacher. There is one aim set before all in the word of God—to be like Him who "went about doing good."

"If any man serve Me," Christ says, "let him follow Me."

John 12:26. By studying the life of Christ let the workers learn how He lived and worked. Let them strive each day to live His life.

Follow on, young men, to know the Lord, and you will know that "His going forth is prepared as the morning." Hosea 6:3. Seek constantly to improve. Strive earnestly for identity with the Redeemer. Live by faith in Christ. Do the work He did. Live for the saving of the souls for whom He laid down His life. Try in every way to help those with whom you come in contact. Strive continually to improve. Let your life fulfill the words: "Thou through Thy commandments hast made me wiser than mine enemies." Psalm 119:98. Talk with your Elder Brother, who will complete your education, line upon line, precept upon precept, here a little and there a little. A close connection with Him who offered Himself as a sacrifice to save a perishing world will make you acceptable workers. When you can lay your hand on truth and appropriate it, when you can say, "My Lord and my God," grace and peace and joy in rich measure will be yours.

Open new fields, is the word from the Lord, and add to your workers. Educate young men to labor, and tarry not. Educate, educate, educate.

"Say not ye, There are yet four months, and then cometh harvest? behold, I say unto you, Lift up your eyes, and look on the fields; for they are white already to harvest. And he that reapeth receiveth wages, and gathereth fruit unto life eternal: that both he that soweth and he that reapeth may rejoice together." John 4:35, 36.

THE CHURCH AND THE MINISTRY

It is high time that the members of our churches made decided efforts to sustain the men who are giving the last message of mercy to the world. Let church members, by a manifestation of practical religion, give weight to the message of warning which is being borne to the world by God's messengers. Intelligent people are alarmed at the outlook in the world. If those who have a knowledge of the truth will practice Bible principles, showing that they have been sanctified by the truth, that they are true followers of the meek and lowly Saviour, they will exert an influence that will win souls to Christ.

Anything less than active, earnest service for the Master gives the lie to our profession of faith. Only the Christianity that is revealed by earnest, practical work will make an impression upon those who are dead in trespasses and sins. Praying, humble, believing Christians, those who show by their actions that their greatest desire is to make known the saving truth which is to test all people, will gather a rich harvest of souls for the Master.

We need to break up the monotony of our religious labor. We are doing a work in the world, but we are not showing sufficient activity and zeal. If we were more in earnest, men would be convinced of the truth of our message. The tameness and monotony of our service for God repels many souls of a higher class, who need to see a deep, earnest, sanctified zeal. Legal religion will not answer for this age. We may perform all the outward acts of service and yet be as destitute of the quickening influence of the Holy Spirit as the hills of Gilboa were destitute of dew and rain. We all need spiritual moisture, and we need also the bright beams of the Sun of Righteousness to soften and subdue our hearts. We are always to be as firm as a rock to principle. Bible principles are to be taught and then backed up by holy practice.

Those in the service of God must show animation and determination in the work of winning souls. Remember that there are those who will perish unless we as God's instrumentalities work with a determination that will not fail nor become discouraged. The throne of grace is to be our continual dependence.

There is no excuse for the faith of our churches to be so faint and feeble. "Turn you to the Stronghold, ye prisoners of hope." Zechariah 9:12. There is strength for us in Christ. He is our Advocate before the Father. He dispatches His messengers to every part of His dominion to communicate His will to His people. He walks in the midst of His churches. He desires to sanctify, elevate, and ennoble His followers. The influence of those who truly believe in Him will be a savor of life in the world. He holds the stars in His right hand, and it is His purpose to let His light shine through these to the world. Thus He desires to prepare His people for higher service in the church above. He has given us a great work to do. Let us do it with accuracy and determination. Let us show in our lives what the truth has done for us.

"Who walketh in the midst of the seven golden candlesticks." Revelation 2:1. This scripture shows Christ's relation to the churches. He walks in the midst of His churches throughout the length and breadth of the earth. He watches them with intense interest to see whether they are in such a condition spiritually that they can advance His kingdom. Christ is present in every assembly of the church. He is acquainted with everyone connected with His service. He knows those whose hearts He can fill with the holy oil, that they may impart it to others. Those who faithfully carry forward the work of Christ in our world, representing in word and works the character of God, fulfilling the Lord's purpose for them, are in His sight very precious. Christ takes pleasure in them as a man takes pleasure in a well-kept garden and the fragrance of the flowers he has planted.

It has cost self-denial, self-sacrifice, indomitable energy, and much prayer, to bring up the various missionary enterprises where they now stand. There is danger that some of those now coming upon the stage of action will rest content to be inefficient, feeling that there is now no need of so great self-denial and diligence, such hard and disagreeable labor, as the leaders in this message experienced; that times have changed; and that since there is now more means in the cause of God, it is not necessary for them to place themselves in such trying circumstances as many were called to meet in the rise of the message.

But were there the same diligence and self-sacrifice manifest at the present stage of the work as at its beginning, we should see a hundred times more than is now accomplished.

If the work is to go forward on the high plane of action upon which it started, there must be no falling off in moral resources. New accessions of moral power must continually be made. If those now entering the field as laborers feel that they may relax their efforts, that self-denial and strict economy not only of means but of time are not now essential, the work will retrograde. The workers at the present time should have the same degree of piety, energy, and perseverance that the leaders had.

The work has been extended so that it now covers a large territory, and the number of believers has increased. Still there is a great deficiency, for a larger work might have been accomplished had the same missionary spirit been manifested as in earlier days. Without this spirit the laborer will only mar and deface the cause of God. The work is really retrograding instead of advancing as God designs it should. Our present numbers and the extent of our work are not to be compared with what they were in the beginning. We should consider what might have been done had every worker consecrated himself, in soul, body, and spirit, to God as he should have done.

———

Our churches are to co-operate in the work of spiritual tilling, with the hope of reaping by and by. There is much perversity to be met, much thwarting of holy plans and consecrated effort, because of the evil heart of unbelief. But the work must be done. The soil is stubborn, but the fallow ground must be broken up, the seeds of righteousness must be sown. Pause not, teachers beloved by God, as though doubtful whether to prosecute a labor which will grow as performed. Fail not, neither be discouraged. They that sow in tears shall reap in joy. "We are laborers together with God: ye are God's husbandry, ye are God's building." 1 Corinthians 3:9. Remember that you cannot trust in self.

———

As never before, we should pray not only that laborers may be sent forth into the great harvest field, but that we may have a clear conception of truth, so that when the messengers of truth shall come, we may accept the message and respect the messenger.

THE HOME MISSIONARY WORK

A WARNING FROM THE CHURCH OF EPHESUS

THE True Witness addresses the church of Ephesus, saying: "I have somewhat against thee, because thou hast left thy first love. Remember therefore from whence thou art fallen, and repent, and do the first works; or else I will come unto thee quickly, and will remove thy candlestick out of his place, except thou repent." Revelation 2:4, 5.

At the first the experience of the church of Ephesus was marked with childlike simplicity and fervor. A lively, earnest, heartfelt love for Christ was expressed. The believers rejoiced in the love of God because Christ was in their hearts as an abiding presence. The praise of God was on their lips, and their attitude of thanksgiving was in accord with the thanksgiving of the heavenly family.

The world took knowledge of them that they had been with Jesus. Sinful men, repentant, pardoned, cleansed, and sanctified, were brought into partnership with God through His Son. The believers sought earnestly to receive and obey every word of God. Filled with love for their Redeemer, they sought as their highest aim to win souls to Him. They did not think of hoarding the precious treasure of the grace of Christ. They felt the importance of their calling, and, weighted with the message, Peace on earth, good will to men, they burned with desire to carry the glad tidings to the earth's remotest bounds.

The members of the church were united in sentiment and action. Love for Christ was the golden chain that bound them together. They followed on to know the Lord more and still more perfectly, and brightness and comfort and peace were revealed in their lives. They visited the fatherless and widows in their affliction, and kept themselves unspotted from the world. A failure to do this would, in their view, have been a contradiction of their profession and a denial of their Redeemer.

In every city the work was carried forward. Souls were converted, and in their turn felt that they must tell of the inestimable treasure. They could not rest till the beams of light which had illumined their minds were shining upon others. Multitudes of unbelievers were made acquainted with the reason of the Christian's hope. Warm, inspired, personal appeals were made to the sinful and erring, to the outcast, and to those who, while professing to know the truth, were lovers of pleasure more than lovers of God.

But after a time the zeal of the believers, their love for God and for one another, began to wane. Coldness crept into the church. Differences sprang up, and the eyes of many were turned from beholding Jesus as the Author and Finisher of their faith. The masses that might have been convicted and converted by a faithful practice of the truth, were left unwarned. Then it was that the message was addressed to the Ephesian church by the True Witness. Their lack of interest in the salvation of souls showed that they had lost their first love; for none can love God with the whole heart, mind, soul, and strength without loving those for whom Christ died. God called upon them to repent and do the first works, else the candlestick would be removed out of its place.

Is not this experience of the Ephesian church repeated in the experience of the church of this generation? How is the church of today, that has received a knowledge of the truth of God, using this knowledge? When its members first saw God's unspeakable mercy for the fallen race, they could not keep silent. They were filled with longing to co-operate with God in giving to others the blessings they had received. As they imparted, they were continually receiving. They grew in grace and in the knowledge of the Lord Jesus Christ. How is it today?

Brethren and sisters who have long claimed to believe the truth, I ask you individually, Have your practices been in harmony with the light, the privileges, and the opportunities granted you of heaven? This is a serious question. The Sun of Righteousness has risen upon the church, and it is the duty of the church to shine. It is the privilege of every soul to make advancement. Those who are connected with Christ will grow in grace and in the knowledge of the Son of God, to the full stature of men and women. If all who claim to believe the truth had made the most of their ability and opportunities to learn and to do, they would have become strong in Christ. Whatever their occupation,—whether they were farmers, mechanics, teachers, or pastors,—if they had wholly consecrated themselves to God they would have become efficient workers for the heavenly Master.

But what are the members of the church doing that they should be designated "laborers together with God"? 1 Corinthians 3:9. Where do we see travail of soul? Where do we see the members of the church absorbed in religious themes, self-surrendered to the will of God? Where do we see Christians feeling their responsibility to make the church prosperous, a wide-awake, light-giving people? Where are those who do not stint or measure their loving labor for the Master? Our Redeemer is to see of the travail of His soul and be satisfied; how is it with those who profess to be His followers? Will they be satisfied when they see the fruit of their labors?

Why is it that there is so little faith, so little spiritual power? Why are there so few who bear the yoke and carry the burden of Christ? Why do persons have to be urged to take up their work for Christ? Why are there so few who can unveil the mysteries of redemption? Why is it that the imputed righteousness of Christ does not shine through His professed followers as a light to the world?

THE RESULT OF INACTION

When men use their powers as God directs, their talents will increase, their ability will enlarge, and they will have heavenly wisdom in seeking to save the lost. But while the church members are listless and neglectful of their God-given responsibility to impart to others, how can they expect to receive the treasure of heaven? When professed Christians feel no burden to enlighten those in darkness, when they cease to impart grace and knowledge, they become less discerning, they lose their appreciation of the richness of the heavenly endowment; and, failing to value it themselves, they fail to realize the necessity of presenting it to others.

We see large churches gathered in different localities. Their members have gained a knowledge of the truth, and many are content to hear the word of life without seeking to impart light. They feel little responsibility for the progress of the work, little interest in the salvation of souls. They are full of zeal in worldly things, but they do not bring their religion into their business. They say: "Religion is religion, and business is business." They believe that each has its proper sphere, but they say: "Let them be separated."

Because of neglected opportunities and abuse of privileges, the members of these churches are not growing "in grace, and in the knowledge of our Lord and Saviour Jesus Christ." 2 Peter 3:18. Therefore they are weak in faith, deficient in knowledge, and children in experience. They are not rooted and grounded in the truth. If they remain thus, the many delusions of the last days will surely deceive them, for they will have no spiritual eyesight to distinguish truth from error.

God has given His ministers the message of truth to proclaim. This the churches are to receive and in every possible way to communicate, catching the first rays of light and diffusing them. Here is our great sin. We are years behind. The ministers have been seeking the hidden treasure and have been opening up the casket and letting the jewels of truth shine forth, but the members of the church have not done a hundredth part of that which God requires of them. What can we expect but deterioration in religious life when the people listen to sermon after sermon and do not put the instruction into practice? The ability God has given, if not exercised, degenerates. More than this, when the churches are left to inactivity Satan sees to it that they are employed. He occupies the field and engages the members in lines of work that absorb their energies, destroy spirituality, and cause them to fall as dead weights upon the church.

There are among us those who, if they would take time to consider, would regard their do-nothing position as a sinful neglect of their God-given talents. Brethren and sisters, your Redeemer and all the holy angels are grieved at your hardness of heart. Christ gave His own life to save souls, and yet you who have known His love make so little effort to impart the blessings of His grace to those for whom He died. Such indifference and neglect of duty is an amazement to the angels. In the judgment you must meet the souls you have neglected. In that great day you will be self-convicted and self-condemned. May the Lord lead you now to repentance.

May He forgive His people for neglecting the work in His vineyard which He has given them to do.

"Remember therefore from whence thou art fallen, and repent, and do the first works; or else I will come unto thee quickly, and will remove thy candlestick out of his place, except thou repent." Revelation 2:5.

Oh, how few know the time of their visitation! How few, even among those who claim to believe present truth, understand the signs of the times or what we are to experience before the end! We are today under divine forbearance; but how long will the angels of God continue to hold the winds, that they shall not blow?

Notwithstanding God's inexpressible mercy toward us, how few in our churches are truly humble, devoted, God-fearing servants of Christ! How few hearts are full of gratitude and thanksgiving because they are called and honored to act a part in the work of God, being partakers with Christ of His sufferings!

Today a large part of those who compose our congregations are dead in trespasses and sins. They come and go like the door upon its hinges. For years they have complacently listened to the most solemn, soul-stirring truths, but they have not put them in practice. Therefore they are less and less sensible of the preciousness of truth. The stirring testimonies of reproof and warning do not arouse them to repentance. The sweetest melodies that come from God through human lips—justification by faith, and the righteousness of Christ—do not call forth from them a response of love and gratitude. Though the heavenly Merchantman displays before them the richest jewels of faith and love, though He invites them to buy of Him "gold tried in the fire," and "white raiment" that they may be clothed, and "eyesalve" that they may see, they steel their hearts against Him, and fail to exchange their lukewarmness for love and zeal. While making a profession, they deny the power of godliness. If they continue in this state, God will reject them. They are unfitting themselves to be members of His family.

WINNING SOULS THE CHIEF AIM

We are not to feel that the work of the gospel depends principally upon the minister. To every man God has given a work to do in connection with His kingdom. Everyone who professes the name of Christ is to be an earnest, disinterested worker, ready to defend the principles of righteousness. Every soul should take an active part in advancing the cause of God. Whatever our calling, as Christians we have a work to do in making Christ known to the world. We are to be missionaries, having for our chief aim the winning of souls to Christ.

To His church God has committed the work of diffusing light and bearing the message of His love. Our work is not to condemn, not to denounce, but to draw with Christ, beseeching men to be reconciled to God. We are to encourage souls, to attract them, and thus win them to the Saviour. If this is not our interest, if we withhold from God the service of heart and life, we are robbing Him of influence, of time, of money and effort. In failing to benefit our fellow men, we rob God of the glory that should flow to Him through the conversion of souls.

BEGIN WITH THOSE NEAREST

Some who have long professed to be Christians, and yet have felt no responsibility for souls perishing within the shadow of their own homes, may think they have a work to do in foreign lands; but where is the evidence of their fitness for such a work? Wherein have they manifested a burden for souls? These persons need first to be taught and disciplined at home. True faith and love for Christ would create in them a most earnest desire to save souls right at home. They would exert every spiritual energy to draw with Christ, learning His meekness and lowliness. Then if God should desire them to go to foreign countries, they would be prepared.

Let those who desire to work for God begin at home, in their own household, in their own neighborhood, among their own friends. Here they will find a favorable missionary field. This home missionary work is a test, revealing their ability or inability for service in a wider field.

THE EXAMPLE OF PHILIP WITH NATHANAEL

The case of Philip and Nathanael is an example of true home missionary work. Philip had seen Jesus and was convinced that He was the Messiah. In his joy he wished his friends also to know the good news. He desired that the truth which had brought such comfort to him should be shared by Nathanael. True grace in the heart will always reveal its presence by diffusing itself. Philip went in search of Nathanael, and as he called, Nathanael answered from his place of prayer under the fig tree. Nathanael had not had the privilege of listening to the words of Jesus, but he was being drawn toward Him in spirit. He longed for light, and was at that moment sincerely praying for it. Philip with joy exclaimed: "We have found Him, of whom Moses in the law, and the prophets, did write, Jesus of Nazareth." John 1:45. At Philip's invitation Nathanael sought and found the Saviour, and in his turn joined in the work of winning souls for Christ.

One of the most effective ways in which light can be communicated is by private, personal effort. In the home circle, at your neighbor's fireside, at the bedside of the sick, in a quiet way you may read the Scriptures and speak a word for Jesus and the truth. Thus you may sow precious seed that will spring up and bring forth fruit.

THE FAMILY A MISSIONARY FIELD

Our work for Christ is to begin with the family in the home. The education of the youth should be of a different order from that which has been given in the past. Their welfare demands far more labor than has been given them. There is no missionary field more important than this. By precept and example parents are to teach their children to labor for the unconverted. The children should be so educated that they will sympathize with the aged and afflicted and will seek to alleviate the sufferings of the poor and distressed. They should be taught to be diligent in missionary work; and from their earliest years self-denial and sacrifice for the good of others and the advancement of Christ's cause should be inculcated, that they may be laborers together with God.

But if they ever learn to do genuine missionary work for others, they must first learn to labor for those at home, who have a natural right to their offices of love. Every child should be trained to bear his respective share of service in the home. He should never be ashamed to use his hands in lifting home burdens or his feet in running errands. While thus engaged, he will not go into paths of negligence and sin. How many hours are wasted by children and youth which might be spent in taking upon their strong young shoulders, and assisting to lift, the family responsibilities which someone must bear, thus showing a loving interest in father and mother. They are also to be rooted in the true principles of health reform and the care of their own bodies.

Oh, that parents would look prayerfully and carefully

after their children's eternal welfare! Let them ask themselves, Have we been careless? Have we neglected this solemn work? Have we allowed our children to become the sport of Satan's temptations? Have we not a solemn account to settle with God because we have permitted our children to use their talents, their time and influence, in working against the truth, against Christ? Have we not neglected our duty as parents and increased the number of the subjects of Satan's kingdom?

By many this home field has been shamefully neglected, and it is time that divine resources and remedies were presented, that this state of evil may be corrected. What excuse can the professed followers of Christ offer for neglecting to train their children to work for Him?

God designs that the families of earth shall be a symbol of the family in heaven. Christian homes, established and conducted in accordance with God's plan, are among His most effective agencies for the formation of Christian character and for the advancement of His work.

If parents desire to see a different state of things in their families, let them consecrate themselves wholly to God and co-operate with Him in the work whereby a transformation may take place in their households.

When our own homes are what they should be, our children will not be allowed to grow up in idleness and indifference to the claims of God in behalf of the needy all about them. As the Lord's heritage, they will be qualified to take up the work where they are. A light will shine from such homes which will reveal itself in behalf of the ignorant, leading them to the source of all knowledge. An influence will be exerted that will be a power for God and for His truth.

INSTRUCT THE CHURCH IN MISSIONARY WORK

"Watchman, what of the night?" Isaiah 21:11. Are the watchmen of whom this demand is made able to give the trumpet a certain sound? Are the shepherds faithfully caring for the flock as those who must give an account? Are the ministers of God watching for souls, realizing that those under their care are the purchase of the blood of Christ? A great work is to be done in the world, and what efforts are we making for its accomplishment? The people have had too much sermonizing; but have they been taught how to labor for those for whom Christ died? Has a line of labor been devised and placed before them in such a way that each has seen the necessity of taking part in the work?

It is evident that all the sermons that have been preached have not developed a large class of self-denying workers. This subject is to be considered as involving the most serious results. Our future for eternity is at stake. The churches are withering up because they have failed to use their talents in diffusing light. Careful instruction should be given which will be as lessons from the Master, that all may put their light to practical use. Those who have the oversight of the churches should select members of ability and place them under responsibilities, at the same time giving them instruction as to how they may best serve and bless others.

Every means should be used to bring the knowledge of the truth before the thousands who will discern the evidence, who will appreciate the likeness of Christ in His people if they can have an opportunity to see it. Let the missionary meeting be turned to account in teaching the people how to do missionary labor. God expects His church to discipline and fit its members for the work of enlightening the world. An education should be given that would result in furnishing hundreds who would put out to the exchangers valuable talents. By the use of these talents, men would be developed who would be prepared to fill positions of trust and influence, and to maintain pure, uncorrupted principles. Thus great good would be accomplished for the Master.

SET THE CHURCH MEMBERS TO WORK

Many who possess real ability are rusting from inaction because they do not know how to set themselves at work in missionary lines. Let someone who has ability lay out before these inactive ones the line of work they could do. Let small missions be established in many places to teach men and women how to use and thus increase their talents. Let all understand what is expected from them, and many who are now unemployed will become true laborers.

The parable of the talents should be explained to all. The members of the churches should be made to understand that they are the light of the world, and according to their several ability the Lord expects them to enlighten and bless others. Whether they are rich or poor, great or humble, God calls them into active service for Him. He depends upon the church for the forwarding of His work, and He expects His professed followers to do their duty as intelligent beings. There is great need that every trained mind, every disciplined intellect, every jot of ability, be brought into the work of saving souls.

Do not pass by the little things and look for a large work. You might do successfully the small work, but fail utterly in attempting a larger work and fall into discouragement. Take hold wherever you see that there is work to be done. It will be by doing with your might what your hands find to do that you will develop talents and aptitude for a larger work. It is by slighting the daily opportunities, neglecting the little things, that so many become fruitless and withered.

There are ways in which all may do personal service for God. Some can write a letter to a far-off friend, or send a paper to one who is inquiring for truth. Others can give counsel to those who are in difficulty. Those who know how to treat the sick can help in this line. Others who have the necessary qualifications can give Bible readings or conduct Bible classes.

The very simplest modes of work should be devised and set in operation among the churches. If the members will unitedly accept such plans, and perseveringly carry them out, they will reap a rich reward; for their experience will grow brighter, their ability will increase, and through their efforts souls will be saved.

THE UNEDUCATED TO BE WORKERS

Let none feel that because they are uneducated they cannot take part in the Lord's work. God has a work for *you* to do. He has given to every man his work. You can search the Scriptures for yourselves. "The entrance of Thy words giveth light; it giveth understanding unto the simple." Psalm 119:130. You can pray for the work. The prayer of the sincere heart, offered in faith, will be heard in heaven. And you are to work according to your ability.

Everyone has an influence for good or for evil. If the soul is sanctified to the service of God and devoted to the work of Christ, the influence will tend to gather with Christ.

All heaven is in activity, and the angels of God are waiting to co-operate with all who will devise plans whereby souls for whom Christ died may hear the glad tidings of salvation. Angels who minister to those that shall be heirs of salvation, are saying to every true saint:

"There is work for you to do." "Go, stand and speak . . .
to the people all the words of this life." Acts 5:20. If
those addressed would obey this injunction, the Lord
would prepare the way before them, putting them in
possession of means wherewith to go.

AROUSE THE IDLERS

Souls are perishing out of Christ, and those who profess to be Christ's disciples are letting them die. Our
brethren have talents entrusted to them for the very
work of saving souls, but some have bound these up in a
napkin and buried them in the earth. How much do
such idlers resemble the angel who is represented as flying in the midst of heaven, proclaiming the commandments of God and the faith of Jesus? What manner of
entreaty can be brought to bear upon the idlers that will
arouse them to go to work for the Master? What can we
say to the slothful church member to make him realize
the necessity of unearthing his talent and putting it out
to the exchangers? There will be no idler, no slothful
one, found inside the kingdom of heaven. Oh, that God
would set this matter in all its importance before the
sleeping churches! Oh, that Zion would arise and put on
her beautiful garments! Oh, that she would shine!

There are many ordained ministers who have never
yet exercised a shepherd's care over the flock of God,
who have never yet watched for souls as they that must
give an account. The church, instead of developing, is
left to be a weak, dependent, inefficient body. The members of the church, trained to rely upon preaching, do
little for Christ. They bear no fruit, but rather increase
in selfishness and unfaithfulness. They put their hope
in the preacher and depend upon his efforts to keep alive
their weak faith. Because the church members have not
been properly instructed by those whom God has placed

as overseers, many are slothful servants, hiding their talents in the earth and still complaining of the Lord's dealing toward them. They expect to be tended like sick children.

This condition of weakness must not continue. Well-organized work must be done in the church, that its members may understand how to impart the light to others and thus strengthen their own faith and increase their knowledge. As they impart that which they have received from God they will be confirmed in the faith. A working church is a living church. We are built up as living stones, and every stone is to emit light. Every Christian is compared to a precious stone that catches the glory of God and reflects it.

The idea that the minister must carry all the burdens and do all the work is a great mistake. Overworked and broken down, he may go into the grave, when, had the burden been shared as the Lord designed, he might have lived. That the burden may be distributed, an education must be given to the church by those who can teach the workers to follow Christ and to work as He worked.

THE YOUTH TO BE MISSIONARIES

Let not the youth be ignored; let them share in the labor and responsibility. Let them feel that they have a part to act in helping and blessing others. Even the children should be taught to do little errands of love and mercy for those less fortunate than themselves.

Let the overseers of the church devise plans whereby young men and women may be trained to put to use their entrusted talents. Let the older members of the church seek to do earnest, compassionate work for the children and youth. Let ministers put to use all their ingenuity in devising plans whereby the younger members of the church may be led to co-operate with them in missionary work. But do not imagine that you can arouse their interest merely by preaching a long sermon at the missionary meeting. Plan ways whereby a live interest may be kindled. Let all have a part to act. Train the young to do what is appointed them, and from week to week let them bring their reports to the missionary meeting, telling what they have experienced and through the grace of Christ what success has been theirs. If such reports were brought in by consecrated workers, the missionary meetings would not be dull and tedious. They would be full of interest, and there would be no lack in attendance.

In every church the members should be so trained that they will devote time to the winning of souls to Christ. How can it be said of the church, "Ye are the light of the world," unless the members of the church are actually imparting light?

Let those who have charge of the flock of Christ awake to their duty and set many souls to work.

LET THE CHURCHES AWAKE

Peculiar and rapid changes will soon take place, and God's people are to be endowed with the Holy Spirit, so that with heavenly wisdom they may meet the emergencies of this age, and as far as possible counteract the demoralizing movements of the world. If the church is not asleep, if the followers of Christ watch and pray, they may have light to comprehend and appreciate the movements of the enemy.

The end is near! God calls upon the church to set in order the things that remain. Workers together with God, you are empowered by the Lord to take others with you into the kingdom. You are to be God's living agents, channels of light to the world, and round about you are angels of heaven with their commission from Christ to sustain, strengthen, and uphold you in working for the salvation of souls.

I appeal to the churches in every conference: Stand out separate and distinct from the world—in the world, but not of it, reflecting the bright beams of the Sun of Righteousness, being pure, holy, and undefiled, and in faith carrying light into all the highways and byways of the earth.

Let the churches awake before it is everlastingly too late. Let every member take up his individual work and vindicate the name of the Lord by which he is called. Let sound faith and earnest piety take the place of slothfulness and unbelief. When faith lays hold upon Christ, the truth will bring delight to the soul, and the services of religion will not be dull and uninteresting. Your social meetings, now tame and spiritless, will be vitalized by the Holy Spirit; daily you will have a rich experience as you practice the Christianity you profess. Sinners will be converted. They will be touched by the word of truth and will say, as did some who listened to Christ's teaching: "We have seen and heard wonderful things today."

In view of what might be done if the church would meet its God-given responsibilities, will its members sleep on, or will they arouse to a sense of the honor conferred upon them through the merciful providence of God? Will they gather up their hereditary trusts, avail themselves of the present light, and feel the necessity of rising to meet the urgent emergency that now presents itself? Oh, that all may arouse and manifest to the world that theirs is a living faith, that a vital issue is before the world, that Jesus will soon come. Let men see that we believe that we are on the borders of the eternal world.

The upbuilding of the kingdom of God is retarded or urged forward according to the unfaithfulness or fidelity

of human agencies. The work is hindered by the failure
of the human to co-operate with the divine. Men may
pray, "Thy kingdom come. Thy will be done in earth,
as it is in heaven;" but if they fail of acting out this prayer
in their lives, their petitions will be fruitless.

But though you may be weak, erring, and sinful, the
Lord holds out to you the offer of partnership with Him-
self. He invites you to come under divine instruction.
Uniting with Christ, you may work the works of God.
"Without Me," Christ said, "ye can do nothing."

Through the prophet Isaiah is given the promise,
"Thy righteousness shall go before thee; the glory of
the Lord shall be thy rearward." Isaiah 58:8. It is the
righteousness of Christ that goes before us, and this is
the glory of the Lord which is to be our rearward. Ye
churches of the living God, study this promise, and consider how your lack of faith, of spirituality, of divine
power, is hindering the coming of the kingdom of God.
If you would go forth to do Christ's work, angels of
God would open the way before you, preparing hearts to
receive the gospel. Were every one of you a living missionary, the message for this time would speedily be proclaimed in all countries, to every people and nation and
tongue. This is the work that must be done before Christ
shall come in power and great glory. I call upon the
church to pray earnestly that you may understand your
responsibilities. Are you individually laborers together
with God? If not, why not? When do you mean to do
your heaven-appointed work?

———

For all who are disheartened there is but one remedy,
—faith, prayer, and work.

Our churches should not feel jealous and neglected because they do not receive ministerial labor. They should themselves rather take up the burden and labor most earnestly for souls.

———

Every talent in our churches should be employed in the work of doing good. The rough places of nature, the wild places, God has made attractive by placing beautiful things among the most unsightly. This is the work we are called to do.

———

We need in our churches youth who are working upon the Christian endeavor principles, and the beginning must be made at home. The faithful performance of home duties has a reflex influence upon the character. In the father's house is to be given the evidence of fitness for work in the church.

———

The Lord does not judge us according to the elevation of our various spheres, but according to the faithfulness with which we fill them.

———

If we do but one third of that which we have entrusted talents to do, the other two thirds are working against Christ.

———

The greatest work that can be done in our world is to glorify God by living the character of Christ.

THE INCREASE OF FACILITIES

A GREAT work must be done all through the world, and let no one conclude that, because the end is near, there is no need of special effort to build up the various institutions as the cause shall demand. You are not to know the day or the hour of the Lord's appearing, for this has not been revealed, and let none speculate on that which has not been given him to understand. Let everyone work upon that which has been placed in his hands, doing the daily duties that God requires.

When the Lord shall bid us make no further effort to build meetinghouses and establish schools, sanitariums, and publishing institutions, it will be time for us to fold our hands and let the Lord close up the work; but now is our opportunity to show our zeal for God and our love for humanity.

We are to be partners in the work of God throughout the world; wherever there are souls to be saved, we are to lend our help, that many sons and daughters may be brought to God. The end is near, and for this reason we are to make the most of every entrusted ability and every agency that shall offer help to the work.

Schools must be established, that the youth may be educated, that those engaged in the work of the ministry may reach higher attainments in the knowledge of the Bible and the sciences. Institutions for the treatment of the sick must be established in foreign lands, and medical missionaries must be raised up who will be self-denying, who will lift the cross, who will be prepared to fill positions of trust and be able to educate others. And besides all this, God calls for home missionaries. The workers for God, in the field or at home, are to be self-denying, bearing the cross, restricting their personal wants, that they may be abundant in good fruits.

A faith that comprehends less than this denies the Christian character. The faith of the gospel is one whose power and grace are of divine authorship. Let us make it manifest that Christ abides in us, by ceasing to expend money on dress, on needless things, when the cause of Christ is crippled for want of means, when debts are left unpaid on our meetinghouses, and the treasury is empty. Do not cultivate a taste for expensive articles of dress or of furniture. Let the work advance as it began, in simple self-denial and faith.

Use your means to create, rather than your influence to diminish, agencies for good. Let no one listen to the suggestion that we can exercise faith and have all our infirmities removed, and that there is therefore no need of institutions for the recovery of health. Faith and works are not dissevered. Since the Lord is soon to come, act decidedly and determinedly to increase the facilities, that a great work may be done in a short time.

Since the Lord is soon coming, it is time to put out our money to the exchangers, time to put every dollar we can spare into the Lord's treasury, that institutions may be established for the education of workers, who shall be instructed as were those in the schools of the prophets. If the Lord comes and finds you doing this work, He will say: "Well done, thou good and faithful servant: . . . enter thou into the joy of thy Lord."

The time has come when no physical, mental, or moral power is to be wasted or misapplied. The Lord desires that His people in America shall no longer confine to a few places at home the great facilities which concern the moral and spiritual advancement of His work. Those to whom He has given much are called upon to impart. Place your means now where it will help in giving light to darkened nations and to the islands of the sea.

———

Work to Be Done. If families would locate in the dark places of the earth, places where the people are enshrouded in spiritual gloom, and let the light of Christ's life shine out through them, a great work might be accomplished. Let them begin their work in a quiet, unobtrusive way, not drawing on the funds of the conference until the interest becomes so extensive that they cannot manage it without ministerial help.

———

When institutes and similar meetings are held, let them not be held in connection with our large, established churches. Let them give character to the work and spread the knowledge of the truth in localities where it is little known. This may not be convenient; but I ask, Was it convenient for Christ to leave the royal courts? Was it convenient for Him to leave His honor, His glory, His high command, and humble Himself to become one with us? He did not go to unfallen beings, but to those who needed Him most. His example we, to whom He has entrusted His work, are to copy.

———

We are to present the word of life to those whom we may judge to be as hopeless subjects as if they were in their graves. Though they may seem to be unwilling to hear or to receive the light of truth, without questioning or wavering we are to do our part.

There is danger in delay. That soul whom you might have found, that soul to whom you might have opened the Scriptures, passes beyond your reach. Satan has prepared some net for his feet, and tomorrow he may be working out the plans of the archenemy of God. Why delay one day? Why not go to work at once?

———

How the angels must feel as they see the end approaching, and see so many of those entrusted with the last message of mercy huddling together, attending meetings for the sake of benefit to their own souls, and feeling dissatisfied if there is not much preaching, while they have little burden and are doing little for the salvation of others. All who are indeed united to Christ by living faith will be partakers of the divine nature. They will be constantly receiving from Him spiritual life, and they cannot be silent.

Life always shows itself in action. If the heart is living, it will send the lifeblood to every part of the body. Those whose hearts are filled with spiritual life will not need to be urged to reveal it. The divine life will flow forth from them in rich currents of grace. As they pray, as they speak, and as they labor, God is glorified.

———

The Workers. It is not the most brilliant or the most talented whose work produces the greatest and most lasting results. Who are the most efficient laborers? Those who will respond to the invitation: "Take My yoke upon you, and learn of Me; for I am meek and lowly in heart."

If men to whom God has entrusted talents of intellect refuse to use these gifts to His glory, after test and trial He will leave them to their own imaginings and will take men who do not appear to be so richly endowed,

who have not large self-confidence, and He will make
the weak strong because they trust in God to do for
them those things which they cannot do for themselves.
God will accept the wholehearted service, and will Himself make up the deficiencies.

———

The Lord Jesus takes those whom He finds will be
molded, and uses them for His name's glory, to meet
His own spiritual conception. He uses material that
others would pass by, and works all who will be worked.
Through very simple means a door is opened in heaven,
and the simplicity of the human agent is used by God
to reveal God to man.

———

Have you tasted of the powers of the world to come?
Have you been eating the flesh and drinking the blood
of the Son of God? Then, although ministerial hands
may not have been laid upon you in ordination, Christ
has laid His hands upon you and has said: "Ye are My
witnesses."

———

Those whom God employs as His instruments may be
regarded by some as inefficient; but if they can pray, if
in simplicity they can talk the truth because they love it,
they may reach the people through the Holy Spirit's
power. As they present the truth in simplicity, reading
from the word or recalling incidents of experience, the
Holy Spirit makes an impression on mind and character.
The will becomes subordinate to the will of God; the
truth heretofore not understood comes to the heart with
living conviction and becomes a spiritual reality.

HELP FOR MISSION FIELDS

There is a burden upon my soul in regard to the destitute mission fields. There is aggressive work to be done in the missions near us; and there is great need of funds for advancing the work in foreign fields. Our foreign missions are languishing. The missionaries are not sustained as God requires. For want of funds, workers are not able to enter new fields.

All around us are souls perishing in their sins. Every year thousands upon thousands are dying without God and without hope of everlasting life. The plagues and judgments of God are doing their work, and souls are going to ruin because the light of truth has not been flashed upon their pathway. But how few are burdened over the condition of their fellow men! The world is perishing in its misery; but this hardly moves even those who claim to believe the highest and most far-reaching truth ever given to mortals. God requires His people to be His helping hand to reach the perishing, but how many are content to do nothing. There is a lack of that love which led Christ to leave His heavenly home and take man's nature, that humanity might touch humanity and draw humanity to divinity. There is a stupor, a paralysis, upon the people of God which prevents them from understanding what is needed for this time.

God's people are on trial before the heavenly universe; but the scantiness of their gifts and offerings, and the feebleness of their efforts in God's service, mark them as unfaithful. If the little that is now accomplished were the best they could do, they would not be under condemnation; but with their resources they could do much more. They know, and the world knows, that they have to a great degree lost the spirit of self-denial and cross bearing.

God calls for men to give the warning to the world that is asleep, dead in trespasses and sins. He calls for freewill offerings from those whose hearts are in the work, who have a burden for souls, that they shall not perish, but have everlasting life. Satan is playing the game of life for the souls of men. He is seeking to secure means, that he may bind it up, so that it shall not be used in advancing the missionary enterprises. Shall we be ignorant of his devices? Shall we allow him to stupefy our senses?

I appeal to our brethren everywhere to awake, to consecrate themselves to God, and to seek wisdom from Him. I appeal to the officers of our conferences to make earnest efforts in our churches. Arouse them to give of their means for sustaining foreign missions. Unless your hearts are touched in view of the situation in foreign fields, the last message of mercy to the world will be restricted, and the work which God desires to have done will be left unaccomplished.

The last years of probation are fast closing. The great day of the Lord is at hand. We should now make every effort to arouse our people. Let the words of the Lord by the prophet Malachi be brought home to every soul: "Even from the days of your fathers ye are gone away from Mine ordinances, and have not kept them. Return unto Me, and I will return unto you, saith the Lord of hosts. But ye said, Wherein shall we return? Will a man rob God? Yet ye have robbed Me. But ye say, Wherein have we robbed Thee? In tithes and offerings. Ye are cursed with a curse: for ye have robbed Me, even this whole nation. Bring ye all the tithes into the storehouse, that there may be meat in Mine house, and prove Me now herewith, saith the Lord of hosts, if I will not open you the windows of heaven, and pour you out a blessing, that there shall not be room enough to receive it. And I will rebuke the devourer for your sakes, and he shall not destroy the fruits of your ground; neither shall your vine cast her fruit before the time in the field, saith the Lord of hosts. And all nations shall call you blessed: for ye shall be a delightsome land, saith the Lord of hosts."

It is time for us to heed the teaching of God's word. All His injunctions are given for our good, to convert the soul from sin to righteousness. Every convert to the truth should be instructed in regard to the Lord's requirement for tithes and offerings. As churches are raised up, this work must be taken hold of decidedly and carried forward in the spirit of Christ. All that men enjoy, they receive from the Lord's great firm, and He is pleased to have His heritage enjoy His goods; but all who stand under the bloodstained banner of Prince Immanuel are to acknowledge their dependence upon God and their accountability to Him by returning to the treasury a certain portion as His own. This is to be invested in missionary work in fulfillment of the commission given to His disciples by the Son of God: "All power is given unto Me in heaven and in earth. Go ye therefore, and teach all nations." "Go ye into all the world, and preach the gospel to every creature," "baptizing them in the name of the Father, and of the Son, and of the Holy Ghost: teaching them to observe all things whatsoever I have commanded you: and, lo, I am with you alway, even unto the end of the world."

Those who are truly converted are called to do a work that requires money and consecration. The obligation that binds us to place our names on the church roll holds us responsible to work for God to the utmost of our ability. He calls for undivided service, for the entire devotion of heart, soul, mind, and strength. Christ has brought us into church capacity that He may engage and engross all our capabilities in devoted service for the salvation of souls. Anything short of this is opposition to the work. There are only two places in the world where we can deposit our treasures—in God's storehouse or in Satan's, and all that is not devoted to Christ's service is counted on Satan's side and goes to strengthen his cause.

The Lord designs that the means entrusted to us shall be used in building up His kingdom. His goods are committed to His stewards that they may be carefully traded upon and bring back a revenue to Him in the saving of souls unto eternal life. And these souls in their turn will become stewards of the truth, to co-operate with the great firm in the interests of the kingdom of God.

Wherever there is life, there is increase and growth; in God's kingdom there is a constant interchange—taking in, and giving out; receiving, and returning to the Lord His own. God works with every true believer, and the light and blessings received are given out again in the work which the believer does. Thus the capacity for receiving is increased. As one imparts of the heavenly gifts, he makes room for fresh currents of grace and truth to flow into the soul from the living fountain. Greater light, increased knowledge and blessing, are his. In this work, which devolves upon every church member, is the life and growth of the church. He whose life consists in ever receiving and never giving, soon loses the blessing. If truth does not flow forth from him to others, he loses his capacity to receive. We must impart the goods of heaven if we desire fresh blessings.

This is as true in temporal as in spiritual things. The Lord does not come to this world with gold and silver to advance His work. He supplies men with resources, that by their gifts and offerings they may keep His work advancing. The one purpose above all others for which

God's gifts should be used is the sustaining of workers in the great harvest field. And if men, and women as well, will become channels of blessing to other souls, the Lord will keep the channels supplied. It is not returning to God His own that makes men poor; it is withholding that tends to poverty.

The work of imparting that which he has received will constitute every member of the church a laborer together with God. Of yourself you can do nothing; but Christ is the great worker. It is the privilege of every human being who receives Christ to be a worker together with Him.

The Saviour said: "I, if I be lifted up from the earth, will draw all men unto Me." John 12:32. For the joy of seeing souls redeemed, Christ endured the cross. He became the living sacrifice for a fallen world. Into that act of self-sacrifice was put the heart of Christ, the love of God; and through this sacrifice was given to the world the mighty influence of the Holy Spirit. It is through sacrifice that God's work must be carried forward. Of every child of God self-sacrifice is required. Christ said: "If any man will come after Me, let him deny himself, and take up his cross daily, and follow Me." Luke 9:23. To all who believe, Christ gives a new character. This character, through His infinite sacrifice, is the reproduction of His own.

The Author of our salvation will be the Finisher of the work. One truth received into the heart will make room for still another truth. And the truth, wherever received, quickens into activity the powers of the receiver. When our church members are truly lovers of God's word, they will reveal the best and strongest qualities; and the nobler they are, the more childlike in spirit they will be, believing the word of God against all selfishness.

A flood of light is shining from the word of God, and

there must be an awakening to neglected opportunities. When all are faithful in giving back to God His own in tithes and offerings, the way will be opened for the world to hear the message for this time. If the hearts of God's people were filled with love for Christ, if every church member were thoroughly imbued with the spirit of self-sacrifice, if all manifested thorough earnestness, there would be no lack of funds for home or foreign missions. Our resources would be multiplied; a thousand doors of usefulness would be opened, and we should be invited to enter. Had the purpose of God been carried out by His people in giving to the world the message of mercy, Christ would, ere this, have come to the earth, and the saints would have received their welcome into the city of God.

If there was ever a time when sacrifices should be made, it is now. Those who have money should understand that now is the time to use it for God. Let not means be absorbed in multiplying facilities where the work is already established. Do not add building to building where many interests are now centered. Use the means to establish centers in new fields. Thus you may bring in souls who will act their part in producing.

Think of our missions in foreign countries. Some of them are struggling to gain even a foothold; they are destitute of even the most meager facilities. Instead of adding to facilities already abundant, build up the work in these destitute fields. Again and again the Lord has spoken in regard to this. His blessing cannot attend His people in disregarding His instruction.

Practice economy in your homes. By many, idols are cherished and worshiped. Put away your idols. Give up your selfish pleasures. Do not, I entreat you, absorb means in embellishing your houses, for it is God's money, and it will be required of you again. Parents, for Christ's sake do not use the Lord's money in pleasing the fancies of your children. Do not teach them to seek after style and ostentation in order to gain influence in the world. Will this incline them to save the souls for whom Christ died? No; it will create envy, jealousy, and evil surmising. Your children will be led to compete with the show and extravagance of the world, and to spend the Lord's money for that which is not essential to health or happiness.

Do not educate your children to think that your love for them must be expressed by indulgence of their pride, extravagance, and love of display. There is no time now to invent ways for using up money. Use your inventive faculties in seeking to economize. Instead of gratifying selfish inclination, spending money for those things that destroy the reasoning faculties, study how to deny self, that you may have something to invest in lifting the standard of truth in new fields. The intellect is a talent; use it in studying how best to employ your means for the salvation of souls.

Teach your children that God has a claim upon all they possess, a claim that nothing can ever cancel; whatever they have is theirs only in trust as a test of their obedience. Inspire them with ambition to gain stars for their crown by winning many souls from sin to righteousness.

Money is a needed treasure; let it not be lavished upon those who do not need it. Someone needs your willing gifts. Too often those who have means fail to consider how many in the world are hungry, starving for food. They may say: "I cannot feed them all." But by practicing Christ's lessons on economy you can feed one. It may be that you can feed many who are hungering for temporal food. And you can feed their souls with the bread of life. "Gather up the fragments that remain, that nothing be lost." John 6: 12. These words were spoken by Him who had all the resources of the universe at His command; while His miracle-working power supplied thousands with food, He did not disdain to teach a lesson in economy.

Practice economy in the use of your time. This is the Lord's. Your strength is the Lord's. If you have extravagant habits, cut them away from your life. Such habits, indulged, will make you bankrupt for eternity. And habits of economy, industry, and sobriety are, even in this world, a better portion for you and your children than a rich dowry.

We are travelers, pilgrims and strangers, on earth. Let us not spend our means in gratifying desires that God bids us repress. Let us rather set a right example before our associates. Let us fitly represent our faith by restricting our wants. Let the churches arise as one, and work earnestly as those who are walking in the full light of truth for these last days. Let your influence impress souls with the sacredness of God's requirements.

If in the providence of God you have been given riches, do not settle down with the thought that you need not engage in useful labor, that you have enough, and can eat, drink, and be merry. Do not stand idle while others are struggling to obtain means for the cause. Invest your means in the Lord's work. If you do less than your duty in giving help to the perishing, remember that your indolence is incurring guilt.

It is God who gives men power to get wealth, and He has bestowed this ability, not as a means of gratifying self, but as a means of returning to God His own. With this object it is not a sin to acquire means. Money is to be earned by labor. Every youth should be trained to habits of industry. The Bible condemns no man for being rich if he has acquired his riches honestly. It is the selfish love of money wrongfully employed that is the root of all evil. Wealth will prove a blessing if we regard it as the Lord's, to be received with thankfulness and with thankfulness returned to the Giver.

But of what value is untold wealth if it is hoarded in expensive mansions or in bank stocks? What do these weigh in comparison with the salvation of one soul for whom the Son of the infinite God has died?

To those who have heaped together treasure for the last days the Lord declares: "Your riches are corrupted, and your garments are moth-eaten. Your gold and silver is cankered; and the rust of them shall be a witness against you, and shall eat your flesh as it were fire."

The Lord bids us: "Sell that ye have, and give alms; provide yourselves bags which wax not old, a treasure in the heavens that faileth not, where no thief approacheth, neither moth corrupteth. For where your treasure is, there will your heart be also. Let your loins be girded about, and your lights burning; and ye yourselves like unto men that wait for their lord, when he will return from the wedding; that when he cometh and knocketh, they may open unto him immediately. Blessed are those servants, whom the lord when he cometh shall find watching: verily I say unto you, that he shall gird himself, and make them to sit down to meat, and will come forth and serve them. And if he shall come in the second watch, or come in the third watch, and find them so, blessed are those servants. And this know, that if the goodman of the house had known what hour the thief would come, he would have watched, and not have suffered his house to be broken through. Be ye therefore ready also: for the Son of man cometh at an hour when ye think not." Luke 12: 33-40.

THE PUBLISHING HOUSE IN NORWAY

[The following appeal, written November 20, 1900, relates to the financial embarrassment of our publishing work in Christiania, Norway. In 1899 word was received by the Foreign Mission Board that the publishing house at Christiania had become involved in debt and was unable to meet its obligations, and that the institution was in danger of falling into the hands of its creditors. To relieve this embarrassment, financial assistance would be required to the amount of $50,000. This the board could not furnish, and though our brethren in Norway continued to hold possession of the publishing house for more than a year after this, little was done for their relief. It seemed that the building must finally be given over to the creditors or be sold to raise funds for meeting the debt. Thus the institution built up by years of labor and sacrifice would be lost to the Lord's work. To prevent this great calamity the Lord has spoken through His servant in the following earnest words of appeal, instruction, and encouragement.]

Our publishing house in Norway is in peril, and in the name of the Lord I appeal to our people in its behalf. All to whose hearts the cause of present truth is dear are called upon to help at this crisis.

Those who love and serve God should feel the deepest interest in all that concerns the glory of His name. Who could see an institution where the truth has been magnified, where the Lord has so often revealed His presence, where instruction has been given by the messengers of God, where the truth has been sent forth in publications that have accomplished great good — who could bear to see such an institution pass into the hands of worldings, to be used for common, worldly purposes? God would certainly be dishonored if His institution were allowed to fall into decay for want of the money which He has entrusted to His stewards. Should this take place, men would say that it was because the Lord was not able to prevent it.

These things mean much to our brethren and sisters in Scandinavia. They will be sorely tried if their facilities are cut off. Let us make an effort to prevent them from falling into depression and discouragement. Let there be a consecrated, united effort to lift the publishing house out of the difficulty into which it has fallen.

There are those who have little faith, who may try to discourage others and thus prevent them from taking part in this good work. It needs only a discouraging word to rouse and strengthen selfishness in the soul. Do not listen to those who would tempt you. Waive the questions that will arise as to how the difficulty has come about. It may have been largely the result of mistakes that have been made; but let us not now devote time to criticism and complaint. Criticisms, complaints, and censure will not bring relief to our brethren in their perplexity and distress.

God has called human agencies to be laborers together with Him in the work of salvation. He uses men encompassed with infirmities and liable to err. Then let us not censure those who have been so unfortunate as to make mistakes. Let us rather seek to be so transformed by the grace of God as to become compassionate, touched with human woe. This will cause joy in heaven; for in loving our fallen brother as God and Christ love us, we give evidence that we are partakers of Christ's attributes.

This is no time to criticize. That which is needed now is genuine sympathy and decided help. We should individually consider the necessities of our brethren. Let every breath devoted to this matter be used in speaking words that shall encourage. Let every power be employed in actions that shall lift.

One part of the ministry of heavenly angels is to visit our world and oversee the work of the Lord in the hands of His stewards. In every time of necessity they minister to those who as co-workers with God are striving to carry forward His work in the earth. These heavenly intelligences are represented as desiring to look into the plan of redemption, and they rejoice whenever any part of God's work prospers.

Angels are interested in the spiritual welfare of all who are seeking to restore God's moral image in man; and the earthly family are to connect with the heavenly family in binding up the wounds and bruises that sin has made. Angelic agencies, though invisible, are co-operating with visible human agencies, forming a relief association with men. The very angels who, when Satan was seeking the supremacy, fought the battle in the heavenly courts and triumphed on the side of God, the very angels who shouted for joy over the creation of our world and its sinless inhabitants, the angels who witnessed the fall of man and his expulsion from his Eden home—these very heavenly messengers are most intensely interested to work in union with the fallen, redeemed race for the salvation of human beings perishing in their sins.

Human agencies are the hands of heavenly instrumentalities, for heavenly angels employ human hands in practical ministry. Human agencies as hand helpers are to work out the knowledge and use the facilities of heavenly beings. By uniting with these powers that are omnipotent, we are benefited by their higher education and experience. Thus as we become partakers of the divine nature, and separate selfishness from our lives, special talents for helping one another are granted us. This is heaven's way of administering saving power.

Is there not something stimulating and inspiring in this thought, that the human agent stands as the visible instrument to confer the blessings of angelic agencies? As we are thus laborers together with God, the work bears the inscription of the divine. The knowledge and activity of the heavenly workers, united with the knowledge and power that are imparted to human agencies, bring relief to the oppressed and distressed. Our acts of unselfish ministry make us partakers in the success that results from the relief offered.

With what joy heaven looks upon these blended influences! All heaven is watching those agencies that are as the hand to work out the purpose of God in the earth, thus doing the will of God in heaven. Such co-operation accomplishes a work that brings honor and glory and majesty to God. Oh, if all would love as Christ has loved, that perishing men might be saved from ruin, what a change would come to our world!

"I will also leave in the midst of thee an afflicted and poor people, and they shall trust in the name of the Lord. . . . They shall feed and lie down, and none shall make them afraid. Sing, O daughter of Zion; shout, O Israel; be glad and rejoice with all the heart, O daughter of Jerusalem. The Lord hath taken away thy judgments, He hath cast out thine enemy: the King of Israel, even the Lord, is in the midst of thee: thou shalt not see evil any more. In that day it shall be said to Jerusalem, Fear thou not: and to Zion, Let not thine hands be slack. The Lord thy God in the midst of thee is mighty; He will save, He will rejoice over thee with joy; He will rest in His love. He will joy over thee with singing." Zephaniah 3: 12-17. What a representation is this! Can we grasp its meaning?

"I will gather them that are sorrowful for the solemn assembly, who are of thee, to whom the reproach of it was a burden. Behold, at that time I will undo all that afflict thee: and I will save her that halteth, and gather her that was driven out; and I will get them praise and fame in every land where they have been put to shame. At that time will I bring you again, even in the time that I gather you: for I will make you a name and a praise among all people of the earth, when I turn back your captivity before your eyes, saith the Lord." Verses 18-20. Read also the first chapter of Haggai.

When human agencies, as stewards of God, will unitedly take of the Lord's own substance and use it to lift the burdens resting on His institutions, the Lord will cooperate with them.

"And the angel that talked with me came again, and waked me, as a man that is wakened out of his sleep, and said unto me, What seest thou? And I said, I have looked, and behold a candlestick all of gold, with a bowl upon the top of it, and his seven lamps thereon, and seven pipes to the seven lamps, which are upon the top thereof: and two olive trees by it, one upon the right side of the bowl, and the other upon the left side thereof. So I answered and spake to the angel that talked with me, saying, What are these, my lord? Then the angel that talked with me answered and said unto me, Knowest thou not what these be? And I said, No, my lord. Then he answered and spake unto me, saying, This is the word of the Lord unto Zerubbabel, saying, Not by might, nor by power, but by My Spirit, saith the Lord of hosts. Who art thou, O great mountain? before Zerubbabel thou shalt become a plain: and he shall bring forth the head-stone thereof with shoutings, crying, Grace, grace unto it. Moreover the word of the Lord came unto me, saying, The hands of Zerubbabel have laid the foundation of this house; his hands shall also finish it; and thou shalt know that the Lord of hosts hath sent me unto you. For who hath despised the day of small things? for they shall rejoice, and shall see the plummet in the hand of Zerubbabel with those seven; they are the eyes of the Lord, which run to and fro through the whole earth. Then answered I, and said unto him, What are these two olive trees upon the right side of the candlestick and upon the left side thereof? And I answered again, and said unto him, What be these two olive branches which through the two golden pipes empty the golden oil out of themselves? And he answered me and said, Knowest thou not what these be? And I said, No, my lord. Then said he, These are the two anointed ones, that stand by the Lord of the whole earth." Zechariah 4: 1-14.

All heaven takes an interest, not only in the lands that are nigh and that need our help, but in the lands that are afar off. The heavenly beings are watching and waiting for human agencies to be deeply moved by the needs of their fellow workmen who are in perplexity and trial, in sorrow and distress.

When one of the Lord's institutions falls into decay, the more prosperous institutions should work to the utmost of their ability in assisting the crippled institution, that the name of God be not dishonored. Whenever the managers of God's institutions close their hearts to the necessities of sister institutions, and neglect to make every effort possible for their relief, selfishly saying, "Let them suffer," God marks their cruelty, and the time will come when they will have to pass through a similar experience of humiliation. But, my brethren, you do not mean to do this. I know that you do not.

Every facility we have in Europe for the advancement of the work is needed; every institution should stand in a healthy, flourishing condition before an ungodly world.

Let not the angels of God who are ministering to those that bear the responsibilities see God's workers disheartened. Already the difficulties have increased by our delay, so that the work of restoration will now require greater labor and expense. In the name of the Lord we ask His people who have means to prove themselves faithful stewards. Repair the machinery so essential to carry forward the work of God, that His people shall not become discouraged and His work be left to languish.

"And the word of the Lord came unto Zechariah, saying, Thus speaketh the Lord of hosts, saying, Execute true judgment, and show mercy and compassions every man to his brother: and oppress not the widow, nor the fatherless, the stranger, nor the poor; and let none of you imagine evil against his brother in your heart." Zechariah 7:8-10. This is the word of the Lord to us also.

I cannot think that the closing part of this chapter will be your experience: "But they refused to hearken, and pulled away the shoulder, and stopped their ears, that they should not hear. Yea, they made their hearts as an adamant stone, lest they should hear the law, and the words which the Lord of hosts hath sent in His Spirit by the former prophets: therefore came a great wrath from the Lord of hosts. Therefore it is come to pass, that as he cried, and they would not hear; so they cried, and I would not hear, saith the Lord of hosts: but I scattered them with a whirlwind among all the nations whom they knew not. Thus the land was desolate after them that no man passed through nor returned: for they laid the pleasant land desolate." Verses 11-14.

Brethren, in your dealings with the Lord's household, "follow after the things which make for peace, and things wherewith one may edify |build up| another." Romans 14:19. Speak no words of censure. Lay no blame on this one or that one. There is need now of the help that all can bring. Seek to heal the breach that has been made. Do it cheerfully. Do it nobly. Come up to the help of the Lord, to the help of the Lord against the mighty. Redeem at once the institution that is in so great peril.

Let all who realize the nearness of the Lord's coming act their faith. When we see one of God's instrumentalities languishing, let those who have heart and soul in the work manifest their interest.

Let those in responsible positions set a right example. Every noble Christian instinct should lead them to plan and work with far greater earnestness for the relief of the Lord's institution than they would for the saving of their own property. Let all try to do something. Look over your affairs, and see what you can do to co-operate with God in this work.

Since there is decided sympathy between heaven and earth, and since God commissions angels to minister unto all who are in need of help, we know that if we do our part, these heavenly representatives of omnipotent power will give help in this time of need. If we will become one in mind and heart with the heavenly intelligences, we can be worked by them. Men to whom God has entrusted capabilities and talents of means will be impressed by Him to take on the burden of responsibility, and help our Scandinavian brethren.

The cause of God in Europe is not to become a stone of stumbling or a rock of offense to unbelievers. The institutions there are not to be closed or given into the hands of worldlings. Let the Lord's servants in Europe make every effort in their power to recover what has been lost, and the Lord will work with them. And I call upon our people in America to co-operate with their brethren in Europe. If all will act their part in His great plan, God's purpose will be accomplished. The difficulty will soon be in the past, no more to harass the cause of God.

Let no hand become slack or palsied. You have the assurance that angels whose home is in the pavilion of the Eternal, and who see the glory of God, are your helpers. Will you co-operate with them in building up every institution that is doing God's service under the supervision of the angelic ministration?

Who can understand the value of the souls for whose salvation their Prince, their King, the Son of the infinite God, gave His spotless life to a shameful death? If all understood this as they should, what a work would be accomplished! Through the Holy Spirit's working they would by their influence, by their words and their talent of means, lead many souls to escape the chain of darkness and the hellish plottings of Satan, and be washed from their sins in the blood of the Lamb. Oh, let the work go deeper and still deeper! Angels of heaven rejoice to see sinners repent and turn to the living God.

If we will restrain the expression of unbelief, and by hopeful words and prompt movements strengthen our own faith and the faith of others, our vision will grow clearer. The pure atmosphere of heaven will surround our souls.

Be strong, and talk hope. Press your way through obstacles. You are in spiritual wedlock with Jesus Christ. The word is your assurance. Approach your Saviour with the full confidence of living faith, joining your hands with His. Go where He leads the way. Whatsoever He says to you, do. He will teach you just as willingly as He will teach someone else.

OUR DANISH SANITARIUM

At Skodsborg, a suburb of Copenhagen, Denmark, our brethren have established a sanitarium. In this they moved forward hopefully, under the conviction that they were doing the very work that God had enjoined upon His people. But our brethren generally have not taken as much interest in the establishment of sanitariums in the European countries as they ought, and our dear brethren having the Skodsborg Sanitarium in hand have moved forward faster than the means in hand warranted, and now they are in difficulty and distress.

I am greatly troubled in regard to the difficulties and dangers surrounding our institutions in Scandinavia. My mind is stirred to appeal to our people, not only in behalf of the Christiania publishing house, but also for the Danish sanitarium. The enemy has been represented to me as waiting eagerly for an opportunity to destroy these institutions, which are instrumentalities of God, used for the redemption of mankind. Shall Satan's desire be gratified? Shall we allow these institutions to be wrested from our hands and their beneficent work to be stopped? Because our brethren have made mistakes, shall we leave them alone to bear the consequences of their miscalculations? Is this the way in which Christ has dealt with us?

When one burdened with a heavy load is at the foot of a difficult hill, surrounded with discouragements, and in need of strong, cheerful helpers, much time is often wasted in criticism, scolding, and fretting. But this does not move the load. The ones upon whom the pressure rests most heavily do not need or deserve the censure. This might more appropriately fall upon those who should have shared the burden earlier. But even then censure might be inappropriate, and it would certainly be useless. Our first thought should be, How can we help to lift the load? Time is precious. There is too much at stake to run the risk of delay.

To charge the managers of the Skodsborg Sanitarium with worldly ambition and a desire to glorify themselves would do them injustice. In the enlarging of the work they were seeking the glory of God, and a work has been accomplished which is far-reaching for good. But they have erred in making investment beyond their means, and have thus placed themselves in the bondage of debt. By this the future of the institution and the honor of the cause are imperiled. Now, instead of adding to the difficulties of the situation, shall we not courageously grapple with the work of lifting the debt?

I am stirred by the Spirit of God to sound an alarm. Oh, what a sight it would be for the angels to see the institutions established for the illustration and promulgation of the principles of reform and Christian living, passing out of the hands of those who can use them in God's work, into the hands of the world! Brethren, it is time that we interested ourselves in behalf of these institutions in Europe that are now suffering for help. As Christ deals with us, so must we deal with our brethren who are in difficulty.

The Lord's treasures are at hand, entrusted to us for just such emergencies. Let our people who love God and His cause come to the help of His imperiled institutions. Our American brethren should rally to the rescue. Our Scandinavian brethren in America should be specially aroused to take decided action. And our brethren in Denmark, Norway, and Sweden should understand that now is the time for them to come up to the help of the Lord. Let all who trust in God and believe His word study diligently to understand their privileges, their responsibilities, and their duty in this matter. If we fail now to do our work as God's helping hand in relieving the Scandinavian publishing house and sanitarium, we shall lose a great blessing.

Who will now place themselves on the Lord's side? Who will be as His helping hand, lifting wholeheartedly? Who will encourage the oppressed to trust in the Lord? Who will manifest that faith which will not fail nor falter, but which presses forward to victory? Who will now strive to build up that which Satan is striving to tear down, a work which should be going forward in strong lines? Who will now do for their brethren in Europe that which they would wish to have done for them in similar circumstances? Who will co-operate with the ministering angels?

The Lord calls upon His people to make offerings of self-denial. Let us give up something that we intended to purchase for personal comfort or pleasure. Let us teach our children to deny self and become the Lord's helping hands in dispensing His blessings.

I plead with my Scandinavian brethren to do what they can. We will unite our efforts with your work of love and helpfulness. There is sufficient means in the hands of the Lord's stewards to do this work if they will unite in tender sympathy to restore, to heal, and to bring health and prosperity to God's instrumentalities.

The sums which you give may be small when compared with the necessities of the work, but be not discouraged. Have faith in God. Hold fast to the hand of Infinite Power, and that which seemed hopeless at first will look different. The feeding of the five thousand is an object lesson for us. He who with five loaves and two small fishes fed five thousand men besides women and children, can do great things for His people today.

Read the account of how the prophet Elisha fed one hundred men: "There came a man from Baalshalisha, and brought the man of God bread of the first fruits, twenty loaves of barley, and full ears of corn in the husk thereof. And he said, Give unto the people, that they may eat. And his servitor said, What, should I set this before an hundred men? He said again, Give the people, that they may eat: for thus saith the Lord, They shall eat, and shall leave thereof. So he set it before them, and they did eat, and left thereof, according to the word of the Lord." 2 Kings 4: 42-44.

What condescension it was on the part of Christ to work this miracle to satisfy hunger! He relieved the hunger of one hundred sons of the prophets, and again and again since then, though not always in so marked and visible a way, He has worked to supply human need. If we had clearer spiritual discernment, so that we could recognize more readily God's merciful, compassionate dealing with His people, we would gain a rich experience. We need to study more than we do into the wonderful working of God. Men who are not united with us in acknowledging the truth, He has moved to favor His people. The Lord has His men of opportunity, like the man who brought the food for the sons of the prophets.

When the Lord gives us a work to do, let us not stop to inquire into the reasonableness of the command or the probable result of our efforts to obey it. The supply in our hands may seem to fall far short of our needs; but in the hands of the Lord it will be more than sufficient. The servitor "set it before them, and they did eat, and left thereof, according to the word of the Lord."

We need greater faith. We should have a fuller sense of God's relationship to those whom He has purchased with the blood of His only-begotten Son. We should exercise faith in the onward progress of the work of the kingdom of God.

Let us waste no time in deploring the scantiness of our visible resources, but let us make the best use of what we have. Though the outward appearance may be unpromising, energy and trust in God will develop resources. Let us send in our offerings with thanksgiving and with prayer that the Lord will bless the gifts and multiply them as He did the food given to the five thousand. If we use the very best facilities we have, the power of God will enable us to reach the multitudes that are starving for the bread of life.

In this work of helping our brethren in Denmark and Norway, let us lift zealously and nobly, leaving the result with God. Let us have faith to believe that He will enlarge our offerings until they are sufficient to place His institutions on vantage ground.

Faith is the spiritual hand that touches infinity.

The simple prayers indited by the Holy Spirit will ascend through the gates ajar, the open door which Christ has declared: I have opened, and no man can shut. These prayers, mingled with the incense of the perfection of Christ, will ascend as fragrance to the Father, and answers will come.

Workers for Christ are never to think, much less to speak, of failure in their work. The Lord Jesus is our efficiency in all things; His Spirit is to be our inspiration; and as we place ourselves in His hands, to be channels of light, our means of doing good will never be exhausted. We may draw upon His fullness and receive of that grace which has no limit.

THE RELIEF OF OUR SCHOOLS

AN EXAMPLE OF LIBERALITY

WHEN the Lord invited Israel to contribute for the building of the tabernacle in the wilderness, there was a hearty response. The people "came, everyone whose heart stirred him up, and everyone whom his spirit made willing, and they brought the Lord's offering to the work of the tabernacle of the congregation." They came, both men and women, as many as were willinghearted. Men came with their gifts of gold and silver, choice fabrics, and valuable wood. The rulers brought precious stones, costly spices, and oil for the lights. "And all the women that were wisehearted did spin with their hands, and brought that which they had spun." They brought "free offerings every morning," until the report was given to Moses: "The people bring much more than enough for the service of the work, which the Lord commanded to make." Exodus 35:21-25; 36:3, 5. This generous-hearted, willing service was pleasing to God; and when the tabernacle was completed, He signified His acceptance of the offering. "A cloud covered the tent of the congregation, and the glory of the Lord filled the tabernacle." Exodus 40:34.

Akin to this example of willing service has been the work done in behalf of our schools in the publication and sale of *Christ's Object Lessons*. We rejoice that so large a number of our people have given themselves to this work and that their efforts are proving so successful. We rejoice that our conference and tract society officers have given their influence and energy to this grand enterprise and that ministers, Bible workers, colporteurs, and church members have engaged so heartily in the special effort for the speedy relief of our schools. The generous, wholehearted way in which our publishing houses and our brethren and sisters in general have taken hold of this enterprise is well pleasing to the Lord. It is in accordance with His plan.

THE LORD'S PLAN

There are, in the divine providence, particular periods when we must arise in response to the call of God and make use of our means, our time, our intellect, our whole being, body, soul, and spirit, in fulfilling His requirements. The present is such a time as this. The interests of God's cause are at stake. The Lord's institutions are in peril. Because of the terrible burden of debt under which our schools are struggling, the work is hindered on every side. In our great necessity, God has made a way through the difficulty and has invited us to co-operate with Him in accomplishing His purpose. It was His plan that the book, *Christ's Object Lessons,* should be given for the relief of our schools, and He calls upon His people to do their part in placing this book before the world. In this He is testing His people and His institutions to see if they will work together and be of one mind in self-denial and self-sacrifice.

ALL TO CO-OPERATE

A good beginning has been made in the sale of *Christ's Object Lessons.* What is needed now is an earnest, united effort to complete the work that has been so well begun. In the Scriptures we read: "Not slothful in business; fervent in spirit; serving the Lord." Romans 12:11. Every branch of God's cause is worthy of diligence; but nothing could be more deserving than this enterprise at this time. A decided work is to be done in accomplishing

God's plan. Let every stroke tell for the Master in the selling of *Christ's Object Lessons*. Let all who possibly can, join the workers.

From the success of the efforts already made, we see that it is far better to obey God's requirements today than to wait for what we might think a more favorable season. We must become men and women of God's opportunity, for great responsibilities and possibilities are within the reach of all who have enlisted for life service under Christ's banner.

God calls us to action, that our educational institutions may be freed from debt. Let God's plan be worked out after His own order.

The present is an opportunity which we cannot afford to lose. We call upon all our people to help to the utmost of their ability just now. We call upon them to do a work that will be pleasing to God in purchasing the book. We ask that every available means be used to assist in its circulation. We call upon the presidents of our conferences to consider how they can forward this enterprise. We call upon our ministers, as they visit the churches, to encourage men and women to go out as canvassers and to make a decided forward movement in the path of self-denial by giving a part of their earnings for the help of our schools.

A general movement is needed, and this must begin with individual movements. In every church let every member of every family make determined efforts to deny self and to help forward the work. Let the children act a part. Let all co-operate. Let us do our best at this time to render to God our offering, to carry out His specified will, and thus make an occasion for witnessing for Him and His truth in a world of darkness. The lamp is in our hands. Let its light shine forth brightly.

Young men, you who think of entering the ministry, take up this work. The handling of the book placed in your hands by the Lord is to be your educator. In improving this opportunity you will certainly advance in a knowledge of God and of the best methods for reaching the people.

The Lord calls for young men and women to enter His service. The youth are receptive, fresh, ardent, hopeful. When once they have tasted the blessedness of self-sacrifice, they will not be satisfied unless they are constantly learning of the Great Teacher. The Lord will open ways before those who will respond to His call.

Bring into the work an earnest desire to learn how to bear responsibilities. With strong arms and brave hearts go forth into the conflict which all must enter, a conflict that will grow more and more severe as we approach the closing struggle.

PREPARATION FOR THE WORK

Those who engage in this work should first give themselves unreservedly to God. They should place themselves where they can learn of Christ and follow His example. He has invited them: "Come unto Me, all ye that labor and are heavy-laden, and I will give you rest. Take My yoke upon you, and learn of Me; for I am meek and lowly in heart: and ye shall find rest unto your souls. For My yoke is easy, and My burden is light." Matthew 11:28-30. Angels are commissioned to go forth with those who take up this work in true humility.

We are to pray without ceasing, and we are to live our prayers. Faith will greatly increase by exercise. Let those who are canvassing for *Christ's Object Lessons* learn the lessons taught in the book for which they are working. Learn of Christ. Have faith in His power to help and save you. Faith is the very lifeblood of the soul. Its presence gives warmth, health, consistency, and sound judgment. Its vitality and vigor exert a powerful though unconscious influence. The life of Christ in the soul is as a well of water springing up unto everlasting life. It leads to a constant cultivation of the heavenly graces and to a kindly submission in all things to the Lord.

I speak to the workers, young and old, who are handling our books, and especially to those who are canvassing for the book that is now doing its errand of mercy: Exemplify in the life the lessons given by Christ in His Sermon on the Mount. This will make a deeper impression and have a more lasting influence upon minds than will the sermons given from the pulpit. You may not be able to speak eloquently to those you desire to help; but if you speak modestly, hiding self in Christ, your words will be dictated by the Holy Spirit; and Christ, with whom you are co-operating, will impress the heart.

Exercise that faith which works by love and sanctifies the soul. Let none now make the Lord ashamed of them because of their unbelief. Sloth and despondency accomplish nothing. Entanglements in secular business are sometimes permitted by God in order to stir the sluggish faculties to more earnest action that He may honor faith by the bestowal of rich blessings. This is a means of advancing His work. Looking unto Jesus, not only as our Example, but as the Author and Finisher of our faith, let us go forward, having confidence that He will supply strength for every duty.

Much painstaking effort will be required of those who have the burden of this work; for right instruction must be given, that a sense of the importance of the work may be kept before the workers, and that all may cherish the spirit of self-denial and sacrifice exemplified in the life of our Redeemer. Christ made sacrifices at every step, sacrifices that none of His followers can ever make. In all the self-denial required of us in this work; amid all the unpleasant things that occur, we are to consider that we are yoked up with Christ, partakers of His spirit of kindness, forbearance, and self-abnegation. This spirit will open the way before us and give us success because Christ is our recommendation to the people.

THE WORK IN ALL LANDS

The work for the relief of our schools should be taken up by our people in all countries. Let it be entered upon by our churches in Australasia. Our school there is in need of help, and if our people will take hold of the work unitedly, they can do much toward lifting the burden of debt; they can encourage the hearts of those who are laboring to build up this, the Lord's instrumentality; and they can aid in extending its influence of blessing to far heathen lands and to the islands of the sea.

We trust that our publishing house in Australia will make liberal terms in the publication of *Christ's Object Lessons*. The Lord has greatly blessed this institution, and it should present to Him a thank offering by making no stinted donation toward freeing the school from debt. We feel sure that it will take up the work and act its part nobly. And this co-operation with God will prove to the Australian publishing house as great a blessing as it has proved to our institutions in America.

Move out in this work, my brethren in Australasia. "Faith is the substance of things hoped for, the evidence of things not seen." Hebrews 11: 1. Have we not proved this in the past? As we have moved out, trusting God's promise, things unseen, except by the eye of faith, have become things seen. As we have walked and worked by faith, God has fulfilled to us every word He has spoken. The evidence we have of the faithfulness of His promises should check every thought of unbelief. It is a sin to doubt, and we do not believe that our brethren in Australasia will be guilty of this.

The Lord has done much for you all through your borders. Lift up your eyes, and look on the fields, already white for the harvest. Praise God that His word has been verified beyond all our conception.

I call upon our people to enter earnestly and disinterestedly upon the work of freeing the school from debt. Let the publishing house do its part in the publication of the book. Let our people throughout Australasia take hold of the sale of *Christ's Object Lessons.* God will bless them in this work.

The workers in England should make every possible effort in the sale of this book, that a school may be established in that country. My brethren in England, Germany, and all other European countries where the light of truth is shining, take hold of this work. Let this book be translated into the different languages and circulated in the different countries of Europe. Let our canvassers in all parts of Europe be encouraged to help in its sale. The sale of this book will do much more than to aid in freeing our institutions from debt. It will open the way for our larger books to find a ready market. Thus the truth will reach many who otherwise would not receive it.

I appeal especially to our brethren in Scandinavia. Will you not take hold of the work which God has given you? Will you not labor to the utmost of your ability to relieve the embarrassed institutions in your field? Do not look on in despair, saying: "We can do nothing." Cease to talk discouragement. Take hold of the arm of Infinite Power. Remember that your brethren in other lands are uniting to give you help. Do not fail or be discouraged. The Lord will uphold His workers in Scandinavia if they will act their part in faith, in prayer, in hopefulness, doing all they can to advance His cause and hasten His coming.

Let a most earnest effort be made by our people in England to inspire their brethren in Scandinavia with faith and courage. Brethren, we must come up to the help of the Lord, to the help of the Lord against the mighty.

Remember that the nearer we approach the time of Christ's coming, the more earnestly and firmly we are to work; for we are opposed by the whole synagogue of Satan. We do not need feverish excitement, but that courage which is born of genuine faith.

RESULTS OF THE WORK

Through the work for the relief of our schools a four-fold blessing will be realized—a blessing to the schools, to the world, to the church, and to the workers.

While funds are gathered for the relief of the schools, the best reading matter is being placed in the hands of a large number of people, who, if this effort had not been made, would never have seen *Christ's Object Lessons*. There are souls in desolate places who will be reached by this effort. The lessons drawn from the parables of our Saviour will be to very many as the leaves of the tree of life.

It is the Lord's design that *Christ's Object Lessons*, with its precious instruction, shall unify the believers. The self-sacrificing efforts put forth by the members of our churches will prove a means of uniting them, that they may be sanctified, body, soul, and spirit, as vessels unto honor, prepared to receive the Holy Spirit. Those who seek to do God's will, investing every talent to the best advantage, will become wise in working for His kingdom. They will learn lessons of the greatest value, and they will feel the highest satisfaction of a rational mind. Peace and grace and power of intellect will be given them.

As they carry this book to those who need the instruction it contains, the workers will gain a precious experience. This work is a means of education. Those who will do their best as the Lord's helping hand to circulate *Christ's Object Lessons* will obtain an experience that will enable them to be successful laborers for God. Very many, through the training received in this work, will learn how to canvass for our larger books which the people need so much.

All who engage in the work aright, cheerfully and hopefully, will find it a very great blessing. The Lord does not force any to engage in His work; but to those who place themselves decidedly on His side, He will give a willing mind. He will bless all who work out the spirit which He works in. To such workers He will give favor and success. As field after field is entered, new methods and new plans will spring from new circumstances. New thoughts will come with the new workers who give themselves to the work. As they seek the Lord for help, He will communicate with them. They will receive plans devised by the Lord Himself. Souls will be converted, and money will come in. The workers will find waste places of the Lord's vineyard lying close beside fields that have been worked. Every field shows new places to win. All that is done brings to light how much more still remains to be done.

As we work in connection with the Great Teacher, the mental faculties are developed. The conscience is under divine guidance. Christ takes the entire being under His control.

No one can be truly united with Christ, practicing His lessons, submitting to His yoke of restraint, without realizing that which he can never express in words.

New, rich thoughts come to him. Light is given to the intellect, determination to the will, sensitiveness to the conscience, purity to the imagination. The heart becomes more tender, the thoughts more spiritual, the service more Christlike. In the life there is seen that which no words can express—true, faithful, loving devotion of heart, mind, soul, and strength to the work of the Master.

———

After we have, by sanctified energy and prayer, done all that we can do in the work for our schools, we shall see the glory of God. When the trial has been fully made, there will be a blessed result.

If it is made in a free, willing spirit, God will make the movement for the help of our schools a success. He will enable us to roll back the reproach that has come upon our educational institutions. If all will take hold of the work in the spirit of self-sacrifice for the sake of Christ and the truth, it will not be long before the jubilee song of freedom can be sung throughout our borders.

BE NOT WEARY IN WELL-DOING

I am glad that there has been such harmonious effort to carry out the purpose of God and to make the most of His providence. This effort to circulate *Christ's Object Lessons* is demonstrating what can be done in the canvassing field. To ministers, students, fathers, mothers, young men, and young women who have engaged in this work I would say: Let not your interest flag. Let this good work go forward steadily, perseveringly, grandly, till the last debt is removed from all our schools and a fund is created for the establishment of schools in important fields, where there is great need of educational work.

As the ministers and Bible workers are called to other

labors, let the members of our churches say to them: "Go forward with your appointed work, and we will continue to labor for the circulation of *Christ's Object Lessons* and for the freedom of our schools." Let no one feel that this work should stop with the special effort of 1900 and 1901. The field is never exhausted, and this book should be sold for the help of our schools for years to come.

Let us have faith in God. In His name let us carry forward His work without flinching. The work He has called us to do He will make a blessing to us. And when His plan for the relief of our schools has been vindicated, when the work pointed out has been fully accomplished, He will indicate to us what to do next.

As long as the message of mercy is to be given to the world, there will be a call for effort in behalf of other institutions and enterprises similar to that for the relief of our schools. And as long as probation continues, there will be opportunity for the canvasser to work. When the religious denominations unite with the papacy to oppress God's people, places where there is religious freedom will be opened by evangelistic canvassing. If in one place the persecution becomes severe, let the workers do as Christ has directed. "When they persecute you in this city, flee ye into another." If persecution comes there, go to still another place. God will lead His people, making them a blessing in many places. Were it not for persecution they would not be so widely scattered abroad to proclaim the truth. And Christ declares: "Ye shall not have gone over the cities of Israel, till the Son of man be come." Matthew 10:23. Until in heaven is spoken the word, "It is finished," there will always be places for labor, and hearts to receive the message.

Wherefore "let us not be weary in well-doing: for in due season we shall reap, if we faint not." Galatians 6:9.

THE CLAIM OF REDEMPTION

Tithes and offerings for God are an acknowledgment of His claim on us by creation, and they are also an acknowledgment of His claim by redemption. Because all our power is derived from Christ, these offerings are to flow from us to God. They are to keep ever before us the claim of redemption, the greatest of all claims, and the one that involves every other. The realization of the sacrifice made in our behalf is ever to be fresh in our minds and is ever to exert an influence on our thoughts and plans. Christ is to be indeed as one crucified among us.

"Know ye not that . . . ye are not your own? For ye are bought with a price." 1 Corinthians 6: 19, 20. What a price has been paid for us! Behold the cross, and the Victim uplifted upon it. Look at those hands, pierced with the cruel nails. Look at His feet, fastened with spikes to the tree. Christ bore our sins in His own body. That suffering, that agony, is the price of your redemption. The word of command was given: "Deliver them from going down to perish eternally. I have found a ransom."

Know you not that He loved us, and gave Himself for us, that we in return should give ourselves to Him? Why should not love to Christ be expressed by all who receive Him by faith as verily as His love has been expressed to us for whom He died?

Christ is represented as hunting, searching, for the sheep that was lost. It is His love that encircles us, bringing us back to the fold. His love gives us the privilege of sitting together with Him in heavenly places. When the blessed light of the Sun of Righteousness shines into our hearts, and we rest in peace and joy in the Lord, then let us praise the Lord; praise Him who is the health of our countenance and our God. Let us praise Him, not in words only, but by the consecration to Him of all that we are and all that we have.

"How much owest thou unto my Lord?" Compute this you cannot. Since all that you have is His, will you withhold from Him that which He claims? When He calls for it, will you selfishly grasp it as your own? Will you keep it back and apply it to some other purpose than the salvation of souls? It is in this way that thousands of souls are lost. How can we better show our appreciation of God's sacrifice, His great donation to our world, than by sending forth gifts and offerings, with praise and thanksgiving from our lips, because of the great love wherewith He has loved us and drawn us to Himself?

Looking up to heaven in supplication, present yourselves to God as His servants, and all that you have as His, saying: "Lord, of Thine own we freely give Thee." Standing in view of the cross of Calvary and the Son of the infinite God crucified for you, realizing that matchless love, that wonderful display of grace, let your earnest inquiry be: "Lord, what wilt Thou have me to do?" He has told you: "Go ye into all the world, and preach the gospel to every creature." Mark 16: 15.

When you see souls in the kingdom of God saved through your gifts and your service, will not you rejoice that you had the privilege of doing this work?

Of the apostles of Christ it is written: "They went forth, and preached everywhere, the Lord working with them, and confirming the word with signs following." Mark 16: 20. Still the heavenly universe is waiting for channels through which the tide of mercy may flow throughout the world. The same power that the apostles had is now for those who will do God's service.

The enemy will invent every device in his power to prevent the light from shining in new places. He does not want the truth to go forth "as a lamp that burneth." Will our brethren consent that he shall succeed in his plans for hindering the work?

Time is rapidly passing into eternity. Will any now keep back from God that which is strictly His own? Will any refuse Him that which, though it may be given without merit, cannot be denied without ruin? The Lord has given to every man his work, and the holy angels want us to be doing that work. As you shall watch and pray and work, they stand ready to co-operate with you. When the understanding is worked upon by the Holy Spirit, then all the affections act harmoniously in compliance with the divine will. Then men will give to God His own, saying: "All things come of Thee, and of Thine own we freely give Thee." May God forgive His people that they have not done this.

Brethren and sisters, I have tried to set things before you as they are, but the attempt falls far short of the reality. Will you refuse my plea? It is not I who appeal to you; it is the Lord Jesus, who has given His life for the world. I have but obeyed the will, the requirement, of God. Will you improve the opportunity of showing honor to God's work and respect for the servants whom He has sent to do His will in guiding souls to heaven?

"But this I say, He which soweth sparingly shall reap also sparingly; and he which soweth bountifully shall reap also bountifully. Every man according as he purposeth in his heart, so let him give; not grudgingly, or of necessity: for God loveth a cheerful giver. And God is able to make all grace abound toward you; that ye, always having all sufficiency in all things, may abound to every good work: (as it is written, He hath dispersed abroad; he hath given to the poor: his righteousness re-maineth forever. Now He that ministereth seed to the sower both minister bread for your food, and multiply your seed sown, and increase the fruits of your righteous-ness;) being enriched in everything to all bountifulness, which causeth through us thanksgiving to God. For the administration of this service not only supplieth the want of the saints, but is abundant also by many thanksgiv-ings unto God; whiles by the experiment of this min-istration they glorify God for your professed subjection unto the gospel of Christ, and for your liberal distribu-tion unto them, and unto all men; and by their prayer for you, which long after you for the exceeding grace of God in you. Thanks be unto God for His unspeakable Gift." 2 Corinthians 9:6-15.

SCRIPTURAL INDEX

Genesis

1 : 31	349
15 : 1	312
18 : 2, 3	341

Exodus

7 : 16	9
12 : 12, 22-24	195
16 : 23	355
18 : 21	215
20 : 3	10
20 : 8	353, 359
31 : 13	350, 361
31 : 16	350
31 : 16, 17	349
33 : 18, 19	221
34 : 6, 7	221
35 : 21-25	468
36 : 3, 5	468
40 : 34	468

Numbers

6 : 22-27	351
11 : 8	355
18 : 20	312

Deuteronomy

4 : 5-8	13
7 : 6	12
7 : 6-14	222
8 : 3	347
15 : 7-11	271
26 : 17-19	223
28 : 9-13	351

Joshua

24 : 14, 15	141

1 Samuel

2 : 30	144, 356
16 : 7, 12	197

1 Kings

17 : 12-24	346
18 : 21	141

2 Kings

4 : 42-44	466

Job

13 15	157
14 : 14	230
38 : 7	349

Psalms

17 : 4	259
19 : 7	221, 365
19 : 7, 8	259
19 : 11	304
23 : 6	368
29 : 1, 2	366
30 : 1-4	366
37 : 3	307
40 : 7, 8	59
41 : 1-3	307
50 : 23	62
51 : 12, 13	43
62 : 5	354
66 : 16	226
73 : 24, 25	368
78 : 25	372
95 : 1-7	351
100 : 3	351
105 : 21, 22	219
119 : 98	416
119 : 130	433
126 : 6	305
127 : 1	109
139 : 14	375
146 : 1-3	109
148 : 1-3	109

Proverbs

2 : 10, 11	69
3 : 9, 10	307
3 : 13-18	218
4 : 22	225
7 : 2	225
8 : 18	258
11 : 24, 25	307
19 : 17	307
19 : 23	225

Ecclesiastes

11 : 6	333

The Song of Solomon

5 : 10, 16	175

Isaiah

1 : 16, 17	149
1 : 18, 19	200
1 : 18-20	150
6 : 8	49, 325, 333
12 : 3	86
21 : 11	431
21 : 12	26
26 : 20	404
35 : 1	308
40 : 9-11	20

Isaiah (continued)

41 : 18	86
42 : 4	125
43 : 10	444
43 : 19, 20	86
53 : 11	309
54 : 2-5	23
55 : 8-13	308
57 : 15	125
58 : 1	17, 61
58 : 6, 7	266
58 : 7	85, 282
58 : 8	267, 438
58 : 8-11	306
58 : 12	126, 265
58 : 12-14	352
58 : 13, 14	266
58 : 14	312
60 : 1	23, 28
61 : 1	54, 225
61 : 4	126
62 : 1	253, 481
66 : 1, 2	184

Jeremiah

9 : 23, 24	149, 258
13 : 20	205
23 : 6	91
29 : 13, 14	53
31 : 1-3	125
33 : 2-9, 16	228

Ezekiel

3 : 18	286
47 : 8-12	228

Daniel

1 : 20	220
2 : 47	220
10 : 1	406

Hosea

2 : 14-20	409
6 : 3	416

Joel

2 : 12-17, 27	409

Micah

6 : 8	149
7 : 18	149

Habakkuk

3 : 17, 18	157

Zephaniah

3 : 12-17	457

(483)

3:14, 17 63
3:18-20 458

Haggai
2:8 102

Zechariah
3:7 298
4:1-14 459
4:6 .... 50, 74
7:8-14 460
9:12 418
9:16 309
12:8 42
13:1 227

Malachi
3:5, 8-12 388
3:7, 9 387
3:7-12 446
3:13-15 389
3:14 266
3:16-18 390
4:2 55

Matthew
4:4 132
4:10 10
5:13 258
5:14 .. 158, 188, 436
5:14-16 33
5:45 284
6:10 438
7:7 95
9:36-38 254
10:23 478
10:40-42 347
11:28, 29 160
11:28-30 ... 247,
               318, 471
11:29 ...... 165, 443
14:16 345
15:8, 9 249
16:24 378
18:10 348
18:20 360
19:17 225
23:8 .... 26, 108
24:31 404
25:21 .. 303, 304, 441
25:35, 36 275
25:40 ...... 303, 348
28:18-20 447
28:20 .. 228, 335, 399

Mark
2:5 232
2:5, 7, 11 234
4:28 187
8:36, 37 78
11:9 203

13:36 410
14:38 410
16:15 ... 89, 273,
          447, 473, 480
16:15, 20 480

Luke
4:18 225
9:23 .. 248, 249, 449
10:29 294
10:35 347
12:14 312
12:33 258
12:33-40 453
14:12-14 305
14:14 312
14:17 ...... 72, 291
14:23 ...... 76, 280
15:6 124
16:5 480
16:10 172
18:7, 8 282
18:13 283
21:34 410
21:35 129
24:32 53

John
1:12 60
1:14 59
1:29 .... 20, 32,
           54, 279
1:45 428
1:45, 46 ..... 37, 38
2:5 415
3:9, 10 155
3:16 .... 66, 88,
           237, 359
3:16, 17 273
4:10-14 64
4:35, 36 .... 23, 416
5:17 187
6:12 452
6:47 88
6:67-69 156
7:37 20
7:38 274
7:46 248
9:4 198
11:25 230
12:26 ...... 312, 416
12:32 449
13:34 284
14:26 249
15:5 ... 45, 247, 438
15:8 42
16:12 55
16:24 364
16:33 307
17:17 403
17:21 401
17:24 309
20:21, 22 292

20:28 416
21:15 284

Acts
1:14 140
4:19, 20 395
4:31, 32 140
5:20 434
9:6 480
10:38 ...... 225, 415
16:30 88
20:18-21 322

Romans
5:5 171
7:24 53
11:16-22 240
11:33 238
12:1, 2 .... 144, 239
12:11 469
12:19 347
14:7 ...... 236, 242
14:19 460
15:1-3 398
16:1, 2 344

1 Corinthians
1:12 401
1:23-25 142
1:30 ...... 160, 258
3:9 ... 187, 232,
       335, 374, 420, 423
4:9 13
6:11 335
6:15, 19, 20 369
6:19, 20 479
9:24-27 374
12:21 288
13:12 309
14:40 98

2 Corinthians
1:4 348
2:14-16 316
3:2 81
6:14-18 195
6:17, 18 91
8:1-6 271
9:6-15 482
9:8 348
10:16 286

Galatians
1:24 413
6:1, 2 398
6:3, 7 399
6:9 .... 305, 478
6:10 85

Ephesians
1:7 258

1:18 309
2:4-6 300
3:8-10 13
4:11-13 . 48, 243, 291
5:8 335
5:25-27 129
6:11, 12 41
6:12 140

Philippians

2:1-5 399
2:5-11 59
2:13 371
2:15, 16 310
4:7 320
4:19 258

Colossians

1:14-17 59
2:10 167
2:17-19 235
3:1 147
3:1-3, 12-17 99
4:14 233

1 Thessalonians

1:19, 20 310
2:19, 20 310
5:4 129
5:6 410

1 Timothy

3:16 59
4:16 330

6:9 374

2 Timothy

2:7, 15 134
2:15 55

Titus

1:8 342

Philemon

19 347

Hebrews

10:32 365
11:1 473
13:2 342
13:5 157

James

1:27 .... 263, 281
2:13 282
2:23 342
4:4 143
5:2, 3 453
5:16 .... 43, 80, 356

1 Peter

1:4, 5 60
2:5 154
2:12 120
3:8-15 121
3:15 325
4:9, 10 343

2 Peter

1:2 148
1:10, 11 147
3:11, 12 13
3:18 425

1 John

1:1-3 90
4:16 283

Jude

14, 15 392
20-23 280

Revelation

1:1-3, 9, 10 128
2:1 ...... 413, 418
2:4, 5 421
2:5 426
2:7 76
3:1-3 77
3:15-19 77
3:16 408
3:18 426
3:20 262
3:21 298
5:11-14 59
13:3 14
14:12 ...... 144, 292
14:12-19 16
18:1, 2 60
22:4 348
22:16 .... 58, 62
22:17 .... 20, 314

GENERAL INDEX

ABEL a believer in Christ 392
Abraham entertains angels 341, 342
Acquaintance with God, safety from deception 13
Action, harmonious, called for 293
Activity, exhortation to 434
Advance, our watchword 157
Advancement, faith required for 73
  in teachers 157
Adventists, warmheartedness of 85
Advertising at camp meetings 36
Advocate, work of Christ as, before mercy seat 364
Afflicted, Holy Spirit stirs to minister for 303
  promises of God's word to 306, 307
Affliction, blessing in 156, 157
Africa, poverty of missions in 27
Aged, sick, poor, burden for 270, 271
Aggressiveness in our work 61
Agitation, everything in 14
Agriculture, A B C of education 179
  spiritual lessons from 182, 187
  teachers awake to necessity of teaching 191
  to be encouraged in our schools 177-180
  wonderful lessons for students in 185
  See also Schools, industries in.
Alarm, sound, throughout earth 22
Alienation, selfishness is root of 43
Ambition, every human, to be merged in Christ 235, 236
America, example of, followed by every country 18

schools and churches to be erected in 109
uniting with papacy 18
work in 25
See also United States.
Amusements, harmful, dancing, theatergoing, card playing 407
  substitute for, visiting poor and sick 276
Anchor, "It is written" to be our 161
Angel, one appointed for every person 366, 367
Angels, good, attend consecrated workers 307, 308
  co-operate and care for men 307, 308
  co-operate with, all who minister to fellow men 456, 457
  gospel workers 29, 130, 260, 303, 433, 459
  medical missionaries 231
  hold four winds 61, 426
  in Christian warfare, bring every blessing 307, 308
  impart spiritual power 285
  minister to heirs of salvation 63
  unite with Christians in worship 366, 367
  in human form are entertained unawares 342
  in soul-saving work, attend truth-filled books same as work of minister 316
  commissioned to oversee the work 456
  employ human hands in practical ministry 456, 457
  unite with human agencies 307, 308

(486)

linger in clean, orderly rooms 171

our companions 307, 308, 366

present at camp meetings, beholding order and arrangement 35

protect against evil angels and Satan's darkness 63

rejoice, at prosperity of God's work 456

when saints obey, glorify, and praise God 366, 367

when sinners give themselves to Saviour 304

Apostasy in advent movement caused by, neglect of light 400, 401

superficiality 132, 133

Appearance, personal 96

world judges by 397

Appetite the law that governs many 374

See also Indulgence.

Arm, right, of third angel's message 229, 288-293, 327

Armageddon soon to be fought 14, 406

Asleep, many today are 22

Association a precious privilege 347

Atmosphere, heavenly, induced by words of hope and faith 462

surrounding workers 306

spiritual, every Christian to be surrounded by 43

Atonement, cross of Christ the means of 236

Father is satisfied with 364

Auditors, wise, to visit schools 216

Australia, advantages of work in 25, 26

children's meetings in 106, 107

health instruction at camp meetings in 112

relief of schools in 473

work to be advanced in 109

Author, Christ the greatest 165

Authors, infidel, words regarding, from heavenly instructor 162-167

supposed great, Christ has not commanded study of 160

worldly, study of, hinders proper education 163

lessens reverence for God's word 162, 163

not to be brought into Lord's schools 160

Authorities, attitude toward 394-401

Avarice prevails 15

Avondale school, farm of 181-192

BABYLON, ancient, Daniel a blessing to 219, 220, 227

Baptism, administration of, solemn occasion 97, 98

conversion before, children to understand 94

examination for, to be thorough 95, 96

meaning of 91

preparation for 91-93

robes for, every church should provide 97, 98

spiritual wedlock to Jesus Christ 462

Baptism and Lord's Supper two monumental pillars 91

Baptismal vows 98, 99

Battle Creek, centering in, means needed elsewhere 138

Battle Creek College, low tuition at 210, 211

size of buildings 137, 212

Battle, men needed now for God's 148

of Armageddon soon to be fought 14, 406

Believers, living epistles 81, 82

new, duty to 85, 86

poor, caring for our own 85

Believers—*continued*
to strengthen one another 239
Bible, authority of, perfect
guide 355
received as God's word,
not written merely,
but spoken 393
Christ in all 392
difficulties in, because of
human tradition 132
flood of light shining from
449
in education, constant education in, demanded 131
foundation for all study
198
gives the only correct ideas
of higher education 163
should have a better place
in our schools 133
takes place of many books
132, 165
to be extolled above every
human production 164
to be the great lessonbook
166
leads church members to reveal best qualities 449,
450
reverence for 393
study, especially needed in
schools 131
more important at camp
meetings than preach-
ing 87
necessary 401
reform in, needed as never
before 131
we should fear to skim surface in 407
with earnest perseverance
132
with holy awe 393
with teachable spirit 90
teachers, best ministerial talent needed as 134, 135
salaries of, paid from tithe
135, 215

to be treated with respect and
deference 393
understanding of, eternity
needed for 59
wisdom inexhaustible in 132
workers, divine instruction
for 58
duty of, to train voice 381
to follow up camp meeting
interests 74
See also New Testament;
Scriptures; Word of God.
Blessings, church members not
to depend on ministers
for 41
God pledges, to command-
ment keepers 388
imparting and withholding
274
Blood of Christ, sanctified by,
unto unity 239
Blood, we must become exponents of efficacy of 82
Body not our own 369
and mind to be preserved in
best health 375
and soul, gospel includes labor
for 225
to be consecrated 375
Books, denominational, educate
young men and women
to sell 330
Holy Spirit impresses minds
as men read 316
neglected, afterward taken
from shelves 313, 314
to be handled by conse-
crated workers 319, 320
harmful, lead into mysticism
and away from truth 132
produce infidels 164, 165
See also Authors.
of record in heaven, every
good impulse noted in
310
Building up instead of tearing
down 465

Bundles, bound in, to be burned 242

Burden Bearer, Jesus was 63

Business, exactness in work of God 338
integrity in canvassing 337
managers, general instruction for 224
meetings at camp meeting 44

Businessmen workers for Christ 29

CALAMITIES coming 389
See also Disasters; Judgments.

Call of hour answered by coming of the man 332, 333

Calvary, cross of, to be kept before people 54

Camp ground, angels on 35, 40
sanitary arrangement on 35

Camp meetings, absence from, detrimental 38, 39
advertising 36, 37
as schools 49
Australian, lectures on health at 112
business meetings at 44
calls for means at 70
children's meetings at 105, 106
discourses at 53-58, 87, 88
economy in 34
establishment of health enterprises to follow 113
example of ancient Israel as to 39, 40
following up interest of 68, 72-74
harmonious co-operation of workers at 46
location of 33, 34
meat, use of, at 112
medical workers at 48, 49, 110-112
ministers at, daily prayer and counsel of 50
depend not on, for blessing 41

duty of 45
plan work for church members 49
strong force of 46-48
murmuring at, an offense to God 52
not a place for instruction in details of work 44, 45
object lesson of neatness, order, good taste 34, 35
object of 31-33, 45, 46
praise meeting at, daily 62-64
preparation for, in home 41-44
presenting Sabbath truth at 38, 60, 61
purpose of, to strengthen spiritually 44
revival efforts at, too few 64-67
saving of souls at 70, 71
special meetings for parents at 32, 33
teach reasons at, for weakness and unhappiness 52, 53
teaching health reform at 112
temperance reform urged at 111
value of small meetings during 87
work for all at 48, 49

Canvassers, as watchmen and messengers 313-315, 329 335-337
assured of divine assistance 340
disqualifications of, carelessness and slackness in secular affairs 337
failing to depend upon God 317
inclination to act the minister and theologian 324, 325
self-exaltation 331
enemy uses every means to divert 332
family lodgings better than hotels for 323

Canvassers—*continued*

God, calls, back to their work 332

has care for books sold by 313, 314

will bless faithful, same as ministers 340

inexperienced, to be connected with experienced 330

intelligent, God-fearing, truth-loving, should be respected 321

Lord imparts fitness to, for work 333

manner of, in presenting the truth may make a decided impression for good 380

many can accomplish more for truth by canvassing than by other means 323, 329

may work as medical missionaries 324

must be both educators and students 335, 339

need and have promise of angelic ministration 314, 319

not all are fitted to be 333, 334

occupy position equal to ministers' 321

opportunity of, to work until close of probation 478

perfect unity should exist among 326, 331

pray for deeper experience 320

qualifications of, ability to explain Scriptures 314, 324

ability to speak clearly and distinctly 380

ability to treat sick and teach others how 324

activity united with firm trust in God 335

burden for souls and service 317, 324

constant improvement 416

courageous 334, 335

deep Christian experience 329

exemplary in health reform 336

genuine humility 335

honesty and integrity of character 337

imbued with Spirit of God 319, 320, 325, 331, 340

praying and working, working and praying 319

ready to give an answer for their hope 325

ready to speak a word to weary 339

tact and humble, prayerful spirit 319, 333

thorough acquaintance with book handled 338

truth inwrought in soul 317-320

well-balanced minds, strong, well educated 329

remuneration of 337

responsible for work that might have been done 332

rewarded by seeing souls converted 315

should, be free to speak to and pray with souls 324, 339

carry tracts, pamphlets, small books, to give away 338

feel that they are God's workmen 333

sow precious seeds by right use of speech 336, 337

success of, affords purest joy and richest recompense 340

to, be educated and trained for work 328-330

be soul winners 325

combine selling books with personal labor 314, 323, 324, 331, 335, 339

give Bible readings when possible 324

report for our papers 336

work as in the sight of heaven 319, 320

work in co-operation with ministers 315

usefulness of, doubled through diligence and presenting Christ 339

visiting ministers to encourage persons to work as 470

work of, after camp meetings 74

Canvassing, benefits of, educates in patience, kindness, affability and helpfulness 322

evangelists, to surrender to workings of Holy Spirit 340

influence upon own and others' lives is incalculable 340

opportunity to use knowledge gained in school 331

preparation for ministry and other fields of usefulness 321, 322, 334

relieving institutions from debt 468-475

strengthens gospel ministry 316

great work done by evangelistic 340

important work of ministering 319

ministers may engage in 321

mistakes in, departure from right principles 318

introducing controverted points of doctrine 325

selling storybooks 315

no higher work than evangelistic 331

should be conducted from missionary standpoint 317

to direct minds to solemn, present truths 319

work, God's means of reaching many otherwise unreached 313, 314

health books and religious books united in 326-328

is missionary work of highest order 313, 317

leaders in, able to discern relation of parts to whole work 328

leaders in, capable of educating others 329, 330

leaders in, to hunt up and train new workers 328

means for extending knowledge of truth 314, 315, 329

not to be left to languish 329

ordained of God to present light in books 313

part of both medical missionary work and ministry 323

presents many opportunities for ministry 322

Capabilities come from God 243

Captivity, Babylonian, God's design in 219

Cause of God, consider, always as a whole 291

needs many skilled workmen 291

neglect no phase of 292, 293

retarded by withholding of tithes and offerings 385-388

tendency to work independent of 235-242

See also Work of God.

Censure, duty to refrain from 292, 293

Changes, peculiar and rapid 436

Channels, men and women needed as 206

Character, building, put best material into 405

deformed by self-indulgence 254

developed by, faith in Christ as personal Saviour 96, 97

influence of solemn truths 97

development of, divine plan for, Peter's ladder 147, 148

now for future 268

good traits of, graces of Peter's ladder 147, 148

is above everything esteemed in earth or heaven 97

now being formed for eternity 268

of Christ, attributes of, sociability 172

beholding, produces miracles in genuine conversion 82, 83

greatest work in world to live the 439

infinitely perfect 60

study carefully 59

of God, attribute of, goodness 349

favorite theme of Christ 55

law transcript of 10

revealed in nature 186

revealed in third angel's message 20

transformation of, testimony of indwelling Christ 43

virtue of, has saving influence 258, 259

Characteristics, most needful, patience, long-suffering, peace, love 398

Cheerfulness, element of religion 365, 366

Children, are younger members of Lord's family 94, 205

home training of, give religious instruction to, from earliest years 93

in character building and overcoming 93, 94

in helpfulness about home 429

in self-denial and giving to missions 102, 451

improperly disciplined, teachers to take special interest in 152

used by Satan to influence the carefully trained 193

management and instruction of, is noblest missionary work 205

meetings and work for, at camp meetings 105-108

orphan, care of, is Christlike work 283-285

religious instruction of, in preparation for baptism 93, 94

Sabbath entertainment of 358, 359

too little attention is given to 196, 197

See also Family; Parents; Home.

Children's meetings, aim of, at camp meeting 105, 106

Australian experience in 106, 107

China, great difficulties to be encountered in 25

workers sustained in, by American businessman 29, 30

Christ, announcement and introduction of public ministry of, Jesus finds Philip, and Philip Nathanael 428

apparent failure of, in His work 307

ascension of 309

as Saviour, able to save and keep saved 66, 67, 240

all who accept, and hold fast will be saved 60
birth and childhood of, Passover visit to Jerusalem when twelve 75
center of all hope 62
chain of dependence through, fast to throne 339, 340
crucified, among us 479
  attention of sinners aroused by preaching 66
  ever fresh theme 60
  for this world 16
  lift up, before people 75, 392
  talk it, pray it, sing it 67
favorite theme of 55
incarnation, life, death, mediation of, glorify Father 364
in Old and New Testament 392
interest of, in struggling followers 309
life and character of, to be studied 59
life of, all who study, will be like Him 96
multitude fed 263, 345, 465
night talk with Nicodemus 154, 155
offices, titles, and appellations of, Author and Finisher of our faith 335, 422
  Author of every blessing 175
  Author of religion 21
  bright and morning Star 20, 21
  Captain of our salvation 76
  Captain of the Lord's host 140
  Commander 342
  Counselor 76
  Creator 342
  divine Attendant 322
  divine Companion 322
  Elder Brother 416

Fountainhead of wisdom 160
General 28
Giver 175
Great Physician 111, 136, 227
Great Teacher 86, 152, 153, 331
Guide 76, 221
Head 242
Holy One 322
I AM 20
Intercessor 67
King 189, 342
Lamb of God 20, 67, 404
Leader 130, 140
Light Bearer 329
Lion of Judah 404
Living One 20
Majesty of heaven 79
Merchantman 426
One "altogether lovely" **175**
Pattern 393
Redeemer 342, 416
Restorer 175, 200
risen Saviour 111
Root and Offspring of David 20
Saviour 175
Sin Bearer 20, 67
Source of all true pleasure and wisdom 175, 331
Sun of Righteousness 67, 114, 479
Teacher 160, 221
Victim 479
Way, the Truth, and the Life 67, 248
parable of lost sheep 124, **125**
paralytic healed 234
pre-existence of, world should know we believe in 58
refused adoration from angels at ascension 309
theme of every discourse 54
to be preached in third angel's message 20, 21

Christ—*continued*
  walked with Enoch 392
  work of, personal interviews
      large part of 115
    to save men from Satan's
        rule 237
      See also Character of
          Christ; Gospel; Grace of
          Christ; Holy Spirit; Love
          of Christ; Parables.
  youth and early manhood of,
      kept life mission ever be-
      fore Him 307
Christ's Object Lessons, sale of
    468-478
  work with, to continue 478
Christian, experience, dark
        and uncertain, may
        be changed 266
    deep, needed by, canvassers
        329
    deeper, all workers to pray
        for 320
      See also Experience.
  help work, duty of church in
      295-297
    for neighbors 276
    importance of 299
    means of strength to church
        266, 267
    promises of God regarding
        306, 307
      See also Medical missionary
          work; Service.
Christians, duties of, to orphans
    282
  early, zeal and enthusiasm of,
      waning 422
  neglect to help the poor
      273, 275
  to be light bearers 145
  types and symbols of power
      of gospel 11
    See also Believers; People of
        God.
Church, case containing jewels
    261
  Christ's interest in 418, 419

garden containing variety of
    flowers 333, 334
God's love for 42
how to waken, from carnal
    slumber 437
in heaven and on earth, one
    366
Laodicean message applicable
    to, now 426
live, a working 435
members, camp meetings to be
    attended by 38-40, 43
  depending too much on
      ministers 30
  goods committed to, as
      stewards 448
  hundredth part of duty of,
      not done 425
  leaders to encourage, to
      save souls 302
  living experience to be
      gained by 64
  make feeble efforts to save
      souls 423, 424, 445, 446
  many dead in sin 426, 427
  neglecting neighbors 294,
      295
  responsibilities of, in train-
      ing children 193
  sins of individual, do not
      prove church wrong 239
  sleeping in meeting 361
  to assist in educating youth
      212, 213
  to be channels of light 405
  to be soul winners 296, 297,
      302, 427, 431
  to care for poor and suffer-
      ing 261, 275
  to do medical missionary
      work 291, 292
  to learn to love neighbors
      by loving God supremely
      303
  to organize for work 432
  to show hospitality 347, 348
  to study how to forward
      work 29

to study methods of personal work 433
trained to rely on preaching 434
urged to labor in hope of reaping 420
world sees, not pulpit 260
membership in large, a disadvantage 198
ministry to be sustained by 417
nothing so dear to God as 42
organization, purpose of 295
responsibilities of, evangelize world 19, 23, 24, 28, 29
uphold standard of reform in neighborhood 292
schools, buildings for 108, 109, 203
criticism and suspicion hinder establishment of 202
expense of, all to share 109, 216, 217
families near, to be good representatives of our faith 204
in America, Australia, Europe, and elsewhere 109
lessonbooks in 203
medical missionary work by children in 203
neglect of establishing 199, 200, 203
object of, children to be witnesses for Christ 202, 203
object of, separation from worldly associations 109, 193
object of, to carry forward interest begun at camp meetings 108
object of, to save the children 193, 195, 199
object of, to train children to be missionaries 198, 201, 203

object of, word of God to be foundation of all study in 195, 198
order and government in 201
responsibility of churches with 204
results of, children give message when older ones cannot 202, 203
thorough education in common branches in 198
to be conducted on basis of financial success 217
two or three churches uniting to establish 109
unity necessary to success of 202
vision of 108
where but few Sabbathkeepers 109, 198, 199
work done in, to be of highest order 200
workers to provide for, in raising up new churches 108
youth from world attending 203, 204
See also Schools.
school teachers, co-operation of parents with 199, 202
difficulties to be met by 201
enter sports of little children 205
qualifications of 200, 201
missionaries 198, 205
tact, skill, special talents 205
to be selected by wise men who can discern character 200
See also Teachers.
sermonizing not supreme need of 49
shortcomings and failures of, feeble faith no excuse for 418

Church—*continued*
lack of burden for souls
424, 445, 446
neglecting Christian help
work 294, 295
simplest methods of work for
433
summoned to universal action
437
unity in 239
waning of early zeal in 422
See also People of God.
Churches, popular, attending,
sometimes beneficial
74, 75
great body of Christ's true
followers in 70, 71, 76
working, for members of 76
for ministers of 77, 78
Circumstances, are helpers, not
hindrances 145
opposing, should create determination to overcome 145
Cities, families should move
from 178, 195
methods of labor in 31, 32
pitiful conditions of poor in
275
reformers to witness for God
in 136
warning to be given, without
delay 32
City missions, treatment rooms
needed in 113
Cleanliness and order, lessons in,
from Israel 170
part of education 169, 171
Clothing, special, for Sabbath
use 355
See also Dress.
College View, money invested
in 210
Colonization around our institutions 184, 187
Commandment keepers, seal of
God upon 15
Commands, divine, Holy Spirit
impresses 10

of God to be obeyed without
question 466
Commission of Christ, someone
must fulfill 295
Communion with God, church
needs members who have
habitual 64
through Bible study and
prayer 47
See also Prayer.
Companionship with Christ
brings a sacred joy 322
Compassion and mercy toward
poor, sick, sinful 262
Complaining, by those who rob
God 389, 390
cure for 367, 368
offense to God 52
Comprehension, disciples re-
proved for slowness
of 248
Confederacy with world, enter
not into 17
Conflict, final, Sabbath to be
issue in 352
terrible, right upon us 407
Consecration, daily, essential to
soul winning 66, 67, 318
result of, constant new endowment of physical,
mental, and spiritual
power 306
Consistency in teaching health
principles 112
Control, exercising, over others
397
Controversy, attitude of, be
slow in taking 62
meetings not appointed for 69
on outside questions to be
avoided 122
Conversation, about Satan
62, 63
at table 173, 174
frivolous, grieves angels 173
See also Expressions; Jesting;
Words.

Conversion, change of heart, thoughts, purposes 95
children to understand meaning of, before baptism 94
entire surrender 92
See also New birth.
Converts, educate, to become laborers 49
labor for 92, 93, 95
reason for so few 371
to be instructed regarding dress 96
walk of, after baptism 98, 99
young, parents to work for 93, 94
Conviction, most irreligious have hours of 71
real, in hearts of men 66, 67
reinforced by daily prayer and study 401
Co-operation between medical missionaries and ministry 288-293
Cornelius a representative of upper classes 79
Counselor, word of God our 161
Courtesy, Christian, to be cultivated in our schools 172, 173
importance of cultivating 262
in, hospitality, illustrations of 342
workers 322
true, source of 257
Crisis, if there was ever, it is now 16
impending 24
preparation for final 404, 405
Criticism, result of inactivity in service 296, 297
Satan author of 42
Cross, bearing, and self-denial, God's people have largely lost spirit of 445, 446
our portion 251, 441
See also Self-denial.
of Christ, atonement on 236

attention of all called to 54, 67
bring sinners by faith to 67
canvasser doubles his usefulness by presenting 339
center of all lines of work 235
center of all religious institutions 235, 236, 241
endured for joy of saving souls 449
enthusiasm inspired by 287
lift up 240
makes yoke easy and burden light 247
medical missionaries will lift 440
mercy and truth meet at 59, 60
stands where Satan set his throne 237
study again and again 59, 60
theme of study in schools 132
triumphs of, God wants men to push 26
viewed aright gives sure foundation 238
of Christian, followers of Christ must take up 251
many fail to bear 338
Crucifixion of self is life to the soul 125

DANGER, many in, of oppressing fellow men 397
Daniel, and the Revelation, demand special study 128
God's will plainly revealed in 131
in presenting, uplift Christ 62
example to institutions 219, 220
light to the world 220
type of God's people 227

Daniel—*continued*
   with his companions, peerless
      in courts of Babylon 220
Darkness, spiritual, joy in
      heaven over efforts
      to dispel 316
   only purpose of workers is
      to enlighten those in 317
David anointed secretly by
      Samuel 197
Death of Christ under most
      humiliating circum-
      stances 230
   See also Cross of Christ.
Debating on questions outside
      truth to be avoided 122
Debt, church buildings dedicated
      free of, if possible 101-104
   duty to remove 207
   gifts and offerings for 103, 104
   incurring, by medical institu-
      tions 464
   methods for liquidating 103,
      213
   not, to be left on churches
      101-104
   to be paid with tithe 391
   on institutions to be avoided
      210-213, 216, 217
   relief plan for liquidating in-
      stitutional 468-478
   shun as disease 211, 217
Demon worship in last days re-
      vealed to John 15
Denominations, work for min-
      isters of other 77, 78
   See also Churches.
Dependence, law of reciprocal,
      to be recognized and
      obeyed 242
Despondency accomplishes
      nothing 472
Destiny, eternal, now being
      decided 16
   sealed by indifference, neglect,
      cherishing sins 404, 405
Destitute, Christlike work for
      283-285

See also Needy; Poor.
Dew, present truth in words
      gentle as the 400
Diet, extremes in 373, 374
   of, Daniel and his companions
      372
      Israelites 372
      students to be simple but
         not meager 209
   on Sabbath 357
   vanity in, for visitors 343
   vegetarian, to be advocated at
      camp meetings 112, 113
Dietetic reform, failure of min-
      isters to take hold of 377
   See also Health reform.
Diet of Spires, object of 402
Difficulties, angels give power to
      combat 285
   work of God soon hedged
      with, beyond imagi-
      nation 22
Dignity, love of, should not
      be once named among
      us 317
   not lowering, to minister to
      suffering 279
   sacred, holy, of the ministry
      414
   workers for higher classes
      should possess true 81
Directions from God, power in
      following 251
Disasters, sign of last days 408
   souls perishing in 445
   See also Calamities.
Disciples, Christ manifested
      deep interest in 309
   reproached at times with
      slowness of compre-
      hension 248
Discipleship, tests of 96
Discouraged, prayer for, in re-
      vival efforts 65, 66
Discouragement, words of, not
      to be uttered 455, 474
   workers for God will meet
      with 335

Discourses, Christ crucified should be theme of 67
followed by Bible study 68
harsh, loud note not to be heard in 67
in too quick succession 56
lost unless hearers' hearts are softened by God's Spirit 68
short, pointed, most helpful 56, 57
See also Sermons.
Disorganization, the gospel is God's remedy for universal 11
Display never makes right impression 318
Distinction from world to be decidedly apparent 146, 147
Disunion is weakness and defeat 293
See also Unity.
Divisions, Christ made no, in His work 242
Doctrine, Christ center of all true 54
Drama of life 145
Dream about unfinished building 72
Dress, Aaron's was symbolic 96
display of, in expensive ornaments or costly array 96
new converts to be instructed regarding 96
Drink, strong, men of wealth and talent overcome by 256

EARTH has concealed treasures 178
Eating and drinking, dispense with unhealthful gratifications in 371
habits of, show whether of world or God 372
intemperate 111
right principle in 374, 375
Economy, false 24

in, daily living to help cause 450
institutions, look after small things 113, 208, 209
of means and time essential 419, 452
Education, Christian experience should be combined with all 154
hindrances to reform in 141-150
in, Christian sociability and courtesy 172-174
domestic duties 169-171
own country 137
word of God needed constantly 131
industries as branch of 176-180
influences life here and for eternity 154
mistakes in, accepting a low standard of knowledge 152
expending time, study, in gaining comparatively useless 130
spending too long time in obtaining 331
study of books leading to reception of false ideas 162-164
most desirable, is knowledge of the Scriptures 130, 131
object of true, to give reasons for our faith 128, 129
of children, church and home schools to be established for 198-200
of medical missionary evangelists 291
of our institutions, must be conducted on Christian principles 145, 146
should be of a different order 126, 142
standard of, is not to be lowered 126, 152

Education—*continued*
to benefit surrounding communities 188, 189
of youth, all to have privileges of 197
molds whole social fabric 150
reform needed in 126
should interest every Seventh-day Adventist 162
true higher, develops character 127
imparts a knowledge of salvation 127
knowledge of God is 97, 131
most earnest attention must be given to 127
produces results as lasting as eternity 154
science of, is the truth 131
true, obtained by going out into field with truth 331
worldly, no time now to fill mind with theories of 130
Satan has woven his plans and principles into 127
Educator, work of true, to thwart Satan's devices 127
Educators, danger of, conforming to worldly customs, practices, traditions 150
missionaries can become industrial 176
should prize more and more God's truth and law 130
teachers to take their position as true 158
Efficiency, Christ is our, in all things 467
Holy Spirit gives, to our work 51
in God's work, how gained 443, 444
Effort, strength in united 289-293
Efforts, determined, to help forward Lord's work 469, 470
public, at camp meetings, following up interest of 72-75
Elements from beneath stirred up 18
Elisha feeding men miraculously 466
End, diligent work needed in view of 148
is near 440
See also Second advent.
Enemies of truth, discretion in referring to 394, 395
England, advantages of work in 25
need of more laborers in 26
Enoch, Christ walked with 392
Entertainment of visitors, elaborate preparations for 343
Entertainments, worldly, in our schools 143
Envy and evil surmising of Satan 42
Ephesus, church of, warning from 421-423
Erring, restoring, in spirit of meekness 121
Error, let truth discover 38
Eternity, millions now deciding for 406
Europe, advantages of work in 25
efforts to strengthen the work in 461, 462
facilities for work in, to be preserved 459, 461
schools to be established in 109
Evangelists, importance of voice culture for 380
work of 76
Example, Christ's, in service to humanity 258
influence of 264
See also Influence.

Executives, need of, in God's cause 80

Experience, daily, living faith like threads of gold to run through, in performance of little duties 171
deeper, pray, pray for 320
of canvasser under Spirit of God becomes deep 320
See also Christian experience.

Expressions, unguarded, against government and law 394, 395

Ezekiel pictures the living stream 227, 228

FACILITIES to be increased for great work in short time 441

Failure, apparent, faith and courage of Christ in face of 307
workers never to speak or think of 467

Failures and mistakes, we cannot blot out 149

Faith, and activity impart assurance 199
and works combined 441
exhortation to live by 171
is the hand to touch infinity 467
lack of, dishonoring God by 63
is hindering coming of kingdom 438
lifeblood of soul 472
prayer, work, only remedy for disheartened 438
strengthened by using our talents 44

Faithfulness, in home duties fits for work in church 439
man judged by, rather than by position 439

Familiarity not to lead to lack of sympathy 232

Families, as light bearers 430
located near schools 183, 187, 204
to locate in dark places as missionaries 442
work of consecrated women for 118

Family, earthly, symbol of heavenly 430
first field for Christian work 429
worship, all to take part in 357, 358
to be object lesson for children 354
See also Children; Home; Parents.

Farming to be encouraged in our schools 177, 178
See also Agriculture.

Fashion, changing apparel for sake of 96

Favor given until work is done 21

Field, every part of, to be worked 24

Fields, foreign, aggressive work in 23-29
results of work in 27, 28
time to work in 18
See also Foreign missions; Mission fields.

Finances of cause, ministers to be relieved from responsibilities of 216
trained men to manage 216

First fruits required of God 384

Fitness, Lord imparts 333

Flesh food, clamor of Israelites for 372
not furnished at camp meetings 112

Food, beneficial, nourishing in place of injurious 373, 374
furnished by Christ to multitude 345
preparation of, for Sabbath 355-357

Foreign missions, call for self-denial to sustain 445-453
needs of 450
Foundation, solid, needed when the wrath of God breaks 16
Fountains of life, God's people to be 227, 228
Friday, preparation day 354
Funds, for orphanages 286
to educate workers 213, 214

GALL, one drop of, poisons hearers or readers 123
Game of life, Satan playing for soul in 148, 264, 446
Generation, youth of this, choosing path to destruction 254
Gentleness in working for souls 400, 401
Germany, facilities to be furnished for work in 25
Gift, widow's mite 310
Gifts, and offerings, God's claims to 384
debts to be lifted by 104
See also Funds; Giving; Means; Money; Offerings.
of God, to men, how to be used 284, 285, 449
of the Spirit 291
Gilboa, souls barren as hills of 417
Giving, condition of receiving 448
example of, set by God 385, 386
widow's mite 310
for building of tabernacle 468
to God's cause 446-453
See also Gifts; Liberality; Sacrifice.
God, appellations, offices, titles of, Creator 349, 350
Deity 186
Eternal 462

Fountain of life and power 364
Great Sower 187
Infinite One 393
King 349
Lawgiver 350
Master Worker 24
Most High 393
Omniscience 14
Sanctifier, the 350
Stronghold 157
personal acquaintance with, necessary to salvation 13
presence of, works through nature's laws 186
Golden chain of, divine love binds men to throne of God 238
obedience, every link a promise 350
Gospel, advance meets opposition 407
and medical missionary work 289
angels prepare hearts to receive 438
different instrumentalities used in 240
extent of, in last days, "regions beyond" 29
remote parts of earth 24
to all mankind 21
to all the world 23, 24, 28, 29, 240, 289, 403
to every creature 296
to every nation, kindred, tongue, and people 31, 100, 133, 438
to thousands of places not yet reached 412
to waste places of earth 24
feast, call to 76, 412
God's remedy for disorganization 11
health reform principles to be bound up with 379
imparts heaven's choicest gifts 238

in, Leviticus, given in precept 392

whole Bible 392

influences of, in life 253

layman to carry, as well as minister 427

live out, in all its bearings 189

medical work combined with 292

ministry, definition of 301 *See also* Ministry.

preachers of, must first be saved by 51, 52

present truth embraces 291

revealed as living power 264

saving truths of, in third angel's message 11, 19, 241

valueless except soul is surrendered 241

wealthy in need of 257

work, for health of body and soul 225

Satan's efforts to counterwork 242

workers in, must be elevated and sanctified 242

Government, civil, limits of authority of, in religious matters 402

recognition of 394-402

Grace, of Christ, apparently hopeless material subjects of 308, 309

everything owing to 268

precious exhibitions of, God has yet 413

precious treasure of, not to be hoarded 421

receive, without limit 467

received is spiritual tide to others 227

rich blessings of, He longs to bestow 262

seekers of, heed instruction given on dress 96

success through 436

transforms faulty character 43

treasures of, revealed to seekers 364

truth spoken in, has quickening power 400

of God, all treasures of, open as Christ pleads 364

atmosphere of faith and courage, result of 43

fresh current of, flows as imparted to others 43, 44, 448

powerful to subdue unsanctified impulse 161

received should stimulate consecrated effort 297

soft, subduing influence of 405

sweeps through chambers of mind 170

to be manifested through His people 253

Gratitude, giving expression to 232

lack of, among professed believers 426

Guidance, divine, in plans 241

Guilt, constantly burdening souls of many 52, 53

HABIT, every, open to inspection of God 372

Hand, and arm, medical missionary work is right, of third angel's message 229, 288-293

God's helping, circulators of *Christ's Object Lessons* 476

missionary nurses are 136

Harmony, God desires, in workers 292, 293

of action essential in crisis 139

Healing, by Christ of paralytic 234

miraculous, why sanitariums instead of 441

Healing—*continued*
  physical, is often accompanied by spiritual 226
  spiritual, many receive 226
Health, and life, prayer and Bible study bring, to the soul 253
  Hebrews', secured through obedience 222
  institute at Battle Creek, instructions regarding work of 223, 224
  institutions, established everywhere as branch of gospel work 113
    give character to work in new fields 113
    to be beacons of light, warning, and reproof 223, 224
    to reach class nothing else can 113
  laws of, obedience to, matter of personal duty 369
  principles, consistency in teaching 112, 113
    promulgation of, preparation for Christ's coming 224
    to be taught by example 112, 113
  publications, indifference regarding, is offense to God 327
  reform, a part of the truth 327
    camp meetings present opportunities for illustrating 112, 113
    canvassers to be examples of 336
    Daniel and companions are sermons on 372
    disregarded brings spiritual and physical degeneracy 371
    disregarded by ministers 299, 300, 327, 376-378

    disregarded unfits one to stand as God's messenger 378
    educate people in, by precept and practice 112
    gospel is to be bound up with 327, 379
    ignored by persons in positions of influence 327
    light regarding, not heartily received in churches 370, 371
    make known principles of 379
    many opposed to, in heart and practice 373
    ministers and people to make advance moves in 299, 300
    ministers to become intelligent on 376
    parents to study and teach children principles of 370
    perverted, is health deform 374
    presented in more positive and decided manner 112
    principles of, will be received with favor by all who want light 379
    purpose of light on 378
    right arm to message 327
    rise higher and still higher in 112, 113
    teachers should have practical knowledge of 370
    those who have never adopted, cannot judge 370
    to bear message regarding, in every church 370
    will rescue many from physical, mental, and moral degeneracy 378
  work, properly conducted, is entering wedge for other truths 327

Healthful living must be made
a family matter 370
Heathen nations, supplying
workers for 25-30
Heaven, believers on earth and
beings in, constitute one
church 366
cry of poor reaches to 385
joy in, over tidings of soul
winning 316
nearness of, to earth 366, 367
preparation for, home on
earth should be 354
we must impart the goods of,
to receive fresh blessings
448
Helping others, necessary for
character development
262
Hesitation will keep things back
192
Higher classes, Christ's work
for 255
exposed to danger 255-257
fruits of work for 79
labors for 255-258
necessity of working for 78,
80, 81, 255
will accept temperance principles 256
Holy Spirit, awaits our demand
175
balancing agent in presenting
message 291
baptism in name of 91
brings life into conformity to
law of God 92
clear way for, by self-renunciation 43
controlling power in our institutions 241
convicts and converts soul 81
convincing power of 316
co-operates with workers 260,
266, 267, 400
creates desire for truth 231
develops true love for God
and man 303

directions of, to be obeyed 241
earnest seeking for 42
elevates and ennobles 241
endows with power from
above 51, 88
given through sacrifice of
Christ 449
harmony with 293
illuminates minds 43, 415
lacking because variance and
bitterness are cherished 42
leads men to Christ 92
Lord longs to pour upon us
in rich measure 43
needed by, all 292, 293
ministers 51, 88
put away variance to
receive 42
qualifies for service 436
resistance of, brings with-
drawal of 366, 367
stirs to ministry for afflicted
303
why not enthused by? 296
Home, angels in human form
entertained in 342
being missionaries in 429, 430
children to share duties of 429
conducting school in 198, 199
field a vital problem 430
light should shine from every
430
invite youth to your 348
made happy by morning and
evening family worship
354
many will not hear truth unless it is brought into 314
missions to be strengthened 27
missionary work, for youth
and children 435, 436
home a mission field for
427-430
how advanced 27
of women 114-118
most effective agency for
formation of Christian
character 430

Home—*continued*
  on earth a preparation for
    heavenly 354
  schools, purpose of 198, 199
  symbolic of heaven 430
  See also Family; Children;
    Parents.
Homeless, blessings in caring
  for 348
Hope, and courage, impart,
    when entertaining needy
    347
  and faith, every worker may
    go forth in 412
    strengthen as talents are
      used 44
  be strong and talk 462
  bring sunshine to those having
    lost 277
  faithful Christians speak
    words of 390
  God looks with pitying ten-
    derness upon youth with-
    out 254, 255
  many put their, in preachers
    434
  multitudes dying without 445
  show discouraged sufferer he
    is prisoner of 279
  souls guarded as long as there
    is 366, 367
  sources of, Christ 88, 311
    God's approval 130
    Holy Spirit 415
    religion in home 119
    truth-filled books 314
  uplift Jesus as center of all 88
Hopeless, present word of life
    to 442
Hospitality, privilege and bless-
    ing of 341-348
House of worship, humble,
    stands as light amid
    darkness 100
  pews in, not to be rented 101
Houses of worship, building of
    100-104

rededication of, after paying
    of debt on 104
  when possible, to be dedicated
    free from debt 100-103
House-to-house work, a place
    for everyone in 428
  ministry in many lines in
    83, 84
  Paul's example of 321, 322
Human agencies, to co-operate
    with heaven 458, 459
  used by God 457
Humility, God uses laymen hav-
    ing, to reach souls minis-
    ters cannot 43
Hundred times more accom-
    plished if self-sacrifice of
    early days manifested 419
Hundredth of blessing not re-
    ceived 362
Hygiene, ministers to have
    knowledge of 301,
    302, 376, 377

IDLERS, arouse, to activity 434
Immortality, Christ alone can
    give 54
Improvement, institutions to be
    examples of 188
  young men to strive for 416
Independence, selfish, in medical
    missionary work would
    weaken message 288-291
  Satan originator of 236
India, difficulties of work in 25
Indifference, dangerous, in view
    of times 408, 409
Individual, every, to be light
    bearer 11
  responsibility, use of 189, 190
Indulgence, health and char-
    acter of youth ruined
    through 254, 255
  See also Appetite.
Industrial reform 176-180
Industries to be taught in our
    schools 176, 182, 191, 208
  See also Trades.

Infidel sentiments in textbooks 165

Infidelity, seeds of, sown by teachers 164

fastens itself on mind with despotic power 162

Influence, law of, to be recognized and obeyed 242

reason for little, upon unbelieving associates 146, 147

religious, in sanitariums inspires guests with confidence 226

See *also* Example.

Influences, disorganizing, Christ corrects 237

Institutes, ministerial 89, 90

Institutions, Christ in charge of 134

dedicated free from debt if possible 207

establishment of, in foreign fields 25-30

in many places 113

no command to cease 440, 441

small, in many localities 212

families gathering around, for selfish convenience 183, 184, 187

in Europe, need of strengthening 461, 462

in Scandinavia, difficult conditions of 463-467

large, harmonious action will do more than 293

lifting burdens that rest on 458

of learning, prisoners of hope 145

relief of 468-478

prosperous, to help those less favored 459, 461

purpose of 219-228

light bearers 11

qualify colaborers with God 134, 135

represent message 18

teach third angel's message 128, 220, 241

religious, the cross the center of 241

selfishness woven into 80

workers in, necessity of prayer and Bible study to 253

spiritual reformation required among 253

Instruction, religious, from earliest years 93

Instructor, heavenly, words from 162-167, 184, 185

Intemperance, peril of men of wealth and talent through 256

Intercession of Christ 364

Intercessor, office work of our 363

Isaiah, book of, chapter 58, reform for this time 265

Israel, cause of weakness of 249

convocations of, example for camp meetings 39, 40

order and cleanliness among 170

purpose of God for, above all nations 222

JEALOUSY bars way against Holy Spirit 42

Jehovah the only true God 166

Jerusalem, Paul assists church in 271

Jesting and joking cause grief to angels 173

See *also* Conversation.

John the beloved, banished to Patmos 128

visions of 59, 128

Joseph, fountain of life to Egyptians 227

light bearer in Egypt, God's design in 219

type of God's people today 227

representative of Christ 220

Judas, warning from selfishness of 264, 265
Judgment, investigative 130
Judgments of God, about to fall 408
    already in land 445
    doing their work while church sleeps 445, 446
    for disobedience preceded by warning 19
    See also Calamities; Disasters.
Justification by faith, sweetest melody from God through human lips 426

KINDERGARTEN at camp meeting 105
Knowledge of God is basis of true education 97

LABOR, evangelistic, defective methods of 87, 88
    for, higher classes 78-81, 255-258
    ministers of other churches 77, 78
    personal, by ministers 68, 76
        by youth 115
        required of all 276
        reward of 305-312
        successful 111
    physical, advantage to girls 176
        co-operation with God in our 187
        dignity of 192
        for students 176, 180
        lessons of truth in 177, 187
        teachers uniting with students in 179
Laborers, evangelistic, most efficient 443
Land for use of schools 181-187
Landmarks of truth, experience, and duty 17
Laodicean message addressed to believers in carnal security 77

Last days, evils of, heresies, delusions 31
    setting aside God's law 10
    spirit of war 14
    unbelief respecting Christ's coming 129
God's people in, need convocations 40
    stand before magistrates 128
    warn wicked 10, 11, 19, 22, 61
    perils of, already here 128, 129
    truths for, proclaimed by Holy Spirit's power 24
Law, civil, appearance of enmity toward, to be guarded against 394-397
    duty to obey 402
    of God, exalted in last days 18
    proclamation of, at Sinai 10
    relation of, to medical missionary work 266
    use to be made of, in sermons 54
Laws, of health and life, sanitariums to show evil of disregarding 225
    of life, converted will conscientiously regard 369
    obedience to, matter of personal duty 369
    violation of, dishonors God 369, 370
    of nature, are laws of God 369
        bring daily practice into harmony with 371
        God not restricted by 186
        ignorance of, is sin 369
        not self-acting, God works through 186
        obedience to, creates life-saving atmosphere about soul 371
        violation of, results in sickness and disease 369, 370
        physical, accountability for light in regard to 372

are indeed laws of God 373
  ministers should understand 376
  obedience to, results in physical, mental, and moral well-being 224
  reformers stand in defense of 136
Leaves of tree of life, lessons drawn from parables as 475
  principles of Bible as 393
Lessonbooks in our schools 203
  See also Books; Textbooks.
Lessons, for young children, from book of nature 178, 179, 186
  from, everyday things 170, 171
  labor 177
  men slow to comprehend 248, 249
Leviticus, gospel given in precept in 392
Liberality, the reward of 390
  See also Giving.
Life, holy trust 379
  of church in relation to medical work 289
  physical, not treated in haphazard manner 372
  spared, physician to thank God for 232
Light, spiritual, all revealed, is for every soul 11
  channels of, Christ's followers to be 11, 145
  communicated most effectively by personal effort 428
  let, shine forth 405
  practices to be in harmony with 423
  promote, among own people 37
London, scarcely touched 26
  should have one hundred workers 26

Lost, tenderness and compassion in work for 268
Loud cry, when given 401
Love, ability cannot take place of 84
  all need to sow a crop of 268
  assemble in God's house to cultivate attributes of 368
  coldness because of lack of 422
  effects of, will do work we cannot comprehend 84
  for children not expressed by indulging selfish desires 451
  for God, lacking 425, 426
  leads to increased love for others 422
  our labors accepted as tokens of 261
  whoever have not, cannot be successful missionaries 84
  for Jesus, golden chain binding believers together 421
  service for Him is proof of 427, 428
  lack of, drives soul away from truth 398
  like that manifested by Christ 445
  loss of first, causes lack of zeal 368, 422
  of Christ, all believers to tell story of 66
  angels watch to see who will manifest 268
  effect of, corrects peculiarities 52
  followers to reflect 413, 425
  fragrance of, workers should reveal 75
  greater than mother's 287
  ministers to present precious 413
  Saviour present when we tell of 267

Love—*continued*
 talk to sinners with heart
  overflowing with 66, 67
 to be burden of every
  message 367
 wealth of, underlies all His
  dealings 221
 yearns for church 261
 of God, Christ's favorite
  theme 55
 depravity of man met by
  237
 embraces all mankind 273
 for church is unspeakable
  42, 261
 God's people channels for 12
 home life should enshrine 76
 perfect 368
 revealed in nature 358
 sense of, immensity and
  diversity of 368
 thousands might rejoice in,
  if Christians did duty 273
 work of bearing message of,
  committed to church 427
 world must hear message of
  120, 427
 pure, sanctified, is sacred
  perfume 84
Lowliness of Jesus 399
Lowly, power of kindness to 259
Luxury, deny, to help poor
 272, 273
 indulging in, while want walks
  streets 257

MAGISTRATES and courts,
 witnessing before 128
Management of schools, importance of 206
Managers, institutional, make
 God first and last 224
 needed 80, 206
 part of, in work of message
  229
 qualifications of, avoiding
  debt like levelheaded
  businessmen 210

faithful financiers who can
 look ahead 80
 study essential duty 161
 some only half converted 141
Mark of the beast unchanged 17
Martha and Mary, characteristics of both needed 118
Masses, reaching 33
Means, accountable to God for
 447, 448
 do not stand idle while others
  struggle to obtain, for
  cause 452
 ever to be flowing into treasury through tithe 386
 gather, from world for work
  among most degraded
  246
 God gives ability to acquire
  214, 215, 452
 less spent in foreign fields than
  in home fields 28
 missions handicapped for
  want of 391
 misuse of, diverting of, from
  needy fields 445
 embellishing homes 450
 expending in self-gratification 452
 multiplying facilities where
  work is established 450
 using for self-service and
  self-glorification 387
 not sin to acquire, if returned
  to God 452
 proper use of, aiding cause of
  God with 384, 452
 building up God's kingdom
  448
 creating agencies for good
  441
 dispensing property before
  death 391
 economizing 441, 451, 452
 employing for salvation of
  souls 451
 establishing centers in new
  fields 450

giving to sustain foreign missions 442, 446

helping poor 451

helping young people get education 213, 214

raising of, at camp meeting, not for minor purposes 70

result of misuse of, unfits steward of, for higher trust of heaven 391

See also Funds; Gifts; Money; Riches; Stewards.

Meat excluded from diet at dining tent at camp meetings 112

Medical, and evangelistic workers, co-operation of 113

men, guardians of people's health 110

labor of, at camp meetings 110

missionaries, responsibilities of, solemn 243

missionary lines, education in 297, 377

work in, years delayed 301

missionary work, and gospel ministry, co-operation between, like that of hand and arm with body 241, 288-293

and gospel ministry never to be divorced 240, 241

bears God's signature 300

bound up inseparably with commandment keeping 265, 266

by church members 267, 289, 299-301

by ministers 298-302

by physicians 229-234, 246

canvassing a part of 323

carried on as part of gospel 292

demonstrates practical work of gospel 240, 241, 289

described in Isaiah 54, 265, 266, 289, 290

enemy determined to counteract God's design in 245, 246

for all classes 301

is entering wedge for truth 293, 327

is gospel in illustration 241

neglected by church 294-297, 300

neglected by ministry 298-303

not to be controlled by unsympathetic 300, 301

not to be made all and in all 240-242

not to be separated from conferences 235

part of God's reform work 291

prepares people for Lord 233

principles of truth kept pure in 289

prosperity of, is in God's order 299

relation of, to canvassing 323, 324

relation of, to church work 292

relation of, to message 229, 241, 267, 288-293, 327

relation of, to ministry 240, 241, 288-293, 300, 301, 377, 378

See also Christian help work.

profession, sacred work of 230

students, education of, how made complete 291

workers not to consider appearance of wealth essential 251

Meekness, and lowliness, success comes to learners of 397

essential to heralds of gospel 397

Meetings, heavenly beings join
in 366, 367
sleeping in 361
Melodies, sweetest, through human lips are justification,
righteousness of Christ
426
Memorials, medical institutions
as 225, 226
Men, of, all ranks and capacities
to co-operate 17
higher classes won for
truth 80
management needed 206
sharp, clear, spiritual sight
needed 150
Mercy and compassion toward
poor and sick, 262
Message, a life-and-death 61
Christ to be central theme of
20, 21
to be given to whole world 133
without delay 32
to be unchanged 17
warnings of, to be presented
with discretion 55
Methods of labor, Christ's to be
copied 230
in teaching 69, 88, 248
in meeting opposition 120-123
less preaching, more teaching
87, 88
Mind, and body, God wants,
preserved in best health
375
eternal, man must place himself under control of 241
Minds polished and refined by
mutual contact 172
Ministers, and physicians engaged in same work
233, 234
are stars in Christ's hand 413,
414
called to be, Christ's representatives 414
educators 302
watchmen 431

dangers and mistakes of, trying to do all the work of
the church 435
disqualifications of, in disregarding health reform
299, 300, 327, 376-378
education of, of primary importance 135
example for, in Christ 48
needs of, close connection
with God 47
freedom from unnecessary
temporal perplexities 216
number of, to be greatly increased 411, 414
of other denominations to be
labored for 77, 78
qualifications of, humble,
learn of Christ, and
true teacher 88
intelligent on, and living
out, health reform 301,
302, 376
knowing how to help sick
302
speak with power and ex-
pression 381, 383
wives of, adopting orphans
285
work of, as Bible teachers
134, 215
as canvassers 321
as educators in gospel work
272
at camp meetings 45-50
for individuals 413
give careful instruction regarding proper Sabbath
observance 353
in ministering to sick and
afflicted 301
organize working forces of
church 49, 302
strengthen churches to care
for sick and poor 272
study subjects for presentation 412, 415
teach health reform 376

teach people how to labor
for souls 49, 50, 431
to educate more than
sermonize 88
young, God calls for 411
not called to work among
churches 415
not to become shadows of
other men 415
trained by older workers
415
Ministry, canvassing a preparation for 322, 334, 415, 471
highest of all work 411
neglecting opportunities for
service 294, 295
no place for idlers in 412
object of gospel, to proclaim
truth to sick and to well
300, 301
of Christ, to all classes 79
those who belittle, belittle
Christ 411
united with medical missionary work 288, 300-302
vivified by Holy Spirit is
needed 88
young men not to be deterred
from 411
Miracles of conversion 82
Mission, of Christ's servants 55
fields, destitute 445-453
to help one another 459-462
See also Fields, foreign;
Foreign missions.
Missionaries, able to teach best
methods of labor 176
advantages of, industrially
trained 176, 177
children and youth to be 435,
436
foreign, not properly
sustained 27
Missionary work, all should
engage in 296, 297
arousing interest in 436
is to be world wide 23-30
true, defined 230

Mistakes, fretting over 463
we cannot blot out 149
Models, worldly, not to fix eyes
upon 147
Money, a trust from God to
carry on His work 214
borrowing 207
for institutions in foreign
lands 25, 28
love of, root of all evil 453
misuse of 451
needed treasure 451
See also Means.
Murmuring an offense to God 52
Music in praise meetings 62
Mysteries taught by remnant
church 19, 20
Mysticism, Bible a substitute
for 132

NATHANAEL, conversion of
37, 38
Nations angry 14
Nature, book of, next to Bible
in importance 185
contemplation of, on Sabbath
358, 359
lessons from, of divine truth
186
marred by sin 358
no virtue in deifying 185, 186
powers of, unseen, manifested
in effects 186
Satan strengthens destructive
tendencies of man's 238
study, brings health and
happiness 179
on Sabbath 358, 359
through, to nature's God 205
Needy, abundance of rich belongs to 272-287
example of care for 271
God tests us by sending,
among us 270
to visit and help, is pure
religion 263
See also Destitute; Poor.

Neighbor, duty toward 270, 271
   who is our? 294, 295
Neighbors, angels unite in work
   for 307, 308
   duty to labor for 276
   help, in industrial and sanitary
      lines 188, 189
   love for, must be fostered
      304, 305
New birth will give success to
   canvassers 319
   See also Conversion.
New Testament, advancement
   and unfolding of Old 392
Nicodemus, taught by Christ
   154, 155
Noah and Enoch were Christians 392
Nurses, God gives wisdom and
   skill to 229
   realize they are on probation
      253
   training of, in schools by well-
      qualified physicians 136
   work of, as missionaries in
      house-to-house work
      83, 84
      at camp meetings 112
      battle with disease and
         show value of nature's
         remedies 136
      open fast-closed doors to
         many hearts 229

OAR nor canvas needed while
   sailing with world 129
Obedience, acceptable, prompt
   466
   example of, Daniel's and his
      three companions' 220
   Joseph's 219, 220
   God sought to teach Israel
      lesson of 140
   results of, health 222
   prosperity 222
   success 140
   victory gained by, to high-
      est General 140

vigor of intellect 222
   wisdom 219, 220
Object lessons from nature, salt,
   preserving and saving element 258, 259
   stars, ministers of Christ 413,
      414
Offering, by, Mary 310
   widow 310
Offerings, today, all must give
   384-387
   complainers withhold 389, 390
   See also Tithes and offerings.
Oil, golden, 11, 12
   holy 116, 117, 123
Ointment, Mary's offering of 310
Old Testament, gospel in types
   and shadows 392
Olive trees, oil of, as symbol 11,
   12, 116, 117, 123
One drop of gall 123
Operating room, Christ present
   in 231
Opponents, bitterest, to be
   treated with respect
   and deference 122
   tenderness and meekness
      toward 121
Opportunity, God has His men
   of 466
Opposers of truth, honest ones
   among 122
Opposition, from ministers of
   other churches 100
   meeting, hurling charges in
      121, 122
   strengthens workers 145
Oppression of fellow men 397
Order, at school 201
   heaven's first law 201
   Israel an example of, in church
      organization and in fam-
      ilies 170
Orphans, adopting of, by ministers' wives 285
   and widows are objects of
      God's special care 281
   care of 281-287

homes for 182, 246, 247, 282, 286, 287
in families 281, 282, 284
of unbelievers 286
take, and present to God as fragrant offering 284
unpromising 282
Others, rescued to help 260
Outcasts, Christians to help 254-256, 259
efforts for, unavailing unless loyalty to God is impressed upon 259
will listen to His word 259
Outdoor life for pupils 179
Overwork, physicians to guard against 245, 246
Ownership of all, acknowledging God's 386

PAPACY, America to unite with 18
Papers and books are God's means of keeping message before people 315, 316
Parables and parabolic sayings of Christ, calling poor to feast 305, 312
harvest 254
light of the world 166
lighted candle 145
lost sheep 124, 125
strong man armed 407
talents 452
well of water springing up 51, 173, 472
Paralytic, healing of 234
Parents, and teachers deal with human minds at most impressible period 204
benefited by care and work for children 199
in some countries compelled to send children to school 199
interest of, in church schools 107, 108
lessons given for instruction of, at camp meeting 49
responsibilities of, for children's entertainment on Sabbath 358, 359
in instructing children preparatory to baptism 93
solicitude of, for salvation of their children 283
to, develop strong character in children 93
establish church schools 195
give education in God's word 195
guard with special interest newly baptized children 93, 94
make children their companions 94, 199
second efforts of teachers 199, 202
set right example before children 94
shield children from temptation 199
study and teach health principles 370
study daily with children 199
surround children with right influences 195
teach children to be missionaries 198
teach obedience 94
teach right habits of speech 381
teach that path of self-denial is only path of safety 370
train children for God's service 429
work of, for children outside family 283
See also Children; Family; Home.

Passover, children gathered in
at time of 195
Past, we cannot blot out record
of 149
Pastors, work of, for young converts 95
See also Ministers.
Patients, blending spiritual healing of, with physical 229-
234
Paul as house-to-house worker
321, 322
Peace, and rest in God shown by
daily lives 47
of Christ gives persuasive
power to voice 47
People of God, angels near to
aid in work of 308
distinguished 12
God's purpose for 445
lives of, observed by world
11-13, 258
need convocations 40
professed state of 445
to be, educated to do missionary work 267
fountains of life 227, 228
to represent God's character
to world 220-222
world recognizes superiority
of 12
See also Church; Seventh-day
Adventists.
Perils of last days 61, 62
Persecution, effect of, upon
God's people 401
relentless, against all reformers 403
Personal work, Christ's work
consisted largely of 115
most effective 428
promises and reward for 305-
312
Pesthouse, atmosphere of world
like 10
Peter's ladder of Christian
progress 147

Pews, renting of 101
Philip called by Christ and calls
Nathanael 428
Physician, Christ is the Great
111, 136, 231, 232
every, in our ranks should be
a Christian 229
in chief to be free from minor
responsibilities 247
Luke the beloved 233
patients to be directed to
Christ as Great 230, 247
registered in heaven as laborer together with
God 229
Physicians, and ministers should
work harmoniously and
unitedly 233, 234, 240
bound to the people by providence 244
dangers of, considering their
capabilities individual
property 243, 244
gathering unnecessary re-
sponsibilities 244-247,
252, 253
hiding principles of faith to
obtain large patronage
250
leading patients to fix
attention on them,
not Christ 244
neglecting to seek counsel
from God and brethren
252
seeking independence from
God's people 244
trusting to outward dis-
play 251
disqualifications of, carelessness and indifference to
human woe 232
selfishness 244
self-sufficiency 252
duties of, to co-operate with
God 250-252
to stand firmly for third angel's message 250, 251

godly, none too many 233
help for Christian, Christ accomplishes work attempted by 230
distinction through Sun of Righteousness revealed in life of 251
divinely guided in surgery 252, 253
speak a word in season to afflicted 248
will receive wisdom and skill from God 229, 252
needs of, being ever under control of divine 247, 248
divine power and wisdom 247
prayers of gospel minister 248
searching of Scriptures and earnest prayer 253
possibilities and opportunities of, bringing to sick a leaf from tree of life 230
doing noble work if connected with Christ 231
opening closed door to many hearts 229
to minister to relatives of patients 231
warning impenitent, cheering hopeless, prescribing mental and physical health 233, 248
qualifications of, converted and sanctified through truth 229
firm connection with God of wisdom 231
following the Lord's ways of working 251, 252
genuine Bible Christians 229
knowing how to pray 247
love for Christ and souls 230
loving and fearing God 251, 252

meekness and lowliness of heart 251
more anxiety to secure God's approval than patronage 252
personal religion 247
resting in Jesus as a constant friend 252
revealing their directions to be from God 251
sense of entire dependence on God 248, 251
understanding their responsibility and accountability 229
responsibilities of, guardianship of physical and moral health 110, 233
Satan seeks to hinder by multiplying 245, 246
standing as God's representatives 234
style of dress, equipage, furniture of, count not with God 251
work of, at camp meetings 110, 112
educate missionary nurses in our schools 136
educate those grown up with deformed characters 247
includes healing of body, mind, soul 229-234
instruct people in principles of true temperance 233
live and teach principles of health reform 247
not especially in dens of iniquity in cities 246
point patients to Christ 230-234
talk to patients of Christ's works of healing 231
win souls to Christ by both public and private effort 234

Physiology and hygiene, ministers should understand 301, 302, 376
Pioneers, self-denial and self-sacrifice of 419
Plan, God has, for each 12
Plans, all, to be presented before God 241
wise, to be laid for giving the message 32
Pleasure, seekers of, fate of 407
selfish, give up, to aid cause 450, 451
Pledge, temperance, call for signers to 110
Politics, discussions of, to be avoided 122
Poor, and invalids to prove a blessing to church 263, 272
bringing, to our homes 276
caring for our own 85
cautions in helping 278
Christ's legacy to church 261
condition of 83
"household of faith" to care for 85, 261-272
how to help 83, 84, 188, 189, 272
means spent for ornament instead of for 274, 275
our duty to relieve needs of 255
Paul's example of care for, at Jerusalem 271
provision for 385
teach, to help themselves 278, 279
two classes of 269, 270
work for, spiritual side prominent in 290
world's, call on world for support of 286
See also Destitute; Needy.
Potentates, earthly, crown of Christ uplifted above diadems of 402

Poverty, and sin, prevalence of 255
cause of, in Christian world 275
withholding gifts and offerings tends to 449
Power, consecrating body, soul, and spirit brings 306
divine, fullness of, imparted to God's people 12
inexhaustible supplies of 306
intellectual and moral, from fountain of wisdom 48
overcoming, to all who trust in Christ 399
special, at this time in presentation of truth 16
Powers, of darkness, power from above to meet 18
working with intense energy from beneath 22
of mind and body proportionately taxed 177, 180
Praise to be given to God 232, 233, 367, 368
meetings, God's desire for 364
how to conduct 62, 175
use of voice in 382
Prayer, and counsel by camp meeting workers 50
answer to, in God's own time 153
by physicians, for council 252
with patients 232
Christ presents child of God's penitential, as His own request 364
convictions reinforced daily by 401
definite object for 199
distinct utterance in 381-383
dry and stale 64
family, long, not in place 358
to be offered distinctly 381, 383
for, progress of cause 80
salvation of souls 80

if properly offered is power
382
indited by Holy Spirit 467
lodged by the throne 153
position in 381
public, clear and distinct 382,
383
Lord's means to communi-
cate precious treasures of
truth 382
recipe to cure lifeless 266
remedy for disheartened 438
seasons of, with those convicted by the truth 65,
66, 413
suppliant in, becomes client
364
three times a day 298
Prayers, we are to live our 471
Preaching, at camp meetings to
be of most spiritual character 53, 57, 58
church members trained to
rely upon 434
less of, more of teaching 87, 88
manner of, melting soul by
presenting Jesus 53, 54
truth and healing sick bound
together 234, 242
See also Sermons.
Precipitancy will retard 192
Prejudice, difficulty of overcoming, not to discourage us
38
not to be aroused 58
swept away 68-70
Preparation of heart for camp
meeting 41
Present, truth, health reform
part of 327
importance of knowledge
of 396
use, diligently before it becomes yesterday 149
Price of redemption 479
Principles, of God's kingdom,
make manifest, to uni-
verse 13

right, institutions to show results of obedience to 224
Printing in our schools 176, 182
Prisoners of hope, our institutions of learning are 145
Privilege of workers to speak as
God's mouthpiece 52
Probation, but few, very few
days of 407
no second 19
years of, fast closing 405, 446
Promises of God to unselfish
workers 306, 307
Properties, purchase of, for advancement of work 113
Prophecies are fulfilling 14
Prosperity, conditions of, always
the same 224
of Sanitarium dependent on
favor of God 223
our, lies in separation from
world 143, 144
result of liberality 390
true, test of 143
Protestants, rise of 403
Publications, denominational, to
be handled by consecrated
workers 319, 320
See also Books, denomina-
tional; Canvassing.
Publishing, sermons in newspapers 37
house in Christiania, Norway
454-462
houses helping schools 469
Purpose of God in the church
9-13

QUARRY of world and the
workshop of God 363
Queensland, camp meeting in 58

RANK and caste, Christ ignores
268
Redeemed, gratitude of, to those
who directed them to
Christ 311, 312

Redemption, claim of 479-482
Refinement, need of, in workers 257
Reform, every true, has place in third angel's message 110
  in observance of Sabbath called for 353
  industrial 176-180
  ministers to 376
  of living conditions in community 188, 189
  temperance, more attention to be given 110
  whole church to hold up standard of 292
Reformation when churches sense nearness of events portrayed in the Revelation 61, 62
Reformatory, movement begins with parents and children 119
  our work is 126
Reformers, not destroyers 151
  Protestant, held aloft religious liberty banner 402, 403
  to be reformed 154
Relatives, labor for 427, 428
Religion, cheerful side of 365, 366
  Christ is author of our 21
  definitions of 379
  faith and power of, give evidence to world 21
  home, hope of church 119
  true, outflowing of God's love to man 379
Religious, exercises prolonged to weariness 174
  liberty, banner of, committed to us 402, 403
Remedies for sin-sick soul, every physician may have 229
Representatives of God's character, our privileges as 220-222
Resources of heaven await Christ's laborers 267

Responsibilities, caution against gathering too many 293
Restoration, work of, in Isaiah 58 for this time 265
Revelation, book of, dwell on, in preaching 61, 62
  study of 59, 127, 128, 131
  to be taught in our schools 127-131
Revival efforts too few at camp meeting 64-67
Reward, future and present, to personal workers 305-312
Rich, labors of Christ for 255
  needs of 255-258
  souls won from among 258
Riches obtained by robbery 15
  See also Means.
Right hand and arm of gospel work 229, 288-293, 327
Righteousness, health reform unites truth with 378, 379
  of Christ, goes before humble workers 438
  goes before workers for higher classes 82
  light of, to shine into soul 202
  loud cry of third angel's message 19
  ministerial institutes necessary because of refusal of light on 89
  only efficiency of ministers 89
  shines through believers to world 424
  sweetest melody from God 426
Robbery of God in tithes and offerings 391, 446, 447
Rooms, angels linger in neat, orderly 171

SABBATH, diet on 357
  false, Protestant churches accept 193

God's sanctified memorial torn down 18
golden clasp uniting God and His people 351
how to welcome 356, 357
kept in heaven 362
most joyful day of week 359
presentation of, great test 60, 61
without hesitancy 38
meetings, all to help make interesting 362, 363
cheerfulness, with no sadness, to characterize 365, 366
short sermon, testimony service 361, 367
observance, acquainting ourselves with God and nature 358, 359
children to be instructed regarding 356, 359
closing by song and prayer 359
in home 356-359
instruction regarding, ministers to give 353
making attractive for children 358, 359
preparation for 355-357
time of, not to be wasted in bed 357
traveling as related to 359, 360
question to be issue in final conflict 352
reform in last days 265, 266
school, instruction in 193
work, training for 136
seal of God 350
sign of, God's creative power 265, 350
obedience 349, 350
special clothing for 355
spiritual bearing of, upon life 353
spurious, exalted as sign of Satan's authority 352

Sacrifice, of Christ, constant realization of, qualifies for service 81
explained to followers at His coming 20
rich men to learn joy of 258
spirit of, in pioneers of cause 419
to be made now 450
See also Self-denial; Self-sacrifice.
Samaritan, good, parable of, Christ illustrates nature of true religion in 294
woman, conversation of Christ with 64
Sanctification, Sabbath a sign of 350
true, in harmony with God and His character 350
Sanitarium, managers, high calling and influence of 223, 224
workers, duty of, to be reformers 223
Sanitariums, danger of, separating from church 240, 241
economy in establishing 113
establish, in all the world 113, 225
establishing small but properly equipped 113
head physicians in 247
operating rooms of, Christ present in 231
patients at, leave with new hearts 226
prosperity of, dependent on favor of God 223
purchase of properties for 112, 113
purpose of, beacon lights of warning and reproof 223
centers of education and healing 225
disseminate light and advance reform 219-228
heal diseased soul, body 226

Sanitariums—*continued*
  memorials for God 225, 226
  representatives of truth 220
  rivers of life and healing
    228
  religious influence in, inspires
    guests with confidence
    226
Satan, accepted as God by
  world 15
  agencies of, all at work to
    deceive, delude, occupy,
    and entrance 31, 66
  all who criticize 42
  communicators of gloomy,
    disagreeable thoughts
    62, 63
  always wide awake to
    deceive 46
  as prince of world, bruised
    under feet of over-
    comers 52
  busily laying plans for last
    mighty conflict 14
  forces of, are uniting for
    perdition 242
  plays game of life for souls
    148, 264, 446
  promises glory of world to
    his worshipers 14
  throne of, where God's
    throne should have
    been 236
  brings discord and bitterness
    among God's people 151
  causes our schools to imitate
    worldly plans and cus-
    toms 142, 143
  incited rebellion in heaven
    236, 237
  misrepresents God's law 10
  originator of, envy, jealousy,
    evil surmising, evilspeak-
    ing 42
  power of, received by world
    as power of God 14
  represents chosen people as
    deluded 11
  strengthens destructive tend-
    encies of man's nature
    238
  talking of, delights him 62
  will bring in every kind of
    theory to pervert truth
    129
  worldly amusements from 143
Scandinavia, relief of institutions in 454-467
  work in 25
Scenes, closing, we are in 129
School, at Avondale, Cooranbong 181-192
  pattern school 187-192
  buildings, erection of, hiring
    money for 207
  strict economy to be prac-
    ticed in erecting 208
  suitable for church schools
    203
  farm, Holy Spirit gives wis-
    dom to managers of 185
  Lord's farm 187, 192
  to be regarded as lesson-
    book 181, 182, 187
  usefulness learned on,
    essential 192
  ground, Lord's property 187
  homes, Christian sociability
    and courtesy taught in
    172-174
  domestic duties in 169, 171
  object of 168, 169
  religious exercises in, plan-
    ning and managing of
    174, 175
  rooms in, students' care
    for 171
  those in charge of, bear
    grave responsibilities
    168, 169
  management, good financial,
    necessary 210
  of Christ, learners in, every-
    one 148
  lessons learned in, how to
    teach 153

meekness and lowliness
learned in 117, 397
obedience learned in 214
soul winning learned in 318
spiritual success only to
those in 397
Schoolroom needed as much as
church building 109
Schools, abundance of wholesome food supplied in
209
Christ's Object Lessons used
to relieve indebtedness
on 468-476
dangers of, imitating worldly
customs and practices
141-151
lowering standard in order
to secure popularity 142-
144
providing worldly enter-
tainments for students
143
through half-converted
teachers and managers
141
too much clinging to old
customs 142
unsuitable persons settling
near 183, 184, 187
using textbooks containing
suppositions of world's
great authors 160
degree of moral power test of
prosperity of 143
economy in erection and management of 208, 209
establishment of, in other
countries 137, 139
in smaller churches 198, 212
in various places 137-139,
212
family or home 198, 199
finances of, to be examined
216, 217
financial management of 210-
218

grounds about, dedicated to
God as His own school-
room 183
not to be occupied with
private dwellings 181-
184, 187
industries and manual training in, agriculture, gar-
dening, general farming
176-180, 182, 191
blacksmithing, painting,
shoemaking 182
bookbinding 176
carpentry 176, 182
cooking 182
laundering and mending 182
not to be dropped because
difficulties arise 176
printing 176
tentmaking 176
typewriting 182
location of, in country where
there is land to cultivate
177, 178, 181-185, 187
missionary nurses trained in
136
missionary work to be fostered
by 189, 190
must be conducted under
God's supervision 191
nonessentials to work of, to
be kept at distance 187
of other denominations not
our pattern 152
of prophets, ours to be like
137, 139, 152
of world, books used in, containing skepticism and infidelity 164-166
physical labor in, promotes
health of students 179,
180
physicians to give instruction
in 136
principals and teachers in,
need baptism of Holy
Spirit 153

Schools—*continued*
 purpose of, as God's instrumentalities to make Himself known to man 206
 fit people to stand in day
  of God's preparation 152
 give all-round education
  152, 177
 object lessons for surrounding communities 188, 189
 prepare young people for
  Sabbath school duties
  136
 save children from evil and
  destruction 195
 third angel's message to be
  given through 127-131
 to be family schools 152
 train youth according to
  God's plan 127
 train youth for service in
  gospel work 133, 207
 rabbinical, at Jerusalem,
  Jesus' visit at 75
 should be free from debt 207,
  213, 217
 studies in Bible to have chief
  place among 131, 132, 163
 studies in bookkeeping of primary importance 182
 studies in common branches,
  thorough education in
  198
 success of, requires union and
  obedience of all connected
  with 139, 140
 test of prosperity of 143
 to be models of heaven in
  order 201
 tuition, placing too low is
  unwise 210-212
 virtue, intelligence, piety in,
  source of joy 143
 See also Church schools.
Science, and religion, relation of,
  in education 131
 education in, not sufficient 131
 not to be inferior 152

of God's word in schoolwork
  192
Scriptures, most effective agency
  in saving souls 288
 passages of, to be on lips of
  parents 354
 reading, contemplation of, an
  audience with the Infinite
  393
 See also Bible; Word of God.
Scroll, not all prophecy understood until unrolling of
  17
Seal of God, John saw company
  with 15
 or mark of beast, all preparing for 130
Second advent, all God's instrumentalities to warn world
  of 18
 experience, parable of ten virgins an illustration of 129
 hope of, to be often presented
  406
 nearness of, approaching with
  stealthy tread 406, 408
 day and hour no man
  knows 440
 delayed by failure of His
  people to finish work 450
 hastening greatly 22
 institutional facilities to be
  increased in view of 440,
  441
 perilous times ominous of
  129
 unbelief respecting 129
 preparation for, adoption of
  health principles 224
 purpose of, explanation of
  mysteries of redemption
  19, 20
 signs of, as in Christ's day 146
 great and wise know not
  406
 unbelieving overtaken as by
  thief 129

universal warning of, to world 18

virgins, ten, parable of, to illustrate time of 129

worldliness destroyed by looking for 406

Seed of righteousness, faith essential in sowing 420

Self-denial, and sacrifice 445, 446

box 103

those unwilling to practice, will be tested 104

to aid mission fields and home missionary work 450-453

works wonders in advancing spirituality of church 102

See also Cross of Christian; Self-sacrifice.

Self-indulgence, fruits of 254, 255

great evil of, must be overcome 208

Self-reliance, teaching students 214, 215

Self-respect destroyed through indulgence in sin 53

Self-sacrifice, required of every child of God 449

widow's mite example of 310

See also Sacrifice.

Selfishness, destroys usefulness in soul winning 264

prevents God's working 80

root of alienation 43

Separation, from world, object of 9

peculiarity of character evidence of 437, 438

to prevent corruption of youth 194, 195

from, worldlings 109

worldly systems 143

Sermons, divine instruction concerning 57, 58

have not developed self-denying workers 431

on health reform in case of Daniel and companions 372

present Christ in all 59, 60

publishing, in newspapers 37

to the point 56

See also Discourses; Preaching.

Service, personal, required of all 276

spirit of, counts more than learning 411, 412

to God in little things 115

Seventh-day Adventists, benevolence of 85

not to conceal the fact of being 81

See also Church; People of God.

Shaking time, we are in 332

Sheep, lost, represents this world 124, 125

to be sought 22

Shepherds, parents as 94, 205

Sick, and poor, minister to educate members to care for 272

benefited by being pointed to Christ 230-233

ministers doubly useful if able to help 302

poor, aged 270, 271

labor for 83, 84

relatives of, to be pointed to Jesus 231

reliance of, on physician 232

Signpost of end 408

Signs of times, few understand 426

Sin, cherished, produces unhappiness 53

Christ, bore penalty of 230

designs to save all mankind from 273

only Saviour from 53

confession of, before receiving Holy Spirit 43

Sin—*continued*
conviction of, men must
have 66
enormity of, seen in light of
cross 66
fashionable with world since
Adam 129, 130
instances of, lack of Christlike
sympathy and love 53
letting interest wane 86
violation of nature's laws
224
poison of, at work in society
136
pride of heart is 53
results of, atmosphere of
world like that of
pesthouse 10
demon now central power
of world 236
ruin and death 83
unhappiness, misery 53, 404
wretchedness and depravity
255, 256, 259
slaves of, can be freed 71
tampering with, forbidden 404
Sin-sick souls, call for our help
254, 255
remedy for, in possession of
Christian physicians 229
Singing, Father Himself joys
over rescued with 125
Sinners, love of God for 273
our attitude toward 268
Slothfulness of church, in soul-
saving work 424, 445, 446
Snares of Satan prepared for
those now asleep 22
Sociability, Christ's example of,
to be taught in our
schools 172, 173
too little, among Christians 343
Society, duty of Christian to,
regenerate and reform
188, 189
work for rich and higher
classes of 78
poison of sin at work in 136

Solomon, apostasy of 250
Song, historical and prophetic,
of Moses 364, 365
of freedom, we shall soon
sing 447
Sons and daughters trained
to shine as lights in
world 33
Soul, conversion of, we should
tax resources to utmost
for 22
destiny of, not to hang on
uncertainty 405
moral powers of, never safe
unless under divine guid-
ance 167
one, saved, flashes heaven's
light all around 22
spiritual needs of, kept prominent 290
value of, more than value of
worlds 21, 22
not to be compared with
mansions or bank stock
21, 22, 453
winners, Christ's presence
with 418, 419
gratitude of redeemed to
311, 312
how to be 443, 444
unlearned can become 318
winning, more being done for,
by heaven than we real-
ize 50
efforts in, for those judged
as hopeless as if in their
graves 442
not dependent on ministers
only 427
selfishness destroys usefulness in 264, 265
uplift Christ in 66, 67
Souls, compelling, to come to
Christ 66
lost, God's servants to seek 255
most hopeless, truth to be
presented to 442

rejoicing over seeing, won in kingdom 480
self-denial required to save 445-453
sin-sick, gospel a cure for 257
 workers to labor for 254-256
 struggling with satanic agencies 234
 without hope 254, 255
 won through work of sanitariums 226
Speech, clear, distinct 380-383
 gift of, no gift more precious than 337
Spewing out of mouth, meaning of figure 408
Spirituality, lack of, hinders coming of Christ 438
Stars, held in Christ's right hand 418
 symbol of God's ambassadors 413, 414
Stewards, of truth urged to vigilance 448
 to invest means for salvation of souls 448
Students, as missionaries in school homes 171
 conversation of, at table 173, 174
 dangers of, becoming involved in debt 217, 218
 depending upon others for education 217, 218
 overstudy 167
 duties of, co-operate with teachers 179
 think for themselves 154
 economy to be studied and practiced by 208, 209
 financial help for, by churches and conferences 213
 health and happiness in nature for 179
 instructed to work in Christ's lines 134
 religious duties of, not to

be neglected for secular study 167
simplicity in diet and appearance of 209
superficial, turn from Christ 133
training of 133-137
 each one, special, individual 152
 who get most out of life 190
Studies, Christ must be brought into all 132
 too many, prevent attendance at religious exercises 167
Study, courses of, short, for ministers 135, 136
Success, conditions of, obedience to every word of God 140
 elements of, in our schools 139, 140
 in sanitariums 223, 224
Suffering, caused by transgression of laws of God 224
 for righteousness' sake 121
 relief of, work of mercy 136
Sufficiency in Christ alone 319
Suicide through wrong practices 373
Sunday, child of papacy 193
Surgeon, most truly successful 252
Surrender, entire, Satan hinders our seeing necessity of 92, 93
 life of daily 116
Suspicion, every thought of, to be put away 42
Sympathy and helpfulness can be understood and appreciated 259

TABLE, conversation of students at 173, 174
 in wilderness, Christ can spread 178
Talents, accountability for improvement of 297, 298

Talents—*continued*
 churches withering up because
  of failure to use 431
 God will help us to improve
  379
 neglect of, by church members
  425
 to be constantly employed to
  best purpose 439
Teacher, Christ as, example for
  teachers 160
 favorite theme of, the
  Father's love 55
 great teacher to mankind
  160, 331
 methods of 69, 248
Teachers, aims of, to advance
  students in all essential
  knowledge 152
 and students, missionary
  efforts of 190
 called to be, laborers together
  with God 156
 light of world 156
 care in selecting 134, 200
 co-operation between students
  and 179
 dangers of, being satisfied
  with worldly standards
  146, 147, 161
 closing hearts of students
  to God 161
 difficulties and discouragements of, bodily infirmities brought by Satan
  156, 157
 labors not always appreciated 156
 prejudice from parents 201
 disqualifications of, being only
  half converted 141
 corrupted by sentiments of
  infidel authors 164
 manifestations of self-importance 159
 proud and unloving 201
 showing partiality 201

 stern, unbending dignity
  169
 unable to distinguish between sacred and com-
  mon 159
 unapproachable, harsh 134
 young, inexperienced, lacking managing ability 201
 help for, God brings good out
  of trial 156, 157
 through Holy Spirit 159
 many, are asleep 166
 have much to unlearn and
  much to learn 155
 should fit themselves to
  train others 207
 needs of, experimental knowledge of how to do God's
  will 161
 Holy Spirit in life 153
 searching Scriptures for
  personal understanding
  155
 sincere, earnest, heartfelt
  devotion 175
 studying Christ's lessons
  and character of teach-
  ing 160
 thorough Christian experience 154, 155
 primary, need to learn to feed
  lambs 205
 qualifications of, able to adapt
  instruction to wants of
  pupils 135
 abstaining from the very
  appearance of evil 201
 administrative ability 169
 attentive to laws of health
  378
 calm, kind, manifesting
  forbearance 201
 can inspire thought 154
 careful, prayerful, serious
  159
 Christlike temper 134

close connection with God 153, 154
companionship with students in joys, sorrows, play, work 169, 205
consecration of 108, 159
constantly advancing in efficiency 153, 154
copying example of Jesus 201
deep sense of value of souls 134
doers of God's word 153
feeling of responsibility to God 152
having attributes of Christ's character 156
having care for students' health and happiness 152
high moral qualities 201
learners 153, 155
linking love and Christlike sympathy with discipline 169
love for children 152, 201, 205
managing ability 160
patience, perseverance, tact 201
piety 175
prayerful, careful, serious 159
sound in faith 127, 201
special care for students' salvation 152
submissive to God 201
teaching by awakening inquiry, thought, expression 154
thorough understanding of God's word 153-155
true missionary spirit 201
true to principle 169
unselfish, devoted, faithful 152
walking with God 201
wise and pitiful in treatment of youth 152

reward of faithful, some lessons linger with even most careless students 159
should be awake to responsibilities 166
should study, the Bible 153-155
to teach, carpentry 176
principles of God's word 131
vital truths 154
to work in Christ's lines 161
work of, carry on educational work in various countries 136, 137
educate students for present and future life 153
educate, train, discipline students' minds 156
entreat students to seek Christ 158
impart higher wisdom to students 159
impart light from throne of God 154
lead students to understand truth for themselves 154
mold minds and character of youth 200
represent God's character and Spirit 156
thwart Satan's devices 127
train students to become missionaries 201
uplift the only true God 166
with students in manual work 179
See also Church school teachers.
Teaching, less preaching and more 87, 88
means much more than many suppose 153
methods of, creating desire for knowledge 154
of Christ, method of 69, 88, 248

Temperance, in all things 374,
    375
  in heathen contests an illustra-
    tion of Christian warfare
    374
  more attention to be given to
    110, 111
  pledge, Christian workers to
    call for signers of 110
  principles, education in,
    needed 256
  wealthy will recognize and
    accept 256
  work 110, 111
  workers in other churches 110
Temple, in heaven, threshold
    of, flushed with glory
    for true church 368
  of soul laid in ruins 279
Tempted, physicians to help 234
Tendencies, destructive, Satan
    strengthens 238
Test, Sabbath the great 60
Testimonies, not needed if word
    of God were treated with
    deference 393
  wrong use of 122
  by mixing in your filling of
    words 122, 123
Textbook, Bible highest and
    most important 131,
    132, 164-166
Textbooks, for our schools to
    direct to God 203
  mere study of, not sufficient
    126
  of worldly schools 164
Third angel to go forth with
    great power 16
Third angel's message, extent
    of 133
  gospel message for last days
    241
  last warning 19, 60
  power to attend 16
  presented, as dry theory 20
    in indefinite manner 60
    in its simplicity 396

  with tact and gentleness
    400, 401
  presents saving truths 11
  proper presentation of, work
    of schools, churches,
    teachers, ministers 131
  relation of, health reform to
    327
    medical missionary work
    to 241, 288-293
  to be taught in all our institu-
    tions 128-131
  true light upon 17
Thorns, and thistles result from
    disobedience 358
  work of Satan 186
Thoughts, new, rich, through
    union with Christ 476,
    477
Three, angel's messages, cre-
    ate schools, publishing
    houses, sanitariums 18
  exert power to close of
    time 18
  linked together 17
  Satan seeks to cast shadow
    about 18
  angel's symbolize work of
    God's people 17
Threshold, upon, of great and
    solemn events 14
Time, economy in use of 452
  none to lose 22, 62
  of trouble, bringing on,
    beforehand 395
    protection for saints in 404
Tithe, Bible teachers to be paid
    from 135, 215
  complainers among withhold-
    ers of 389, 390
  disloyalty in withholding
    387, 388
  not to be used in paying
    debts 391
  paying, instruction in, to be
    given 447
    test of obedience 386
  required by God 384, 387

use of, for gospel support 386,
387, 447

Tithes and offerings, acknowledgment of God' claim
by creation and redemption 479

Tomb of faithful brightened by
Christ 230

Tools, students to learn use of
192

Trades, advantage of, for missions 176, 177
See also Industries.

Training, duty of parents in 202
of workers by labor in connection with experienced
men 90
of youth by schools to be
workers 133
See also Schools.

Transformation great, in fulfillment of Isaiah 55:13
308

Transgressions of law bring human sufferings 224, 225

Traveling soon hedged with
dangers 22

Treasure, earthly, only two
places for depositing—
God's storehouse or Satan's 448
value of, in contrast to one
soul 453

Treatment rooms, need of, in
cities 113

Tree of life, leaves from, physician to bring into sickroom 230
principles of Bible as 393
reserved as reminder of God's
ownership 386

Trials, received as educators,
will produce joy 365

Trust in God, impregnable 157

Truth, how to be presented 58
landmarks of, stand by 17
many will not hear, unless it is
brought to homes 314

mistakes of advocates of,
marring by defective
utterances 380
presentation of, dry, lifeless,
belittles message 47, 48
great power in, at this time
16
tact and gentleness in 400,
401
to most hopeless subjects
442
without addition of self
122, 123
responsibility regarding, to
communicate to others 16
to impart to world 424
word of, tree of life 19

Tuition fees, increasing, to keep
from debt 210, 211

Types and symbols of power of
gospel, Christians to be 11

UNEDUCATED to be workers
433, 434

Unfortunates, Christ's legacy
261-264

Union with Christ, great blessing from 476, 477

United States, foreign nations
will follow example of,
in persecution 395
See also America

Unity, and harmony of action
will bring blessing 50
between medical workers and
ministry 235-242, 288-293
of action needed in work
292, 293
our great need 300
Satan's effort to destroy 236
strength in 293

Universe, earth the lessonbook
of 13
principles of God's kingdom
manifested to, through
church 13, 21
watching closing scenes of
drama 144, 145

Urgency, spirit of, to be manifested in our efforts 65

Utterance, clear, distinct 380-383

VEILS upon faces, many have, today 146

Victory, for sinners when they fix eyes on Saviour 67

gained amid clouds of darkness is more complete 157

gained through, fulfilling obligations to God 262, 263

laying hold of God through Christ 111

obedience, not ceremonies 140

putting on whole armor of God 41

patiently press on to gain 22

Victories, Christian life to be a series of uninterrupted 307

Vigilance necessary to spiritual safety 148

Vineyard of the Lord, appeal for workers in 304

includes whole world 24

Violence and crime, earth filled with 15

Vision of Ellen G. White relating to Avondale school 181-192

Visiting poor and sick a substitute for amusement 276

Visitors, excessive preparations for 343

workers entertaining many 344

Voice culture important to workers 380

WARFARE, aggressive, our duty 22

Warning, churches to receive 76, 77

last, God's people to give 403

message, discretion in giving 55

no time to lose in giving 62

to be given by our institutions 18

Watchfulness, call for, as end draws nigh 410

Watchmen in our schools asleep 166

Watchword, our 303

Weakness, depending on men is cause of 249, 250

Wealth, source of temptation 255, 256

spending, in self-serving while want stalks streets 256, 257

value of, in contrast to one soul 453

Wealthy, conversion of some, to aid cause 82, 83

labor for, manner of 257, 258

special temptations of 256, 257

will unite in work of beneficence 258

Well-doing, continue patiently in 477, 478

White, Ellen G. gives instruction regarding, reservation of land around schools 181-187

missionary labor, highest training 189-192

need of church schools 198-205

school management and finance 206-218

Widow casting in two mites, example of 310

Widows and orphans, care for 281

Willingness to minister 118

Windows of soul to be closed earthward 202

Winds, angels holding four, 14, 21, 61, 408, 426

Wisdom, finite, honor, far less 156

human, buries wisdom of
　　God 132
Women, work of, as gospel
　　workers 114-118
Word of God, bread from
　　heaven 132
　　fear to skim surface of 407
　　leaves from tree of life 393
　　supreme authority 402, 403
　　See also Bible; Scriptures.
Words, carefulness in, increases
　　influence tenfold 122, 123
　　discouraging, grieve Christ
　　　292
　　gentle, in working for souls
　　　400
　　in season 69
　　See also Conversation.
Work, and prayer 319
　　of Christ, apparent failure
　　　in 307
　　of God, business integrity
　　　in 337
　　　character given to, by med-
　　　　ical missionary work 229
　　　extension of, to many local-
　　　　ities to be encouraged 330
　　　Holy Spirit needed to
　　　　balance 291
　　　no change in general fea-
　　　　tures of 17
　　　not time to cease 440, 441
　　　will soon be more difficult
　　　　than we can imagine 22
　　　See also Cause of God.
　　spiritual, all lines of, to re-
　　　ceive equal attention 329
　　appointed by God for all
　　　to do 481
　　appointed for medical
　　　workers 243-253
　　before us, world-wide
　　　evangelization 31
　　doing, during twenty-four
　　　hours of day 29, 30
　　earnest, to be done 21, 65
　　excellence of, to be object
　　　lesson 24, 25

for those nearest 427, 428
greatest, in world, living
　　character of Christ 439
hundredfold greater if same
　　diligence as in 1844 419
Lord will preside over 289
method of, simplest, for
　　churches 433
progress of, not as should
　　be 420
remedy for discouragement
　　438
Worker, Master, God is great 24
　　God to be acknowledged
　　　as 234
Workers, co-operation, of all,
　　needed at camp meet-
　　　ings 46
　　of heavenly agencies needed
　　　by, to restore the fallen
　　　260
　　duties and responsibilities of,
　　　becoming acquainted with
　　　people 75
　　laboring for poor and sick
　　　55, 254, 255
　　reaching higher classes
　　　257, 258
　　warning wealthy 82, 83,
　　　255-258
　　energies, entire, called for 237
　　entertainment of visitors by
　　　344
　　from men now controlled by
　　　human ambitions and
　　　passions 237
　　God designs all to be 423
　　needed who will labor as
　　　Christ did 254, 255
　　preparation of, speedy 331
　　promises to, all may become
　　　useful 48
　　angels as helpers 456
　　co-operation of Christ 418,
　　　419
　　reward 305-312
　　qualifications of, animation
　　　and determination 418

Workers—*continued*
　baptism of Holy Spirit
　　292, 293
　clear-sightedness, spirit-
　　uality 150
　consecration 318
　soul winning as chief aim
　　427
　vigilance 46
　zeal 396
　tide of spiritual life from 227
　voices of, should be trained
　　381-383
　women as 114-118
　young, feeling content with
　　small efforts 419
Workmen, God has, in every
　　age 332
World, dominion of Satan over,
　　Christ came to disprove
　　236, 237
　in present evil state, come out
　　from 147
　condition and needs of 254-
　　260
　conformity to, in customs,
　　maxims, practices 142-144
　God's people to impart
　　spiritual and temporal
　　blessings to 273-280
　lost sheep 124
　needs powerful, spiritual
　　preaching 53
　observes lives of God's
　　people 258
　sin-sick, needs of 254-260
Worldlings, examples of, not to
　　be followed 249, 250
　God moves upon, to favor
　　His people 466
Worlds, unfallen, represented by
　　ninety-nine sheep 124
Worship, pleasantness to be
　　brought into 174, 175
　public, duty to attend 360
Worth, true, God's love and

purity woven into life
　127
Wrath of God, terrible reve-
　　lation to souls without
　　foundation 16

YOKE made easy by cross of
　　Calvary 247
Young, men, duty of, to learn
　　from Great Teacher 415
　duty of, to strive continu-
　　ally to improve 416
　not to commence efforts in
　　churches 415
　to serve as canvassers 415
　training of, for ministry
　　135, 136, 411-416
　Men's Christian Association,
　　to attend 75
　ministers, appeal to 411-416
Youth, dangers of, in choosing
　　path to destruction 254
　misuse of money 214
　wrong, intemperate habits
　　254, 255
　development of, gradual as
　　in plants and flowers
　　204, 205
　education given to, molds
　　whole social fabric 150
　exhorted to enter God's
　　service 471
　invite homeless, to your
　　homes 348
　labors for, at all camp meet-
　　ings 105-107
　by ministers and church
　　members 435, 436
　much lost to cause from loss
　　of 196, 197
　point, to Peter's ladder 147
　training of, church to aid in
　　212-214
　for efficient service 435, 436
　to help other youth 115
　to like responsibilities 435

Shaking 332 , IT 429, EW 50,51, ITI 79,181